ARAB HISTORIANS OF THE CRUSADES

Arab Historians of the Crusades

Selected and translated
from the Arabic sources
by
FRANCESCO GABRIELI

*Translated from the Italian
by E. J. Costello*

DORSET PRESS
New York

This edition published by Dorset Press
a division of Marboro Books Corporation,
by arrangement with Routledge.
1989 Dorset Press

ISBN 0-88029-452-3

Printed in the United States of America

M 9 8 7 6 5 4 3 2 1

CONTENTS

PART THREE

THE AYYUBIDS AND THE INVASION OF EGYPT

PART FOUR

THE MAMLŪKS AND THE LIQUIDATION OF THE CRUSADERS

I

2

3

INTRODUCTION

The purpose of this book is to help the European reader to see the period of the Crusades from 'the other side', through the eyes and the minds of the men who at that time were the enemy. Such an experience is particularly interesting and informative in the case of the mediaeval conflict between Christianity and Islam, two civilizations which then had a great deal in common. They were founded on similar attitudes of mind and religious concepts, and it was their common struggle for universality that brought them into conflict and drove them to fanaticism. Nowadays the fanaticism has died down, at least among Christians, and the battles are fought on other fields, although the issues are still the same. We no longer speak of *daggers* and *hammers* of the Faith; in fact a sympathetic and conciliatory attitude to Islam is characteristic of Christians today; an attitude that may not be shared by the other side. But the violence of the old antagonism still blazes from the pages of the mediaeval chroniclers and polemicists, and we tend still to see the 'enemy' of the Crusades in the light of that old theological and racial hatred, which later conflicts have deepened and embittered. It is only in poetry that Clorinda is brought from the camp of Sulaiman and Argantes to die reconciled with the Faith. Those who wish to rise above this view of history and to see more than one aspect of the situation must take a closer look at the enemy's attitudes and ideals, his way of life and methods of warfare, as they appear in the pages of the Arab chroniclers and historians of the time. The evidence they present is as plentiful and as valuable as that of their European contemporaries. Of course the slogans are back-to-front: 'Christian swine' has been substituted for 'Saracen dog', and the vision of the Holy Rock, upon which the Prophet's foot rested on the night of his miraculous ascent into heaven, for that of the Holy Sepulchre. The saintly Godfrey is replaced by the saintly Saladin. This is not the place for religious and philosophical pronouncements. All we have tried to do is to offer to the historian and the interested layman a selection of the opposition's views to set beside the picture presented by European writers.

The Crusades burst upon the Muslim empire at a crucial moment in its history. The wave of Arab conquests had passed and Arab military activity was confined to defence, while the Turks were still building up their military supremacy within the Muslim empire before their great onslaught on the Christian world. Islam had already suffered at Christian hands during the Byzantine wars, particularly during the tenth century, but this violent attack by the Latin empire, on grounds that were fundamentally and conspicuously religious, took the Muslim world completely by surprise and found it in a state of political disunity that obstructed the speed and efficiency of its preparations for war. Grousset's formula—initial Muslim anarchy versus Frankish monarchy—is an accurate summary of the situation in Syria during the last decade of the eleventh century and the first decade of the twelfth. The land was divided among rival Turkish amīrs, Seljuqid Ata-begs and their vassals. The Fatimids of Egypt maintained a tenuous control of Palestine. In Baghdād the 'Abbasid Caliph reigned under the tutelage of the Turkish Sultan, the dignity of his position a mere shadow of what it had been in the days of al-Mansūr and al-Ma'mūn'. The potentates of southern Syria and the Fatimid commanders in Palestine did their feeble best to put up a resistance, but the Crusaders spread like a stain through the empire, while the

Anti-Crusade, vainly urged and hoped for by Baghdād, remained as ineffective as ever.

During the third and fourth decades of the twelfth century Muslim resistance stiffened as a result of the efforts of the Artuqids of Mardīn, Tughtikīn of Damascus and, in particular, Zangi and Nur ad-Din, Ata-begs of Mosul. When the frontier county of Edessa fell to the Crusaders, Zangi turned his attention to Syria with the double aim of uniting it under his rule and driving the Franks back to the sea. Arabism as a political force was now of only secondary importance. The dynasties that led the counter-attack were Turkish in race and in social and military organization, although their culture was still Arabic. Saladin's rise to power in some ways interrupted and in others continued this movement toward Turkish supremacy. He was of Kurdish origin, educated in both the Turkish and the Arabic cultures, and profoundly orthodox in his faith and his way of life. He brought Egypt back to the path of orthodoxy as the centre of his empire and gave Arabism new prestige. The two monarchs faced one another on the plain of Hittīn, and the Latin crown of Jerusalem rolled in the dust.

The Third Crusade succeeded in stemming the Muslim advance and propping up the tottering Christian states in Palestine. By the use of diplomacy and force the Ayyubids al-'Adil and al-Kamil maintained the equilibrium throughout the middle years of the century. They drove back the Fifth Crusade and kept Frederick II within bounds, but they failed to mount an effective counter-offensive against the Christian states. This was left to the Mamlūk Sultans, Turkish slaves from southern Russia and the Caucasus who by the middle of the thirteenth century had taken over the control of Egypt from the enfeebled Ayyubids. It was to these uncivilized soldiers, who perfected the system of military feudalism introduced by the Seljuqids and continued by the Ayyubids, that Islam owed its deliverance both from the Mongol invasions (the victory at

'Ain Jalūt in 1260 saved Syria) and from the Crusaders. The West could not maintain forever its artificial empire across the Mediterranean. The Papacy had diverted the lofty religious impulse of the first Crusades to serve its own ends in the struggle for power in Europe, reducing the Cross to a mere symbol on a flag carried into battle against baptized Christians (in the Crusade against the Albigenses and the war against the Hohenstaufen). Now it had to look on helplessly while Antioch, Tripoli and Acre fell one after the other and the Muslims finally regained control of Palestine. The Templars' last stand in the Holy Land was also, unknown to them, a foretaste of the catastrophe that was to befall them in the West.

These two eventful centuries, which brought the whole Christian world into conflict with Islam (although the Greek Church was the innocent victim of Western diplomatic errors) on territory that the Muslims had held for five hundred years, are faithfully recorded by Muslim historians of this and the succeeding era.

We have used the term 'Muslim' because many of the authors are not Arabic by birth, but 'Arabic' would be justifiable on the grounds of the language used (for the Persian historians and those few who had so far written in Turkish, add almost nothing to the history of the Crusades), or 'Arabo-Muslim' on the grounds of the spirit that inspired them, although the Arabic-speaking Christian historians of Egypt also had a part to play.

The Frankish invasions, by which the Muslims meant invasions by European Christians as opposed to the Byzantine *Rumi*, in spite of the havoc and loss of life that they caused, and the cost to Islam of the resistance that led up to the final victory, were never, for Muslim chroniclers, a single subject to be treated in isolation. Although of the greatest importance to them, as to the West, they were always incorporated into the customary literary forms, given their place in annals recording general history, or used in the writing of biographies of the

Muslim individuals or dynasties who set themselves up as champions of the Faith. One would search Muslim historical writings in vain for a composite, specific *History of the Wars against the Franks.*

Such a work can be composed, however, by juxtaposing and interweaving material from the various types of historical writing of the period. First come the general histories of the Muslim world, like Ibn al-Athīr's classic work, lesser-known annals by Sibt Ibn al-Jauzi and Ibn al-Furāt and later compilations. Next come chronicles of cities and regions: Ibn al-Qalānisi's of northern Syria and Kamāl ad-Din's of Mesopotamia, histories of regions and their dynasties like those of al-Maqrizi and Ibn Wasil and purely dynastic ones like Abu Shama's. Finally there are the biographies or records of the deeds of a certain person. Among these are the biographies of Saladin by 'Imād ad-Din and Bahā' ad-Din and the official biographies of the first Mamlūk Sultans by Ibn 'Abd az-Zahir. A unique work of the greatest historical and literary value is Usama's brilliant autobiography. The range of styles is wide: some works are simply dry lists of events, some are written in turgid rhymed prose (*saj'*); some are intelligent and accurate, others merely superficial compilations of unsubstantiated facts. What they have in common is, as one would expect, a scornful and hostile attitude toward the impious, fanatical infidels who invaded the territories of Islam.

There are few analyses or discussions of the enemy's military aims. Polemics of this sort had only a brief popularity, during the peace negotiations of the Third Crusade. The presence of an armed enemy on Muslim soil could arouse only one response —the military reprisals enjoined by the Qur'ān, which commands the faithful to press on into enemy territory until the foe is either exterminated or converted to the True Faith. There could be no real peace (*sulh*) with the Franks or with any other infidel enemy, only a temporary truce (*hudna*) when opportune or necessary. The celebrated peace, or truce, of 1192 between Richard and Saladin, was strongly opposed by many Muslims, in principle if not in fact. The two hundred years of the Crusades could not have passed in continuous warfare. There were of course periods of truce, and even, in the twelfth century, cases of 'unholy alliance' between Muslims and Christians against the co-religionists of one side or the other. (Ibn al-Qalānisi gives a frank account of the most scandalous of these alliances, that between the Franks and Damascus to block Zangi's advance in 1140.)

Peace was not however the favourite subject of the Muslim historians—nor perhaps of any historian. Muslim accounts of the Crusades are endless, often merely monotonous, descriptions of battles, skirmishes, ambushes, raids. Slaughter, pillage and devastation are the most common words in the accounts of the Holy War. Only the names of the combatants change. Where the early historians describe the fall of the coastal cities of Syria to the Franks in a welter of blood and flame, two hundred years later we can read of the same scenes, often in the same words but with the roles reversed. *Qui gladio ferit gladio perit*, although there is always admiration for valour and self-sacrifice, qualities to be found on both sides. The most intense conflicts of the two centuries took place during the Third Crusade, at Hittīn and the siege of Acre, when the opposing personalities were thrown into highest relief, the fighting was more widespread and its implications more dramatic. The monotonous military chroniclers sound almost inspired. Their accounts of daily life in the camp of Tiberias, of fights to the death under the walls of Acre, of marches and counter-marches at Saladin's command, have something of the atmosphere of religious epic. Equally important, though sometimes tiresomely detailed and confused, are their accounts of the long peace negotiations. It is a pity that the original text has not been preserved as Qalawūn's treaties were by the Mamlūk historians.

For two hundred years Christianity and Islam, face to face in the Holy Land, were officially enemies bound to ceaseless warfare, interspersed only with precarious truces. This official attitude was accepted by the Muslim historians of the time and limited the range and depth of their approach. They reveal no interest in the social, economic or cultural organization of the Frankish states. Occasionally self-congratulation or contempt leads them to mention cases in which Islam's superior culture and way of life have made their mark on the enemy, for example the case of the ruler of Shaqīf Arnūn mentioned in biographies of Saladin. He spoke Arabic and studied literature and Islamic law, but the only use he made of his knowledge was to try to deceive the enemy (Saladin, that noble Prince, punished him with nothing worse than imprisonment). The only hint to be found of interest in Frankish customs, ideas and way of life appears not in the serious histories but in the autobiography of the unprejudiced Usama; his accounts have not been forgotten in this volume. When mediaeval Muslims write of Christian beliefs or observances they create a grotesque caricature (see for example 'Imād ad-Din on the fall of Christian Jerusalem), based on misconceptions that can only be equalled in Christian accounts of Islamic beliefs and practices. In this respect each side gives as good as it gets and the Crusades were totally ineffective as a means of acquainting either side with the nobler aspects of the other's faith. It is also clear from the Muslim sources that what little exchange there was of men and ideas was almost always the result of Frankish initiative. William of Tyre, who learnt Arabic and who wrote a history of the Orient (now lost) from Arabic sources, had no parallel in the Muslim camp.

The main interest of the Muslim historians is, naturally, their own side and its heroes. It is this aspect of their work, complementing the European sources, that is also of greatest interest to Western readers. In their opening chapters the Arab historians give us frank and lucid discussions of the success of the First

Crusade (there is a bitter passage in Kamāl ad-Din accusing the rival amīrs in Syria of blindly and selfishly welcoming the Frankish invasion and profiting by it). They greet with relief, although sometimes with reservations about the claims to legitimacy that were advanced, the rise of the great champions of the Muslim resistance: Tughtikīn, Zangi, Nur ad-Din, Saladin. Damascus' brave fight against the besieging Franks is the most distinguished example of resistance in open warfare by local and municipal troops. Not long after this, still in the first stage of the war, Zangids, Ayyubids and Mamlūks in succession took over the responsibility for controlling and unifying the defence, theoretically the duty of the Caliph in Baghdād. The Caliphate, already a mere shadow of its former self, disappeared altogether in the course of the Crusades, having done nothing more effective than issue pious exhortations and homilies, and messages of congratulation to the victorious champions of the Faith. The annals of the Anti-Crusade are those of certain Muslim dynasties—Zangid, Mamlūk and others—whose members carried the burden of the Holy War for a variety of reasons, both religious and political, and sometimes sacrificed their whole lives to the cause. It is understandable that their chroniclers, out of piety, gratitude and devotion to the dynasty, have been generous with their eulogies.

Towering above them all, wringing admiration even from the enemy, is Saladin himself. His origins were obscure, his rise to power unorthodox and violent. He was destined to become the incarnation, for good or ill, of the power and prestige, and also the humanity and nobility, of the oriental civilization of the Middle Ages. At the same time, he was an inflexibly orthodox defender of its faith. The portrait of him drawn by Bahā' ad-Din and 'Imād ad-Din, clearly that of the Muslim *optimus princeps*, is that of the pious leader rather than of a gallant knight, and it fails to explain the fascination that this man exerted on his contemporaries and successors, friends and enemies alike. But the legend which gives him a place in Dante's Limbo and in so many tales and epics is not to be found in his own country where the deeds of the less humane Baibars are more widely celebrated. There are vivid accounts in Muslim chronicles of both these heroes of the Islamic counter-offensive, as well as of Zangi, Nur ad-Din, al-Kamil and other great defenders of Islam.

Faithful characterization is one of the great merits of Muslim historians and is practised (with other motives) in the brief but illuminating sketches of enemy leaders: Baldwin II's shrewdness, Richard Cœur de Lion's prowess in war, the indomitable energy of Conrad of Montferrat, Frederick II's diplomacy and sceptical irony; all were noted and independently confirmed by Muslim historians. Other judgments carry less authority; for example the description of the saintly Louis IX as a cunning rogue: is it cunning to end a life of austere faith and quixotic idealism in a foolish expedition to Tunisia in the height of summer? (Yet how vividly he springs to life, in all his dignified affability, in Ibn Wasil's account of his conversation with an Egyptian plenipotentiary in the prison at Mansura.)

The Arab histories of the Crusades compare favourably with their Christian counterparts in their rich accumulation of material and chronological information (although this is not always consistent either internally or with the dating given in European sources) and in their faithful characterization. We would not expect from them either serene impartiality in their attitude to the enemy, or originality and depth of understanding. The views expressed are those of mediaeval Muslim historians in general, alternating between pragmatism and mechanical, pietistic theology. One man stands out as a true historian from the ranks of more or less diligent chroniclers: Ibn al-Athīr. His reputation among Orientalists has recently diminished, because of the free and tendentious use he makes of his sources, but the qualities that reduce his reliability as documentary evidence are those of an original thinker, outstanding among so many passive compilers of facts.

Although for this period the Arabs have no historian of the stature of William of Tyre, their general level of scholarship is probably higher than that of their Christian contemporaries. It is noticeable that the Arabs are for the most part more experienced in the techniques of their art and more professional in their approach. The reason for this has been mentioned: the Arab histories of the Crusades are usually only a section of a general historical panorama.

This volume is by no means the first attempt in the West to show the other aspect of the Crusades. More than a century ago, at the end of Michaud's *Bibliothèque des Croisades*, that great scholar Reinaud, Michele Amari's teacher, produced a volume of *Chroniques Arabes* (Paris, 1829), in which he strung together as a continuous narrative translations and paraphrases of passages from various mediaeval Arab historians. They were taken from the manuscripts of the *Bibliothèque du Roi*, then almost entirely unedited. This pioneer work, which is still of use to the non-Arabist, was designed to give a coherent account of the Crusades from Arabic sources rather than to present those sources for their own sakes. This was also the aim of the section called 'Historiens Orientaux' of the great *Recueil des Historiens des Croisades*, published in the second half of the nineteenth century under the auspices of the Académie des Inscriptions et Belles Lettres. Most of the Oriental section was edited by Barbier de Meynard, and the five volumes published (Paris, 1872–1906) contain extracts, in the original and in translation, of such historians as Ibn al-Athīr, Abu Shama and Abu l-Fidā. This imposing work is ill-adapted for reading as a continuous narrative, and has also been criticized for its choice of extracts and for errors in the text and the translations. Nevertheless it remains a standard work of reference for both Orientalists and mediaevalists.

This volume—a very modest work compared with either of these two—of course includes passages from both. Most of the excerpts, however, are taken directly from the original texts, nearly all of which have now been published or are available in the collection of photostats of historical manuscripts at the Fondazione Caetani per gli studi musulmani in Rome. Seventeen authors are represented; certainly not an exhaustive list of all the Muslim sources for the Crusades, but including all the most important ones and as many as possible of the various types of historical literary writings mentioned earlier. The translation is inevitably fairly free, for a literal translation would be impossible to read easily for any length of time. The precise references given will enable Arabists to verify particular points. While acknowledging our debt to earlier translators, where they have existed, and apologizing for our inevitable errors, we hope that the best interpretation of these passages will be found here, based on emendations to the text that will easily be reconstructed by the specialist.

The criteria of choice will be quite obvious: historical importance, human or literary interest and amusing or picturesque detail—without much historical importance perhaps, but the sort of vivid image that remains fixed in the memory, and is almost too appealing to Muslim historians and modern anthologists.

The second section of the book, devoted to Saladin and the Third Crusade, is inevitably, by both these criteria, the largest. We hope that the book as a whole will give a picture of the period that is both clear in outline and accurate in detail, and that as far as space allows the authors' characteristic styles will be revealed.

I have come to the end of several months spent in the company of these Muslim historians of the Crusades, listening again to their fierce and fanatical hostility to our ancestral faith, their zeal and love for their own faith and its traditions, and their admiration for the champions and martyrs who devoted themselves to its defence. I have studied the Muslim world for many years, but I must confess that never before have I experienced such a sympathetic comprehension and respect for a civilization whose faults and failings need no emphasis but which possessed inspiring qualities of endurance, dedication and self-sacrifice, amazing elasticity and powers of recuperation, and an unyielding faith in the absolute and supreme Law. When qualities such as these are shown by an enemy they tend to be described in terms of their associated defects. It is time for us, without either denying our own faith or shirking the facts, to give them the name they deserve.

Rome, September 1957.

In this second edition certain errors have been corrected and the bibliography brought up to date.

June 1963.

FRANCESCO GABRIELI

TRANSLATOR'S NOTE

In transcribing Arabic proper nouns we have ignored, for the sake of typographical simplicity, the distinction between long and short vowels and the normal and emphatic consonants. As a guide to pronunciation where the stress does not fall on the penultimate syllable words have been accented by a bar if long or by an acute accent if short. The titles of the sections are sometimes the author's and sometimes the editor's; it did not seem necessary to complicate the layout by distinguishing between the two.

F.G.

A standard transliteration of Arabic words into English has been used except in a few cases, where we have kept a very familiar anglicized form.

E.J.C.

BIBLIOGRAPHIC NOTE

General modern histories of the Crusades written by non-Orientalists who have however made use of Reinaud and the *Recueil* (see above) are R. Grousset, *Histoire des Croisades et du Royaume Franc de Jérusalem*, Paris, 1934–36; S. Runciman, *A History of the Crusades*, Cambridge, 1951–54, both in three volumes with enormous bibliographies (R. Grousset has also produced a popular general outline of the period, *L'épopée des Croisades*, Paris, 1939); and A. Waas, *Geschichte der Kreuzzüge*, Freiburg, 1956, 2 vols. Two volumes have so far appeared of the great *History of the Crusades*, the work of many collaborators edited by La Monte and Setton: *The first hundred years* and *The later Crusades, 1189–1311*, Philadelphia, 1955 and 1962.

The definitive work on Muslim historiography and its varieties is F. Rosenthal, *A History of Muslim Historiography*, Leiden, 1952; for a review and fundamental evaluation of the Arab historians of the Crusades see C. Cahen, *La Syrie du Nord à l'époque des Croisades et la principauté franque d'Antioche*, Paris, 1940, pp. 33–93 ('Les sources arabes'), which has been brought up to date by Cahen in his article on the Crusades in *Encyclopédie de l'Islam*, 2nd ed. (1961), pp. 64–67. See also my own chapter *Historiography of the Crusades* in *Historians of the Middle East*, Oxford, 1962, pp. 98–107. A bibliography of individual authors and subjects would, I think, be too specialized to be useful; I shall only mention H. A. R. Gibb's three important studies: 'Notes on the arabic materials for the history of the early Crusades', in *Bulletin of the School of Oriental Studies*, VII

(1935), pp. 739–54; 'The arabic sources for the life of Saladin', in *Speculum*, XXV (1950), pp. 58–72; and 'The achievement of Saladin', in *Bulletin of the John Rylands Library*, XXXV (1952), pp. 44–60 (for Saladin see also my own profile in *Storia e civiltà musulmana*, Naples, 1947 and Florence, 1948); also J. Kraemer, *Der Sturz des Königreiches Jerusalem (583–1187) in der Darstellung des 'Imād ad-Dīn al-Kātib al-Iṣfahānī*, Wiesbaden, 1952; B. Lewis, 'The sources for the history of the Syrian Assassins', in *Speculum*, XXVII (1952), pp. 475–89; F. Gabrieli, 'Gli Ospitalieri di San Giovanni negli storici musulmani delle Crociate', in *Annuario della R. Scuola Archeologica di Atene*, VIII–IX (1929), pp. 345–56.

THE AUTHORS AND WORKS

IBN AL-QALĀNISI[1]

Abu Ya'la Hamza ibn Asad at-Tamīmī, known as Ibn al-Qalānisi (Damascus, *c.* 465/1073–555/1160). He is the earliest Arab historian to write about the Crusades, in his chronicle known as *Dhail ta'rīkh Dimashq* (*Appendix to the History of Damascus*, referring to a chronicle of that title by Hilāl as-Sabi). This work, which is attached to as-Sabi's in a single MS., covers the period 363/974–555/1160, the year of the author's death, and deals to some extent with the history of Mesopotamia, but chiefly of Syria and Damascus, where Ibn al-Qalānisi held various municipal and administrative posts. He writes from first-hand experience of the First and Second Crusades up to the time of Nur ad-Din's entry into Damascus. The narrative is circumstantial and accurate, showing a certain partiality for Tughtikīn's dynasty in Damascus. The style is dry and objective, apart from a few chapters in more stylised prose. His objectivity about most matters, his eye-witness accounts of events through which he lived and his use of documents make Ibn al-Qalānisi's chronicle a basic source for the first period of the Crusades.

Text: Amedroz' edition, Leiden, 1908.

[1] The order of these notes, which in all cases but the first corresponds to that in which the authors appear in the book, is only roughly related to their chronological order.

IBN AL-ATHĪR

'Izz ad-Din Ibn al-Athīr (Jazirat Ibn 'Umar, 555/1160–Mosul 630/1233) came of a Mesopotamian family and is the most famous of three brothers, all well known to Muslims of Arabic education. His most important work is *Kamil at-Tawarikh* (*The Perfect History*, or *The Collection of Histories*), an enormous history of the whole Muslim world from Arabic and Hebrew legends and the history of pre-Muhammedan times to the year 628/1231. For the earlier period (to the beginning of the tenth century A.D.) he reproduces for the most part at-Tábari's great collection, but for the last three centuries and in particular for his own period the breadth and balance of his statements, the wealth of material collected and above all his robust and personal view of history make him a very important source; some would call him the only real Arab historian of the period. This marked individuality is also the cause of his defects as an author: a tendency sometimes to favour the Zangid dynasty (Zangi, Nur ad-Din and their successors), inaccurate chronology and sometimes a certain lack of respect for his sources. But with these reservations one can only admire the unity of a work that embraces the whole Muslim world from Transoxiana to the farthest Maghrib and Spain, one in which the author seeks to trace the causal links of events, and is able to overcome the difficulties of the annalist's technique and present his facts clearly and convincingly.

For his history of the Crusades Ibn al-Athīr was an eye-witness, although not always a sympathetic one, of Saladin's career, and made use of Ibn al-Qalānisi, Bahā' ad-Din and 'Imād ad-Din as sources. The clarity and simplicity of his style, which avoids archaisms and embellishments and aims at presenting the essential facts, has contributed to his reputation as the chief historian of the later Crusades.

Text: Tornberg's edition, vols. X, XI, XII, Leiden, 1853–64.

KAMĀL AD-DIN

Kamāl ad-Din Ibn al-'Adīm (Aleppo 588/1192–Cairo 660/1262) was the historian of his native city, in particular in an enormous biographical work, not yet published in modern times, (*Bughyat at-Talab*, *The Students' Desire*), of which only a part remains, and also in a history of the city (*Zubdat al-halab fi ta'rīkh Halab*, *The Cream of the Milk in the History of Aleppo*), based on material collected for the larger work and extending to 641/1243. This work does for Aleppo of the twelfth and thirteenth centuries what Ibn al-Qalānisi's chronicle does for twelfth-century Damascus. Its value to historians of the Crusades is as an Arabic account of the events in northern Syria.

Text: Sami Dahhān's edition, II, Damascus, 1954.

USAMA

Usama ibn Munqidh, Amīr of Shaizar (Shaizar 488/1095–Damascus 584/1188) is one of the most interesting of the Syrian Arabs living during the Crusades. A man of action and a writer, horseman and huntsman, lover of books and courtier, and an unscrupulous political intriguer, he spent most of his long life in contact with the Franks, the amīrs of Syria and the Fatimid Caliphs of Egypt, but in the end died in obscurity at the height of Saladin's triumphs. He owes his reputation to his autobiography (*Kitāb al-I'tibār*, *Book of Instruction with illustrations*), which has come down to us in an incomplete MS. in the Escurial. It is a sincere if rather verbose self-portrait, and a storehouse of anecdotal information about his Muslim and Frankish contemporaries. Only fragments of the rest of his rich literary production are preserved, among them the *Kitāb al-'Asa* (*The Book of the Stick*), a collection in the traditional Arabic manner of anecdotes, rhymes, sayings and proverbs on the subject of sticks. The last of our selections from his work is taken from this book.

Text: Derenbourg's edition, Paris, 1886 (and for the last example, H. Derenbourg, *Ousama ibn Mounkidh. Un émir syrien au premier siècle des Croisades*, I, Paris, 1893, pp. 528–29).

BAHĀ' AD-DIN

Bahā' ad-Din Ibn Shaddād (Mosul 539/1145–632/1234) entered Saladin's service in 1188, was made Qadi to the army and remained a faithful member of the Sultan's household until Saladin's death. Under his immediate successors he was Grand Qadi of Aleppo. His biography of the Sultan (*an-Nawadir as-Sultaniyya wa l-mahasin al-yusufiyya*, *Sultanly Anecdotes and Josephly Virtues*, Joseph being Saladin's personal name) is an excellent historical and biographical source, dictated by sincere devotion and admiration unmixed with servile flattery and based for the most part on personal observation. The style is simple and free from literary affectations. Bahā' ad-Din gives us the most complete portrait we have of Saladin as the Muslims saw him, and a vivid chronicle of the Third Crusade.

Text: in *Recueil des Historiens des Croisades, Historiens Orientaux*, III, Paris, 1884.

'IMĀD AD-DIN

'Imād ad-Din al-Isfahani (Isfahan 519/1125–Damascus 597/1201) was secretary to Nur ad-Din and then to Saladin, whose chancellor he was under the Qadi al-Fadil. He was a scholar and a rhetorician to the marrow and left a valuable anthology of twelfth-century Arabic poetry as well as various historical works, written from start to finish in the most ornate and artificial style of which the language is capable: blank and rhyming verse, uninterrupted sequences of alliteration, metaphors and puns. This difficult and tedious literary form soon led other anthologists such as Abu Shama (see below) to give the gist of 'Imād ad-Din's history elsewhere, but there are facts of vital historical importance not included in these synopses for which we must go back to the original. Preserved and published in the same volume is 'Imād ad-Din's history of the fall of Jerusalem, which extends as far as Saladin's death (*al-Fath al-qussi fi l-fath al-qudsi*, which might be translated *Ciceronian Eloquence on the Conquest of the Holy City*: puns find their way even into the title); we also have a part, still unedited, of the *Barq ash-Shami*, or *Lightning of Syria*, which chronicles Saladin's life and deeds from 1175. In these two works modern research is revealing, beneath the impossible style, an important source for Saladin's career and for events in Syria and Mesopotamia, in which 'Imād ad-Din was a protagonist and which he describes circumstantially, accurately and faithfully. We have, however, to contend with the fact, clearly revealed in the passages chosen, that the concrete details are almost lost in an appalling mass of verbiage.

Text: Landberg's edition, Leiden, 1888.

ABU SHAMA

Shihāb ad-Din Abu l-Qasim Abu Shama (Damascus 599/1203–665/1267) was a philologist, teacher and industrious anthologist. His *Kitāb ar-Raudatáin*, *The Book of the Two Gardens*, concerning the two dynasties of Saladin and Nur ad-Din, brings together valuable material, for most of which we also have his original sources. He quotes (giving his references) from Ibn al-Qalānisi, 'Imād ad-Din (reduced to a more sober and endurable style), Bahā' ad-Din, Ibn al-Athīr and others. More important to us are his quotations from the lost Shi'ite historian of Aleppo, Ibn Abi t-Tayy, among other things the author of a biography of Saladin. *The Two Gardens* also reproduces numerous documents from the Sultan's chancellery, most of them from the chief secretary, individual collections of whose letters also exist.

Text: Cairo 1287/1870.

MANAQIB RASHID AD-DIN

We use this name to refer to a writer of the Isma'ilite sect in Syria (the Assassins). The *Virtues of our Lord Rashid ad-Din*, as the full title of his work may be translated, is a collection of recollections and anecdotes about the Great Master Rashid ad-Din Sinān, a contemporary of Saladin and thus leader of the sect in Syria at the time of Saladin's greatest power. These records, in which edification is given a much more important place than historical information, were collected in 1324 by an obscure follower of the sect, Shaikh Abu Firās of Máinaqa, at a time when the influence of the Isma'ilites was on the wane. The passage translated here appears, under its cloak of legend, to be an account of the assassination of Conrad of Montferrat.

Text: 'Journal Asiatique' series VII, IX (1877), pp. 324–489 (S. Guyard, *Un grand Maitre des Assassins au temps de Saladin*).

IBN WASIL

Jamāl ad-Din Ibn Wasil (Hamāt 604/1207–697/1298) held several offices under the last Ayyubids and early Mamlūks. In 1261 he went as Baibars' ambassador to Manfred, and ended his career as Grand Qadi of his native city. His greatest work (*Mufarrij al-Kurūb fi akhbār Bani Ayyūb, The Dissipator of*

Anxieties Concerning the History of the Ayyubids) is chiefly concerned with Saladin's career, but first deals with the history of the Zangids, and after Saladin with the Mamlūks up to 680/1282. It is therefore one of the best sources for the thirteenth-century Crusades (the Fifth Crusade, Frederick II's journey, St. Louis' Crusade); later anthologists have drawn from it. It has long remained unpublished, for no good reason, and an edition is only now under way.[1]

Text: MS. Paris Ar. 1702 (photostat from the Caetani collection).

SIBT IBN AL-JAUZI

The grandson (*sibt*) of an earlier chronicler, Ibn al-Jauzi, was a famous preacher who lived for most of his life in Damascus as a friend of the Ayyubid princes (Baghdād 582/1186–Damascus 654/1256). His enormous and prolix universal history (*Mir'āt az-zamān*, *The Mirror of the Times*), of which two versions have come down to us, is particularly important because of the period of the author's life and the course of Syrian history at that time. It is to this work, for example, that we owe the fascinating details of Frederick's visit to Jerusalem, as well as some illuminating details of the siege of Damascus by the Crusaders a century before.

Text: a partial edition by Jewett, Chicago, 1907 (covering the years of the *hijra* 495–654). For the siege of Damascus, see a note in Amedroz' edition of Ibn al-Qalānisi.

Ta'rīkh Mansuri

The chronicle, taking us up to 631/1233, of an obscure functionary of the Ayyubid princes of Syria, a certain Abu l-Fada'il of Hamāt; dedicated to al-Malik al-Mansūr, Amīr of Hims

[1] Three volumes, edited by M. Shayyāl (Cairo 1954–62) have so far appeared.

(from whom the title comes; *A Mansurite History*). Its importance lies in the facts it gives about Frederick II in the Holy Land, and the end of the Muslims in Sicily as described by Sicilian Arabs who came to Syria as emissaries and refugees. These valuable fragments, from the Asiatic Museum in Petersburg, were edited by Amari.

Text: in *Biblioteca Arabo-Sicula*, Second Appendix, Leipzig, 1887.

IBN ʻABD AZ-ZAHIR

Muhyi ad-Din Ibn ʻAbd az-Zahir (Cairo 620/1233–692/1293) was secretary to the Mamlūk Sultans Baibars and Qalawūn, compiler of their official acts of chancellery and later their biographer, drawing on the material he had collected. Parts of Baibars' biography (*Sirat al-Malik az-Zahir*) still exist, and so does the anthology edited by his nephew Shafiʻ al-ʻAsqalani. The greater part of the biography of Qalawūn is to be found in the anonymous *Tashrīf al-ayyām wa l-ʻusūr bi-sirat as-Sultān al-Malik al-Mansūr* (*The Honouring of the Years and the Days, through the Life of the Sultan al-Malik al-Mansūr*). Ibn ʻAbd az-Zahir also wrote a life of Qalawūn's son al-Ashraf, conqueror of Acre, of which a fragment has been published. The rest of this author's work is so far unedited, despite his importance as a contemporary and witness of the events narrated and a transmitter of precious official documents (letters, treaties etc.). Naturally his obsequious attitude to his masters makes it necessary to use his information with caution.

Text: Shafi''s anthology of the life of Baibars, MS. Paris Ar. 1707, and *Tashrīf* (Life of Qalawūn) MS. Paris Ar. 1704 (photostat from the Caetani collection).

Tashrīf

See Ibn ʻAbd az-Zahir.

MAQRIZI

Taqi ad-Din al-Maqrizi (Cairo 776/1364–845/1442), a great scholar and antiquarian, collected valuable material on the historical topography of Egypt. His importance for our period lies in one of his historical works which is almost entirely compiled from other writers (Ibn Wasil, Sibt Ibn al-Jauzi, Ibn 'Abd az-Zahir and other lesser-known sources) but which is indispensable in our present state of knowledge: his *Kitāb as-sulūk fi má'rifa ta'rīkh al-mulūk, The Book of Proceeding to the Knowledge of the History of the Kings*, which includes Ayyubid and Mamlūk history from 577/1181 to 840/1436. It therefore covers the two Frankish expeditions to Egypt and the Mamlūks' final victory in Syria.

Text: M. Ziyade's edition, Cairo, 1934.

IBN AL-FURĀT

Nasir ad-Din Ibn al-Furāt (Cairo 735/1334–807/1405) was, like Maqrizi and almost all his contemporaries, a great anthologist whose importance depends on that of the sources transcribed by him. His great *Ta'rīkh ad-duwal wa l-mulūk, The History of the Dynasties and the Kings*, of which parts of an unpublished MS. are in existence, brings us up to the end of the fourteenth century and contains interesting material on the early Mamlūks. Another long-recognized value of Ibn al-Furāt, as of Abu Shama, is his quotations from the lost Ibn Abi t-Tayy on Saladin's life and times.

Text: Wien Ar. 814 A.F., vols. VI, VII (photostat from the Caetani collection).

AL-‘AINI

Badr ad-Din al-‘Aini (‘Aintāb 762/1360–Cairo 855/1451) was a Mamlūk official and courtier as well as a philologist and student of *hadīth*. He also compiled a general history (*‘Iqd al-Jumān fi ta'rīkh ahl az-zamān, The Necklace of Pearls concerning the History of the People of the Time*) which is usually consulted for sources not yet attributed to known authors or directly accessible.

Text: *Recueil des Historiens des Croisades, Historiens Orientaux*, II, Paris, 1887.

ABU L-FIDĀ'

Abu l-Fidā' 'Imād ad-Din Isma'īl ibn 'Ali al-Ayyubi, the *Abulfeda* of eighteenth- and nineteenth-century Arabists, is a sympathetic figure, an amīr who is also a man of letters, rather in the style of Usama. He was a member of the Ayyubid house after it had lost all autonomous power, supplanted in Syria and Egypt by the Mamlūks, and he succeeded in getting them to recognize his rights to Hamāt, where he ruled with the title of al-Malik al-Mu'ayyad until his death. His two main literary works, the history (*Mukhtasar ta'rīkh al-Bashar, Historical Compendium of the Human Race*) and the geography (*Taqwīm al-buldān, Determination of the Longitude of the Lands*), happened to be among the first works of Arabic literature to be known and partially edited in Europe since the beginning of the modern Arabist movement here. This led at first to an over estimation of the value of these two anthologies, which have been almost supplanted by the older originals discovered since then. The section of the history dealing with the author's own lifetime retains its interest. He saw service as a young man at the fall of

Tripoli and Acre and so was an eye-witness of the tragic ending of the Crusades.

Text: *Recueil des Historiens des Croisades, Historiens Orientaux*, I, Paris, 1872.

ABU L-MAHASIN

Abu l-Mahasin Ibn Taghribirdi (Cairo 813/1411–874/1469) was also one of the group of soldiers and scholars who flourished in the Mamlūk era. His great history of Egypt (*An-Nujūm az-Zāhira fi mulūk Misr wa l-Qāhira, The Shining Stars concerning the Kings of Egypt and Cairo*), is a vast general chronicle of Egyptian history until 857/1453. It is however entirely an anthology of other men's work. His account of the siege and conquest of Acre under al-Ashraf (from a contemporary source), when compared with that of Abu l-Fidā', is the most interesting Muslim account of the event known to us. In the published fragment of Ibn 'Abd az Zahir's biography of the Sultan there is no reference to this event.

Text: MS. Paris Ar. 1873 (photostat from the Caetani collection).[1]

[1] The relevant period is not included in the two Western editions of the *Nujūm*, those of Juynboll and Matthes and of Popper. I have not been able to consult the Cairo edition.

Part One

FROM GODFREY TO SALADIN

CHAPTER ONE

Our main sources for the First Crusade are Ibn al-Qalānisi of Damascus and the Mesopotamian Ibn al-Athīr. Whereas Ibn al-Qalānisi limits himself to a chronological list of events, Ibn al-Athīr relates the various stages of the Crusade to the whole picture of Christian uprisings against Islām, beginning with the reconquest of Spain and the Norman invasion of Sicily. He gives the most complete and convincing, if not the most strictly factual, account of the fall of Antioch and Jerusalem, the establishment of Christian kingdoms in the Holy Land and the first Muslim attempts at retaliation.

THE FRANKS SEIZE ANTIOCH

(IBN AL-ATHĪR, X, 185–8)

The power of the Franks first became apparent when in the year 478/1085–86 they invaded the territories of Islām and took Toledo and other parts of Andalusia, as was mentioned earlier. Then in 484/1091 they attacked and conquered the island of Sicily[1] and turned their attention to the African coast. Certain of their conquests there were won back again but they had other successes, as you will see.

In 490/1097 the Franks attacked Syria. This is how it all began: Baldwin, their King,[2] a kinsman of Roger the Frank who had conquered Sicily, assembled a great army and sent word to Roger saying: 'I have assembled a great army and now I am on my way to you, to use your bases for my conquest of the African coast. Thus you and I shall become neighbours.'

Roger called together his companions and consulted them about these proposals. 'This will be a fine thing both for them

[1] This date clearly refers to the end of the Norman conquest.

[2] This Baldwin (*Bardawīl*) is a mythical character, compounded of the various Baldwins of Flanders and Jerusalem; or else the first Baldwin is mistakenly thought to have been already a king in the West.

and for us!' they declared, 'for by this means these lands will be converted to the Faith!' At this Roger raised one leg and farted loudly, and swore that it was of more use than their advice.[1] 'Why?' 'Because if this army comes here it will need quantities of provisions and fleets of ships to transport it to Africa, as well as reinforcements from my own troops. Then, if the Franks succeed in conquering this territory they will take it over and will need provisioning from Sicily. This will cost me my annual profit from the harvest. If they fail they will return here and be an embarrassment to me here in my own domain. As well as all this Tamīm[2] will say that I have broken faith with him and violated our treaty, and friendly relations and communications between us will be disrupted. As far as we are concerned, Africa is always there. When we are strong enough we will take it.'

He summoned Baldwin's messenger and said to him: 'If you have decided to make war on the Muslims your best course will be to free Jerusalem from their rule and thereby win great honour. I am bound by certain promises and treaties of allegiance with the rulers of Africa.' So the Franks made ready and set out to attack Syria.

Another story is that the Fatimids of Egypt were afraid when they saw the Seljuqids extending their empire through Syria as far as Gaza, until they reached the Egyptian border and Atsiz[3] invaded Egypt itself. They therefore sent to invite the Franks to invade Syria and so protect Egypt from the Muslims.[4] But God knows best.

When the Franks decided to attack Syria they marched east

[1] It is disagreeable to find the great Count acting like a barbarian on the very first page, but the passage is characteristic of the contemptuous crudity with which the Muslims usually spoke of their enemies, as well as giving a fairly accurate picture of Roger's political acumen.

[2] The Zirid amīr of Tunisia Tamīm ibn Mu'ízz.

[3] A general of the Seljuqid Sultan Malikshāh, who in 1076 attacked Egypt from Palestine.

[4] Of course the Fatimids were also Muslims, but they were heretics and so opposed to the rest of *sunni* Islām.

to Constantinople, so that they could cross the straits and advance into Muslim territory by the easier, land route. When they reached Constantinople, the Emperor of the East refused them permission to pass through his domains. He said: 'Unless you first promise me Antioch, I shall not allow you to cross into the Muslim empire.' His real intention was to incite them to attack the Muslims, for he was convinced that the Turks, whose invincible control over Asia Minor he had observed, would exterminate every one of them. They accepted his conditions and in 490/1097 they crossed the Bosphorus at Constantinople. Iconium and the rest of the area into which they now advanced belonged to Qilij Arslān ibn Sulaimān ibn Qutlumísh, who barred their way with his troops. They broke through[1] in rajab 490/July 1097, crossed Cilicia,[2] and finally reached Antioch, which they besieged.

When Yaghi Siyān, the ruler of Antioch, heard of their approach, he was not sure how the Christian people of the city would react, so he made the Muslims go outside the city on their own to dig trenches, and the next day sent the Christians out alone to continue the task. When they were ready to return home at the end of the day he refused to allow them. 'Antioch is yours,' he said, 'but you will have to leave it to me until I see what happens between us and the Franks.' 'Who will protect our children and our wives?' they said. 'I shall look after them for you.' So they resigned themselves to their fate, and lived in the Frankish camp for nine months, while the city was under siege.

Yaghi Siyān showed unparalleled courage and wisdom, strength and judgment. If all the Franks who died had survived they would have overrun all the lands of Islām. He protected the families of the Christians in Antioch and would not allow a hair of their heads to be touched.

[1] At Dorylaeum.

[2] Literally 'the land of the son of Armenus' as the Arab writers call the Lesser Armenia of the Cilician Roupenians.

After the siege had been going on for a long time the Franks made a deal with one of the men who were responsible for the towers. He was a cuirass-maker called Ruzbih[1] whom they bribed with a fortune in money and lands. He worked in the tower that stood over the river-bed, where the river flowed out of the city into the valley. The Franks sealed their pact with the cuirass-maker, God damn him! and made their way to the water-gate. They opened it and entered the city. Another gang of them climbed the tower with ropes. At dawn, when more than 500 of them were in the city and the defenders were worn out after the night watch, they sounded their trumpets. Yaghi Siyān woke up and asked what the noise meant. He was told that trumpets had sounded from the citadel and that it must have been taken. In fact the sound came not from the citadel but from the tower. Panic seized Yaghi Siyān and he opened the city gates and fled in terror, with an escort of thirty pages. His army commander arrived, but when he discovered on enquiry that Yaghi Siyān had fled, he made his escape by another gate. This was of great help to the Franks, for if he had stood firm for an hour, they would have been wiped out. They entered the city by the gates and sacked it, slaughtering all the Muslims they found there. This happened in jumada I (491/April/May 1098).[2] As for Yaghi Siyān, when the sun rose he recovered his self control and realized that his flight had taken him several *farsakh*[3] from the city. He asked his companions where he was, and on hearing that he was four *farsakh* from Antioch he repented of having rushed to safety instead of staying to fight to the death. He began to groan and weep for his desertion of his household and children. Overcome by the violence of his grief he fell fainting from his horse. His companions tried to lift him back into the saddle, but they could not get him to sit up, and so left him for dead while they escaped.

[1] *Firūz* is an alternative reading.
[2] June 3 according to European sources.
[3] One *farsakh* (parasang) is about four miles.

He was at his last gasp when an Armenian shepherd came past, killed him, cut off his head and took it to the Franks at Antioch.

The Franks had written to the rulers of Aleppo and Damascus to say that they had no interest in any cities but those that had once belonged to Byzantium. This was a piece of deceit calculated to dissuade these rulers from going to the help of Antioch.

THE MUSLIM ATTACK ON THE FRANKS, AND ITS RESULTS

(IBN AL-ATHĪR, X, 188–90)

When Qawām ad-Daula Kerbuqā[1] heard that the Franks had taken Antioch he mustered his army and advanced into Syria, where he camped at Marj Dabiq. All the Turkish and Arab forces in Syria rallied to him except for the army from Aleppo. Among his supporters were Duqāq ibn Tutūsh,[2] the Ata-beg Tughtikīn, Janāh ad-Daula of Hims, Arslān Tash of Sanjār, Sulaimān ibn Artūq and other less important amīrs. When the Franks heard of this they were alarmed and afraid, for their troops were weak and short of food. The Muslims advanced and came face to face with the Franks in front of Antioch. Kerbuqā, thinking that the present crisis would force the Muslims to remain loyal to him, alienated them by his pride and ill-treatment of them. They plotted in secret anger to betray him and desert him in the heat of battle.

After taking Antioch the Franks camped there for twelve days without food. The wealthy ate their horses and the poor ate carrion and leaves from the trees. Their leaders, faced with this situation, wrote to Kerbuqā to ask for safe-conduct through his territory but he refused, saying 'You will have to fight your

[1] The Turkish amīr of Mosul.

[2] The Seljuqid Lord of Damascus, soon to be succeeded by his general, the Ata-beg Tughtikīn, whose name comes next on the list and who was to be one of the most active and tenacious opponents of the Crusades during this first phase of conquest.

way out.' Among the Frankish leaders were Baldwin,[1] Saint-Gilles, Godfrey of Bouillon, the future Count of Edessa, and their leader Bohemond of Antioch. There was also a holy man who had great influence over them, a man of low cunning, who proclaimed that the Messiah had a lance buried in the Qusyān, a great building in Antioch:[2] 'And if you find it you will be victorious and if you fail you will surely die.' Before saying this he had buried a lance in a certain spot and concealed all trace of it. He exhorted them to fast and repent for three days, and on the fourth day he led them all to the spot with their soldiers and workmen, who dug everywhere and found the lance as he had told them.[3] Whereupon he cried 'Rejoice! For victory is secure.' So on the fifth day they left the city in groups of five or six. The Muslims said to Kerbuqā: 'You should go up to the city and kill them one by one as they come out; it is easy to pick them off now that they have split up.' He replied: 'No, wait until they have all come out and then we will kill them.' He would not allow them to attack the enemy and when some Muslims killed a group of Franks, he went himself to forbid such behaviour and prevent its recurrence. When all the Franks had come out and not one was left in Antioch, they began to attack strongly, and the Muslims turned and fled. This was Kerbuqā's fault, first because he had treated the Muslims with such contempt and scorn, and second because he had prevented their killing the Franks. The Muslims were completely routed without striking a single blow or firing a single arrow. The last to flee were Suqmān ibn Artūq and Janāh ad-Daula, who had been sent to set an ambush. Kerbuqā escaped with them. When the Franks saw this they were afraid that a trap was being set for them, for there had not even been any fighting to

[1] Baldwin of Le Bourg, later Baldwin II.

[2] The Church of St. Peter in Antioch, called in Byzantine sources *Κασσιανός* and in Arabic sources *Qusyān*, from the name of the man whose son was raised from the dead by St. Peter.

[3] The Finding of the Sacred Lance, at the instigation of Peter Bartholomew, seen through rationalistic Muslim eyes.

flee from, so they dared not follow them. The only Muslims to stand firm were a detachment of warriors from the Holy Land, who fought to acquire merit in God's eyes and to seek martyrdom. The Franks killed them by the thousand and stripped their camp of food and possessions, equipment, horses and arms, with which they re-equipped themselves.

THE FRANKS TAKE MA'ARRAT AN-NU'MĀN

(IBN AL-ATHĪR, X, 190)

After dealing this blow to the Muslims the Franks marched on Ma'arrat an-Nu'mān and besieged it. The inhabitants valiantly defended their city. When the Franks realized the fierce determination and devotion of the defenders they built a wooden tower as high as the city wall and fought from the top of it, but failed to do the Muslims any serious harm. One night a few Muslims were seized with panic and in their demoralized state thought that if they barricaded themselves into one of the town's largest buildings they would be in a better position to defend themselves, so they climbed down from the wall and abandoned the position they were defending. Others saw them and followed their example, leaving another stretch of wall undefended, and gradually, as one group followed another, the whole wall was left unprotected and the Franks scaled it with ladders. Their appearance in the city terrified the Muslims, who shut themselves up in their houses. For three days the slaughter never stopped; the Franks killed more than 100,000 men and took innumerable prisoners. After taking the town the Franks spent six weeks shut up there, then sent an expedition to 'Arqa, which they besieged for four months. Although they breached the wall in many places they failed to storm it. Munqidh, the ruler of Shaizar, made a treaty with them about 'Arqa and they left it to pass on to Hims. Here too the ruler Janāh ad-Daula made a treaty with them, and they advanced to Acre by way of an-Nawaqir. However they did not succeed in taking Acre.

THE FRANKS CONQUER JERUSALEM

(IBN AL-ATHĪR, X, 193–95)

Taj ad-Daula Tutūsh[1] was the Lord of Jerusalem but had given it as a feoff to the amīr Suqmān ibn Artūq the Turcoman. When the Franks defeated the Turks at Antioch the massacre demoralized them, and the Egyptians, who saw that the Turkish armies were being weakened by desertion, besieged Jerusalem under the command of al-Afdal ibn Badr al-Jamali.[2] Inside the city were Artūq's sons, Suqmān and Ilghazi, their cousin Sunij and their nephew Yaquti. The Egyptians brought more than forty siege engines to attack Jerusalem and broke down the walls at several points. The inhabitants put up a defence, and the siege and fighting went on for more than six weeks. In the end the Egyptians forced the city to capitulate, in sha'bān 489/August 1096.[3] Suqmān, Ilghazi and their friends were well treated by al-Afdal, who gave them large gifts of money and let them go free. They made for Damascus and then crossed the Euphrates. Suqmān settled in Edessa and Ilghazi went on into Iraq. The Egyptian governor of Jerusalem was a certain Iftikhār ad-Daula, who was still there at the time of which we are speaking.

After their vain attempt to take Acre by siege, the Franks moved on to Jerusalem and besieged it for more than six weeks. They built two towers, one of which, near Sion, the Muslims burnt down, killing everyone inside it. It had scarcely ceased to burn before a messenger arrived to ask for help and to bring the news that the other side of the city had fallen. In fact Jeru-

[1] A Syrian Seljuqid, Malikshāh's brother. [2] The Fatimid vizier.

[3] If this date were correct the connection with the fall of Antioch would no longer exist. In fact the date given here is wrong: the Egyptians took Jerusalem in August 1098.

salem was taken from the north on the morning of Friday 22 sha'bān 492/15 July 1099. The population was put to the sword by the Franks, who pillaged the area for a week. A band of Muslims barricaded themselves into the Oratory of David[1] and fought on for several days. They were granted their lives in return for surrendering. The Franks honoured their word, and the group left by night for Ascalon. In the Masjid al-Aqsa the Franks slaughtered more than 70,000 people, among them a large number of Imams and Muslim scholars, devout and ascetic men who had left their homelands to live lives of pious seclusion in the Holy Place. The Franks stripped the Dome of the Rock[2] of more than forty silver candelabra, each of them weighing 3,600 drams, and a great silver lamp weighing forty-four Syrian pounds, as well as a hundred and fifty smaller silver candelabra and more than twenty gold ones, and a great deal more booty. Refugees from Syria reached Baghdād in ramadan, among them the qadi Abu Sa'd al-Hárawi. They told the Caliph's ministers a story that wrung their hearts and brought tears to their eyes. On Friday they went to the Cathedral Mosque and begged for help, weeping so that their hearers wept with them as they described the sufferings of the Muslims in that Holy City: the men killed, the women and children taken prisoner, the homes pillaged. Because of the terrible hardships they had suffered, they were allowed to break the fast.

* * *

It was the discord between the Muslim princes, as we shall describe, that enabled the Franks to overrun the country. Abu

[1] The *Mihrāb Dawūd*, called the Tower of David in the European sources, in the citadel at Jerusalem. Not to be confused with a small sanctuary of the same name in the Temple precinct.

[2] The rock from which, the Muslims believe, Muhammad ascended into heaven. Over it was built the so-called 'Mosque of 'Umar', the chief Islamic monument in Jerusalem. It was from this Mosque that the conquerors took their booty. Near by, but separate from it, is the 'Farthest Mosque' (al-Masjid al-Aqsa), where according to Ibn al-Athīr the armies of the Cross showed even greater barbarity. The two sanctuaries are often confused in both Arabic and European sources.

l-Muzaffar al-Abiwardi[1] composed several poems on this subject, in one of which he says:

We have mingled blood with flowing tears, and there is no room left in us for pity(?)
To shed tears is a man's worst weapon when the swords stir up the embers of war.
Sons of Islām, behind you are battles in which heads rolled at your feet.
Dare you slumber in the blessed shade of safety, where life is as soft as an orchard flower?
How can the eye sleep between the lids at a time of disasters that would waken any sleeper?
While your Syrian brothers can only sleep on the backs of their chargers, or in vultures' bellies!
Must the foreigners feed on our ignominy, while you trail behind you the train of a pleasant life, like men whose world is at peace?
When blood has been spilt, when sweet girls must for shame hide their lovely faces in their hands!
When the white swords' points are red with blood, and the iron of the brown lances is stained with gore!
At the sound of sword hammering on lance young children's hair turns white.
This is war, and the man who shuns the whirlpool to save his life shall grind his teeth in penitence.
This is war, and the infidel's sword is naked in his hand, ready to be sheathed again in men's necks and skulls.
This is war, and he who lies in the tomb at Medina seems to raise his voice and cry: 'O sons of Hashim![2]
I see my people slow to raise the lance against the enemy: I see the Faith resting on feeble pillars.
For fear of death the Muslims are evading the fire of battle, refusing to believe that death will surely strike them.'
Must the Arab champions then suffer with resignation, while the gallant Persians shut their eyes to their dishonour?

[1] An Iraqi poet of the eleventh and twelfth centuries.

[2] The Prophet, who from the tomb raises his voice to rebuke his descendants (the sons of Hashim), that is, the unworthy Caliphs whose opposition to the Crusades is only half-hearted.

THE CAPTURE OF BOHEMOND OF ANTIOCH

(IBN AL-ATHĪR, X, 203–4)

In dhu l-qa'da of this year (493/September 1100) Kumushtikīn ibn ad-Danishmánd Tailū, Prince of Malatia, Siwās and other territories, met Bohemond the Frank, one of the Frankish leaders, near Malatia. The former governor of Malatia had a treaty of friendship with Bohemond and asked for his help. Bohemond came with 5,000 men, but was defeated in battle by Ibn ad-Danishmánd and taken prisoner. Then seven Frankish Counts came from across the sea to seek Bohemond's release. They came to a fortress called Ankuriyya, took it and killed the Muslims they found there, before passing on to another fort, which they besieged. Isma'īl ibn ad-Danishmánd, who was defending the fort, mustered his great army, set an ambush for the Franks and then challenged them to battle. Battle was joined, the ambush sprung and of the 300,000 Franks only 3,000 escaped, during the night, and even they were wounded and exhausted. Ibn ad-Danishmánd attacked Malatia, took it and imprisoned the governor. The Frankish army from Antioch came out to challenge him, but he fought and defeated them. All this happened in the space of a few months.

THE DEATH OF GODFREY AND THE FRANKISH CONQUESTS THAT FOLLOWED IT

(IBN AL-ATHĪR, X, 222)

In this year (493/1100) Godfrey, the Frankish King of Syria and ruler of Jerusalem, marched on the coastal city of Acre and besieged it, but was killed by an arrow.[1] Before his death he had fortified the city of Jaffa and handed it over to a Frankish Count

[1] All the Muslim sources say that Godfrey was killed in battle.

named Tancred. At Godfrey's death his brother Baldwin marched on Jerusalem with 500 cavalry and infantry. When Ibn Duqāq, King of Damascus, heard of this he led his army out against them, accompanied by Janāh ad-Daula of Hims, and together they defeated the Franks.

In the same year the Franks took Sarūj in Mesopotamia. They already held Edessa by agreement with its inhabitants, most of whom were Armenians with only a few Muslims. At this point Suqmān mustered a strong Turcoman army in Sarūj and attacked the Franks, but was defeated (in rabī' I January–February 1100). When the Franks had smashed the Muslim army in this way they marched on Sarūj, besieged it and took it. They slaughtered most of the men, enslaved the women and sacked the city. Only those who succeeded in getting out of the city escaped with their lives.

In the same year the Franks took the port of Haifa, near Acre, by storm and by a treaty with Arsūf, and expelled the population. In rajab/May they attacked and took Caesarea, murdered the inhabitants and sacked the city.

SAINT-GILLES THE FRANK BESIEGES TRIPOLI

(IBN AL-ATHĪR, X, 236–37)

Saint-Gilles the Frank[1]—God damn him!—and Qilíj Arslān ibn Sulaimān ibn Qutlumīsh, ruler of Iconium, met in battle. Saint-Gilles had 100,000 men[2] and Qilíj Arslān only a few. In the battle the Franks were routed, many of them killed or captured, and Qilíj Arslān returned home with the booty of this unexpected victory. Saint-Gilles, defeated, retired into Syria with 300 men. The Prince of Tripoli, Fakhr al-Mulk ibn 'Ammār,

[1] Raymond of Saint-Gilles, Count of Toulouse and founder of the Frankish dynasty in Tripoli.

[2] It is hardly necessary to point out that this is a ridiculous exaggeration, as is often the case with figures given by the Muslim chroniclers.

sent to the Amīr Yakhūz, who governed Hims for Janāh ad-Daula, and to Duqāq ibn Tutūsh, King of Damascus, to tell them of the opportunity to take advantage of Saint-Gilles' weakness. So Yakhūz went in person and Duqāq sent 2,000 men, who were joined by reinforcements from Tripoli. They gathered at the gates of Tripoli and challenged Saint-Gilles to battle. The Frankish prince ordered 100 of his men to attack the detachment from Tripoli, 100 more the army from Damascus, and another 50 the party from Hims. He kept the remaining 50 at his side. The men from Hims fled at the mere sight of the enemy, followed by the men from Damascus. Only the men from Tripoli stood firm and gave battle. When Saint-Gilles understood what had happened, he led a charge of the other 200 Franks against the Muslims, scattered them and killed 7,000 of them. Then he settled down to besiege Tripoli, aided by local men from the hills and the surrounding countryside, most of them Christians. The citizens defended themselves stubbornly, and 300 Franks were killed. Saint-Gilles made a pact with them, and in return for money and horses left Tripoli to attack Tortosa in the same province. The siege was successful: the Franks killed most of the inhabitants and then moved on to the fort of at-Tubān, near Rafaniyya, which was commanded by a certain Ibn al-'Arīd. In the battle that took place the Muslims were victorious and captured one of the leading Franks, for whom Saint-Gilles offered a ransom of 100,000 *dinar*[1] and 1,000 prisoners; but the offer was refused.

BOHEMOND IS LIBERATED, AND BALDWIN DEFEATED AT RAMLA

(IBN AL-ATHĪR, X, 237–8)

In this year (495/1102), Danishmánd freed Bohemond the

[1] Various standards of *dinar* were current in the mediaeval Muslim world; the weight of the 'legal' standard was 4.25 grams of fine gold.

Frank, ruler of Antioch, whose capture has just been described. The ransom was 100,000 *dinar* and the return of Yaghi Siyān's daughter, whom Bohemond had captured. On his release Bohemond went straight to Antioch, where his arrival gave his people new enthusiasm. It was not long before he sent emissaries through Syria to Qinnasrīn and the surrounding area to demand tribute. This caused the Muslims suffering that cancelled out the effects of Danishmánd's glorious exploits.

In the same year Saint-Gilles besieged Hisn al-Akrād.[1] Janāh ad-Daula was mustering an army to attack the Franks from the rear when he was murdered in the Great Mosque at Hims by one of the Batinite sect.[2] It is said that his kinsman King Ridwān put the knife into the assassin's hand. On the morning after his death Saint-Gilles appeared at the walls of Hims, which he besieged and took. From Hims he took over the control of all Janāh ad-Daula's domains.

In jumada II/April 1102 the Count besieged Acre and almost captured it. He brought up siege engines and towers, and blockaded the harbour with sixteen galleys. Muslims gathered from all along the coast, burnt the enemy's siege engines and towers and sank their ships. God gave the Muslims a glorious victory and cast down the infidels.

The Frankish Count of Edessa spent many months besieging Beirūt, but in the end he abandoned his efforts and withdrew his troops.

Finally in rajab/May 1102, the Egyptian armies marched on Ascalon to prevent the Franks from occupying what was left of the former Egyptian possessions in Syria. When Baldwin of Jerusalem heard the news he marched out against them at the head of 700 cavalry. But God granted the Muslims victory and

[1] 'Krak des Chevaliers', the mighty fortress north-east of Tripoli that played so important a part in the history of the Crusades.

[2] A member of the sect of Batinites, Isma'ilites or Assassins. Their terrorist activities, to which every history of the Crusades contains numerous references, were as unwelcome to the Muslims as to the Franks.

the Franks were routed with heavy losses. Baldwin tried to escape by hiding in a cane-brake but he was smoked out, badly burned. He fled to Ramla, closely pursued by the Muslims, and succeeded in reaching Haifa, although many of his followers died or were captured.

THE FRANKS TAKE JUBÁIL AND ACRE

(IBN AL-ATHĪR, X, 225)

In this year (497/1103–4) some ships reached Laodicea from the land of the Franks bringing merchants, soldiers, pilgrims and so on. Saint-Gilles used these as land and sea reinforcements in his siege of Tripoli, and continued his attack on the city. But he could not force an issue and so moved on to attack Jubáil vigorously. When the inhabitants realized that further resistance was useless they sued for peace and handed over the city. But the Franks failed to keep to the terms of the surrender; they seized the Muslims' possessions, using every form of violence and torture to extort them. After Jubáil they marched on to Acre to assist Baldwin, King of Jerusalem. The city was besieged by land and sea. The governor was a certain Bannā, known as Zahr ad-Daula al-Juyushi after the (Fatimid) vizier al-Malik al-Juyushi al-Afdal. He put up a vigorous resistance under repeated attacks, but finally capitulated and abandoned the city. The Franks took it by assault, and unleashed the full violence of their brutality on the population. The governor escaped to Damascus but after a while returned to Egypt to defend his conduct before al-Afdal, who accepted his explanation.

CHAPTER TWO

The following pages, also taken from Ibn al-Athīr, describe two important developments: the vigorous Muslim reaction to the Frankish drive on Harrān, an advance-post on the road to Baghdād, and the even more important Franco-Muslim coalitions that developed at this time to wage war among themselves. The Muslims' lack of any sort of unified policy, which had been of such advantage to the Crusaders, infected the victors as well, and Baldwin of Edessa and Tancred of Antioch had no scruples about entering into opposing alliance with rival Muslim amīrs.

SUQ ĀN AND CHEKERMĪSH LEAD AN EXPEDITION AGAINST THE FRANKS

(IBN AL-ATHĪR, X, 256–7)

While the Franks—God damn them!—were conquering and settling in a part of the territories of Islām, the rulers and armies of Islām were fighting among themselves, causing discord and disunity among their people and weakening their power to combat the enemy. The city of Harrān was ruled by one of Malikshāh's mamlūks, a man called Qaraja who a year before this had left the city under the command of a certain Muhammad al-Isfahani. This man, with popular support, rebelled against Qaraja because he was a tyrant, whereas al-Isfahani was an intelligent and energetic man. Qaraja's only supporter in Harrān was a Turkish page called Jawalī, whom al-Isfahani befriended and made commander of the army. One day, when they were drinking together and al-Isfahani was drunk, Jawalī killed him, with the connivance of one of his servants. Then the Frankish army from Edessa marched on Harrān.

Mu'īn ad-Daula Suqmān and Shams ad-Daula Chekermīsh[1] were involved in a vendetta caused by Chekermīsh's murder of Suqmān's nephew, as will be narrated later on, God willing. When they heard what had happened they suggested joining forces to save the situation at Harrān. Each declared that he offered himself to God and sought a reward in heaven alone. They welcomed one-another's overtures and set out for a rendezvous on the bank of the river Khabūr, where they sealed their alliance. Together they moved off to attack the Franks, Suqmān with 7,000 Turcoman cavalry and Chekermīsh with 3,000 Turkish, Arab and Kurdish cavalry. They encountered the enemy on the bank of the river Balīkh and a battle took place (May 1104). The Muslims pretended to retreat, and were followed for about two *farsakh* by the Franks. Then they turned on their pursuers and massacred them. The Turcoman troops loaded themselves with booty; the loot was immense and very valuable because they were close to the regions under Frankish cultivation. Bohemond of Antioch and Tancred of Galilee were at some distance from the main body of the army, hidden behind a hill from which they were to fall on the Muslims from the rear at the height of the battle. When they emerged they found the Franks in flight and their land being pillaged. They waited for nightfall and then retreated, followed by the Muslims, who killed and captured many of their number. Bohemond and Tancred, with six knights, escaped to safety. Baldwin of Edessa fled with a group of his counts. They made for the Balīkh, but their horses stuck fast in the mud and they were captured by a band of Suqmān's Turcomans. Baldwin was taken to their master's tent, but Suqmān had gone off with his company in pursuit of Bohemond. Chekermīsh's troops realized that Suqmān's army had seized the booty from the Frankish camp, while they returned empty-handed, so they said to

[1] The former, as mentioned earlier, was the Artuqid amīr of Hisn Kaifa, the latter was amīr of Mosul.

Chekermīsh; 'What shall we say to our people, or to the Turcomans, if Suqmān's men take all the spoils and we have nothing?' They persuaded him to seize the Count from Suqmān's tent. When Suqmān returned he was exceedingly angry, and his followers leapt into the saddle and were on the point of setting out in pursuit, but he called them back and said: 'The Muslims will be as dismayed at our quarrel as they were delighted at our reconciliation. I should not want to give the enemy the satisfaction of seeing me give vent to my anger at Islām's expense.'

Suqmān at once returned to the battlefield, took the arms and standards left by the Franks, ordered his men to dress in Frankish clothing and to mount Frankish horses, and sent them off towards the forts held by the Franks at Shaihān. Thinking that their companions were returning in victory the Franks came out of the first of the forts, and were killed. The Muslims took the fort and repeated the trick with the other strongholds. Meanwhile Chekermīsh marched on Harrān, occupied it and left a trustworthy officer there while he went on and spent a fortnight besieging Edessa. Then he returned to Mosul, taking with him Baldwin, whom he had seized from Suqmān's tent. He fixed the ransom at 35(000) *dinar* and a hundred and sixty Muslim prisoners. The Frankish dead numbered about 12,000.

BALDWIN OF EDESSA AND TANCRED OF ANTIOCH

(IBN AL-ATHĪR, X, 321–6)

When Jawali[1] reached Makisīn he freed the Frankish count who was a prisoner in Mosul and whom he had brought with him. The Count's name was Baldwin, and he was lord of Edessa, Sarūj, and other towns; he had spent all this time (from 1104–1108) in prison, offering enormous sums as ransom but unable to gain his freedom. Now after having been in prison

[1] The Turkish amīr who seized Mosul from Chekermīsh, the captor of Baldwin.

for almost five years, Jawalī released him and gave him robes of honour. It was agreed that his ransom should be a certain sum of *dinar*, the release of the Muslims held captive by him, and a promise to help Jawalī, when requested, with all that his armies, his presence and his money could offer. When the terms had been agreed Jawalī sent the Count to the fort of Ja'bar, into the custody of its ruler Salim ibn Malik, until the arrival of his nephew Joscelin, a gallant Frankish knight and Prince of Tall Bashīr; he had been captured at the same battle as the Count but had ransomed himself for 20,000 *dinar*. Joscelin came to Ja'bar as hostage for the Count, who went to Antioch in freedom. Then Jawalī released Joscelin, accepting as hostages in his place his and the Count's brothers-in-law, and sending Joscelin to join the Count and strengthen his resolve to release his prisoners, pay the ransom and fulfil his other obligations. When Joscelin reached Manbij he captured and sacked it. Some of Jawalī's men who were with him reproached him with a violation of his undertaking, but he replied that what he did to this city was no affair of theirs.

The Count, free and safely back in Antioch, was given 30,000 *dinar*, horses, arms, and clothing, by Tancred, who had taken over the city while the Count was in prison. Now Baldwin applied to Tancred to restore the city to him, but met with no response. He moved to Tall Bashīr, where the arrival of Joscelin, released by Jawalī, delighted and encouraged him. Meanwhile Tancred was preparing to attack him before he had time to muster his army and collect reinforcements, and before Jawalī could come to his aid. These men used to fight one-another and then after the contest would meet to dine and talk.[1]

The Count freed a hundred and sixty Muslim prisoners, all from the county of Aleppo. He gave them clothes and sent them on their way. Tancred returned to Antioch with the problem of Edessa still unresolved. Baldwin and Joscelin made

[1] The Muslim historian is struck by the chivalry of these medieval knights.

a series of raids on Tancred's forts, with the help of Kawasīl, an Armenian who controlled Ru'bān, Kaisūm and other forts north of Aleppo, and whose army was a miscellaneous band including a number of Muslim renegades. Baldwin's reinforcements from him numbered 2,000 cavalry and 2,000 infantry, all converts. Tancred prepared to fight, and sent the Patriarch of Edessa, whose status, like that of the Caliph among Muslims, commanded everyone's obedience, to mediate about Edessa. A group of metropolitans and priests gave evidence that Bohemond, Tancred's uncle, who had been planning to return to Europe, told Tancred to restore the city to the Count on his release from prison. So on 9 safar (501/29 September 1108) Tancred restored Edessa to Baldwin. Baldwin crossed the Euphrates and gave Jawalī's emissaries the money and men he had promised, together with a number of prisoners from Harrān and elsewhere as a *douceur*. At Sarūj Jawalī's emissaries repaired a mosque belonging to three hundred poor Muslims. The governor of Sarūj was a convert from Islām, and Jawalī's men heard him speaking ill of Islām and beat him up. This led to a brawl. The whole matter was referred to the Count, who said, 'This man is of no use either to you or to us', and had him killed.

In safar of the next year (502/September 1109) a battle was fought between Jawalī Saqau and Tancred the Frank, Prince of Antioch. The cause was a letter sent by Ridwān (of Aleppo) to Tancred of Antioch, putting him on his guard against Jawalī by informing him of Jawalī's treacherous plot to attack Aleppo. Ridwān said that with Jawalī in Aleppo Tancred's Franks would no longer be able to maintain their hold on Syria. He asked for Tancred's help and co-operation in repulsing him. Tancred welcomed this appeal and set out from Antioch with six hundred cavalry sent by Ridwān. When Jawalī heard the news he sent to Baldwin of Edessa to ask for his help in return for the rest of the ransom money. Baldwin left Edessa and met Jawalī at Manbij. At this moment news reached Jawalī that the Sultan's army[1] had taken Mosul and seized all the money and treasure that Jawalī had there. This was a heavy blow to him, and many of his followers abandoned him, among them the Atabeg Zangi ibn Aq Sunqūr and Baktāsh an-Nahawandi. Jawalī had a thousand cavalry left, as well as a band of volunteers who had attached themselves to him. When the two armies were drawn up outside Tall Bashīr, Tancred had 1,500 of his own cavalry, six hundred from Ridwān, and infantry as well. Jawalī put the amīrs Aqsiyān and Aluntāsh al-Abarri on his right, Badrān ibn Sádaqa, Ispahbād Sabau and Sunqur Dirāz on his left, and in the centre the two Franks, Count Baldwin and Joscelin. In the battle that followed the men from Antioch charged the Count of Edessa, and after some violent fighting Tancred forced the enemy's centre to retreat. But Jawalī's left wing charged the infantry from Antioch and killed so many of them that Tancred's defeat seemed certain. At this point some of Jawalī's men fell on the chargers belonging to Baldwin, Joscelin and certain others, mounted them and galloped off. Jawalī rode after them to bring them back to the fight, but they did not owe him obedience since the loss of Mosul, and refused to turn back. When he realized that they would not obey him he was afraid to stay at his post, and led his army in a retreat. Ispahbād Sabau made for Syria; Badrān ibn Sádaqa for the fortress of Ja'bar; Ibn Chekermīsh for Jazirat Ibn 'Umar, and Jawalī himself for Rahba. Many Muslims were killed and their possessions taken by Tancred. The Frankish armies unleashed all their ferocity on the Muslims. Baldwin and Joscelin fled to Tall Bashīr, and many of the Muslims sought refuge with them. They were well treated: the wounded were cared for, the naked clothed, and all set on their way home.

[1] The Seljuqid Sultan Muhammad ibn Malikshāh (1104–17), the feudal overlord of all these amīrs.

CHAPTER THREE

The extracts from Ibn al-Qalānisi that follow give a vivid first-hand account of the fall of the Syrian coastal cities (Tripoli, Beirūt, Sidon, and later, Tyre), and of the effect on Islām's spiritual capital of the influx of Frankish invaders into the empire. Muslim public opinion, alarmed by the tales of the Syrian refugees, demanded substantial military action by the central authorities; the Caliph and the Seljuqid Sultan, who, as usual, 'promised to provide'.

THE FALL OF TRIPOLI

(IBN AL-QALĀNISI, 163–4)

In sha'bān of 502/March 1109 Bertrand,[1] the son of Saint-Gilles (who was attacking Tripoli) arrived by sea from his homeland with sixty vessels carrying Franks and Genoese, and encamped under the city walls. He was contesting the claims of Saint-Gilles' nephew, the Count of Cerdagne. Tancred supported Cerdagne and Baldwin supported Bertrand. Baldwin succeeded in making peace between them, and Cerdagne and his men returned to 'Arqa. In a field there he encountered a Frank. He was about to kill him, but the Frank struck back and killed Cerdagne. When Bertrand was told he sent men to take over 'Arqa from the dead man's followers.

After this the Franks turned their full attention to Tripoli. They brought up all their troops to attack it and to press the inhabitants to surrender. This continued from the beginning of sha'bān until 11 dhu l-hijja (6 March to 12 July 1109). They brought siege-towers against the walls, and when the inhabi-

[1] Here and elsewhere the text has 'Raymond', confusing the son with his father, Raymond of Saint-Gilles. The father died in 1105, still vainly hoping to become Lord of Tripoli, and was succeeded by his cousin's son, William-Jordan, Count of Cerdagne, until Bertrand arrived to contest his claim.

tants saw this display of force they lost heart and were sure that there was no hope for them. This state of mind led to despair when the Egyptian fleet was late in bringing supplies and reinforcements, delayed, by God's will, by lack of provisions and contrary winds. The Franks pressed their advantage, stormed the ramparts and took the city by force on Monday 11 dhu l-hijja/12 July 1109. They sacked the city, captured the men and enslaved the women and children. They seized an immense quantity of loot and treasure as well as the contents of the city library,[1] works of art and heirlooms belonging to the local notables. The lives of the governor and his soldiers were spared. They had in fact asked for safe-conduct out of the city before it was taken, and after its capture they were allowed to go free. They soon arrived in Damascus, but the rest of the population was subjected to terrible ordeals and cruel tortures, its possessions confiscated and its hidden treasures dragged to light. The Franks and Genoese agreed each to take a third of the land and booty and to leave a third for Bertrand. As for Baldwin, they put aside from the total a share that would satisfy him.

After Tancred's failure to achieve his aim by supporting Cerdagne he had turned back and laid siege to Baniyās, which made a treaty with him in shawwāl/May of the year 1109. Then he attacked the city of Jubáil, where Fakhr al-Mulk ibn 'Ammār (amīr of Tripoli) was staying. Supplies were very short and the citizens hard-pressed. On Friday 22 dhu l-hijja/23 July 1109 they began negotiations with Tancred. He offered them their lives in exchange for the city, and they accepted his terms. Fakhr al-Mulk got away with his life and promises that he would be treated with respect and consideration by the Franks.

[1] *Dar al-'ilm*, literally 'house of learning', which was both a library and a college, and the pride of the Banu 'Ammār, the amīrs of Tripoli. Jubáil, the ancient Byblos (the *Gibelet* of the Crusaders), had in fact already been taken by Saint-Gilles in 1104 (see above). The reference here must be to Jábala (*Zibel*), which lies north of Tripoli and south of Laodicea.

Soon after this the Egyptian fleet arrived. In manpower, number of vessels and quantity of equipment and stores it was larger than any that had ever sailed from an Egyptian port. It brought enough men, money and supplies to keep Tripoli's besiegers at bay for a year, as well as supplies for the rest of the Egyptian territories in Syria. The fleet reached Tyre eight days after the fall of Tripoli, by God's will. So the supplies were unloaded at Tyre and distributed throughout the various regions, which was a help to the people of Tyre, Sidon and Beirūt, who had been complaining of their lack of resources and weakness in the face of Frankish aggression. But the fleet could delay no longer, and set sail with the next fair wind for Egypt.

THE FALL OF BEIRŪT

(IBN AL-QALĀNISI, 167–8)

In this year (503/1109–10) Tancred and his minions swarmed out of Antioch and over the surrounding regions of Syria. They took Tarsus, imprisoned the governor and overran the district. After returning to Antioch they set out again for Shaizar, and demanded a tribute of 10,000 *dinar*, after devastating the province. Next they besieged Hisn al-Akrād, and when the garrison surrendered went on to 'Aqra. Meanwhile Baldwin and Saint-Gilles' son were blockading Beirūt by land and sea, and while Tancred was on his way back to Antioch Joscelin of Tall Bashīr went to Beirūt to strengthen Baldwin's hand and to ask for his help against the amīr Mawdūd's army, which was threatening Edessa. The Franks set to work to build a siege-tower to use against the walls of Beirūt, but as soon as it was finished and put into service the Muslims smashed it to pieces with stones flung from catapults. The Franks began to build another, and Saint-Gilles' son undertook to provide a third.

At this moment twelve Egyptian men-of-war appeared, overwhelmed the Frankish fleet, capturing some of the ships, and brought provisions into Beirūt. This helped the inhabitants to recover their enthusiasm. Then Baldwin sent to Suwaidiyya[1] to ask for the help of the Genoese fleet there. Forty ship-loads of troops duly arrived at Beirūt, and the Franks mustered all their forces, on land and sea, for an assault on the city on Friday 21 shawwāl/13 May 1110. They brought up the two siege-towers and fought ferociously. In the end the defenders lost heart, seeing no escape from certain death. In the evening the Franks made a breakthrough and forced their way into the city. The governor fled with a few companions, but they were brought back by the Franks, the whole party executed and the money they had with them confiscated. The city was sacked, the inhabitants captured and enslaved and their money and goods seized. A short time later a party of 300 cavalry arrived to assist the city. When they came to the Jordan they met a small band of Franks, turned tail and fled into the mountains, where many of them perished.

From Beirūt Baldwin led his army to besiege the city of Sidon, and forced the inhabitants to surrender. They begged him to defer the date set (for the payment of the tribute they owed him) and he agreed, after setting the sum at 6,000 *dinar* instead of the 2,000 that he had demanded before that. Then he returned to Jerusalem for the pilgrimage.

THE FALL OF SIDON

(IBN AL-QALĀNISI, 171)

In this year (503/1109–10) news came of the arrival by sea of a Frankish King[2] with more than sixty ships full of pilgrims and soldiers for the war against Islām. They made for Jerusalem, and King Baldwin came out to meet them and to decide with them their plans for the invasion of the Muslim empire. From

[1] The port of Antioch.

[2] Sigurd I, King of Norway.

Jerusalem they went to besiege Sidon, and from 3 rabī' II (504/19 October 1110) they blockaded the city by land and sea. The Egyptian fleet was still at Tyre, but could not come to Sidon's aid. The Franks spent several days building a siege-tower covered with brushwood, matting and fresh ox-hides, to repulse stones and Greek fire. They mounted the tower on wheels, and on the day of battle they provided it with weapons and water and vinegar to put out fires. Then they moved into attack with it. The sight of it filled the people of Sidon with despair, for they feared a fate like that of Beirūt. The qadi of the city and a group of elders came out and appeared before the Franks to ask Baldwin to spare their lives. He guaranteed the safety of the citizens and the army, as well as of their possessions, and promised that any who wanted to go to Damascus should be free to leave Sidon. Reassured by Baldwin's oath the governor, the treasurer and all the armed forces of the city, as well as many of the citizens, left and went to Damascus. This was on 20 jumada I 504/4 December 1110, after a siege lasting forty-seven days. Baldwin restored the city to order, installed a garrison and then returned to Jerusalem. A short while later he returned to Sidon and imposed a tax of more than 20,000 *dinar* on the remaining Muslim inhabitants, taxing their last penny and reducing them to poverty. They used force to extort money from those they knew to be concealing some.

THE EFFECTS IN BAGHDĀD OF THE EVENTS IN SYRIA

(IBN AL-QALĀNISI, 173)

In jumada II 504/November–December 1110 the Sultan Ghiyāth ad-Dunya wa d-Din Muhammad ibn Malikshāh travelled from Hamadhān to Baghdād. Messengers and messages reached him there from Syria reporting on the situation there, the movements of the Franks after their retreat from the Euphrates, and events in Sidon, Ātharib and the province of Aleppo. On the first Friday of sha'bān a Hashimite Sharīf[1] from Aleppo appeared in the Sultan's mosque at Baghdād, with a group of sufis, merchants and lawyers, and began to beseech aid for Syria. They made the preacher come down from the pulpit and then smashed it to pieces. They wept and groaned for the disaster that had befallen Islām with the arrival of the Franks, for the men who had died and the women and children who had been sold into slavery. They made such a commotion that the people could not offer the obligatory prayers. To calm them, the servers and imāms promised, on the Caliph's behalf, that troops would be sent to support Islām against the infidel. On the following Friday the men came back and repeated their noisy laments and cries for help, in the Caliph's mosque. Not long after this the Sultan's sister, who was the wife of the Caliph, arrived in Baghdād from Isfahān, bringing a train of endless and indescribable splendour: jewels, rich furnishings, horses and trappings, clothes and equipage, slaves and pages, handmaids and servants. The Sharīf's cries for help disturbed the gaiety and joyousness of the occasion. The Caliph, the Prince of the Faithful al-Mustazhir bi-llāh, was extremely annoyed and wanted to arrest the offenders and punish them severely. But the Sultan intervened, pardoned the offenders and ordered the amīrs and army commanders to return to their posts and prepare to march in the Holy War against the infidel enemies of God.[2]

In jumada II/December 1110–January 1111 an ambassador arrived from the Byzantine Emperor[3] with valuable gifts, and

[1] A true or presumed descendant of Muhammad; a privileged class that enjoyed great prestige among the Muslims.

[2] Baghdād at this time contained two rulers: the 'Abbasid Caliph, the nominal sovereign and leader of orthodox Islām, and the Seljuqid Sultan, the real ruler of Persia, Irāq and feudal lands in Syria. Unity between the two, sometimes strengthened by marriage bonds, was not always perfect.

[3] Alexius Comnenus (1081–1118).

letters inviting the Muslims to unite with him to drive the Franks out of Syria. He called on them to rouse themselves and summon all their energies to strike before the damage was beyond repair and reached too serious proportions. He for his part had already tried by force to prevent the Frankish armies from passing through his lands into Islamic territory. But if their armies and reinforcements came pouring into the Muslim empire by the direct route, necessity would force him to treat with them and allow them to pass through his lands, and to help them to achieve their aims and objects. He begged and prayed that all would unite to combat the Franks and would make common cause with him to extirpate them from these realms.

THE SIEGE OF TYRE

(IBN AL-QALĀNISI, 178–81)

In this year (505/1111–12) Baldwin assembled the largest army he could muster and marched on Tyre. Its governor 'Izzal-Mulk and the people of Tyre hurriedly wrote to the Ata-beg of Damascus, Zahīr ad-Din (Tughtikīn) asking for his help and offering to hand the city over to him. They begged him not to delay in sending a large contingent of his Turks to their aid and assistance, for if help did not come soon they would be forced to hand the city over to the Franks, as they despaired of getting any help from al-Afdal in Egypt.[1] The Ata-beg responded at once and sent to Tyre a large contingent of Turks, fully equipped, and consisting of more than 200 cavalry and skilled archers. Voluntary foot-soldiers from the surrounding region, from Mount 'Āmila and even from Damascus arrived at Tyre in large numbers, while the Ata-beg sent further reinforcements.

[1] The Fatimid vizier, mentioned above, who should have been the first to come to the aid of these coastal towns, which were all nominally Egyptian.

As for Baldwin, when he heard of the Ata-beg's interest in Tyre he hastily surrounded the city with all the troops at his disposal. This was on 25 jumada I 505/29 November 1111. He ordered his men to cut down all the trees and date-palms and to build permanent living-quarters under the city walls. Several vain attempts were made to take the city by storm. It was said that in one day's fighting the citizens used 20,000 arrows.

When Zahīr ad-Din heard that the Franks had besieged Tyre he came down from Damascus as far as Baniyās and sent out flying columns and bands of foot-soldiers to raid the Frankish provinces, with licence to kill, pillage, burn, destroy, and in every way to create difficulties for the Franks and lure them away from the city while reinforcements were brought up. But the reinforcements failed to get into the city. Zahīr ad-Din went to attack the great fortress at al-Habīs, across the Jordan, took it after some fierce fighting and killed its garrison. Meanwhile the Franks had begun work on two wooden towers for use against the walls of Tyre. Time and again Zahīr ad-Din tried to hinder them by coming down to attack them, so that the garrison inside Tyre could come out and fire the towers; the Franks realized what he was trying to do, and dug trenches all round their position. They set guards over the trenches and the towers and were able to ignore his manoeuvres as well as his raids into their territories.

Winter came on, causing little harm to the Franks on the hard, sandy region where their camp was sited, but bringing much suffering to the Turkish army. None the less they continued their raids and their efforts to cut the Frankish supply lines and intercept their convoys. They cut the bridge on the road to Sidon to prevent reinforcements from arriving by that route. The Franks reverted to bringing in all their supplies by sea. When Zahīr ad-Din heard what they were doing he took a section of the army round to the north side of the city, overrunning the area outside the city walls. A number of sailors were killed and about twenty ships fired where they lay drawn up on the shore. Meanwhile Tughtikīn did not omit to send letters to the people of Tyre encouraging them and urging them to keep up their resistance to the Frankish attacks.

In about eleven weeks the building of the two towers and their battering-rams was completed. On 10 sha'bān/11 February the Franks brought them into use against the city walls, and battle raged around them. The smaller of the two was more than forty cubits high; the larger, more than fifty. On 1 ramadān/2 March the people of Tyre made a sortie and attacked the two towers with Greek fire, wood, pitch, and the means to set fire to them. They failed to set fire directly to either of their objectives, but they started a blaze near the smaller one in a place where the Franks could not extinguish it, and the wind blew it on to the tower. In spite of the fierce struggle put up by the men inside the tower, it burnt down. The Muslims took a lot of booty from it: cuirasses, shields and other things, and then the fire caught the other tower. When the Muslims realized that the Franks, occupied with fighting the fire in the towers, had given up their attack on the walls, they too let the attack from the ramparts drop. Then the Franks turned on them, drove them back from the towers, extinguished the fires, and set a large detachment of picked guards to protect the towers and the catapults.

Until the end of ramadān the Franks kept up their attack on the city. They brought one of the towers up close to the wall, filling in the three trenches in front of it. The Muslims broke through the wall at the point where the Frankish tower faced it and started a fire there. The props caught fire, the wall fell down in front of the tower, and it was no longer possible to bring the tower up close under the wall and assault the city from there. The wall where they had attacked it was quickly repaired, while the towers to either side of it dominated it and prevented the mobile tower from getting any closer on that side. So the Franks cleared away the accumulation of rubble and dragged the tower up to another part of the city wall, which they began to batter with rams slung in the tower. The wall cracked, stones fell out in places, and the defenders were on the brink of disaster. Then an officer of the fleet from Tripoli, an experienced, intelligent and observant man, thought of making iron hooks to pinion the heads and sides of the rams when they struck the wall, by means of ropes guided by men from the walls, so that the pull on them caused the towers to heel over. The Franks themselves were forced to cut down some of the rams for fear of destroying the tower. At other times the ram would bend and break, and at other times it was smashed to pieces by two boulders roped together and flung from the walls. The Franks made several rams, which were all smashed in the same way. Each one was sixty cubits long, with a block of iron at one end weighing more than twenty pounds, and was attached to the tower with ropes.

Again and again the rams were repaired and the tower brought up to the wall again. Then the sailor of whom we spoke invented another weapon. A long beam of unseasoned timber was set up on the wall in front of the tower. At the top of it, forming a cross,[1] another beam forty cubits long swung on pulleys worked by a winch in the manner of a ship's mast, at the direction of whoever was operating the machine. At one end of the pivoting beam was an iron spar, and at the other end ropes running on pulleys, by means of which the operators could hoist buckets of dung and refuse and empty them over the Franks working in the tower, and so prevent their working the rams. The Franks found themselves working under great difficulties and unable to keep up the attack. Then the sailor had grape-panniers and baskets filled with oil, pitch, wood-shavings, resin and cane-bark, set on fire and hoisted up, in the manner described, to the level of the Frankish tower. The

[1] A T-cross, as the context makes clear.

flames caught the top of the tower, and as fast as the Franks put them out with vinegar and water, the Muslims hurried to send over more fire-buckets; they also poured small vessels of boiling oil over the tower to feed the flames. The fire grew and spread, overcame the two men working at the top of the tower, killing one and forcing the other to go down, enveloped the top platform and crept down to the next and then the next, consuming the wooden structure and overcoming the men working on the platforms. Unable to extinguish it, the Franks in and around the tower fled. The citizens of Tyre came out, raided the tower, and took away vast quantities of arms, equipment and supplies.

The Franks despaired of taking the city and began to withdraw. They burnt down the encampment that they had built and many of the ships drawn up on the shore, from which they had taken masts, rudders and implements to build the towers. In all they had about two hundred vessels of all sizes, of which about thirty were men-of-war. They loaded some with their light baggage and left Tyre on 10 shawwāl/10 April 1112. The siege had lasted for four and a half months. The Franks went to Acre and from there dispersed to their cities. The people of Tyre emerged from their city to reap the reward of their victory. The Turks who had been sent to help them returned to Damascus, less about twenty men killed in the fighting, and there received their pay[1] and their monthly stipends. There is no other case of a Frankish tower being burnt down, as this one was, from top to bottom. This achievement was partly due to the tower's being the same height as the ramparts,[2] for if their heights had been different the lower of the two would have been destroyed.

[1] The 'there' may refer to Damascus, on their return, or it could mean 'during the war', i.e. at Tyre itself.

[2] Literally 'the two towers', referring to the mobile tower and the section of the city wall that looked down on it. The same word is used here for both, which is sometimes confusing.

Tyre lost 400 men, and the Franks about 2,000, according to reliable witnesses. The people of Tyre took back the offer they had made to Tughtikīn to hand over the city to him, but he simply said: 'I did what I did for the love of God and his Muslims, not in hope of money and power.' This noble deed brought him blessings and gratitude, and he promised that in a similar situation he would be quick to help them. Then, after labouring hard and battling with the Franks until God freed Tyre of its troubles, he returned to Damascus. The citizens of Tyre began to rebuild their walls where the Franks had broken them down, restored the trenches to their former shape and size, and fortified the city. The volunteer infantry dispersed.[1]

[1] After this successful defence, Tughtikīn helped and protected Tyre on other occasions, but was finally forced to yield to the Crusaders in 1124.

CHAPTER FOUR

The first serious blow to the Franks came not from Baghdād but from the united action of Ilghazi, the Artuqid amīr of Mardīn, and Tughtikīn, Ata-beg of Damascus. In 1119 Ilghazi made a surprise attack on the Norman Prince Roger of Antioch at Balāt (or Sarmadā, to the west of Aleppo) and defeated and killed him after a violent battle. Two accounts of it are given here: first that of Kamāl ad-Din, the most faithful and accurate record of the events, and then Ibn al-Qalānisi's version, in which he comments on the failure of the Muslims to recapture Antioch, left unprotected during the crisis.

THE DEFEAT AND DEATH OF ROGER OF ANTIOCH AT BALĀT

(KAMĀL AD-DIN, II, 187–90)

Ilghazi and Tughtikīn went together to Mardīn and from there sent messages to the Muslim armies and to Turcoman soldiers far and near, to join them in the great army they were mustering. In 513/1119 Ilghazi and more than 40,000 men crossed the Euphrates at the Badayā and Sanja fords. The troops dispersed over the regions of Tall Bashīr and Tall Khalid, killing and looting where they could. Messengers arrived from Aleppo begging Ilghazi to hurry there as the Franks were raiding al-Atharib, south of Aleppo, and morale was low. Ilghazi marched through Marj Dabiq, Maslamiyya and Qinnasrīn, and by the end of safar 513/June 1119 his bands of raiders had entered Frankish territory in the region of ar-Ruj and taken the near-by fort of Qastūn. Sir Roger (*Sirjāl*), ruler of Antioch, assembled the Frankish and Armenian armies and made straight for the iron bridge (over the Orontes) and went from there to take up his position at Balāt, between two mountains near the Sarmadā pass, north of al-Ātharib. He encamped there on Friday 9 rabī' I/20 June 1119.

The (Muslim) amīrs grew tired of the long delay while Ilghazi awaited the arrival of Tughtikīn so that they could agree on a plan of action. They goaded Ilghazi into an immediate encounter with the enemy. He made all the amīrs and commanders renew their oath to fight bravely, to stand firm without retreating, and to offer their lives in the Holy War. To this they cheerfully swore. The Muslims, drawn up in echelon formation, left their tents at Qinnasrīn on Friday 16 rabī' I/27 June, and passed the night close to the Frankish army, which was building a fort to dominate the Tall 'Afrīn and imagined that the Muslims were besieging al-Ātharib or Zardanā. As dawn broke they saw the Muslim standards advancing to surround them completely. The qadi Abu l-Fadl ibn al-Khashshāb was at their head, mounted on a mare and carrying a lance, and urging the Muslims on to war. One of the soldiers, seeing him, said scornfully: 'So we have left home and come all this way to march behind a turban!'[1] but the qadi at the head of the troops rode up and down the lines haranguing them and using all his eloquence to incite them to summon every energy and rise to the highest pitch of enthusiasm, until men wept with emotion and admiration. Then Tughān Arslān ibn Dimlāj[2] led the charge, and the army swept down on the enemy tents, spreading chaos and destruction. God gave victory to the Muslims. The Franks who fled to their camp were slaughtered. The Turks fought superbly, charging the enemy from every direction like one man. Arrows flew thick as locusts, and the Franks, with missiles raining down on infantry and cavalry alike, turned and fled. The cavalry was destroyed, the infantry

[1] Religious and legal scholars wore the turban; the Christian equivalent would be the friar's or monk's hood.

[2] Amīr of Arzan, in the Jazira, and a vassal of Ilghazi.

cut to pieces, the followers and servants were all taken prisoner. Roger was killed, but (only) twenty Muslims were lost, among them Sulaimān ibn Mubarak ibn Shibl, whereas only twenty Franks escaped. A few of the leaders got away, but almost 15,000 men fell in the battle, which took place on Saturday (28 June) at midday. A signal of victory reached Aleppo as the Muslims were assembled for the noon prayer in the Great Mosque. They felt a great groan go up, seeming to come from the west; and yet none of the soldiers from the victorious army reached the city until the hour of the afternoon prayer.

The peasants burned the Frankish dead; in one charred corpse more than forty arrows were found. Ilghazi took over the Frankish camp and his soldiers brought to him the booty they collected, but he took only some arms to be sent to the rulers of Islām and left the rest to his troops. When the prisoners were brought before him he noticed one of magnificent physique, who had been captured by a small, thin, ill-armed Muslim. As he passed before the Prince the Turcoman soldiers said to him: 'Aren't you ashamed to have been captured by this little man, with a physique like yours?' and he replied: 'By God, this man did not capture me; he is not my conqueror. The man who captured me was a great man, greater and stronger than I, and he handed me over to this fellow. He wore a green robe and rode a green horse!'[1]

(IBN AL-QALĀNISI 200–1)

When the Ata-beg Zahīr ad-Din (Tughtikīn) came to Aleppo to collaborate with Najm ad-Din (Ilghazi) in the action that they had agreed to take together in the hope of a result that

[1] The reference to green, the heavenly colour, makes it clear that he is speaking of the Prophet or of someone sent by him, who intervened to ensure a Muslim victory.

both desired, he found that large numbers of Turcoman troops had already assembled from everywhere to be with him, like lions seeking their prey, or hawks wheeling above the creatures they are about to tear to pieces. News came that Roger of Antioch, with over 20,000 cavalry and innumerable foot-soldiers, fully armed and equipped, had left the city and encamped near Sarmadā, or Danīth al-Baqal, between Antioch and Aleppo. When they heard this the Muslims flew toward them like hawks flying to protect their nests, and in less time than it took for their glances to meet the two armies came to blows. The Muslims charged and surrounded the Franks, driving them back with swords and arrows. And God—to whom be the praise!—gave the Muslims victory over the infidel rabble. On Saturday 7 rabī' I 513/28 June 1119, in less than an hour, the Franks were all lying dead, cavalry and infantry with their horses and armour, and none escaped to bear the news. Even Roger, their leader, was found stretched out among the dead. Some who were there said that they had walked over the battlefield, to witness the splendid miracle sent by God, and had seen dead horses bristling like hedgehogs with the arrows sticking out of them. Meanwhile Antioch lay open, with no one to protect it, deserted by its champions, a prize for whoever came first to claim it, waiting for the man who could take it. But because the Ata-beg Zahīr ad-Din was not there, no one thought to occupy the city. The Turcomans were thrust headlong into action without time to prepare themselves, such being God's decree, while the rest of the troops were wholly occupied with seizing booty, of which there was enough to enrich, delight and satisfy everyone. So 'their dwellings stood desolate and deserted';[1] God, Lord of the worlds, be praised!

[1] A Qur'anic phrase (Qur'ān XXVII, 53), here applied to the conquered enemy. The whole passage is written in *saj'*, rhymed prose full of rhetorical tropes used at times of high emotion.

BALDWIN, HIS DEATH AND HIS CHARACTER

(IBN AL-QALĀNISI, 233)

In this year (526/1131–32) news came from the Franks of the death of Baldwin, 'the little leader' (*ar-ru'ayyis*), King of the Franks and Lord of Jerusalem. He died in Acre on Thursday 25 ramadān/8 August 1132.[1] He was an old man, rich in experience and inured to every trial and hardship of life. Several times he had been imprisoned by the Muslims, in war and in peace, but his famous stratagems and skilful manœuvring had got him out. At his death he was succeeded by a man who lacked his good sense and gift for kingship; the new King was Fulk, Count of Anjou, who came out by sea from his homeland. Baldwin's death caused trouble and disturbance among the Franks.

[1] The date given here is a year too late; Baldwin died at Jerusalem on 21 August 1131, which corresponds to 25 ramadān 525.

CHAPTER FIVE

With the appearance on the scene of Zangi, the Ata-beg of Mosul and Aleppo, (1129–46), the real Muslim counter-offensive began. Ibn al-Athīr was the faithful servant and historian, and enthusiastic eulogist of the brief Zangid dynasty of Mesopotamia and Syria. According to his religious view of history it was Providence that put into Zangi's hands the kingdom left by Tughtikīn of Damascus, the first opponent of the Crusades to be worthy of the name, who died in 1128. Zangi's real aim, even when fighting the Crusaders, was Damascus, nominally ruled by Tughtikīn's incompetent descendants, and controlled in fact by Mu'īn ad-Din Unur. Faced with the threat of Zangi, none of these hesitated to make an alliance with the Franks. In the following extracts Ibn al-Athīr presents an exalted image of his hero, and Ibn al-Qalānisi the opposite view; that of civil patriotism and loyalty to the local dynasty of Tughtikīn.

ZANGI, MAN OF DESTINY FOR ISLĀM

(IBN AL-ATHĪR, X, 458)

If God in his mercy had not granted that the Ata-beg (Zangi) should conquer Syria, the Franks would have overrun it (completely). They had laid siege to this town and that, but Zahīr ad-Din Tughtikīn had barely heard the news before he was mustering his men and marching on the Frankish territories. He besieged them and raided them, and in this way forced the Franks to abandon their campaign and return home. Now in this year (522/1128), by God's decree, Tughtikīn died, and Syria would have been left completely at their mercy, with no one to defend its inhabitants; but that God in His mercy to the Muslims was pleased to raise to power 'Imād ad-Din (Zangi), whose deeds in the battle with the Franks we shall, God willing, record here.

ZANGI TAKES THE FORTRESS OF BA'RĪN. THE DEFEAT OF THE FRANKS

(IBN AL-ATHĪR, XI, 33–34)

In shawwāl of this year (531/1137), Zangi left Hims and laid siege to Ba'rīn,[1] a strongly defended fortress near Hamāt, held by the Franks. He surrounded it and began to attack it and try to storm it. The Franks marshalled their cavalry and infantry and set out, kings, counts and barons together, against the Ata-beg Zangi to make him lift the siege. But Zangi was unmoved. He stood firm to await them, and when they arrived he faced them in a battle which after some bitter fighting resolved itself into a rout of the Franks, who fled, closely pursued by the Muslims. The Frankish King[2] shut himself up inside the near-by fort of Ba'rīn, and was besieged there by the Muslims. The Ata-beg cut off all means of communication with the fort, so that not even news of their homelands got inside, so closely were movements controlled by Zangi and so great was the fear of him.

Then priests and monks traversed the Byzantine empire, the countries of the Franks and the neighbouring Christian states raising armies to fight the Muslims and declaring that if Zangi took Ba'rīn and the Franks inside it he would overrun all their lands in no time, for there would be no one to defend them. They said that the Muslims had but one ambition: to march on Jerusalem. So the Christians flocked to Syria by land and sea. Among them was the Byzantine Emperor.[3] Meanwhile Zangi continued to wage war on the Franks, who held out but were running short of food and other essentials, for the siege had been sprung on them unexpectedly, leaving them no time

[1] The Crusaders 'Mont Ferrand', which stood between Tortosa and Hamāt.
[2] King Fulk of Jerusalem and his barons.
[3] John II Comnenus (1118–43).

to make preparations. They had not believed that anyone could put them on the defensive—they had been expecting to take over the whole of Syria themselves. When they ran out of food they ate their horses, and then they were forced to ask for terms. They requested Zangi to guarantee their lives until they reached their own domains. At first he refused to accept their terms, but hearing that the Emperor and the rest of the Franks were approaching Syria he granted the men in the fort their lives and fixed the ransom at 50,000 *dinar*. They accepted his terms and yielded up the fort to him. When they emerged they learnt that a great concourse was on its way to save them, and reproached themselves for having surrendered, unaware of what was happening outside the fort.

While the siege of Ba'rīn was going on Zangi had taken Ma'arra and Kafartāb from the Franks. Like the population of the whole region between there and Aleppo and Hamāt, as well as of Ba'rīn, the inhabitants of these two towns had been reduced to a state of squalid misery by the constant pillaging and slaughter, for this region had been a theatre of war since the beginning. When Zangi assumed command the people breathed again, the countryside blossomed and soon began to bring in a large revenue. It was an unqualified victory, as anyone who saw it knows.

One of Zangi's finest acts was his treatment of the people of Ma'arra. When the Franks took the town they seized their possessions, and at the reconquest their descendants and survivors presented themselves before Zangi to ask for restitution of their belongings. He asked to see the documents giving proof of ownership, but they replied that the Franks had taken everything, including the title-deeds. He had the land registers in Aleppo examined, and anyone for whom there was an entry for the land tax on a particular holding was given that land. Thus he restored their land to the people of Ma'arra, the finest act of justice and generosity that I ever heard of.

DAMASCUS AND THE FRANKS IN ALLIANCE AGAINST ZANGI

(IBN AL-QALĀNISI, 270–3)

In this year (534/1139–40) news came that the Ata-beg 'Imād ad-Din (Zangi) had finished repairing the damage to Baalbek and its fort and had begun preparations for a siege of Damascus. Soon came the news that he had left Baalbek in rabī' 1/November 1139 and had encamped in the Biqā'.[1] From there he sent a message to Jamāl ad-Din[2] inviting him to exchange the city for another of his own choice or suggestion. Jamāl ad-Din refused, and so on Wednesday 13 rabī' II/6 December Zangi left the Biqā' and camped at Darayya, immediately outside Damascus. On his arrival at Darayya the advance parties of the two sides came to blows. Jamāl ad-Din's men were defeated, and some took refuge inside the city. On Friday 28th Zangi advanced in force on the side of the city where the Musalla[3] was, and won a victory against a great host composed of the citizen militia and peasants. There was wholesale slaughter. Survivors were killed or imprisoned. Those who could, whether or not they were wounded, escaped to the city. That day, but for God's grace, the city would have fallen. Zangi took his prisoners back to camp, and for the next few days undertook no operations. He sent out messengers and exerted himself to obtain peace by courtesy and diplomacy, offering the amīr of Damascus, Baalbek and Hims and other towns that he suggested. Jamāl ad-Din Muhammad ibn Taj al-Mulūk would have preferred to accept these terms and to come to a peaceful agreement without bloodshed, in a way that would bring peace and prosperity to the people. But his advisers

[1] The ancient Coelesyria, between Lebanon and Antilebanon.
[2] The nephew and fourth successor of Tughtikīn to the amirate of Damascus.
[3] The place of (public) prayer.

rejected this view. For several days Zangi sent out his troops in raiding parties, without deploying his full force or completing the blockade, in order to avoid violence and to act like a man restrained by peaceful intentions and a reluctance to indulge in bloodshed and pillage. In jumada I Jamāl ad-Din showed the first signs of an illness that was finally to gain complete mastery of him, its grip tightening and loosening, its tide ebbing and flowing until he was absolutely at its mercy. Medicine and magic art had no effect on him, and in the end his destiny fulfilled itself, and on the night of Friday 8 sha'bān/29 March 1140, at the very hour of his brother and forerunner Shihāb ad-Din Mahmūd's assassination, he passed to his Creator. The people were overcome by this coincidence of day and hour, and gave praise and glory to God. He was given a place in his grandmother's sepulchre at al-Faradīs.[1] After his burial the commanders and notables decided to fill the gap left by his death by putting in his place his son, the amīr Adab ad-Daula Abu Sa'īd Abaq Ibn Jamāl ad-Din Muhammad. They swore solemn oaths of loyalty and obedience, faithful service and counsel. Thus the matter was settled. The city had an effective government, all discord ceased, and confusion was replaced by calm, so that after a time of unrest men's spirits were once more tranquil.

When the Ata-beg 'Imād ad-Din learnt of Jamāl ad-Din's death he brought his troops up close to the city, in the hope that on their leader's death disunity among the military commanders would give him the opportunity to realize some of his ambitions. But things did not go as he had anticipated: he found the civil and military authorities of Damascus firm in their decision to fight it out and to continue their resistance and opposition to him. He returned to camp discouraged and furious. At this point the Franks agreed to give Damascus support and help in driving Zangi back and prevent his getting

[1] Bab al-Faradīs, one of the gates of Damascus.

what he wanted. The agreement was sealed with a solemn oath, and each side gave guarantees that it would honour its obligations. The Franks asked for a certain sum of money for them to use on any operations that they undertook, and also for hostages, for their own peace of mind. This was agreed, and money and hostages—relatives of the army commanders—were handed over. Then the Franks began their preparations for assisting Damascus, and messages passed between them in which it was agreed that the Franks should concentrate their resources on the other forts and towns in the area, to drive off Zangi and prevent his achieving his ambition of taking Damascus, before he became so powerful and well-equipped that he could break through the Frankish lines and attack their own territories.

When Zangi heard what was afoot, and that the Frankish troops were assembling ready to move at the same time as the army from Damascus, he left his camp, and on Sunday 5 ramadān moved off toward Haurān to confront the Franks if that was what they wanted, or to follow them if they moved off. After using these tactics for a while he turned aside at the Ghuta[1] of Damascus and camped at 'Adhrā' on Wednesday 24 shawwāl/12 June. He burnt some villages in the Marj and the Ghuta as far as Harastā at-Tin, and on the following Saturday left for the north on the receipt of definite information that the Franks were encamped in force at al-Madān. One of the conditions of the Franco-Damascene agreement was that the Muslims should hand over Baniyās, which was held by Ibrahīm ibn Turghūt. This man, you will understand, had taken his men on a raiding mission in the region of Tyre and there crossed the path of Raymond of Antioch,[2] who was on his way to reinforce the Franks at Damascus. In the battle Ibrahīm

[1] The Ghuta is the fertile belt of gardens and orchards around Damascus; all the place-names in this passage refer to places in and around Damascus.

[2] Raymond of Poitiers.

was defeated and killed, together with a few of his men. The rest returned to Baniyās and mustered reinforcements from the tribes of the Wadi t-Taim and elsewhere in sufficient numbers to defend the fortress. Then the amīr Mu'īn ad-Din[1] attacked and besieged the fort with the army from Damascus, using catapults and various other methods. He had a large Frankish contingent with him, and the siege continued throughout shawwāl (May–June 1140). Then came the news that in shawwāl the Ata-beg 'Imād ad-Din, from his camp at Baalbek, had summoned the Turcomans to attack Baniyās and drive off the besiegers. This was the situation at the end of dhu l-hijja of that year.... Baniyās was beleaguered until all its stores were gone and there was no food for the defenders, then it surrendered to Mu'īn ad-Din. The governor was recompensed with other fiefs and benefices, and Mu'īn ad-Din handed the city over to the Franks as he had agreed, and returned in triumph to Damascus at the end of shawwāl.

On the morning of Saturday 7 dhu l-hijja/22 June the Ata-beg 'Imād ad-Din appeared with his army outside Damascus. At the Musalla he had attacked the city wall unnoticed, for the citizens were all deep in the final hours of sleep. As dawn broke they realized what was happening and a great cry of anguish went up as they rushed to their posts on the walls. The gates opened and the citizen cavalry and infantry came out. Zangi had sent his own men out on raiding missions in Haurān, the Ghuta, the Marj and other places, and confronted the army from Damascus with his guards, to prevent their pursuing their raiding parties. The two sides came to blows and a large number of troops were involved in the fighting on both sides, but Zangi withdrew his men, for his main concern was to act as cover for the raiders. These rounded up vast numbers of horses

[1] Mu'īn ad-Din Unur (the *Aynard* of the Frankish sources) was an old Turkish general and the real ruler of Damascus during these years, on behalf of the young amīr Abaq.

and cattle, sheep, lambs, oxen, and household goods, for their action had taken the city completely by surprise. That night Zangi camped at Marj Rahit, so that his men could reassemble with their booty, and then left by the northern route, taking a vast quantity of booty with him.

CHAPTER SIX

After his setback at Damascus Zangi recovered his position by conquering Edessa (1144) and breaking up the county, the first of the four Christian states born of the First Crusade to disappear. We give versions of the story by Ibn al-Qalānisi and Ibn al-Athīr. The latter, as usual, covers the wider field, giving in anecdotal form both the local events and their effect on the whole struggle between Christianity and Islām. Barely two years after this triumph his hero was assassinated while fighting other Muslims. He bequeathed his political and military ambitions to his son Nur ad-Din (Norandin), Sultan of Aleppo. Ibn al-Athīr's eulogy of Zangi, with due allowance made for its emotional bias, reveals traits of character of which we have independent confirmation.

ZANGI TAKES EDESSA

(IBN AL-QALĀNISI, 279–80)

In this year (539/1144) news came from the north that Zangi had taken Edessa by storm, in spite of its strength and state of readiness to face even a powerful besieging army. Zangi had always coveted Edessa and watched for a chance to achieve his ambition. Edessa was never out of his thoughts or far from his mind. At last he heard that Joscelin (II) Prince of Edessa, with a large part of his army, the flower of his gallant company of knights, had been killed in battle far away from the city. It seemed as if it was God's will. When Zangi heard the news he hastened to besiege and blockade Edessa with a large force. He sent to summon the aid of the Turcomans, in fulfilment of their obligations in the Holy War. Large numbers answered his appeal and they completely surrounded the city, intercepting all supplies and reinforcements. It was said that even the birds dared not fly near, so absolute was the desolation made by the besiegers' weapons and so unwinking their vigilance. Catapults drawn up against the walls battered at them ceaselessly, and nothing interrupted the remorseless struggle. Special detachments of sappers from Khurasān and Aleppo began work at several suitable places, digging into the bowels of the earth until their tunnels, propped up with beams and special equipment, reached under the towers of the city wall. The next step was to light the fires, and they applied to Zangi for permission. This was given after he had been into the tunnels to inspect them and had admired their imposing work. The wooden supports were fired, flames spread and devoured the beams, the walls above the tunnels crumbled, and the Muslims took the city by storm. Many men of both sides were killed when the walls collapsed, and many more Franks and Armenians were killed, wounded or put to flight. The city was taken at dawn on Saturday 26 jumada II/23 December 1144. Then the looting and the killing began, the capturing and pillaging. The hands of the victors were filled with money and treasure, horses and booty enough to gladden the heart and make the soul rejoice. Then Zangi ordered that the carnage should come to an end, and began to rebuild the walls where they had been damaged. He appointed suitable men to govern and defend the city and to look after its interests. He reassured the inhabitants with promises of good government and universal justice. Then he left Edessa for Sarūj, to which the Franks had fled, and took it. Indeed every region and town through which he passed was immediately handed over to him.

(IBN AL-ATHĪR, XI, 64–6)

On 6[1] jumada II of that year the Ata-beg 'Imād ad-Din Zangi ibn Aq Sunqūr seized from the Franks the city of Edessa and

[1] A '2' must have fallen out here; the real date is that given by Ibn al-Qalānisi.

other forts in the Jazira.[1] The Franks had penetrated far into this area, as far as Amid and Nusaibīn, Ras al-'Ain and ar-Raqqa. Their influence extended from near Mardīn to the Euphrates, and covered Edessa, Sarūj, al-Bira, Sinn ibn 'Utaīr, Jamlīn, al-Mu'azzar, Quradi and other cities as well. All these and other regions west of the Euphrates belonged to Joscelin, the most famous of the Franks and the leader of their army by virtue of his valour and command of strategy. Zangi knew that if he made a direct attack on Edessa the Franks would concentrate there to defend it, and it was too well fortified to be an easy conquest. He moved to Diyār Bakr, to give the Franks the impression that his interests lay elsewhere and that he was in no position to attack their kingdom. When the Franks felt sure that he could not extract himself from the war he was fighting with the Artuqids and other princes at Diyār Bakr, and so felt safe from him, Joscelin left Edessa and crossed the Euphrates to move westwards. As soon as Zangi's spies informed him of this, he issued orders to his army to set out the next day for Edessa. His amīrs were summoned to his presence, and he ordered food to be served. 'No one', he said, 'shall eat with me at this table unless he is prepared to hurl his lance with me tomorrow at the gates of Edessa.' The only ones who dared to come forward were a solitary amīr and a youth of humble birth whose bravery and prowess were known to all, for he had no equal in battle. The amīr said to him; 'What are you doing here?' but the Ata-beg intervened: 'Leave him, for his, I can see, is not a face that will be lagging behind me in battle.'

The army set out and reached the walls of Edessa. Zangi was the first to charge the Franks, but the young man was at his side. A Frankish knight lunged at Zangi from the side, but the amīr faced him and transfixed him with his lance,[2] and Zangi was saved.

They besieged the city and attacked it for three weeks. Zangi

[1] Northern Mesopotamia.

[2] Could also mean 'fell, struck by him'.

made several assaults on it, and used sappers to mine the walls. He was straining every nerve in the struggle, for fear that the Franks should marshal their forces and march on him to relieve the fortress. Then the sappers undermined the wall and it collapsed, and Zangi took the city and besieged the citadel. The citizens and their goods were seized, the young taken captive, the men killed. But when Zangi inspected the city he liked it and realized that it would not be sound policy to reduce such a place to ruins. He therefore gave the order that his men should return every man, woman and child to his home together with the goods and chattels looted from them. This was done in all but a very few cases, in which the captor had already left the camp. The city was restored to its former state, and Zangi installed a garrison to defend it. Then he received the surrender of Sarūj and other cities west of the Euphrates. The only exception was al-Bira, a strongly defended fort on the bank of the Euphrates.[1] So he marched on it and besieged it, but it was well stocked and well guarded, and so after some time, as by God's will we shall describe, he lifted the siege.

It is said that a great authority on genealogies and biographies tells the following story: the King of Sicily sent a naval expedition that ravaged Tripoli in North Africa. Now there was in Sicily a learned, God-fearing Muslim whom the King held in great respect, relying on his advice rather than that of his own priests and monks; so much so that the people used to say that the King was really a Muslim. One day, as the King was standing at a window overlooking the sea, he saw a small boat come into the harbour. The crew told him that his army had invaded Muslim territory, laid it waste and returned victorious. The Muslim sage was dozing at the King's side. The King said to him: 'Did you hear what they said?' 'No.' 'They told me that we have defeated the Muslims in Tripoli. What use is Muhammad now to his land and his people?' 'He was not there,'

[1] Now Birecik in Turkey.

replied the old man, 'he was at Edessa, which the Muslims have just taken.' The Franks who were present laughed, but the King said: 'Do not laugh, for by God this man is incapable of speaking anything but the truth.' And a few days later news came from the Franks in Syria that Edessa had been taken.[1] Certain honest and godly men have told me that a holy man saw the dead Zangi in a dream and asked him: 'How has God treated you?' and Zangi replied, 'God has pardoned me, because I conquered Edessa.'

ZANGI'S DEATH, AND A EULOGY OF HIM

(IBN AL-ATHĪR, XI, 72–4)

In this year (541), on 5 rabīʿ II/14 September 1146, the Ata-beg ʿImād ad-Din Zangi ibn Aq Sunqūr, martyr for the Faith, ruler of Mosul and Syria,[2] was killed while he was besieging Jaʿbar as we have narrated. He was killed at night, murdered by a group of his courtiers. They fled to the fortress, whose inhabitants joyfully shouted the news to the (besieging) camp. When Zangi's servants came to his bedside they found that there was still a spark of life in him. My father, one of Zangi's close friends, recalled: 'I went straight to him; he was still alive, and when he saw me, clearly wanting to make an end of it he made a sign to me with his fingers imploring me to take pity on him. At the very suggestion I fell to the ground and said: "My Lord, who has done this?" but he was beyond speech, and yielded up his soul, may the Lord have mercy on him.'

Zangi was a handsome man, with a swarthy complexion, fine eyes, and hair that was beginning to go grey. He was more

[1] Faulty synchronization, possibly with the Sicilian expedition of 1142, or perhaps with the more successful one of 1146. This anecdote is another confirmation of Roger II's tolerant interest in the Muslim world. The nodding sage at his side might even be Idrisi.

[2] Although Zangi died while attacking another Muslim (the ʿUqailid ruler of Jaʿbar), the faithful Ibn al-Athīr endows him here and elsewhere with the title 'Martyr for the Faith' (*shahīd*), for his unceasing battle with the Franks.

than 60 years old, for he had been a baby when his father was killed,[1] as has been narrated. After his death he was buried at Raqqa. His subjects and his army went in awe of him; under his government the strong dared not harm the weak. Before he came to power the absence of strong rulers to impose justice, and the presence of the Franks close at hand, had made the country a wilderness, but he made it flower again. The population increased, and so did its prosperity. My father told me that he had seen Mosul in such a state of desolation that from the cymbal-makers' quarter one could see as far as the old Great Mosque, the *maidān* and the Sultan's palace, for not a building in between remained standing. It was not safe to go as far as the old Great Mosque without an escort, so far was it from human habitation, whereas now it is the centre of a mass of buildings, and every one of the areas mentioned just now is built up. My father also told me about the occasion when Zangi arrived in the Jazira one winter. One of his chief amīrs, 'Izz ad-Din ad-Dubaisi, who held the city of Daquqā as a fief from him, billeted himself on a Jew. The Jew appealed to the Ata-beg, who sympathized with him. He had only to give ad-Dubaisi a look to make him pack his bags and move.

Then the Sultan himself entered the city and had his baggage and tents unpacked. My father said: 'I remember seeing his men putting up his tents in the mud, spreading straw on the ground to keep them out of the mire. Then he appeared and took up residence there. Such was the strictness of his principles.'[2] Mosul had been one of the most impoverished regions before Zangi's time, but during and after his reign it blossomed with

[1] The amir Aq Sunqūr, who in 1094 rebelled against Tutūsh, Sultan of Aleppo, and was executed.

[2] The chroniclers are unanimous in their praise of Zangi for his unfailing defence of the civilian populations from intimidation and extortion by his troops. According to Kamāl ad-Din, the historian from Aleppo, when Zangi's troops left that city 'they seemed to be walking between two ropes,' so careful were they not to trample the crops. They knew from experience that the Ata-beg was not a man to be trifled with.

crops, sweet-smelling flowers and other plants as fruitfully as anywhere else in the world.

Zangi also used to take care to protect the honour of his subjects' women, especially his soldiers' wives. He used to say that if the soldiers' wives were not kept under strict control during their husbands' long absences on campaigns they would certainly go astray. He was the bravest man in the world. Of the time before he came to power it is enough to say that he went with the amīr Maudūd of Mosul to Tiberias, in Frankish territory, and flung a lance at the city gates that left a scar in the wood. In the same way he attacked the Humaidi fortress of 'Aqar, which was at the top of a lofty mountain, and flung a lance that reached as far as the walls. There are other similar stories. During his reign in Mosul he was entirely surrounded by hostile states, all doing their best to seize his kingdom. But he, far from merely defending himself from his enemies, never let a year pass without taking over a piece of enemy territory. His neighbour on the Takrīt side was the Caliph al-Mustarshid bi-llāh, who besieged Mosul. On the Shahrazūr side was the Sultan Mas'ūd, then Ibn Suqmān of Khilāt, then Dawūd ibn Suqmān of Hisn Kaifa, then the Prince of Amid and Mardīn, then the Franks, from Damascus to Mardīn, and finally the Princes of Damascus itself. All these states were trying to encroach on his lands, but he attacked now this one, now that, making a conquest here, a treaty there, until at his death he had taken over several tracts of land at the expense of all his neighbours. You will find the details in the book in which we describe his reign and those of his sons.[1]

[1] The *History of the Ata-begs of Mosul*, in which Ibn al-Athīr displays to the full his patriotism and loyalty to the Zangid dynasty.

CHAPTER SEVEN

The most significant episode of the inconclusive Second Crusade, which was begun under the shadow of the loss of Edessa, was the short and ineffective siege of Damascus (1148). Ibn al-Qalānisi was an eye-witness, and his account completes and complements that of Ibn al-Athīr. Sibt Ibn al-Jauzi adds some picturesque details. The heroic death for his Faith and his country of the old *faqīh* al-Findalawi could be taken as a symbol of the most noble and austere aspects of the Muslim resistance.

THE SECOND CRUSADE. THE SIEGE OF DAMASCUS

(IBN AL-QALĀNISI, 297–300)

At the beginning of 543/1148 news was brought from several sources of the arrival of a Frankish fleet on the Syrian coast. Troops disembarked at the ports of Tyre and Acre to link up with the Franks already there. These were estimated at 100,000 men, allowing for the depredations of war, plague and famine. After the new arrivals had completed the obligatory pilgrimage to Jerusalem and returned, some by land and some by sea, they assembled in the camps of the King of Germany,[1] the leading Frankish noble there, and of other, lesser princes. They had not decided which of the Muslim cities of Syria to attack. In the end they decided to besiege Damascus, for in their evil hearts they deluded themselves that they could take it, since the town and country districts merge into one another. The amīr of Damascus, Mu'īn ad-Din Unur, received several warnings of the invasion and made preparations to defend his realm and

[1] The Emperor Conrad III. The part played by Louis VII of France is almost entirely ignored by Muslim writers.

repulse the enemy. He fortified the more exposed positions, manned the communication trenches and the loopholes, cut off supplies to enemy bases and blocked up water-holes and springs. Meanwhile about 50,000 infantry and cavalry, with trains of camel and oxen, were marching on Damascus. As they approached the city they made for the district known as *Manazil al-'Askar* (Military Encampment) but found that the water supply had been cut off. So they moved on to al-Mizza and encamped there, in order to be near water. They besieged the city with cavalry and infantry. On Saturday 6 rabī' I 543/24 July 1148 the Muslims challenged them to fight, and the battle began. The army from Damascus had large numbers of auxiliaries; experienced Turkish storm-troopers, the citizen militia and volunteers fighting for the Faith. After a fierce struggle the Franks, superior in numbers and equipment, overwhelmed the Muslims, seized the water supplies and encamped in the gardens surrounding the city. They closed in on the city walls, coming up closer than any army in ancient or modern times had ever been. On this day the Malikite lawyer and scholar, the imām Yusuf al-Findalawi—God have mercy on him!—fell in battle, a martyr for the Faith, by the river at ar-Rabwa. He was facing the enemy and refusing to withdraw, in obedience to the precepts of God Almighty in His noble Book.[1] The devout 'Abd ar-Rahmān al-Halhuli met the same fate.

The Franks set to work to cut down the trees and build fortifications with them, and to destroy the bridges. This occupied them for the whole of the night. The population of Damascus, after the experiences of the last hours, were disheartened and uncertain what to do. But at dawn on the Sunday the Muslim army made a sortie, attacked the Franks, and defeated them, killing and wounding large numbers. The amīr

[1] I.e. the Qur'anic teaching about the Holy War; no particular passage is referred to here.

Mu'īn ad-Din performed prodigious feats in this battle, showing unparalleled valour, tenacity and indefatigable prowess in his onslaught on the enemy. The battle raged long and furiously. The infidel cavalry waited to make the charges, for which it is famous, until a favourable opportunity presented itself. Fighting was still going on at sunset. Night fell, the battle had to cease for a while, and the troops retired to their billets. The regular soldiers spent the night facing the enemy, while the population mounted guard on the walls as a security measure against an enemy so close at hand.

Meanwhile letters had been sent to the provincial governor to ask his help. Turcoman cavalry and infantry from the province poured into the area. In the morning, reinforced and heartened, the Muslims returned to the battle. They stood firm and sent clouds of arrows from long-bows and cross-bows to rain down on the enemy's cavalry and infantry, horses and camels.

That day a large detachment of archers arrived on foot from the Biqā', increasing the number of defenders and doubling their supply of arms. That day both sides stood firm, but on the Tuesday our army attacked like eagles on mountain partridges, or sparrow-hawks on the quails' nest. They surrounded the Frankish camp, which had been barricaded with tree-trunks from the orchards, and broke down the defences with arrows and stones. The Franks, frightened and disheartened, dared not come out. When not one showed himself the Muslims began to think that some plot or ambush was afoot. The only troops to appear were cavalry and infantry patrols on raiding missions. They dared not take the initiative until they could see an opportunity to charge the Muslims, or an avenue of escape. Anyone bold enough to come within range of the Muslims was struck down by an arrow, stone or lance. Men of the Damascus militia and from the surrounding regions lay in wait for the Franks along paths they thought safe and killed anyone who used them. The heads were taken to Damascus to be exchanged for a reward; in this way a large number of heads was collected.

News reached the Franks from many sources that the Muslims were bearing down on them to attack them and wipe them out, and they felt that their defeat was certain. They consulted among themselves, and decided that the only escape from the trap or abyss that loomed ahead of them was to take flight. At dawn on the following Wednesday they retreated in miserable confusion and disorder.

When the Muslims saw that they had gone, and observed the traces that they left in their flight, they set off the same morning to pursue them. They showered them with arrows and killed many of their rearguard in this way, and horses and pack animals as well. Innumerable corpses of men and their splendid mounts were found in their bivouacs and along the route of their flight,[1] the bodies stinking so powerfully that the birds almost fell out of the sky. That very night they set fire to ar-Rabwa and al-Qubba al-Mamduda.

This gracious sign of God's favour brought rejoicing to Muslim hearts, and they gave thanks to the Most High for hearing the prayers raised unceasingly to Him in the days of their distress. For which let God be praised and blessed!

(IBN AL-ATHĪR, XI, 85–6)

In this year (543/1148) the King of Germany left his homeland with a large army of Franks to attack the Muslim empire. He had no doubt that with his vast supplies of men, money and equipment he would be victorious after only a brief struggle. On his arrival in Syria the Franks there presented themselves

[1] Among whom, perhaps, 'freed from the deceptive world', lay Cacciaguida, the great-great-grandfather of Dante, the only relative of his to figure significantly in the *Divine Comedy* (Paradiso XV).

to offer their obedience and put themselves at his command. He ordered them to follow him to Damascus, to besiege and take it, as he thought. They marched off with him and surrounded the city.

The ruler of Damascus was Mujīr ad-Din Abaq ibn Muhammad ibn Buri ibn Tughtikīn, but he wielded no effective power, the real commander being Mu'īn ad-Din Unur, one of his grandfather Tughtikīn's mamlūks. It was he who had put Mujīr ad-Din on the throne. He was a wise and just man, upright and God-fearing. He assumed responsibility for mustering an army and defending the city. For a while the Franks kept up the siege, and then on 6 rabī' I/24 July they moved in to attack, cavalry and infantry together. The army came out of Damascus to meet them and fought relentlessly. Among the soldiers was the lawyer Hujjat ad-Din Yusuf ibn Dibās al-Findalawi of the Maghrib, a very old man and a lawyer of absolute probity. When Mu'īn ad-Din saw him marching on foot he went to meet him, greeted him and said: 'Sir, your age gives you dispensation; *I* will concern myself with the defence of Islām!' and he begged him to retire. But the old man refused, saying: 'I have offered myself for sale, and He has bought me. By God, I neither agreed nor asked that the contract should be annulled!' He was referring to the words of Almighty God: 'God has bought the faithful, both themselves and their possessions, and given them Paradise in exchange.'[1] He went on to fight the Franks until he was killed, near an-Nairab, half a *farsakh* from Damascus.

The Franks gained ground and the Muslims weakened. The German king advanced as far as al-Maidān al-Akhdar (the Green Square), and everyone was convinced that he would take the city. Meanwhile Mu'īn ad-Din had sent a message to Saif ad-Din Ghazi, son of the Ata-beg Zangi and ruler of Mosul, calling on him to come to the aid of the Muslims and to

[1] Qur'ān IX, 112.

drive off the enemy. Saif ad-Din marshalled his army and marched into Syria, bringing with him his brother Nur ad-Din Mahmūd[1] from Aleppo. When they reached Hims, Saif ad-Din sent to Mu'īn ad-Din to say: 'I have come with every man in my realm capable of bearing arms. I ask that a condition of my attacking the Franks shall be the presence of my representatives in Damascus. If I am defeated, I shall take my army inside the city and defend it from within. If we are victorious, the city is yours, and I shall not question your right to it.' To the Franks he sent a threatening message urging them to retreat from Damascus. The Franks broke off the fight, for they had many casualties, and were alarmed at the prospect of having to face Saif ad-Din as well as the army from Damascus. They decided to conserve their forces, while the citizens repaired the defences and drew breath after the labour of unceasing combat. Meanwhile Mu'īn ad-Din sent to the Franks to say: 'The King of the East has arrived; if you do not retreat I shall hand the city over to him, and then by God you will repent.' To the Syrian Franks he wrote: 'What reason have you for supporting these people against us when you know that if they take the city they will seize your possessions on the coast? I warn you that if I feel that I am losing the battle I shall hand the city over to Saif ad-Din, and you may be sure that if he becomes ruler of Damascus you will not be allowed to keep a foothold in Syria.' This message persuaded them to break their alliance with the King of Germany in exchange for the fortress of Baniyās from Mu'īn ad-Din. So the Syrian Franks had a private discussion with the King of Germany and frightened him with their tales of Saif ad-Din, his vast army, his constant reinforcements, and the probability that he would take Damascus despite anything that they could do to prevent him. They were so persuasive that the king withdrew his troops from Damascus. The Syrian Franks took over Baniyās and the German Franks returned to

[1] The 'Norandin' of the Crusaders; Islām's champion before Saladin.

their homeland, which is north of Constantinople and to one side. Thus God delivered the believers from their distress. Abu l-Qasim ibn 'Asakir, in his history of Damascus, says that a certain learned lawyer said that he saw al-Findalawi in a dream and asked him: 'How has God treated you and where are you?' and received the reply, 'God has pardoned me. I am in the garden of Eden (among the blessed) stretched on couches set to face one another.'[1]

(SIBT IBN AL-JAUZI, 300)

. . . It was harvest time. The Franks went down into the valley and ate much of the crop, and this gave them dysentery. Many died of it, and all the others were ill. The people of Damascus were in great need, but gave alms of what they had, each in proportion to his possessions. The whole population, men, women and children, assembled in the Great Mosque. Uthmān's Qur'ān[2] was displayed, and the people sprinkled their heads with ashes and wept tears of supplication. And God heard their prayers.

The Franks had with them a great Priest with a long beard, whose teachings they obeyed. On the tenth day of their siege of Damascus he mounted his ass, hung a cross round his neck, took two more in his hand and hung another round the ass's neck. He had the Testaments and the crosses and the Holy Scriptures set before him and assembled the army in his presence; the only ones to remain behind were those guarding the tents. Then he said: 'The Messiah has promised me that today I shall wipe out this city.' At this moment the Muslims opened the city gates and in the name of Islām charged as one man into the face of death. Never, in pagan times or since the

[1] Qur'ān XXXVII, 42–43.

[2] A precious copy of the Holy Book dating from the time of the first collation of the text under the Caliph 'Uthmān (644–56); it might even be the very copy he was reading when he was murdered.

coming of Islām, was there a day like this. One of the men of the Damascus militia reached the Priest, who was fighting in the front line, struck his head from his body and killed his ass too. As the whole Muslim army bore down upon them the Franks turned and fled. The Muslims killed 10,000, smote their crosses and their cavalry with Greek fire, and pursued the army as far as the tents. Night separated them, and in the morning the Franks were gone and no trace of them remained.

CHAPTER EIGHT

In 1154, six years after Damascus had successfully resisted the Crusaders, Nur ad-Din, Zangi's son, realized his father's old dream and became ruler of the Syrian metropolis without bloodshed. From here and from his ancestral home, Aleppo, he put new enthusiasm and efficiency into the fight against the Crusaders. Fighting continued, with mixed fortunes, for twenty years, until Nur ad-Din's death in 1174. For some time before this date his reputation had paled before the new star shining in Egypt: Saladin. This obscure official at Nur ad-Din's court was destined to crown with success a century of Muslim struggles against the Christian invaders. Ibn al-Athīr gives an idealized picture of Nur ad-Din, as he did of his father. We can credit him with at least one quality not shared by Zangi: a certain spiritual awareness and humanity.

NUR AD-DIN'S VICTORIES AND HIS TRIUMPH AT DAMASCUS

(IBN AL-QALĀNISI, 340–2)

Nur ad-Din reached the well-guarded city[1] on Friday 27 rabī' I (552/9 May 1157) to see that supplies of military equipment were being prepared for the troops. He intended to stay there for a few days and then to move directly to where his army of Turcoman and Arab troops were mustered for the Holy War against the infidel enemy. God, if He so willed, would assist in their discomfiture and hasten their downfall.

As soon as he arrived he set to work on the task that had brought him to Damascus: ordering the building of siege-engines and the manufacture of arms that his victorious army would need, and summoning the warriors and champions of

[1] Damascus.

Damascus, its volunteer militia of young citizens and men from the north, to equip themselves and prepare for battle against the polytheist and heretic Franks. Then he left Damascus to join his victorious army, and pressed on without rest or delay. He left on the last Saturday of rabī' I and was followed by a huge throng made up of militia, volunteers, imāms, sufis[1] and holy men. Almighty God was pleased to crown his plans and decisions with glittering success, casting down the rebellious infidels and hastening their death and utter destruction and the coming of the time when no trace of them should remain. Such a thing is not difficult for God the Omnipotent, the Almighty.

On the following Saturday, 7 rabī' II/18 May, a short while after the just King Nur ad-Din had surrounded Baniyās with his victorious army, set up his siege-engines and begun the attack, a messenger-pigeon arrived in Damascus from the victorious army encamped around Baniyās, with the good news[2] from Asad ad-Din,[3] who was stationed at Hunīn with Arab and Turcoman troops. The Franks—God damn them!—had sent a column of more than a hundred of their commanders and other knights to make a lightning raid on Asad ad-Din's forces, thinking that there were only a few of them, and not the thousands that were really there. When they approached, our men came out upon them from the rear like lions on their prey, and there followed an orgy of slaughter, capture and looting. Few of the Franks escaped. On the following Monday the prisoners and the heads of those killed arrived in Damascus together with their equipment and a selection of horses, shields and lances. These were paraded around the city, and the spectacle caused great joy, and gratitude to God for this second manifestation of His grace. Men have faith in His power to

[1] The mystics of Islām, members of religious fraternities.

[2] Nur ad-Din was the first Muslim ruler to organize a regular information service by pigeon post.

[3] Asad ad-Din Shirkūh, Nur ad-Din's faithful Kurdish general, Saladin's uncle.

hasten the destruction and downfall of their enemies, for such a thing is easy for Him.

This double blessing was followed by the arrival on Tuesday of a carrier-pigeon from the well-guarded camp at Baniyās with the news that on that day, at the fourth hour, the fort had been taken by storm. Tunnels had been dug under the walls, and when they were fired the towers had crumbled and our army had rushed in, slaughtering the defenders and pillaging the fort. The survivors fled to the citadel and barricaded themselves in there, but their capture, God willing, was not far off, with God's help and blessing.

However, it was the will of fate that the Franks should decide to band together to release Honfroi[1] of Baniyās and his companions besieged in the citadel. These men had reached the end of their resistance, and urgently entreated our Lord Nur ad-Din to have pity on them. They offered to hand over the citadel and all its contents in exchange for their lives. He refused. When, soon after this, the King of the Franks[2] and all his army appeared from the mountains and took the besieging army by surprise, as well as the troops stationed on the road to intercept supplies, the only prudent thing to do was to retire and allow him to reach the defenders and bring them help. But when Baldwin saw that the walls of the lower city were in ruins and its houses destroyed he saw no hope of making the place habitable. This was the end of rabī' II/first ten days of June 1157.

On Wednesday 9 jumada I/19 June more carrier-pigeons arrived with letters from Nur ad-Din's well-guarded camp. The just King had learnt that the Franks were encamped at Mallaha, between Tiberias and Baniyās, and had pursued them with his victorious army of Turks and Arabs. As the Muslim army came upon them from behind, the Franks saw the shadow that their banners cast on them as they closed in. They seized their arms and leapt on to their horses, dividing into four de-

[1] Humphrey of Toron. [2] Baldwin III.

tachments to attack the enemy. Then Nur ad-Din and his knights dismounted and crushed them beneath the blows of their arrows and swords. In less time than it takes to tell the enemy was completely overwhelmed and the fighting was over. Almighty and all-conquering God had sent His virtuous supporters victory and condemned the infidel rebels to hell. The Frankish cavalry was killed or captured and a great number of their infantry put to the sword; one authority says that not more than ten survived, delivered from death for the time being, but overwhelmed with terror. Some say that their King was among the survivors; some that he was killed; certainly nothing more was heard of him, although the Franks searched for him far and wide. God will help us to subdue them! The Muslim army lost only two men: one of the champions mentioned earlier, who killed four infidel champions before his time came and he reached the end of his allotted span and was killed; and one other, an unknown foreigner. Both died as martyrs for the Faith, deserving a heavenly reward. May God have mercy on them. The soldiers filled their hands with booty: horses, harnesses, flocks, and provisions of all sorts. Their church with its famous treasure was Nur ad-Din's share. This was a great victory and a glorious triumph sent by Almighty God the bringer of victory to honour Islām and its believers and to debase polytheism and its faction.

The prisoners and the heads of the slain reached Damascus on the Sunday after the victory. On each camel the Muslims set two captive knights, and spread one of their standards filled with a certain number of scalps of hair. Their generals, commanders and governors were each mounted on a horse, fully armed and in their helmets and each carrying a standard. The infantry, Turcopules[1] and sergeants walked bound together by a single rope in small groups. A huge crowd of citizens, old

[1] 'Sons of the Turks'; local troops serving as auxiliaries in the armies of the Crusaders.

men, young men, women and children came out to see the glorious victory granted by God to all Muslims, and they praised and blessed Him for permitting His friends to triumph and enabling them to defeat the adversary. They praised the just King Nur ad-Din sincerely and unceasingly for being their defender and champion, honouring him for the kingly gifts with which he was endowed. Poems were also composed on the subject, one of which said:

Thus the day came for the Franks when the shame of capture, defeat and disaster engulfed them.
They were led in procession on their camels, with their standards, downcast in anguish and pain,
After they had been proud, honoured and famous, in battle and in conflict.
Thus, thus enemies perish when devastation is let loose upon them.
Taken shamefully like sheep in the pasture, shrouded night and morning in disaster.
They, fools, broke the peaceful truce after it had been legally sealed.
They reaped the reward of their perfidy, and brought down the ruin and hatred that engulfed them.
May God not defend their assembled hosts, assailed by the sharpest swords ever to strike a blow!
The result of ungratefulness is death or imprisonment; the result of gratitude is the highest reward.
Let us therefore praise and thank God ceaselessly, and may His grace endure for ever.

THE DEATH OF NUR AD-DIN

(IBN AL-ATHĪR, XI, 264–7)

On Wednesday 11 shawwāl 569/15 May 1174 Nur ad-Din Mahmūd ibn Zangi ibn Aq Sunqūr, ruler of Syria, Mesopotamia and Egypt, died of a heart attack. He was buried in the citadel at Damascus, and later transferred to the *madrasa*[1] that he had founded in Damascus near the osier-workers' market.

[1] A school of higher learning, teaching Muslim law and theology.

An amazing coincidence occurred: on 2 shawwāl he was riding out with a pious amīr, who said: 'Praise be to Him who alone knows whether or not we shall meet here again in a year's time.' Nur ad-Din replied, 'Do not say that, but rather, praise be to Him who alone knows whether we shall meet here in a month's time.' And Nur ad-Din, God have mercy upon him, was dead at the end of eleven days, and the Amīr before the year's end, so that they both died as their words had foreshadowed. Nur ad-Din was making preparations to invade Egypt and take it from Saladin,[1] in whom he divined a certain reluctance to fight the Franks as he should. He knew that it was fear of himself, Nur ad-Din, and of finding himself face to face with his Lord, that weakened Saladin's enthusiasm, and made him content to have the Franks as a bulwark between them. Nur ad-Din sent messengers to Mosul, in the Jazira, and to Diyār Bakr to mobilize troops for the assault. He intended to leave his nephew Saif ad-Din in command of Mosul and Syria, and to lead his army to Egypt, but in the midst of his preparations there came a command from God that he could not disobey.

A distinguished doctor who attended Nur ad-Din told me: 'when Nur ad-Din was struck down by the illness from which he died he sent for me together with other doctors. When we arrived we found him lying in a small room in the citadel in Damascus, in the clutches of an attack of angina and even then at the point of death—he could not even speak loudly enough to be heard. He was taken ill in the room to which he used to withdraw to pray, and he had not been moved. When we entered the room and I saw the condition he was in I said: "You should not have waited until you were as ill as this to call us.

[1] Saladin was sent to Egypt by Nur ad-Din as his representative, and after removing the Fatimid Caliphate had himself made ruler there, but he had not yet brought himself to break the normal bond of subjection to Nur ad-Din. The latter is therefore described here as 'ruler of Egypt', although in fact he never exercised any real power there.

You should be moved at once to a large, well-lit room. In an illness such as this it is important." We gathered round to examine him, and blood-letting was advised. Then he spoke: "You would not bleed a man of sixty"; and he refused to be treated. So we tried other specifics, but they did him no good, and he grew worse and died; may God show him mercy and compassion.'

Nur ad-Din was a tall, swarthy man with a beard but no moustache, a fine forehead and a pleasant appearance enhanced by beautiful, melting eyes. His kingdom extended far and wide, and his power was acknowledged even in Medina and Mecca and the Yemen, when Shams ad-Daula ibn Ayyūb entered them and proclaimed himself their ruler.[1] He was born in 511/1117, and was known throughout his realms as a wise and just ruler. I have read the lives of the kings of old, and after the right-guided Caliphs and 'Umar ibn 'Abd al-'Azīz[2] I have not found one more upright or a sterner advocate of justice. I have written about him at length in my history of the dynasty,[3] and am giving only an extract here, in the hope that men in authority will read it and take him for their model.

Among his virtues were austerity, piety and a knowledge of theology. His food and clothing and all his personal expenditure came out of income from properties bought with his legal share of booty and money allocated for communal Muslim interests. His wife complained to him of his austerity, and so he allotted to her, from his private property, three shops in Hims that would bring her in about twenty *dinar* a year. When she objected that this was not much he said: 'I have no more.

[1] In the Hijāz ('the two Holy Places': Medina and Mecca) and in the Yemen conquered by Saladin's brother, Nur ad-Din's authority was no more real than in Egypt; they were in fact part of the Ayyubid empire.

[2] The 'rightly guided' or orthodox Caliphs were Muhammad's first four successors: Abu Bakr, 'Umar, 'Uthmān, 'Ali. These, with the Umayyad Caliph 'Umar ibn 'Abd al-'Azīz (Umar II, 717–19), are the ideal rulers of orthodox tradition, the eternal example of just government.

[3] *History of the Ata-begs of Mosul.*

Of all the wealth I have at my disposal, I am but the custodian for the Muslim community, and I do not intend to deceive them over this or to cast myself into hell-fire for your sake.'

He often got up to pray at night, and his vigils and meditations inspired praise. As the poet said:

He unites prowess in war with devotion to his Lord; what a splendid sight
is the warrior at prayer in the Temple!

He had a good knowledge of Muslim law (*fiqh*) of the Hanafite school[1] but he was not a fanatic. He had heard canonic traditions (*hadīth*) being transmitted, and had himself transmitted them, which is a meritorious act in God's eyes. As an example of his justice; he would not permit the imposition of any illegal duty or tax anywhere in his domains, but abolished them all, in Egypt, Syria, the Jazira and Mosul. He held the Holy Law in the deepest respect and applied its precepts; for example, a man summoned him to appear before a tribunal, so he appeared, together with the plaintiff, and sent to the qadi, Kamāl ad-Din ibn ash-Shahrazuri, to say: 'I am here to defend myself before the tribunal. You are to proceed as you would with any other litigants.' In the event he won the case, but he gave the disputed object to the man who had cited him, saying: 'I had in any case intended to give him the object that he claimed, but I was afraid that my real motive might be pride and disdain to appear before the tribunal. So I appeared there, and now I am giving him what he claimed was his.' He set up 'Houses of Justice' throughout his realm, and with his qadi sat to administer justice to the oppressed, Jew or Muslim, at the expense of the oppressor, even if it were his own son or his chief amir.

On the battlefield he had no equal; he carried two bows and quivers into the fray with him. The lawyer Qutb ad-Din an-Nāsawi said to him: 'In God's name, do not endanger yourself

[1] One of the four principal schools or systems of Islamic law. The other three are the Shafi'ite, the Malikite and the Hanbalite.

and all Islām! If you fell in battle, every Muslim alive would be put to the sword.' Nur ad-Din replied: 'And who is Mahmūd[1] to be spoken to like this? Before I was born there was another to defend Islām and this country, and he is God, apart from whom there is no God!' Among his public works he built walls for all the cities and fortresses of Syria, among them Damascus, Hims, Hamat, Aleppo, Shaizar, Baalbek, and many others. He built numerous Hanifite and Shafi'ite *madrasas*, the Great Mosque of Nur ad-Din at Mosul, hospitals and caravanserai along the great roads, Dervish monasteries in every town, and left generous endowments to each. I have heard that the monthly income of all his foundations amounted to 9,000 Tyrian *dinar*. He honoured scholars and men of religion, and had the deepest respect for them. He would rise to his feet in their presence and invite them to sit next to him. He was always courteous to them and never contested what they said. He used to conduct correspondences with them in his own hand. His expression was grave and melancholy, because of his great humility. Many were his virtues, innumerable his merits; this book is not large enough to encompass them all.

[1] The Sultan's personal name; Nur ad-Din was simply an honorific title.

CHAPTER NINE

The following chapter, which might be called 'Frankish scenes and Frankish customs, seen through the eyes of a Muslim', consists largely of extracts from the celebrated *Autobiography* of Usama ibn Munqidh, the gallant and cultured amīr of Shaizar whose life spanned almost the whole of the first century of the Crusades. His memoirs, a rich jumble of juicy anecdotes and references to historical events, are stuffed with passages recalling his encounters with the Franks in peace and in war, passages in which hostility, curiosity and sympathy appear in turn. These little episodes are sometimes delightfully paradoxical, and offer a welcome relief from the monotonous scenes of warfare that fill the pages of the professional historians.

THE FRANKISH CAVALRY

(USAMA, 48)

Among the Franks—God damn them!—no quality is more highly esteemed in a man than military prowess. The knights have a monopoly of the positions of honour and importance among them, and no one else has any prestige in their eyes. They are the men who give counsel, pass judgment and command the armies. On one occasion I went to law with one of them about some herds that the Prince of Baniyās seized in a wood; this was at a time when there was a truce between us, and I was living in Damascus. I said to King Fulk, the son of Fulk:[1] 'This man attacked and seized my herd. This is the season when the cows are in calf; their young died at birth, and he has returned the herd to me completely ruined.' The King turned to six or seven of his knights and said: 'Come, give a judgment on this man's case.' They retired from the audience chamber and discussed the matter until they all agreed. Then they re-

[1] Fulk of Jerusalem (1131–43). For his relationship with Usama, see below.

turned to the King's presence and said: 'We have decided that the Prince of Baniyās should indemnify this man for the cattle that he has ruined.' The King ordered that the indemnity should be paid, but such was the pressure put on me and the courtesy shown me that in the end I accepted four hundred *dinar* from the Prince. Once the knights have given their judgment neither the King nor any other commander can alter or annul it, so great an influence do their knights have in their society. On this occasion the King swore to me that he had been made very happy the day before. When I asked him what had made him happy he said: 'They told me that you were a great knight, but I did not believe that you would be chivalrous.' 'Your Majesty', I replied, 'I am a knight of my race and my people.'[1] When a knight is tall and well-built they admire him all the more.

FRANKISH PIRACY

(USAMA, 25–6)

I entered the service of the just King Nur ad Din—God have mercy on him!—and he wrote to al-Malik as-Salih[2] asking him to send my household and my sons out to me; they were in Egypt, under his patronage. Al-Malik as-Salih wrote back that he was unable to comply because he feared that they might fall into Frankish hands. He invited me instead to return to Egypt myself:[3] 'You know,' he wrote, 'how strong the friendship is between us. If you have reason to mistrust the Palace, you could go to Mecca, and I would send you the appointment to the governorship of Aswān and the means to combat the Abyssinians. Aswān is on the frontier of the Islamic empire.

[1] This exchange, and the whole paragraph, depends on a play on the terms 'chivalry' and 'cavalry', for which Arabic has only one word.

[2] In spite of his title ('the good king') al-Malik as-Salih was in fact the Fatimid vizier Tala'i' ibn Ruzzīk, who ruled Egypt under its Caliph al-Fa'iz and died in 1161.

[3] Usama was deeply implicated in the intrigues and bloody revolutions of Muslim politics; this explains the reference in one of the letters mentioned in the text to his fear of 'the Palace'.

I would send your household and your sons to you there.' I spoke to Nur ad-Din about this, and asked his advice, which was that he would certainly not choose to return to Egypt once he had extricated himself. 'Life is too short!' he said. 'It would be better if I sent to the Frankish King for a safe-conduct for your family, and gave them an escort to bring them here safely.' This he did—God have mercy on him!—and the Frankish King gave him his cross, which ensures the bearer's safety by land and sea. I sent it by a young slave of mine, together with letters to al-Malik as-Salih from Nur ad-Din and myself. My family were dispatched for Damietta on a ship of the vizier's private fleet, under his protection and provided with everything they might need.

At Damietta they transferred to a Frankish ship and set sail, but when they neared Acre, where the Frankish King[1] was—God punish him for his sins—he sent out a boatload of men to break up the ship with hatchets before the eyes of my family, while he rode down to the beach and claimed everything that came ashore as booty. My young slave swam ashore with the safe-conduct, and said: 'My Lord King, is not this your safe-conduct?' 'Indeed it is,' he replied, 'But surely it is a Muslim custom that when a ship is wrecked close to land the local people pillage it?' 'So you are going to make us your captives?' 'Certainly not.' He had my family escorted to a house, and the women searched. Everything they had was taken; the ship had been loaded with women's trinkets, clothes, jewels, swords and other arms, and gold and silver to the value of about 30,000 *dinar*. The King took it all, and then handed five hundred *dinar* back to them and said: 'Make your arrangements to continue your journey with this money.' And there were fifty of them altogether! At the time I was with Nur ad-Din in the realm of King Mas 'ūd[2], at Ru'bān and Kaisūn; compared with the safety

[1] Baldwin III (1143 62)

[2] The Seljuqid Sultan of Iconium. The two forts are in the region of Samosata. These events took place in about 1155.

of my sons, my brother and our women, the loss of the rest meant little to me, except for my books. There had been 4,000 fine volumes on board, and their destruction has been a cruel loss to me for the rest of my life.

FRANKISH MEDICINE

(USAMA, 97–8)

The ruler of Munáitira[1] wrote to my uncle asking him to send a doctor to treat some of his followers who were ill. My uncle sent a Christian called Thabit. After only ten days he returned and we said 'You cured them quickly!' This was his story: They took me to see a knight who had an abscess on his leg, and a woman with consumption. I applied a poultice to the leg, and the abscess opened and began to heal. I prescribed a cleansing and refreshing diet for the woman. Then there appeared a Frankish doctor, who said: 'This man has no idea how to cure these people!' He turned to the knight and said: 'Which would you prefer, to live with one leg or to die with two?' When the knight replied that he would prefer to live with one leg, he sent for a strong man and a sharp axe. They arrived, and I stood by to watch. The doctor supported the leg on a block of wood, and said to the man: 'Strike a mighty blow, and cut cleanly!' And there, before my eyes, the fellow struck the knight one blow, and then another, for the first had not finished the job. The marrow spurted out of the leg, and the patient died instantaneously. Then the doctor examined the woman and said; 'She has a devil in her head who is in love with her. Cut her hair off!' This was done, and she went back to eating her usual Frankish food, garlic and mustard, which made her illness worse. 'The devil has got into her brain,' pronounced the doctor. He took a razor and cut a cross on her head, and removed the brain so that the inside of the skull was

[1] The Crusaders' *Moinestre*, in the Lebanon about ten miles east of Jubáil.

laid bare. This he rubbed with salt; the woman died instantly. At this juncture I asked whether they had any further need of me, and as they had none I came away, having learnt things about medical methods that I never knew before.[1]

THE FRANKS AND MARITAL JEALOUSY

(USAMA, 100–1)

The Franks are without any vestige of a sense of honour and jealousy. If one of them goes along the street with his wife and meets a friend, this man will take the woman's hand and lead her aside to talk, while the husband stands by waiting until she has finished her conversation. If she takes too long about it he leaves her with the other man and goes on his way. Here is an example of this from my personal experience: while I was in Nablus I stayed with a man called Mu'ízz, whose house served as an inn for Muslim travellers. Its windows overlooked the street. On the other side of the road lived a Frank who sold wine for the merchants; he would take a bottle of wine from one of them and publicize it, announcing that such-and-such a merchant had just opened a hogshead of it, and could be found at such-and-such a place by anyone wishing to buy some; '. . . and I will give him the first right to the wine in this bottle.'

Now this man returned home one day and found a man in bed with his wife. 'What are you doing here with my wife?' he demanded. 'I was tired,' replied the man, 'and so I came in to rest.' 'And how do you come to be in my bed?' 'I found the bed made up, and lay down to sleep.' 'And this woman slept with you, I suppose?' 'The bed,' he replied, 'is hers. How could I prevent her getting into her own bed?' 'I swear if you do it

[1] Not all Frankish doctors were butchers like the fiend portrayed here, but the air of ironic superiority that this passage conveys was justified by the supremacy of the great medical tradition of the East at that time.

again I shall take you to court!'—and this was his only reaction, the height of his outburst of jealousy!

I heard a similar case from a bath attendant called Salim from Ma'arra, who worked in one of my father's bath-houses. This is his tale: I earned my living in Ma'arra by opening a bath-house. One day a Frankish knight came in. They do not follow our custom of wearing a cloth round their waist while they are at the baths, and this fellow put out his hand, snatched off my loin-cloth and threw it away. He saw at once that I had just recently shaved my pubic hair. 'Salim!' he exclaimed. I came toward him and he pointed to that part of me. 'Salim! It's magnificent! You shall certainly do the same for me!' And he lay down flat on his back. His hair there was as long as his beard. I shaved him, and when he had felt the place with his hand and found it agreeably smooth he said: 'Salim, you must certainly do the same for my *Dama*.' In their language *Dama* means lady, or wife. He sent his valet to fetch his wife, and when they arrived and the valet had brought her in, she lay down on her back, and he said to me: 'Do to her what you did to me.' So I shaved her pubic hair, while her husband stood by watching me. Then he thanked me and paid me for my services.

You will observe a strange contradiction in their character: they are without jealousy or a sense of honour, and yet at the same time they have the courage that as a rule springs only from the sense of honour and a readiness to take offence.

ORIENTALIZED FRANKS

(USAMA, 103–4)

There are some Franks who have settled in our land and taken to living like Muslims. These are better than those who have just arrived from their homelands, but they are the exception, and cannot be taken as typical. I came across one of them once when I sent a friend on business to Antioch, which was governed by Todros ibn as-Safi,[1] a friend of mine. One day he said to my friend: 'A Frankish friend has invited me to visit him; come with me so that you can see how they live.' 'I went with him,' said my friend, 'and we came to the house of one of the old knights who came with the first expedition. This man had retired from the army, and was living on the income of the property he owned in Antioch. He had a fine table brought out, spread with a splendid selection of appetizing food. He saw that I was not eating, and said: 'Don't worry, please; eat what you like, for I don't eat Frankish food. I have Egyptian cooks and eat only what they serve. No pig's flesh ever comes into my house!'[2] So I ate, although cautiously, and then we left. Another day, as I was passing through the market, a Frankish woman advanced on me, addressing me in her barbaric language with words I found incomprehensible. A crowd of Franks gathered round us and I gave myself up for lost, when suddenly this knight appeared, saw me and came up. 'What do you want with this man?' 'This man,' she replied, 'killed my brother Urso.' This Urso was a knight from Apamea who was killed by a soldier from Hamāt. The old man scolded the woman. 'This man is a merchant, a city man, not a fighter, and he lives nowhere near where your brother was killed.' Then he turned on the crowd, which melted away, and shook hands with me. Thus the fact that I ate at his table saved my life.

THE TEMPLARS AT JERUSALEM

(USAMA, 99)

This is an example of Frankish barbarism, God damn them! When I was in Jerusalem I used to go to the Masjid al-Aqsa, beside which is a small oratory which the Franks have made

[1] Theodore Sophianos, the Greek commander (*ra'īs*) of the municipality of Antioch.

[2] It is fear of this 'unclean' food that troubles the Muslim guest, who even when reassured eats cautiously.

into a church. Whenever I went into the mosque, which was in the hands of Templars who were friends of mine, they would put the little oratory at my disposal, so that I could say my prayers there. One day I had gone in, said the *Allāh akhbar*[1] and risen to begin my prayers, when a Frank threw himself on me from behind, lifted me up and turned me so that I was facing east. 'That is the way to pray!' he said. Some Templars at once intervened, seized the man and took him out of my way, while I resumed my prayer. But the moment they stopped watching him he seized me again and forced me to face east, repeating that this was the way to pray. Again the Templars intervened and took him away. They apologized to me and said: 'He is a foreigner who has just arrived today from his homeland in the north, and he has never seen anyone pray facing any other direction than east.' 'I have finished my prayers,' I said, and left, stupefied by the fanatic who had been so perturbed and upset to see someone praying facing the *qibla*![2]

I was present myself when one of them came up to the amīr Mu'īn ad-Din—God have mercy on him—in the Dome of the Rock, and said to him: 'Would you like to see God as a baby?' The amīr said that he would, and the fellow proceeded to show us a picture of Mary with the infant Messiah on her lap. 'This,' he said, 'is God as a baby.' Almighty God is greater than the infidels' concept of him![3]

THE RANSOMING OF PRISONERS

(USAMA, 60–2)

I had sought an opportunity to visit the King of the Franks to sue for peace between him and Jamāl ad-Din Muhammad ibn

[1] The beginning of the canonic sequence of prayers.

[2] The Muslim at prayer must face the *qibla*, the direction of Mecca. The custom of facing east to pray was widespread among mediaeval Christians.

[3] A Qur'ānic formula, used with particular relevance here in reporting what is to a Muslim a blasphemy.

Taj al-Mulūk[1]—God have mercy on him!—basing my hopes of success on a service that my late father had once performed for King Baldwin, the father of King Fulk's wife.[2] The Franks brought their prisoners for me to ransom, and I ransomed those whose survival was God's will. There was a fanatic called William Jibā who had gone off to sea as a pirate in his own ship and captured a vessel carrying four hundred men and women who were coming from the Maghrib on the Pilgrimage. Some were brought before me with their owners, and I ransomed as many as I could. Among them was a young man who greeted me and then sat without speaking. I asked who he was, and was told that he was a young devout, who was owned by a tanner. 'How much do you want for this one?' I asked. 'Well,' he said, 'I shall only sell him if you buy this old man as well, for I bought them together. The price is forty-three *dinar*.' I redeemed a certain number on my own account, and another group for Mu'īn ad-Din—God have mercy on him—for a hundred and twenty *dinar*. I paid in cash as much as I had on me, and gave guarantees for the rest. On my return to Damascus I said to Mu'īn ad-Din: 'I redeemed some captives on your behalf for whom I could not pay cash. Now that I am back, you can pay for them yourself if you like, or if not then I will pay for them.' 'No,' he said, 'I insist on paying, for my dearest wish is to gain merit in God's eyes.' He was outstanding in his eagerness to do good and earn a heavenly reward. He paid the sum I owed the Franks, and I returned to Acre a few days later. William Jibā had thirty-two prisoners left, among them the wife of one of the men I had been able to ransom. I bought her, but did not pay for her at once. Later that day I rode to his house—God damn him!—and said to him: 'Sell me ten of these.' He swore that he would only sell the whole lot together. 'I have not

[1] The treaty of 1140 between Damascus and the Franks (see above). This passage suggests that the author had a hand in drafting the treaty.

[2] Baldwin II had been the guest of the amīr of Shaizar during one of his periods of captivity, as Usama himself informs us elsewhere.

brought enough money for all of them,' I said; 'I will buy some of them now and the rest later.' But he insisted that he would sell the whole group together, so I went away. That night, by God's will, they all escaped, and the inhabitants of that quarter of Acre, who were all Muslims, sheltered them and helped them to reach Muslim territory. The accursed Jibā searched for them in vain, for God in his mercy saved them all. Then Jibā began to demand the money from me for the woman whom I had bought from him but not yet paid for, and who had fled with the rest. I said: 'Hand her over, and I will give you the money for her.' 'The money was due to me yesterday, before she escaped,' he said, and forced me to pay. But it meant little to me beside the joy of knowing that these poor things were safe.

A PROPOSAL TO SEND MY SON TO EUROPE

(USAMA, 97)

A very important Frankish knight was staying in the camp of King Fulk, the son of Fulk. He had come on a pilgrimage and was going home again. We got to know one another, and became firm friends. He called me 'brother' and an affectionate friendship grew up between us. When he was due to embark for the return journey he said to me: 'My brother, as I am about to return home, I should be happy if you would send your son with me,' (the boy, who was about fourteen years old, was beside me at the time), 'so that he could meet the noblemen of the realm and learn the arts of politics and chivalry. On his return home he would be a truly cultivated man.' A truly cultivated man would never be guilty of such a suggestion; my son might as well be taken prisoner as go off into the land of the Franks. I turned to my friend and said: 'I assure you that I could desire nothing better for my son, but unfortunately the boy's grandmother, my mother, is very attached to him, and she would not even let him come away with me without extracting a promise from me that I would bring him back to her.' 'Your mother is still alive?' 'Yes.' 'Then she must have her way.'[1]

THE FALCON OF ACRE

(USAMA, 142–3)

I went to Acre with the amīr Mu'īn ad-Din—God have mercy on him—to visit the court of the Frankish King Fulk, the son of Fulk.[2] There we met a Genoese who had brought from the land of the Franks a great falcon on a lure. It worked together with a young bitch, hunting crane. When the bird was set at a crane the dog ran behind, and as soon as the bird had attacked the crane and struck it down, she seized it so that it could not escape. The amīr asked the King to give him the falcon, and the King took the bird and the dog from the Genoese and gave it to him. They travelled back with us, and on the road to Damascus I saw the falcon savaging gazelles as it did the food we gave it. We brought it back to Damascus, but it did not survive long enough to be taken out hunting.

CHRISTIAN PIETY AND MUSLIM PIETY

(USAMA, *Kitāb al-'asa* 528–9)

I paid a visit to the tomb of John the son of Zechariah—God's blessing on both of them![3]—in the village of Sebastea in the

[1] It is characteristic of the mediaeval Muslim family that in the excuses he invents Usama invokes not the boy's mother but his grandmother. What a pity that he did not agree to the proposal; Usama's son, visiting the Christian world, might have left us some fascinating comparisons between the two civilizations.

[2] See above.

[3] Both Zechariah and John the Baptist were believed to be prophets and venerated as such by the Muslims.

province of Nablus. After saying my prayers, I came out into the square that was bounded on one side by the Holy Precinct. I found a half-closed gate, opened it and entered a church. Inside were about ten old men, their bare heads as white as combed cotton. They were facing the east,[1] and wore (embroidered?) on their breasts staves ending in crossbars turned up like the rear of a saddle. They took their oath on this sign, and gave hospitality to those who needed it.[2] The sight of their piety touched my heart, but at the same time it displeased and saddened me, for I had never seen such zeal and devotion among the Muslims. For some time I brooded on this experience, until one day, as Mu'in ad-Din and I were passing the Peacock House[3] (*Dar at-Tawawīs*), he said to me: 'I want to dismount here and visit the Old Men (the ascetics).' 'Certainly,' I replied, and we dismounted and went into a long building set at an angle to the road. For the moment I thought there was no one there. Then I saw about a hundred prayer-mats, and on each a sufi, his face expressing peaceful serenity, and his body humble devotion. This was a reassuring sight, and I gave thanks to Almighty God that there were among the Muslims men of even more zealous devotion than those Christian priests. Before this I had never seen sufis in their monastery, and was ignorant of the way they lived.

[1] Normal practice among Christians of the time (see above).

[2] The text and meaning of the last words here are uncertain: the cross in the form of staves was probably on the habits of these monks of the Chapter of St. John.

[3] A monastery (*khanqā*) belonging to an order of Muslim mystics, or sufis.

Part Two

SALADIN AND THE THIRD CRUSADE

CHAPTER ONE

The Muslim sources for Saladin and his deeds are, first, his officials and household retainers 'Imād ad-Din and Bahā' ad-Din: the former with his history of the conquest of Jerusalem (which continues in fact up to the death of Saladin). The extremely artificial style overlays an eye-witness account of the events described whose value is being increasingly realized. The latter, the author of a biography of Saladin written in a less flamboyant style, shows a warmth of sympathy and devotion that rarely slips into unctuous apologia. The third and frequently quoted authority on Saladin is Abu Shama, in a section of his *Book of the Two Gardens*, which is an anthology containing extracts from 'Imād ad-Din (shorn of the flowers of his style), Bahā' ad-Din and Ibn al-Athīr. Its only real value lies in the inclusion of other sources now lost (Ibn Abi t-Tayy) and for its selection of acts and documents from the Sultan's Chancellery. Ibn al-Athīr, although his attitude to Saladin was tainted by his political loyalties, preserves his unusual qualities of clear, informed exposition, using his sources with independent judgment.

The best all-round portrait of Islām's great champion is the one that opens Bahā' ad-Din's biography, and it is reproduced here in its entirety.

SALADIN'S CHARACTER

(BAHĀ' AD-DIN, 7–41)

One of the authentic canonical traditions[1] contains these words of the Prophet: 'Islām rests on five pillars: the asseveration that there is no god but God; prayer; the paying of the legal tithe; the fast of ramadān; and the Pilgrimage to God's Sacred House (at Mecca).' Now Saladin was a man of firm faith, one who often had God's name on his lips. He drew his faith from the evidence duly studied in the company of the most authoritative

[1] *Hadīth*, mentioned several times in the following sections. They are sayings attributed to the Prophet and transmitted in a standard form, each with a chain of guarantors, the purpose of which is to establish its authenticity. The 'science of *hadith*' became an important branch of Muslim theology.

scholars and the greatest lawyers, acquiring sufficient competence to take his part in a theological discussion should one arise in his presence, although of course he did not adopt the technical language used by the specialists. The result of this was that his faith was free of any taint of heterodoxy, and speculation never led him into any theological error or heresy. His faith was firm, within the bounds of healthy speculation, and it had the approval of the highest authorities. The imām Qutb ad-Din an-Nisaburi compiled for him a catechism containing all the essential elements of dogma, and he was so deeply attached to this that he taught it to all his little sons so that it should be impressed on their minds from earliest childhood. I myself have heard him instructing them and heard them repeat it before him.

As for the canonic prayers, he performed them assiduously, and used to pray in public; in fact one day he remarked that it was years since he had performed them any other way. When he was ill he would send for one imām and would force himself to rise and pray with him. He was assiduous in his performance of the extra-canonic prayers; if he woke up during the night he would make two raka'āt,[1] and if not he would perform them before the morning prayer. He never omitted the canonic prayer except when he was at death's door in the last three days of his life, during which time he was unconscious. If the hour of prayer came round while he was travelling he would dismount from his horse and pray.

As for the legal alms-giving, he died without leaving a large enough estate to be subject to it, for his extra-canonic gifts had consumed all his wealth. Of all that he had been master of, he left in his treasury when he died forty-seven Nasirite drachmas[2] and a single piece of Tyrian gold. Nor did he leave houses, estates, gardens, villages, fields or any other material possession.

[1] The *rak'a* (plural *raka'āt*) is the complex of prostrations and elevations and formulae that together constitute the unit of the canonic prayer.

[2] I.e. stamped with his official name, al-Malik an-Nasir (king-champion of the Faith).

As for ramadān, there were ramadāns that he should have made up, because of illness at various times. The qadi al-Fadil[1] kept an exact record of these days, which Saladin began to make up when he was at Jerusalem in the year of his death, persevering in the fast for more than the prescribed month. He had still two ramadāns to make up for, that illness and involvement in the Holy War had kept him from observing; fasting did not suit his temperament, and God inspired him to fast in that year to make good his omissions. In the absence of the qadi I kept count of the days on which he fasted. The doctor was not in favour of it, but Saladin would not listen to him. 'Anything might happen,' he said, as if he had been inspired to pay his debt of conscience, and fasted long enough to discharge whatever he had owed to God.

As for the Pilgrimage, he had always wanted and intended to go, in particular in the year of his death. He made a decision to go then, and ordered the preparations to be made. We got together provisions for the journey and were ready to set out when lack of time and shortage of the money necessary to equip himself as became a man of his standing prevented his departure. He put it off until the next year, but God decreed otherwise, as often happens in the experience of men both great and small.

He loved to hear the noble Qur'ān recited; he examined the imām whose job it was and required him to be learned in Qur'anic studies and to have a perfect knowledge and understanding of the text. At night, when he was in his room, he would ask anyone who was awake to recite two, three or four suras of the Qur'ān while he listened. In public audiences he would ask whoever had been appointed to the office to recite twenty or so verses. Once he passed a child reciting the Qur'ān to its father, and the recitation pleased him so much that he

[1] Head of Chancellery and Saladin's intimate councillor; he is referred to several times further on.

called the child to him and assigned to him a part of his personal daily food and bequeathed to the child and his father part of an estate. He was humble and sensitive of heart, quick to weep, and used often to be moved to tears by hearing the Qur'ān recited. He enjoyed hearing *hadīth* delivered by a profound scholar of tradition and doctrine. When any were present at court he would summon them and listen to their teachings, and would make his sons and the mamlūks in his service listen too, bidding them all sit down to listen as a sign of respect. Or if a certain scholar was not the sort of man to knock on sultans' doors, but rather shunned audiences at court, he would himself go to the scholar to hear his readings. In this way he heard the *hafiz*[1] al-Isfahani in Alexandria and transmitted many *hadīth* from him. He loved to read *hadīth* himself and often he would summon me when he was alone, send for the books of *hadīth* and read from them himself. When he came upon a tradition containing an edifying parable it would move him to tears.

He venerated deeply the laws of the Faith, believed in the resurrection of the body, the reward of Paradise for the virtuous and of Hell for the sinners, and accepted all the teachings of Holy Scripture with an open heart. He hated philosophers, heretics, materialists and all the opponents of the Law. For this reason he commanded his son al-Malik az-Zahir, Prince of Aleppo, to punish a young man called as-Suhrawardi[2] who called himself an enemy of the Law and a heretic. His son had the man arrested for what he had heard of him and informed the Sultan, who commanded that he be put to death. So he was killed, and left hanging on the cross for several days.

He put his whole faith and confidence in God and turned to Him (for help). As an illustration of this I shall recount an

[1] In Islam a *hafiz* (from which comes the name of the celebrated Persian poet) is one who either knows the Qur'ān by heart or is versed in *hadīth*.

[2] Philosopher and mystic of Aleppo who in 1191 fell victim to the intolerance of orthodoxy sanctioned by Saladin. This aspect of his real character bears little relation to the fantasies created by historians of the new enlightenment.

incident of which I was a witness. The Franks—God damn them!—had come up and camped at Bait Nuba, a few days' march from Jerusalem. The Sultan was there, having posted advance guards in close contact with the enemy and sent out spies and reconnaissance troops. Thus he obtained the news of a firm decision taken by the enemy to besiege Jerusalem and give battle. This frightened the Muslims. The Sultan summoned the amīrs and informed them of the critical situation in which the Muslims found themselves, and consulted them on the advisability of staying in Jerusalem. The amīrs began by blustering, but their real intentions were quite different, each of them asserting that he would not in the least mind staying in the city, that the whole of Islām would be exposed to danger: they, they said, would remain, and he was to take a detachment of the army and go out to encircle the enemy, as had happened at Acre. His job would be to cut off the enemy's supplies and to harry them. Theirs would be to defend the city. On this decision the council broke up, but Saladin remained firm in his resolve to stay in the city in person, well aware that if he did not stay no one would. When the amīrs had gone home, one of them returned to say that they would not stay unless Saladin's brother al-Malik al-'Adil, or one of his (own) sons, stayed behind to command and support them. Saladin realized that what they really meant was that they would not hold out, and this troubled and perplexed him. That night, the Thursday night, I was on duty beside him from sunset until it was almost dawn. It was winter, and we were alone but for God. We discussed this project and that, examining the implications of each in turn, until I began to feel concerned for him and to fear for his health, for he seemed to be overwhelmed by despair. I begged him to lie down on his bed, in the hope that he might sleep a while. He replied: 'Perhaps *you* are tired,' and rose. Scarcely had I returned to my rooms and settled to a task than dawn broke and the muezzin's call to prayer resounded. I almost always made my morning prayer with Saladin, so I went back to his room, where he was washing himself. 'I have not shut an eye,' he said. 'I knew that,' I replied. 'How did you know?' 'I did not sleep either, there was no time for it.' We prayed together, and again took up the usual problem. 'I have had an idea,' I said, 'that may be of use, God willing.' 'What is it?' 'Turn to Almighty God, call on him and have trust in him to resolve this terrible dilemma.' 'How should we do it?' 'Today,' I said, 'is Friday. Your Majesty should wash before going to the Friday prayer and should perform the public prayer as usual in the Masjid al-Aqsa, on the spot from which the Prophet ascended on his journey to Heaven. Offer certain alms secretly by the hand of someone you trust and then pray two *raka'āt* between the muezzin's first and second call, prostrating yourself and invoking God Almighty—on this subject there is an authentic *hadīth* of the Prophet saying: "My God, all my earthly power to bring victory to your Faith has come to nothing; my only resource is to turn to You and to rely on Your help and trust in Your goodness. You are my sufficiency, You are the best preserver!" God is too generous to let your prayers go to waste.' Saladin did exactly as I advised. As usual I was at his side during the prayers: he performed two *raka'āt* between the first and second call, and I saw him prostrate, with tears running down his white beard and on to his prayer-mat, but I could not hear what he said. . . . The very same day a message came from 'Izz ad-Din ibn Jurdik, captain of the advance guard, to say that the Franks were on the move. Their whole army was mounted and moving that day toward the plain. There they halted until the afternoon and then retired to their tents. On the Saturday morning a second messenger brought word that they had repeated this manoeuvre, and during the day a spy reported that a quarrel had broken out among the Franks. The French held that it was absolutely essential to besiege Jerusalem, while the King of England and his supporters did not want to put all Christendom in jeopardy and his own men in danger in that mountainous, waterless land—for Saladin had ordered that all the springs around Jerusalem were to be blocked up. So they went out to take council, for their custom is always to hold councils of war in the saddle, mounted on their horses. They decided to put the whole matter into the hands of ten men and to abide by their decision. On Monday morning came the joyful news that they had withdrawn and were returning to the region of ar-Ramla. I saw with my own eyes this evidence of Saladin's faith in God.

HIS JUSTICE

Abu Bakr the Truthful[1]—God look kindly on him—said that the Prophet—God bless and preserve him—said: 'The just prince is God's shadow on earth, and his mercy. Those who act loyally to him, in private and before others, will be set in the shadow of God's throne on the day when there shall be no other shade but that. Those who betray him, privately or publicly, shall be abandoned by God on the day of Resurrection. The just prince's day's work shall be held equal in value to that of sixty pious men, each devoted to worshipping God and working for the benefit of his own soul.' Saladin was just, benign, merciful, quick to help the weak against the strong. Every Monday and Thursday he would give an audience and administer justice in public session, in the presence of the lawyers, qadis and scholars. He listened to the litigants, for all had access to him, great and small, old, hale and sick. Whether on journeys or at home he was ready to perform this office, always ready to receive the supplications addressed to him and to remove the abuses brought to his notice. Every day he ordered the pleas to be collected and opened the Gate of Justice. He never turned away anyone who had suffered injustice and was

[1] The first Caliph, Muhammad's successor (632–34).

seeking recompense. In a sitting held night and morning with his secretariat he affixed the sentence appointed by God to each wrongdoer. No one ever implored his help without his stopping, listening to the complaint, examining the case and receiving the plea. I myself saw a man from Damascus, one Ibn Zuháir, come with a complaint against Saladin's nephew Taqi ad-Din. He sent requesting the latter to appear before a tribunal, and although Taqi ad-Din was one of the people he loved and respected most he did not allow personal feeling to affect his judgment.

Even more important than this episode as an illustration of his justice was the case of the merchant 'Umar al-Khilati. I happened to be at the tribunal in Jerusalem one day when this fine old man came before me with a legal document in his hand that he invited me to open. I asked who the defendant was, and he said: 'The defendant is the Sultan himself, but this is the seat of justice and we have heard that you are not partial in your judgments.' 'What is the matter at issue?' 'Sunqur al-Khilati,' he replied 'was one of my slaves, and remained so until his death. He had control of large sums of money belonging to me, and at his death the Sultan seized them, so I am suing him for their restitution.' 'Old man,' I said, 'what made you wait so long?' 'A man's rights are not annulled by his waiting to seek justice, and this legal opinion states clearly that this property is mine until I die.' I took the paper from him and read it, and found that it contained a description of Sunqur al-Khilati and stated that he had bought him from a certain merchant in Arjīsh, on a certain day of a certain month of a certain year, and that he had remained in his possession until his death in such and such a year. It was clear to the witnesses of this document that he had never forfeited his legal right to the man. The document was perfectly in order. I was baffled by the problem and said to the man: 'You cannot sue for restitution of property except in the presence of the defendant. I will inform him and tell you what he has to say about it.' The man was satisfied and went away. Later on the same day I had an audience of the Sultan and informed him of the dispute. He found it very strange. 'Have you studied the document?' he asked. 'I have studied it and I found it perfectly in order and correctly registered at Damascus.' Indeed a legal certificate had been attached to it at Damascus bearing the testimonies of distinguished witnesses in the presence of the qadi of Damascus. The Sultan was amazed. 'Send for this man,' he said, 'and we shall contest the case before the tribunal. We must act in this matter as the law requires.' Some time later, when I was alone with Saladin, I said to him: 'That fellow keeps coming to me; the least I can do is to hear the case.' 'Send one of my legal representatives to hear his claim,' said Saladin, 'then let the witnesses make their depositions, but wait to open the document until the man himself appears here.' I did this, the man presented himself, and the Sultan called him to approach and made him sit down in front of him while I stood at his side. Then he descended from his sofa and came down to his level and said: 'If you have a claim to make, make it.' The man said: 'I have evidence to prove my case,' and asked for the document to be opened. I opened it and found that it was as we had said. The Sultan listened to the evidence, then said: 'I have a witness who will say that this Sunqur was at that time my property and in my possession in Egypt, and that I bought him with eight others at a date earlier than the year stated here, and that he remained in my possession until I freed him.' Then he summoned a group of distinguished amīrs who were fighting in the Holy War, who attested to this and put the same case as he had, confirming the facts that he had stated. The man was speechless. Then I said: 'My Lord, this man acted as he did only because he relied on Your Majesty's benevolence. He came here into Your Majesty's presence, and it would be a bad thing for him to go away disappointed in his faith.' 'This is quite a different matter,' said

Saladin, and ordered that the man should be given a garment of honour and a large gift of money—I have forgotten now how much.

Is this not a fine example of his humility and submission to the Law, and of his mortification of his pride and generosity to one whom he could have punished with full authority?

EXAMPLES OF HIS GENEROSITY

The Prophet said: 'When the generous man stumbles God takes his hand,' and many other *hadīth* speak of generosity. Saladin's was too widespread to be recorded here and too well known to need mention: I shall restrict myself to one significant fact; that he, ruler of all those lands, died leaving forty-seven Nasirite *drachmas* of silver in his treasury and a single piece of Tyrian gold whose weight I have forgotten. He used to give away whole provinces; when he conquered Amida,[1] Qara Arslān's son[2] asked him for it and he gave it to him. I myself saw a whole series of deputations appear before him in Jerusalem when he had decided to leave for Damascus and there was no gold left in the treasury to give these people. I was so insistent on his giving them something that he sold a village belonging to the public revenue and distributed to them what he was given for it without keeping a single *drachma*. He was as generous when he was poor as when he was rich, and his treasurers kept certain reserves concealed from him for fear that some financial emergency might arise. For they knew that the moment he heard of their existence he would spend them.

I heard Saladin say in the course of conversation, 'There might be a man here who looks on money as one looks on the dust in the road,' by which he seemed to be referring to himself. He would give even more than the postulant asked, but I

[1] In Mesopotamia.

[2] Muhammad Ibn Qara Arslān, Artuqid amīr of Hisn Káifa (1174–85).

have never heard him say 'We gave so-and-so so much.' He spread largesse with a generous hand, smiling as cheerfully on the recipient as if he had hardly given him anything. His gifts bestowed honour even more than money. The people knew what he was like and solicited his generosity at every moment, but I never heard him say 'I have already given over and over again; how much more must I give?' Most of the documents on this subject were drawn up by me and written in my own hand. I used to feel ashamed at the exorbitant demands but never of him, whatever I had to ask of him for others, knowing his generosity and the absence of any scruple or demur on his part. No one in his service ever had to turn to others for help. As for enumerating his gifts or giving details, no one could hope to get them straight. Let me just say that I heard his chief administrator say, when we were discussing Saladin's bounty: 'We counted the horses he gave away on the plain of Acre and the number reached 10,000,' and anyone with experience of his generosity would find even that a small number. O Lord, You inspired his generosity, You who are the most generous, therefore be generous to him in your mercy and grace, O most merciful of the merciful!

HIS COURAGE AND STEADFASTNESS

The Prophet is reported to have said: 'God loves courage, even in the killing of a serpent.' Saladin was indeed one of the most courageous of men; brave, gallant, firm, intrepid in any circumstance. I remember when he was encamped facing a great Frankish army which was continuously growing with the addition of reinforcements and auxiliaries, and all the time his strength of will and tenacity of purpose increased. One evening more than seventy enemy ships arrived—I counted them myself—between the *'asr*[1] prayer and sunset, and their only

[1] The first hour of the afternoon.

effect seemed to be to incense him the more. When winter came he had disbanded his army and faced the enemy with only a small detachment of troops. I asked Baliān ibn Barzān[1] how many there were—he was one of the great Frankish kings of Palestine, and had an audience of the Sultan on the day when peace was signed—and he replied through the interpreter: 'The Prince of Sidon (another of their kings and commanders) and I came from Tyre to join our army. When we came within sight of them we laid a wager on the size of the army. He guessed 500,000, I guessed 600,000.' 'And how many of them are dead?' 'Killed in battle, 100,000; died of sickness or drowned, God alone knows.' And of all that multitude only a small minority returned home.

Every day for as long as we were in close contact with the enemy he made it an inflexible rule to make one or two circuits of the enemy camp; in the thick of battle he would move through the ranks, accompanied only by a page with a warhorse led on a bridle. He would traverse the whole army from the right wing to the left, creating a sense of unity and urging them to advance and to stand firm at the right time. He directed his troops from a commanding height and followed the enemy's movements from close at hand. He had certain sections of *hadīth* read up and down the army's ranks. This arose from my observation that *hadīth* had been read in every noble place, but one never heard of their being read before the ranks drawn up for battle, 'and if Your Majesty were willing for this to be done it would be a fine thing'. He authorized it, and a section of the *hadīth* was taken down to the troops, together with one who had made a regular study of them, and the reading was held while we were all in the saddle, sometimes advancing and sometimes at a halt between the ranks of the two armies.

I never saw him find the enemy too numerous or too power-

[1] Baliān II of Ibelīn; one of the Frankish plenipotentiaries at the negotiations of 1192 Greater detail of these affairs in later chapters.

ful. He would ponder and deliberate, exposing each aspect of the situation and taking the necessary steps to deal with it, without becoming angry, for he was never irate. On the day of the great battle on the plain of Acre the centre of the Muslim ranks was broken, drums and flags fell to the ground, but he stood firm with a handful of men until he was able to withdraw all his men to the hill and then lead them down into battle again, shaming them into turning and fighting, so that although there were almost 7,000 infantry and cavalry killed that day God gave the Muslims victory over their enemies. He stood firm before overwhelming hordes of enemy soldiers until it became clear to him that the Muslims were exhausted, and then he agreed to a truce at the enemy's request. The Franks were also exhausted and had suffered even heavier losses than we, but they could expect reinforcements, as we could not, so that peace was in our interest, as emerged clearly from the developments that followed.[1] When he was ill, which happened often, or throughout the most appalling crises he stayed firmly in camp; the camp-fires of each side could be seen clearly by the other; we heard the sound of their bells[2] and they heard our call to prayer, until everything resolved itself in the pleasantest and most acceptable manner.

HIS ZEAL IN THE HOLY WAR

Almighty God has said. 'And those who fight for Our cause, We shall guide them in Our path, and God is with those who act with nobility,'[3] and the sacred works are full of passages referring to the Holy War. Saladin was more assiduous and zealous in this than in anything else. If one said that once Saladin

[1] The polemic and apologetic reasons for this argument are perfectly clear, and will appear again in discussions of the 1192 peace.

[2] More accurately *nawaqīs*; wooden clappers used instead of bells by Christians in the East.

[3] Qur'ān XXIX, 69.

had gone forth on the Holy War he did not spend a *dinar* or a *drachma* except on the war or in gifts and donations one would speak the truth and one's statement would be accurate. The Holy War and the suffering involved in it weighed heavily on his heart and his whole being in every limb; he spoke of nothing else, thought only about equipment for the fight, was interested only in those who had taken up arms, had little sympathy with anyone who spoke of anything else or encouraged any other activity. For love of the Holy War and on God's path he left his family and his sons, his homeland, his house and all his estates, and chose out of all the world to live in the shade of his tent, where the winds blew on him from every side—so much so that on one stormy night on the plain of Acre his tent fell down, and if he had not happened to be in the turret he would have been killed. All this only increased his zeal, constancy and passion. Anyone who wanted to ingratiate himself with him had only to encourage him in his efforts and recount some anecdote of the war. Several books on the subject were written for him; I was one of those who compiled one for his use, containing all the laws, Qur'anic verses and *hadīth* relating to the subject, with elucidations of the obscure terms; he often read it until his son al-Malik al-Afdal took it from him.[1]

I want to tell what I heard from him personally on the subject. In dhu l-qa'da 584/January 1189 he took Kaukab[2] and mustered his troops there while the Egyptians, commanded by his brother al-Malik al-'Adil, prepared to return to Egypt. Saladin accompanied him, to enjoy his company and to perform the prayer of the Feast[3] at Jerusalem, and we went with him. After the prayer at Jerusalem it occurred to him to go on to Ascalon, disband his troops there and return by the coastal route, inspecting the territories as far as Acre in order to provide for their

[1] Or; 'so much so that his son learnt it from him'.
[2] Fort near Tiberias held by the Hospitallers.
[3] The Feast of the Sacrifice, which ends the days of the Pilgrimage in dhu l-hijja.

needs. He was advised against this on the grounds that once the army was disbanded there would be only a few of us left, whereas the Franks were all concentrated in Tyre, and we should be exposing ourselves to great danger. He took no notice, said farewell to his brother and the army at Ascalon, and then we all set off after him along the coast to Acre. It was deepest winter, the sea was very rough 'with waves like mountains' as God says in the Qur'ān.[1] I had little experience of the sea and it made a deep impression on me; in fact I thought that if anyone had said to me that if I spent a whole day sailing on the sea he would make me master of the whole world I could not have done it. I thought that anyone who earned his living from the sea must be mad, and that those who hold that evidence given by men who have been on the sea is invalid are correct in their judgment.[2] All these thoughts were caused by the sight of the tempestuous sea. While I was standing thus Saladin turned to me and said: 'I think that when God grants me victory over the rest of Palestine I shall divide my territories, make a will stating my wishes, then set sail on this sea for their far-off lands and pursue the Franks there, so as to free the earth of anyone who does not believe in God, or die in the attempt.' I was deeply impressed by what he said, so contrary to all my own thoughts, so I said: 'There is no one on earth braver than Your Majesty or more firmly intent upon bringing victory to God's religion.' 'Why do you say that?' 'As for courage,' I replied, 'because this terrifying sea does not frighten you, and as for helping God's religion, because Your Majesty, not content with extirpating God's enemies from a certain part of the earth, wishes to purify the whole world', and asked permission to recount to him the thoughts that had passed through my mind. He gave me permission and I told him, adding, 'this is a splendid

[1] Qur'ān XI, 44.

[2] It was considered foolish to sail on the sea, and in some schools of law the sailor's evidence was not legally valid.

proposal, but Your Majesty should send your troops by ship, but yourself, the bulwark of Islām, should not risk your life.' 'Now I shall put a question to you; what is the most noble death?' 'Death in God's path,' I said. 'Well then, the worst that can befall me is the most noble of deaths!'

Behold, what purity of ambition, what a brave and burning soul! My God, You know that he expended every energy to make Your Faith victorious and fought the Holy War in the hope of Your mercy; be merciful, O most piteous of the merciful!

HIS ENDURANCE AND DETERMINATION TO WIN MERIT IN GOD'S EYES

Almighty God said: '. . . and then they fought for God's cause, and endured, and your Lord is forgiving and merciful.'[1] I saw him on the plain of Acre smitten with such a painful malady; boils covering him from waist to knees, so that he could not sit down, but lay on his side in his tent. He could not be served his food, since he could not sit, so he ordered that it should be divided among those present. In spite of all this he remained in his tent in the camp, close by the enemy, and when he had disposed his troops in left and right wings and a central block, in battle order, he (mounted his horse and) remained on horseback from the dawn to the midday prayer, and from early afternoon to sunset, inspecting his battalions notwithstanding the painful throbbing of his abscesses. When I marvelled at him he said: 'When I am on my horse all pain ceases until I dismount'—a gift of Providence!

He fell ill when we were on our way to Kharruba[2] and had to abandon Tall al-Hajal as a result. When the Franks learnt this they sallied forth to strike a blow at the Muslims. This was the episode of the river: the enemy reached the wells below the Tall on the first day's march. Saladin ordered the baggage-

[1] Qur'ān XVI, 111. [2] Between St. John of Acre and Haifa.

train to withdraw to Nazareth and as 'Imād ad-Din of Sinjār was also ill he gave him permission to withdraw with the baggage, but he himself remained firmly at his post. On the second day, the enemy moved in to confront them and Saladin, suffering as he was, commanded the army to prepare for battle. He set al-Malik al-'Adil on the right wing, Taqi ad-Din on the left and his sons al-Malik az-Zahir and al-Malik al-Afdal at the centre. He stationed his own troops so as to attack from the enemy's rear. No sooner had he come down from the Tall than a Frank captured from the enemy army was brought to him. He invited the man to embrace Islām and when he refused gave the order for his head to be cut off, which was done in his presence. The enemy marched on and as they advanced, seeking the source of the river, he executed a deceptive manœuvre behind them to cut them off from their followers. He would advance a little and then dismount to rest, putting a handkerchief over his head to shield him from the violence of the sun but refusing to allow a tent to be pitched for him lest the enemy should see it as a sign of weakness. Thus he continued until the enemy reached the source of the river, when he halted in front of them on a hill dominating the place, until night fell. He commanded his victorious army to pass the night sword in hand and he, with us in attendance, retired to the top of the hill where a small tent was pitched for him, and here we passed the whole night, the doctor and I tending and distracting him, he now sleeping and now waking, until dawn broke. The trumpets sounded, and he mounted and deployed his troops so as to encircle the enemy. They retreated upon the tents pitched on the western side of their camp, along the river, pressed heavily by the Muslims throughout the day. It was on this day that to gain merit in God's eyes he sent forward his sons al-Malik al-Afdal, al-Malik az-Zahir and al-Malik az-Zafir with the rest of the army, and went about sending everyone with him to the front, until there remained at his side only the doctor and myself, the army inspector and the pages bearing the standards and oriflams, and no one else, but we were so disposed that anyone looking at us from far off would think that beneath those standards was a great force. The enemy continued on their march in spite of severe losses. They buried every casualty and carried all their wounded with them so that we should not learn the extent of their losses. They marched on under our eyes in ever more precarious conditions and halted by the bridge. We despaired of being able to attack them effectively in that position for they had closed ranks so as to present a close-knit line of defence. Saladin remained at his post, with the army mounted and facing the enemy, until night fell. He then commanded them to spend that night as they had the previous one, and we returned to the position we had held that night and remained on the alert until morning. Then we returned to harassing the enemy as we had the day before, and the enemy continued on its march, fighting off continual guerrilla attacks, until they drew near to their tents and reinforcements came out to help them reach their camp. Behold the heights of patience and valour reached by Saladin! O Lord, You inspired his virtues and aided him in using them; do not deprive him of his reward, O most merciful of the merciful!

I was there when news came to him of the death of his little son Isma'il; he read the letter, and spoke to no one; we had to learn about it from others. He betrayed no reaction except that as he read the letter his eyes filled with tears. I saw him one night at Safad, which we were besieging, when he said: 'We shall not sleep tonight until five catapults have been mounted.' He ordered a squadron of men to work on each one and we spent the whole night on duty beside him, in the most peaceful conversation and relaxation, while reports came in one after another of the progress of the operation. At dawn the work was finished except for mounting the lever bars. It had been a very long, cold, wet night.

I was there too when he was brought the news of the death of Taqi ad-Din (his nephew). We were with a small detachment of men attacking the Franks below Ramla, and the enemy were at Yazūr, a short gallop away. He sent for al-Malik al-'Adil, 'Alam ad-Din Sulaimān ibn Jandar, Sabiq ad-Din ibn ad-Daya and 'Izz ad-Din ibn al-Muqaddam, and sent the rest back to the tents at the distance of a bow-shot. Then he took out the letter, read it, and wept pitifully enough to move to tears even those who did not know the reason for his weeping. Finally, in a voice thick with tears, he said: 'Taqi ad-Din is dead.' He began to weep again, as did everyone else. After a time I took a hold on myself and said: 'God forgive us for the state we are in: consider where you are and on what you are engaged, then leave off weeping and turn to other things.' The Sultan replied: 'Yes, God forgive us.' He repeated this several times, adding, 'Let no one know of this!' He called for rose-water and bathed his eyes, then sent for food and summoned the others to approach again. No one knew what had happened until the enemy withdrew to Jaffa and we to Natrūn, where our supplies were.

He was deeply attached to his infant sons and showed great affection for them. Nevertheless he endured separation and resigned himself to their being far away from him, putting up with the discomforts of a life of squalor when he could have behaved quite differently, in order to gain merit in God's eyes and dedicate himself to the Holy War against God's enemies. My God, he left all this in the hope that You would approve of him; approve of him therefore and have mercy on him!

EXAMPLES OF HIS HUMANITY AND FORGIVENESS

God has said: '... and those among men who pardon others, and God loves those who act rightly.'[1] He was indulgent to

[1] Qur'ān III, 128.

those who failed and slow to wrath. I was on duty at his side at Marj ʿUyūn before the Franks attacked Acre—may God make its reconquest easy!—It was his custom to ride on for as long as possible and then to dismount and have food served, which he would eat in company with his men before retiring to sleep in his private tent. When he awoke he would pray, and then withdraw, with me in attendance on him, to read a section of *hadīth* or Law: among other works that he read with me was an anthology of Suláim ar-Razi, including the four sections of the Law. One day he dismounted as usual and food was served. He was about to rise when he was told that it was almost the hour of prayer, so he sat down again and said: 'Let us pray, and then let us go to bed.' He sat and talked wearily. Everyone except his personal servants had withdrawn, when suddenly there appeared an ancient mamlūk whom he held in high esteem, who presented him with a plea from someone fighting in the Holy War. 'I am tired now,' said the Sultan, 'present it again a little later', but the man would not comply with this request. He held the plea up to the Sultan's august face, opening it so that he could read it. Saladin read the name written at the top, recognized it and said: 'A worthy man.' 'Well then,' said the other, 'Your Majesty will inscribe your *placet*.' 'But there is no inkwell here,' said the Sultan, for he was sitting at the opening of the tent, blocking the entrance, while the inkstand was at the back of the tent, which was a big one. But his interlocutor observed: 'There is the inkstand, at the back of the tent!' which was nothing if not an invitation to Saladin to bring that very inkwell out. The Sultan turned, saw the inkstand and said: 'By Allāh, you are right!' He leaned on his left elbow, stretched out his right hand, took the inkstand, signed the plea. . . . Then I said: 'God said to His prophet: "You are truly a magnanimous man",[1] and it seems to me that Your Majesty shares this quality with him,' to which

[1] Qur'ān LVIII, 4.

Saladin replied: 'It did not cost anything: we heard what he wanted, and we wanted to recompense him.' If a similar thing had happened to a private individual he would have lost his temper; and who would have been capable of replying to one of his subordinates in this way? This is the perfection of kindness and generosity, 'and God will not let such goodness go unrewarded'.[1]

Sometimes, when the crowd thronged round him to present their pleas, the cushion on which he sat ended up crushed underfoot, yet he did not seem to mind at all. Once, while I was riding beside him, my mule took fright at the camels and kicked his thigh, injuring it; and he simply smiled. One rainy windy day as I was entering Jerusalem with him and the road was terribly muddy the mule splashed him and ruined all his clothes; but he smiled and refused to allow me to ride further back because of the incident.

Sometimes he was addressed in the most insulting manner by postulants and plaintiffs; his reaction to it was always cheerful and benevolent. Here is a splendid anecdote on the subject: The Frankish King's brother was making for Jaffa, while our army had withdrawn toward Natrūn, two days' forced march from Jaffa or three days' normal march. Saladin sent out a detachment of troops on reconnaissance and then set out for Caesarea to confront a troop of enemy reinforcements whom he hoped to drive off. The Franks of Jaffa, among them the King of England[2] and some of his men, heard of this, and the King sent most of his troops by sea to Caesarea for fear that some harm might befall the reinforcements, keeping only a few men with him for he knew that Saladin and his army were far away. When Saladin and his army reached Caesarea he found that the reinforcements had already arrived in the city and strengthened its defences. When he saw that he could not touch them he left that evening, marched all night and reached

[1] Qur'ān IX, 121. [2] Richard Cœur de Lion.

Jaffa in the morning. The English King with seventeen knights and about three hundred infantry had camped outside the city in one of their tents, and at dawn was attacked by our army. The King—God damn him!—who was excitable, valorous and shrewd in warfare, mounted his horse and planted himself in front of us, not entering the city. The Muslim army surrounded him on every side except that of the city and ranged itself in battle order. The Sultan gave his troops the command to charge, taking advantage of the propitious circumstances. Suddenly a Kurdish amīr replied in openly disrespectful terms, upbraiding him for a fief that he considered less than munificent. The Sultan pulled his horse round on its rein in contempt, realizing that on that day absolutely nothing would be achieved. He left them and turned back, ordering that the tent that had been pitched for him should be struck. The army broke contact with the enemy, certain that today the Sultan would have several people killed and crucified; his own son al-Malik az-Zahir told me that on that day he was so afraid of his father that he did not dare to appear in his presence, although he had led a charge and pushed forward until Saladin had stopped him. The Sultan went as far as Yazūr, a short day's march; a small tent was pitched for him where he dismounted, while the army encamped under small shelters, as was usually done on these occasions. All the amīrs trembled with fear, certain that they would be rebuked and come under the shadow of the Sultan's wrath. 'I could not bring myself to appear before him,' said al-Malik az-Zahir, 'until he sent for me. I went in and saw that he had received a quantity of fruit from Damascus. "Send for the Amīrs to come and eat some of this," he commanded. My fear dissolved, I sent for the amīrs, who appeared in fear and trembling, and saw that his face was cheerful and that his affability calmed and soothed them. They left him to prepare for departure as if nothing had happened. You see what humanity he showed, so difficult to maintain in these times, and unknown in the stories of the kings of old!'

HIS UNFAILING GOODNESS

The Prophet said: 'I was sent to reveal clearly the soul's most noble qualities' and when someone seized his hand he did not withdraw it until the man let go of his own accord. The Sultan too was distinguished by the nobility of his conduct, the benevolence of his regard, his great modesty and extraordinary affability to his guests. He would not permit anyone who visited him to leave without eating with him, or to ask for something without receiving it. Everyone who appeared before him was treated with honour, even an infidel; the Prince of Antioch came to visit him, appearing unexpectedly at the mouth of his tent, after the truce of shawwāl 588/November 1192 had been signed and the Sultan was returning from Jerusalem to Damascus. He came upon him suddenly on the journey and presented a plea to him, and the Sultan made him a gift of al-'Umq, a territory that he had taken from him in the year of his conquest of Palestine in 584/1188–89. Again, when the ruler of Sidon came to Nazareth I saw him receive him with reverence and honour and divide his food with him, even offering him the chance of embracing Islām, describing its prayers and exhorting him to be converted. He showed equal generosity to religious leaders,[1] scholars and men of virtue and reputation, and directed us that every well-known religious leader visiting the camp should be presented to him, so that he could show him his hospitality. In 584 a man who was well known as a scholar and mystic passed by the camp. He was a member of a distinguished family, his father was ruler of Tabrīz but the son had dissociated himself from his father's occupation and dedicated

[1] *Masha'ikh*, leaders of the mystical fraternities, or other old and devout men famous for their virtue and holiness.

himself to learning and acts of piety. He had undertaken the Pilgrimage and had come on a visit to Jerusalem where, having seen the Sultan's pious acts, he had the idea of visiting him. He came to our camp and entered my tent unexpectedly. I received him, welcomed him and asked the reason for his visit. He told me about it, saying that he had desired to visit the Sultan because of the noble and praiseworthy works of his that he had seen. That evening I informed the Sultan of the man's visit and he sent for him, heard some *hadīth* from him and encouraged him in the path of virtue. Then we retired and the man spent the night in my tent with me. After the morning prayer he began to take his leave of me. It seemed discourteous to let him go without saying goodbye to the Sultan, but the man refused: 'I have received what I wanted of him,' he said. 'I only wanted to see him and pay him a visit.' Whereupon he left. Some days later the Sultan asked me about him and I told him what he had done. Saladin seemed upset that I had not told him of his departure and said: 'How could a man like that come and knock on our door and then go away without enjoying our beneficence?' He disapproved so strongly of my conduct that I was obliged to write to Muhyi ad-Din, qadi of Damascus, charging him with the task of searching for the man and handing over to him the letter enclosed in his, which informed the man that the Sultan was very sorry that he had left without seeing him again and that the friendship between us should lead him to return. One day unexpectedly he did appear again. I led him to the Sultan, who received him with joy and detained him for several days. After that he gave him a fine robe of honour, a suitable mount and a pile of clothes to take to his family, disciples and neighbours, as well as a sum of money for the journey. So he parted from him, deeply grateful and offering up sincere prayers to God to grant the Sultan a long life.

Once a Frankish prisoner was brought before him in whom the Sultan aroused such fear that the marks of terror and agitation were visible in his face. The interpreter asked him: 'What are you afraid of?' God inspired him to reply: 'At first I was afraid of seeing that face, but after seeing it and standing in his presence, I am sure that I shall see only good in it.' The Sultan was moved, pardoned him and let him go free.

One day when I was on duty I was riding with him ahead of the Franks when a sentry brought up a woman who was in a distracted state, weeping and beating her breast. 'This woman,' said the sentry, 'has come from the Frankish camp and asked to be brought before the Sultan, so we brought her here.' The Sultan told the interpreter to ask her what was the matter, and she said that Muslim raiders had come into her tent the day before and had carried off her little daughter. 'All night long I have been seeking help, until this morning our leaders told me: "The Muslim King is merciful; we will let you leave the camp to go to him, and you can ask him for your daughter." So they let me come, and you are my only hope of getting my baby back again.' Saladin was moved to pity by her plight, and tears came into his eyes. His generous spirit prompted him to order someone to take her to the market-place in the camp to ask who had bought the child, repay him and bring her back. All this occurred in the morning; not an hour passed before the knight returned with the child on his shoulders. As soon as her mother caught sight of her she fell to the ground, rubbing her face in the dust, while everyone there wept with her. She raised her face to heaven, but we could not understand what she said. Her daughter was handed over to her and she was conducted back to her own camp.

Saladin did not like to treat his servants harshly even when they were guilty of serious dishonesty; two purses of Egyptian gold were taken from his treasury and two of copper substituted, and he punished the treasurers only with the loss of their jobs.

Prince Arnāt of al-Karak[1] was brought before him, together

[1] Reynald of Châtillon.

with the King of the Palestinian Franks, both captured at the battle of Hittīn in 583/1187, the famous battle of which we shall speak at length in its place.[1] This villain Arnāt was a powerful and violent infidel; during a period of truce between them and the Muslims a caravan from Egypt was passing by his territory and he broke the truce to attack and capture it, ill-treating and torturing the men and imprisoning them in narrow dungeons. When they invoked the truce his only reply was: 'Call on your Mahomet to save you.' When this was reported to the Sultan he vowed that when God put the man in his power he would kill him with his own hand. On that day, when God did put him in his power, he reaffirmed his decision to kill him to fulfil his vow, and sent for him and the King. As the King was complaining of thirst he had a cup of sherbet brought for him. The King drank and offered it to Arnāt, but Saladin said to the interpreter: 'Tell the King, it was to you I gave the drink, and for my part I shall give him neither my water to drink nor my food to eat!' meaning that if a man had eaten his food honour forbade him to do that man any harm. After that he struck off Arnāt's head with his own hand, in fulfilment of his vow. At the fall of Acre he released all the prisoners, more than 4,000 of them, from their dungeons and gave each a subsidy to enable him to reach his country and his people. So much I have heard from various people, for I was not present at this event.

Saladin was a pleasant companion, affectionate and shrewd, well versed in genealogy and the battles of the Arabs, their history and the genealogy of their horses, and the wonders and curiosities of the country; so much so that anyone who had the pleasure of his company would learn things that he could have heard from no one else. He put his companions at their ease and drew them out; he would ask one about one's health, how

[1] In accounts of the events of Hittīn we find references to the dramatic episode described here.

one looked after oneself, how one was eating and drinking and all about oneself. Conversation in his circle was unusually honest, though no one was spoken of except in praise; he liked to hear only good of people and had a very restrained tongue; in fact I have never heard him speak ill of someone with enjoyment. It was the same when he wrote; he never wrote a line of insult to a Muslim. He observed all his obligations faithfully. Every time an orphan was brought before him he invoked God's mercy on his dead parents, consoled the child and provided the father's bread.[1] If there were a trustworthy old man in the orphan's family he would entrust the child to him, and if not he secured to the child an adequate portion of his father's salary and entrusted him to someone who would see to his upbringing. The sight of an old man moved him to pity, and he would give him alms. He kept these noble qualities all his life, until God raised him to the seat of His mercy and the home of His grace.

All these are simply examples of his soul's lofty and noble qualities. I have limited myself in this way in order not to extend this book unduly and bore the reader, and have included only things seen with my own eyes or witnessed by trustworthy persons and checked by myself. This is only a part of what I myself saw when I was in his service, and is trivial compared with what others knew who had spent more time in his company and served him longer. This much however is enough to show the intelligent reader the purity of his noble character.

[1] As is explained in the sentence that follows, he awarded the child a pension equal to a whole or a part of his father's salary, in the case of civil or military officials.

CHAPTER TWO

The year of triumph for Saladin's counter-offensive was, as mentioned above, 583/1187. The decisive battle of Hittīn, which smashed for a time the crusading forces in the Holy Land, was followed by the loss of a large number of their strongholds in Palestine and, the deeper loss to the Christian world, by the fall of Jerusalem, recaptured for Islām in a conquest that added lustre to Saladin's reputation for humanity and moderation. Our narrators for these events are 'Imād ad-Din and Ibn al-Athīr. (Bahā' ad-Din was an eye-witness only of events from 1188 onward.) For Hittīn and the fall of Jerusalem we give both accounts; their style and content make a useful contrast. Ibn al-Athīr's clear and sober version is deliberately placed before 'Imād ad-Din's wearisome obscurities, but the latter contain the most direct and authoritative testimony available.

Events preceding Hittīn

(IBN AL-ATHĪR, XI, 347–51)

DISCORD BETWEEN THE FRANKS IN SYRIA; THE COUNT OF TRIPOLI JOINS SALADIN

The ruler of Tripoli, known as Count Raymond son of Raymond of Saint-Gilles[1] married the Countess of Tiberias[2] and moved to Tiberias to be with her. The King of the Franks in Syria died of leprosy[3] and left the kingdom to his sister's son, a minor,[4] with the Count as Regent. He took over the government and administration of the kingdom, and indeed at that time the Franks had no one braver or shrewder than he. The Count aspired to become King himself through the agency of the child, but the young King died and the kingdom passed to his mother, and the Count's ambitions were frustrated. Then the

[1] Raymond III. [2] Eschiva, Countess of Bures. [3] Baldwin IV (1174–85).
[4] Baldwin V, died in 1186 after a few months of nominal rule.

Queen[1] fell in love with a knight called Guy who had come from the West to Syria, married him and handed over the crown and the royal authority to him. The Patriarch, the priests and monks, the Hospitallers, Templars and Barons were summoned, and she announced her abdication in favour of her husband. She called on them to be witnesses of the deed, and they swore loyalty and obedience to him. This displeased the Count, who was stripped of his authority and asked to account for the moneys collected during his regency. He swore that he had spent them on the young King's behalf, but his loyalty to the new King was strained so far that he reached a position of open secession and rebellion. He began a correspondence with Saladin, established a cordial relationship with him and turned to him for help in achieving his ambition to rule the Franks. Saladin and the Muslims were pleased and Saladin promised to help him and to give him every possible assistance in his plans. He guaranteed to make him King of all the Franks. He freed some of the Count's knights whom he held prisoner, which made the best possible impression on Raymond, who openly displayed his obedience to Saladin. A certain number of Franks followed his example, which led to discord and disunity and was one of the chief reasons why their towns were reconquered and Jerusalem fell to the Muslims, as we shall narrate. Saladin sent guerrilla bands from the Tiberias region who devastated the Frankish lands and returned unscathed. This weakened the Franks but gave the Muslims energy and enthusiasm for attacking them.

PRINCE ARNĀT'S TREACHERY

Prince Arnāt of al-Karak[2] was one of the chief Frankish barons

[1] Sibylla, sister of Baldwin IV, mother of Baldwin V, in second marriage wife of Guy of Lusignan.

[2] Al-Karak in Moab, Transjordan, a fort dominating the overland route between Egypt and Syria, and Syria and the Hijaz.

and one of the most arrogant; a violent and most dangerous enemy of Islām. Saladin knew this and on several occasions attacked him and sent raiding parties into his territories. Arnāt humbled himself to sue for peace, which Saladin conceded, and both swore to observe a truce which would allow caravans to move freely between Syria and Egypt. In 582/1186–7, however, a great caravan passed close to his territory, richly laden and accompanied by a great host of people and a large armed escort. This infamous man broke the truce and attacked them, captured the whole caravan, seized the booty, animals and weapons, and threw all his prisoners into dungeons. Saladin sent letters rebuking him and reproaching him with his treachery, and threatening him with reprisals if he did not release the prisoners and their possessions. The Count persistently refused to comply. Saladin vowed that if ever he laid hands on him he would kill him, and what followed will be recounted, God willing.

SALADIN ATTACKS AL-KARAK

In 583/1187 Saladin wrote to all the provinces to call them to arms in the Holy War. He wrote to Mosul in the Jazira, to Arbela and other eastern states, to Egypt and to the Syrian domains, calling them to arms and exhorting them to fight in the Holy War, and commending as many as possible to arm themselves for battle. At the end of muharram/April 1187 he and his army and the Damascene guard left Damascus and marched to Ras al-Ma', where the Syrian contingents joined them. He gave his son al-Malik al-Afdal 'Ali command of them and marched with a contingent of his own troops to Busra. This was because he had heard that Arnāt of al-Karak was going to attack the pilgrims and cut off their advance, making it clear that once he had dealt with them he would return to bar the way to the Egyptian army and prevent its joining up with the Syrians.

Saladin therefore marched on Busra to prevent Arnāt's attack on the pilgrims and to make him stay quietly at home for fear of the Sultan. Among the pilgrims was a whole group of Saladin's relations, including the son of one of his sisters: Muhammad ibn Lajīn. When Arnāt learned that Saladin was at the boundary of his territories he stayed where he was and abandoned his plans, and so the Pilgrimage went through in safety. When it had passed and all was quiet in that region Saladin marched on al-Karak and sent his raiding parties throughout the regions of al-Karak, ash-Shaubak and elsewhere, pillaging, breaking and burning, while the Prince was besieged and powerless to defend his lands, and fear of al-Afdal's army kept the other Franks immobilized at home. So Saladin was free to besiege and pillage, burn and ravage the whole region, which he did.

AN INCURSION INTO THE REGION OF ACRE

Saladin sent orders to his son al-Afdal to send a large detachment of the army into the region of Acre to plunder it and lay it waste. He took Muzaffar ad-Din Kiökbarī ibn Zain ad-Din, ruler of Harrān and Edessa, with Qaimāz an-Najmi and Yildirīm al-Yaquti, two of the leading amīrs, and several others. They left by night at the end of safar/May 1187 and attacked Saffuriyya in the morning. A body of Templars, Hospitallers and others came out of the city to repulse them and a terrible battle followed. God gave the Muslims victory at last and the Franks turned and fled. Some were killed and the rest captured. Among the dead was the Grand Master of the Hospital,[1] one of the most famous Frankish noblemen, who had done much harm to the cause of Islām.

The Muslims sacked the regions round about, then returned safe and sound with their booty and prisoners to Tiberias, where

[1] Roger des Moulins.

the Count was. He had done nothing to prevent the Christians' defeat. It was a great victory, for the Templars and Hospitallers were the backbone of the Frankish armies. The joyful news spread far and wide.

SALADIN RETURNS TO HIS ARMY AND INVADES FRANKISH TERRITORY

When Saladin received the joyful news that the Templars and Hospitallers had been defeated and many of them slaughtered or taken prisoner he returned from al-Karak to the army under al-Afdal's command, where all the other amīrs and troops were gathered. There he reviewed his army and estimated that he had 12,000 cavalry with regular fiefs and military stipends, as well as volunteers. The Sultan disposed the army in battle order, with a central column and two wings, a vanguard and a rearguard. He assigned to each man a post and commanded him not to desert it, and so marched out and encamped at Uqhuwana near Tiberias. We have already said that the Count was on Saladin's side. Saladin received a stream of letters from him with promises of help and support; 'But the Devil makes promises to them only to deceive them'.[1] Now when the Franks saw the Muslim armies and realized that they were bent on attacking them, they sent the Patriarch, with priests and monks and a large number of knights to Raymond to reproach him with having taken Saladin's side. 'You must have become a Muslim,' they said, 'otherwise you could not have endured what the Muslims have just done to the Franks by massacring and enslaving those Templars and Hospitallers, nor could you let them pass through your lands without objecting or intervening to stop them.' The local militias of Tiberias and Tripoli joined in the remonstrances and the Patriarch threatened, among other things, to excommunicate him and to annul his

[1] Qur'ān XVII, 66.

marriage. When the Count saw what a serious situation he had created he took fright and said that he repented. They accepted his apologies, forgave him for his defection and begged him to join them against the Muslims and to give them his help in the defence of their lands. The Count agreed to make his peace and be reunited with them and returned with them to the Frankish King, and so peace was restored between them after all that had happened. But God saw to it that it did them no good. Infantry and cavalry mustered and marched from Acre to Saffuriyya, but they were reluctant and demoralized.

The Battle of Hittīn

(IBN AL-ATHĪR, XI, 351–5)

While the reunited Franks were on their way to Saffuriyya, Saladin called a council of his amīrs. Most of them advised him not to fight, but to weaken the enemy by repeated skirmishes and raids. Others however advised him to pillage the Frankish territories, and to give battle to any Frankish army that might appear in their path, 'Because in the East people are cursing us, saying that we no longer fight the infidels but have begun to fight Muslims instead. So we must do something to justify ourselves and silence our critics.' But Saladin said: 'My feeling is that we should confront all the enemy's forces with all the forces of Islām; for events do not turn out according to man's will and we do not know how long a life is left to us, so it is foolish to dissipate this concentration of troops without striking a tremendous blow in the Holy War.' So on Thursday, 23 rabī' II/2 July 1187, the fifth day after we encamped at Uqhuwana, he struck camp and moved off up the hill outside Tiberias, leaving the city behind him. When he drew near to the Franks, however, there was no one to be seen, for they had not yet left their tents. So he went back down the hill with his army. At night he positioned troops where they would prevent the enemy from giving battle and then attacked Tiberias with a small force, breached the wall and took the city by storm during the night. The inhabitants fled for refuge to the citadel, where the Countess and her children were, and defended themselves there while the lower town was sacked and burned.

When the Franks learned that Saladin had attacked Tiberias and taken it and everything in it, burning the houses and anything they could not remove, they met to take counsel. Some advised the King to meet the Muslims in battle and chase them out of Tiberias, but the Count intervened to say: 'Tiberias belongs to me and my wife. There is no question that Saladin is master there now and that only the citadel remains, where my wife is immured. For my part, if he takes the citadel, my wife and all my possessions there and then goes away I shall be happy enough. By God, I have observed the armies of Islām over the course of the years and I have never seen one equal to Saladin's army here in numbers or in fighting power. If he takes Tiberias he will not be able to stay there, and when he has left it and gone away we will retake it; for if he chooses to stay there he will be unable to keep his army together, for they will not put up for long with being kept away from their homes and families. He will be forced to evacuate the city, and we will free our prisoners.' But Prince Arnāt of al-Karak replied: 'You have tried hard to make us afraid of the Muslims. Clearly you take their side and your sympathies are with them, otherwise you would not have spoken in this way. As for the size of their army, a large load of fuel will be good for the fires of Hell. . . .' 'I am one of you,' said the Count, 'and if you advance then I shall advance with you, and if you retreat I shall retreat. You will see what will happen.' The generals decided to advance and give battle to the Muslims, so they left the place where they had been encamped until now and advanced on the Muslim army. When Saladin received the news he ordered his army to withdraw from its position near Tiberias; his only reason for besieging Tiberias was to make the Franks abandon their position and offer battle. The Muslims went down to the water (of the lake). The weather was blazingly hot and the Franks, who were suffering greatly from thirst, were prevented by the Muslims from reaching the water. They had drained all the local cisterns, but could not turn back for fear of the Muslims. So they passed that night tormented with thirst. The Muslims for their part had lost their first fear of the enemy and were in high spirits, and spent the night inciting one another to battle. They could smell victory in the air, and the more they saw of the unexpectedly low morale of the Franks the more aggressive and daring they became; throughout the night the cries *Allāh akbar* (God is great) and 'there is no God but Allāh' rose up to heaven. Meanwhile the Sultan was deploying the vanguard of archers and distributing the arrows.

On Saturday 24 rabī' II/4 July 1187 Saladin and the Muslims mounted their horses and advanced on the Franks. They too were mounted, and the two armies came to blows. The Franks were suffering badly from thirst, and had lost confidence. The battle raged furiously, both sides putting up a tenacious resistance. The Muslim archers sent up clouds of arrows like thick swarms of locusts, killing many of the Frankish horses. The Franks, surrounding themselves with their infantry, tried to fight their way toward Tiberias in the hope of reaching water, but Saladin realized their objective and forestalled them by planting himself and his army in the way. He himself rode up and down the Muslim lines encouraging and restraining his troops where necessary. The whole army obeyed his commands and respected his prohibitions. One of his young mamlūks led a terrifying charge on the Franks and performed prodigious feats of valour until he was overwhelmed by numbers and killed, when all the Muslims charged the enemy lines and almost broke through, slaying many Franks in the process. The Count saw that the situation was desperate and realized that he could not withstand the Muslim army, so by agreement with his companions he charged the lines before him. The commander of that section of the Muslim army was Taqi ad-Din 'Umar, Saladin's nephew. When he saw that the Franks charging his lines were desperate and that they were going to try to break through, he sent orders for a passage to be made for them through the ranks.

One of the volunteers had set fire to the dry grass that covered the ground; it took fire and the wind carried the heat and smoke down on to the enemy. They had to endure thirst, the summer's heat, the blazing fire and smoke and the fury of battle. When the Count fled the Franks lost heart and were on the verge of surrender, but seeing that the only way to save their lives was to defy death they made a series of charges that almost dislodged the Muslims from their position in spite of their numbers, had not the grace of God been with them. As each wave of attackers fell back they left their dead behind them; their numbers diminished rapidly, while the Muslims were all around them like a circle about its diameter. The surviving Franks made for a hill near Hittīn, where they hoped to pitch their tents and defend themselves. They were vigorously attacked from all sides and prevented from pitching more than one tent, that of the King. The Muslims captured their great cross, called the 'True Cross', in which they say is a piece of the wood upon which, according to them, the Messiah was crucified.[1] This was one of the heaviest blows that could be inflicted on them and made their death and destruction certain. Large numbers of their cavalry and infantry were killed or captured. The King stayed on the hillside with five hundred of the most gallant and famous knights.

I was told that al-Malik al-Afdal, Saladin's son, said: 'I was

[1] According to the Qur'ān, which preaches the Docetic doctrine, it was not the true person of Christ, but only a simulacrum, that was crucified.

at my father Saladin's side during that battle, the first that I saw with my own eyes. The Frankish King had retreated to the hill with his band, and from there he led a furious charge against the Muslims facing him, forcing them back upon my father. I saw that he was alarmed and distraught, and he tugged at his beard as he went forward crying: "Away with the Devil's lie!" The Muslims turned to counter-attack and drove the Franks back up the hill. When I saw the Franks retreating before the Muslim onslaught I cried out for joy: "We have conquered them!" But they returned to the charge with undiminished ardour and drove our army back toward my father. His response was the same as before, and the Muslims counter-attacked and drove the Franks back to the hill. Again I cried: "We have beaten them!" but my father turned to me and said: "Be quiet; we shall not have beaten them until that tent falls!" As he spoke the tent fell, and the Sultan dismounted and prostrated himself in thanks to God, weeping for joy.' This was how the tent fell: the Franks had been suffering terribly from thirst during that charge, which they hoped would win them a way out of their distress, but the way of escape was blocked. They dismounted and sat down on the ground and the Muslims fell upon them, pulled down the King's tent and captured every one of them, including the King,[1] his brother, and Prince Arnāt of Karak, Islām's most hated enemy. They also took the ruler of Jubáil, the son of Humphrey (of Toron), the Grand Master of the Templars, one of the Franks' greatest dignitaries,[2] and a band of Templars and Hospitallers. The number of dead and captured was so large that those who saw the slain could not believe that anyone could have been taken alive, and those who saw the prisoners could not believe that any had been killed. From the time of their first assault on Palestine in 491/1098 until now the Franks had never suffered such a defeat.

When all the prisoners had been taken Saladin went to his

[1] Guy of Lusignan. [2] The Grand Master, Gerard of Ridfort.

tent and sent for the King of the Franks and Prince Arnāt of Karak. He had the King seated beside him and as he was half-dead with thirst gave him iced water to drink. The King drank, and handed the rest to the Prince, who also drank. Saladin said: 'This godless man did not have my permission to drink, and will not save his life that way.' He turned on the Prince, casting his crimes in his teeth and enumerating his sins. Then he rose and with his own hand cut off the man's head. 'Twice,' he said, 'I have sworn to kill that man when I had him in my power: once when he tried to attack Mecca and Medina, and again when he broke the truce to capture the caravan.' When he was dead and had been dragged out of the tent the King began to tremble, but Saladin calmed and reassured him. As for the ruler of Tripoli, when he escaped from the battle, as we have described, he went to Tyre and from there made his way to Tripoli. He was there only a few days before he died of rage and fury at the disaster that had befallen the Franks in particular, and all Christendom in general.

When Saladin had brought about the downfall of the Franks he stayed at the site of the battle for the rest of the day, and on the Sunday returned to the siege of Tiberias. The Countess sent to request safe-conducts for herself and her children, companions and possessions, and he granted her this. She left the citadel with all her train, and Saladin kept his word to her and let her escape unmolested. At the Sultan's command the King and a few of the most distinguished prisoners were sent to Damascus, while the Templars and Hospitallers were rounded up to be killed. The Sultan realized that those who had taken them prisoner were not going to hand them over, for they hoped to obtain ransoms for them, and so he offered fifty Egyptian *dinar* for each prisoner in these two categories. Immediately he got two hundred prisoners, who were decapitated at his command. He had these particular men killed because they were the fiercest of all the Frankish warriors, and in this way he rid the Muslim people of them. He sent orders to his commander in Damascus to kill all those found in his territory, whoever they belonged to, and this was done.

A year later I crossed the battlefield, and saw the land all covered with their bones, which could be seen even from a distance, lying in heaps or scattered around. These were what was left after all the rest had been carried away by storms or by the wild beasts of these hills and valleys.

THE SULTAN SALADIN AND HIS ARMY ENTER FRANKISH TERRITORY

(ʿIMĀD AD-DIN, 18–29)

In the morning the Sultan began to review the army in the field, like a cloud heavy with rain, a tempestuous sea of dust, a swelling ocean of whinnying chargers, of swords and cuirasses. He marshalled his gallant knights and his battalions who swept like a cloud over the face of the earth, making the dust fly up from earth to the Pleiades and sending the crows, to escape the dust, flying as far as Vega. The plain broke the seal of dust, lethal messages of impending disasters were fixed on the messenger-pigeons of death; the ribs of the bows longed to enclose their embryos the arrows, the curved arrow was careful to keep to its place on the right, the shot arrow was united to the bow-string; the bows were faithful to their oaths of vengeance and every battalion rose up in search of retribution. On the day of the review the Sultan came forward to set the army in order, to divide it into sections and to draw up its ranks far and near. To every amīr he assigned a duty, to every knight a post, to every lucky champion a station, to every ambush a place, to every combatant an opponent, to every burning spark someone to extinguish it, to every company (of Franks) someone to destroy it, to every flintstone someone to strike it, to every blade someone to whet it, to each action a command, to each arrow a point, to each right hand a sword, to each sword a hilt, to every courser an arena, to every outrider a defence, to every archer a target, to every leader a follower, to everything rising a place to which to rise, to every name an object. To each amīr he assigned a place on the left or the right from which he was not to move, whence his body was not to absent itself, nor was any one of them to depart. He brought forward the front line of gallant archers of each battalion, advising each section of what would bring it into contact with another section. He said: 'When we enter the enemy's terrain this is our army's battle order, our method of advancing and retreating, the position of our battalions, the place where our knights rise up, where our lances are to fall, the paths by which to direct our horses, the arenas for our coursers, the gardens for our roses, the site of our vicissitudes, the outlets of our desires, the scene on which we shall be transfigured.' He reinforced men's hopes with the amounts of his largesse and realized, by fulfilling his promises and crowning his intentions, the desires of his men. When the ranks were drawn up and the arms distributed he made gifts of war-horses and scattered largesse, devoted himself to making donations and giving coveted prizes, scattered stores of gifts and emptied quivers of arrows, spent hidden reserves, using the choicest and best parts, and distributed bundles of arrows, of which the soldiers received more than a quiverful. He made chargers gallop and brought forth an ample harvest of troops. He spurred on brave coursers and called on the witnesses to bear witness, he drew up in succession his squadrons' virtues and won over to his side the sympathies of the swords; he strengthened the cutting blades, gave drink to the terrible lances, and returned to his tents happy and content, received with welcome and gratitude, generous and appreciated after having deployed and organized his men, arrayed them in squadrons and platoons, confirmed and well-established, with pious works, well-founded hopes, perfume poured out, glowing face, fragrant odour, radiant aspect, certain of victory and in firm possession of certainty; saying 'amen' to the auguries that demanded it, drawing auspicious omens from the white markings of his headstrong coursers, clearly drawing up his terms for recovering the debt owed to the Faith. He delighted in the beauty of the war-horses and in the voices wishing him well, and his spirit rejoiced at the prospect of the march; he tightened the belts of firmness and confirmed a definite decision; he ordered his men to mount for the journey and harnessed the Arab steeds to cross the desert. He left on Friday 17 rabī' II/27 June 1187, accompanied by victory, aided by unfailing supplies, supported by power, buttressed by good fortune, augmented by luck, with success in attendance, conversant with glory, the companion of victory, with the thanks of Islām and the support of God Almighty. He advanced with his ranks of embattled squadrons drawn up as we have said, each platoon flanked by others, ordered ranks, well-arranged formations, long-bodied horses on leading-reins, lethal arrows in quivers, drawn swords in hand, old wolves, cleaving blades, runners in sandals, rending lions; the tents of Khisfīn wept, there where God was bringing near the eclipse and downfall of the enemy, the darkening and disappearance of unbelief. Thus he passed the night surrounded by radiant faces and eyes watchful on God's path, the hands unsheathing the mighty swords, the tongues giving thanks for God's goodness, the hearts flowering with devotion, the souls conversing in heavenly love, the feet guided by the destiny they were to fulfil. In the morning he marched forward and descended to the Jordan, determined to attack and sure of his defence; the vast sea of his army surrounded the lake of Tiberias, while the spread of his tents made that plain seem narrow. The earth adorned itself in its new clothes, heaven opened so that the angels could descend from its gates; the ship-like tents rode at anchor in this expanse and the battalions flooded in wave upon wave. A second sky of dust spread out, in which swords and iron-tipped lances rose like stars. Uqhuwana was changed into burgeoning flowerbeds and flowering orchards by bay chargers and knights like proud lions, by crescent swords like arches of myrtle, by Yemeni blades like garden trees, by yellow banners like unfurled pennons of jasmin, by standards red as anemones and coats of mail glittering like pools, by swords polished white as streams of water, by feathered arrows blue as birds and curved as branches, by helmets gleaming like sweet-smelling many-petalled camomile flowers, by helmets like bubbles on a sea of breastplates, by neighing horses like eagles, roused to delight at the sight and sound of war.

The Franks meanwhile had ranged their standards at Saffuriyya and unfurled their banners. Their javelins were like bridges over the billows of their slim curvetting chargers, and their swords kindled in the shadowy clouds of dust. They were deployed in circles around their centres, to protect them with their bows and swords. They had mustered their hordes, drawn up their army, with spirits strengthened, cavalry and infantry, lancers and archers side by side, the pennons on their lances unfurled to the wind, the champions of error assembled, the 'True Cross' elevated, with the adorers of the false God gathered around it, the delirious madmen of human and divine nature. They had recruited the army in the lands of the Hypostatics,[1] and raised the Sublime Cross on high in adoration; no one with a stick to call his own was exempt from the summons, and they set out in numbers defying account or reckoning, numerous as pebbles, 50,000 or even more, they and their scheming plots. They assembled at Sa'īd, where they gathered from far and near. There they remained, unwilling to move or depart, and every morning the Sultan Saladin marched to within sight of them and opened fire on them from a commanding position and harassed them openly to make them confront him in an attempt

[1] I.e. Christians; those who venerate the three Hypostates or divine persons.

to remove his sword from their necks and his floods from their throats. But they had supplies of water and would not move, but sat where they were, for if they had ventured out, death would have come out of its lair to slaughter them. And they would have met someone who would strike them down and hand them over to death. They were terrified by the situation in which they found themselves, and fled shamefully from what should have made them glow with ardour. Then the Sultan decided to bathe in the waters of Lake Tiberias and from there to dominate the region with lance and sword, to take possession of the land and make himself its master. So he brought the lance-handles to the Jordan and made the dust rise over the lake from the hooves of the chargers, with which he found it easy without any difficulty to take the lovely Arab women by surprise. He gave orders to his troops, the amīrs and leaders of his army, to station themselves in front of the Franks and to bring them crisis in place of calm. If they came out to fight the Muslims would fall on them with just vengeance; if they moved anywhere the Muslims would spring on them like lions on hares; if they tried to reach Tiberias to defend it and seek help there they would betray the fact at once and the Muslims would immediately set out to attack them.

THE FALL OF TIBERIAS

Saladin surrounded Tiberias with his personal guard and his most faithful troops. He advanced the infantry and sappers, the Khurasani and the artillery, surrounded the walls and began to demolish the houses, giving battle fiercely and not sparing the city in the attack. This was Thursday, and he was at the head of his troops. The sappers began to mine one of the towers. They demolished it, knocked it down, leapt on to it and took possession of it. Night fell, and while the dawn of victory was breaking for them, the night of woe was darkening for the enemy. The citadel put up resistance and the Countess shut herself up there with her sons. When the Count heard that Tiberias had fallen and his Princedom been taken he was seized with consternation and lost all his strength of purpose, putting himself completely in the hands of the Franks. 'From today onwards,' he said, 'not to act is no longer possible. We must at all costs drive the enemy back. Now that Tiberias is taken and the whole Princedom with all my possessions, acquired or inherited, is lost, I cannot resign myself or recover from this reverse.'[1] The King was his ally and offered no opposition, but consented to this without hypocrisy, with sincere and unmixed affection, in a friendly manner completely lacking in coldness. He gave him precise promises without having to be asked twice, and set out on the march with his army, his sight and his hearing, his dragons and demons, beasts and wolves, the followers of his error and the faction of his evil deeds. The earth trembled beneath their feet, the heavens were clouded with the dust thrown up by them. News came that the Franks had mounted and were on the move with the ranks of their steadfast faith, who leapt into the attack, drawn up for battle and flooding over the ground, creeping forward on the defensive, kindling the fire of war, responding to the cry of vengeance, running to reach their dwellings. This was Friday 24 rabī' II. As soon as the news was verified the Sultan confirmed that his decision, based on his earlier judgment, was accurate, and rejoiced to hear that they were on the march; 'If our objective is gained,' he said, 'our request will have been heard in full and our ambition will have been achieved. Thanks be to God, our good fortune will now be renewed, our swords sharp, our courage valiant, our victory swift. If they are really defeated, killed and captured, Tiberias and all Palestine will have no one left to defend them or to impede our conquest.'

[1] In this account the Count expresses quite different loyalties from those described by Ibn al-Athir on the eve of the battle.

Thus he sought God's best (fortune) and set off, casting all delay aside. On Friday 24 rabi' II the Franks were on the march toward Tiberias with all their forces, moving as fast as if they were always going downhill. Their hordes rolled on, their lions roared, their vultures flew above them, their cries rose up, the horizon was hidden by the clouds of them, their heads sought eagerly for those who were to strike them off. They looked like mountains on the march, like seas boiling over, wave upon wave, with their crowding ranks, their seething approach-roads and mutilated barbarian warriors. The air stank, the light was dimmed, the desert was stunned, the plain dissolved, destiny hung over them, the Pleiades sent dust down upon them, the chargers' saddle-cloths brushed the ground and swept it, their hurrying hooves scored the earth. The knights clad in mail went with raised visors amid the swords, the hardened warriors and heroes of battle were loaded down with the apparel of war, and their number was complete. Ahead of them the Sultan had drawn up his battalions and strengthened all his resolve for the fight. He set his army to face them and kept a watch on their vanguard in case they should charge; he cut off their access to water and filled in the wells, which caused them great hardship. He prevented their getting down to the water and set himself between them and their objective, keeping them at a distance. This was on a burningly hot day, while they themselves were burning with wrath. The Dog Star was blazing with merciless heat that consumed their water supplies and offered no support against thirst.

Night separated the two sides and the cavalry barred both the roads. Islām passed the night face to face with unbelief, monotheism at war with Trinitarianism, the way of righteousness looking down upon error, faith opposing polytheism. Meanwhile the several circles of Hell prepared themselves and the several ranks of Heaven congratulated themselves; Malik (the Guardian of Hell) waited and Ridwān (the Guardian of

Paradise) rejoiced. Finally, when day dawned and the morning gleamed out, when dawn sent waves of light across the sky and the clangour of the trumpets startled the crow from the dust, when the swords awoke in their sheaths and the lances flamed with eagerness, when the bows stirred and the fire glowed, when blades were unsheathed and prevarication ripped away, then the archers began to scorch with their burning shafts men destined for Hell fire; the bows hummed and the bowstrings sang, the warriors' pliant lances danced, unveiling the brides of battle, the white blades appeared naked out of the sheath amid the throng, and the brown lances were pastured on entrails. The Franks hoped for a respite and their army in desperation sought for a way of escape. But at every way out they were barred, and tormented by the heat of war without being able to rest. Tortured by the thirst they charged, with no other water than the 'water' of the blades they gripped. The fire of arrows burned and wounded them, the fierce grip of the bows seized tenaciously upon them and struck them dead. They were impotent, driven off, pushed to extremes and driven back, every charge thrown off and destroyed, every action or attack captured and put in chains. Not even an ant could have escaped, and they could not defend themselves by charging. They burned and glowed in a frenzied ferment. As the arrows struck them down those who had seemed like lions now seemed like hedgehogs. The arrows beat them down and opened great gaps in their ranks. They sought refuge on the hill of Hittīn to protect them from the flood of defeat, and Hittīn was surrounded by the flags of destruction. The sword-blades sucked away their lives and scattered them on the hillsides; the bows found their targets, the wild fates stripped them, disasters crushed them, destruction picked them out, they became death's target and fate's prey. When the Count realized that they were defeated his anguish was clear to see. He gave up all effort and planned a way of escape. This was even before the main body of the army was roused and the embers were fanned, before the war was set alight and the flame burned. His band went off to find a way of escape and took the road across the wadi, refusing to stop. He went off like a flash of lightning in his folly, before the leak became too big; he fled with a few followers and did not return to the attack. Thus he absented himself from the fight, seized by an unconquerable terror that forced him to flee. The fighting grew more violent as lance crossed lance and sword struck sword. The Franks were surrounded whichever way they turned and completely encircled. They began to pitch their tents and to rally their troops, setting up their pavilions on Hittīn, while the gallant archers hammered away at their swords. But they were prevented from planting and raising their tents, and plucked from the roots and branches of life. They hoped to improve their position by dismounting from their horses, and they fought tenaciously, but the swords went through them as a torrent flows and our army surrounded them as Hellfire surrounds the damned. Finally they resorted to saddling the ground, and their girth clasped the nipples of the plain.[1]

The devil and his crew were taken, the King and his counts were captured, and the Sultan sat to review his chief prisoners, who came forward stumbling in their fetters like drunken men. The Grand Master of the Templars was brought in in his sins, and many of the Templars and Hospitallers with him. The King Guy and his brother Geoffrey were escorted in, with Hugh of Jubáil, Humphrey, and Prince Arnāt of al-Karak, who was the first to fall into the net. The Sultan had vowed to have his blood and had said: 'When I find him I shall kill him immediately.' When the Prince was brought before him he made him sit beside the King, and reproached him for his treachery and paraded his wickedness before him. 'How often have you made a vow and broken your oath; how many obligations have you

[1] Ibn al-Athīr puts the meaning of this elegant metaphor in simpler words; they had dismounted, now 'they sat on the ground'.

failed to honour, how many treaties made and unmade, and agreements reached and repudiated!' The interpreter passed on this reply from him: 'This is how kings have always behaved; I have only followed the path of custom.' Meanwhile the King was dying from thirst and was shaking with fear like a drunkard. But Saladin addressed him affably, calmed the wave of terror that had swept over him, assuaged his fear and reassured him in his heart; he sent for iced water for him, to soothe his burning throat and quench his tormenting thirst. Then the King passed the goblet to the Prince for him too to quench his thirst, and he took it in his hand and drank. The Sultan said to the King: 'You did not have my permission to give him drink, and so that drink does not imply his safety at my hand.' Then he mounted his horse and left him to roast himself at the fire of his fear; he stayed out riding until his tent had been pitched, his standards and banners planted and his troops had returned from the battle to their base. Then he entered the pavilion, summoned the Prince, raised his sword and struck him on the shoulder, and as he fell ordered that his head should be struck off. He was dragged out by the feet. This was done in the King's presence and filled him with despair and terror. The Sultan realized that the King was consumed with fear and assaulted by terror and consternation, and so he called him to his side, made him come up close and reassured and calmed him. He put him at his ease as he stood at his side and calmed him by saying: 'This man's evil deeds have been his downfall, and as you saw his perfidy has been his destruction. He died for his sins and wickedness; the spark he struck from life is extinguished and the source of his being has dried up.'

This defeat of the enemy, this our victory occurred on a Saturday, and the humiliation proper to the men of Saturday was inflicted on the men of Sunday, who had been lions and now were reduced to the level of miserable sheep.[1] Of these

[1] I.e. the Christians were humiliated like despised Jews.

thousands only a few individuals escaped, and of all those enemies only a few were saved. The plain was covered with prisoners and corpses, disclosed by the dust as it settled and victory became clear. The prisoners, with beating hearts, were bound in chains. The dead were scattered over the mountains and valleys, lying immobile on their sides. Hittīn shrugged off their carcasses, and the perfume of victory was thick with the stench of them. I passed by them and saw the limbs of the fallen cast naked on the field of battle, scattered in pieces over the site of the encounter, lacerated and disjointed, with heads cracked open, throats split, spines broken, necks shattered, feet in pieces, noses mutilated, extremities torn off, members dismembered, parts shredded, eyes gouged out, stomachs disembowelled, hair coloured with blood, the praecordium slashed, fingers sliced off, the thorax shattered, the ribs broken, the joints dislocated, the chests smashed, throats slit, bodies cut in half, arms pulverized, lips shrivelled, foreheads pierced, forelocks dyed scarlet, breasts covered with blood, ribs pierced, elbows disjointed, bones broken, tunics torn off, faces lifeless, wounds gaping, skin flayed, fragments chopped off, hair lopped, backs skinless, bodies dismembered, teeth knocked out, blood spilt, life's last breath exhaled, necks lolling, joints slackened, pupils liquefied, heads hanging, livers crushed, ribs staved in, heads shattered, breasts flayed, spirits flown, their very ghosts crushed; like stones among stones, a lesson to the wise.[1]

This field of battle had become a sea of blood; the dust was stained red, rivers of blood ran freely, and the face of the true Faith was revealed free from those shadowy abominations. O sweet rivers of victory over such evil! O burning, punishing blows on those carcasses! O sweet heart's comforter against that confusion! O welcome prayers at the joyful news of such an event! Such is the number of the slain that the tongues of all

[1] Our author must surely have considered this macabre tirade one of the most successful examples of his literary style.

the peoples would not be capable of counting and enumerating them; as for the prisoners, all our tents could not produce enough tent-cords to bind and fetter them, and I saw thirty or forty on a single rope, led by a single rider, and in one place a hundred or two hundred captives guarded by a single man. Here rebels became prisoners, enemies were denuded, sovereigns made subject, great men humiliated, Counts reduced to game, horsemen hunted down, honoured men reviled, the faces of the infernal Templars ground in the dust, skulls trampled underfoot, the bodies they were blessed with hewn to pieces and scattered. How many proud men were taken, how many leaders bound and led, how many polytheists were grinding their teeth, how many infidels filled with gloomy thoughts, how many Trinitarians cut in half, how many impious enquirers after God had their arms bound; how many wounders were wounded, and injurers injured, and kings enslaved, and profaners profaned, and destroyers destroyed, and plunderers plundered, and noble lords in fetters, and violent men in chains, and freemen in servitude, and followers of error in the hands of the followers of truth!

THE CAPTURE OF THE GREAT CROSS ON THE DAY OF BATTLE

At the same time as the King was taken the 'True Cross' was also captured, and the idolaters who were trying to defend it were routed. It was this cross, brought into position and raised on high, to which all Christians prostrated themselves and bowed their heads. Indeed, they maintain that it is made of the wood of the cross on which, they say, he whom they adore was hung, and so they venerate it and prostrate themselves before it. They had housed it in a casing of gold, adorned with pearls and gems, and kept it ready for the festival of the Passion, for the observance of their yearly ceremony. When the priests exposed it to view and the heads (of the bearers) bore it along all would run and cast themselves down around it, and no one was allowed to lag behind or hang back without forfeiting his liberty. Its capture was for them more important than the loss of the King and was the gravest blow that they sustained in that battle. The cross was a prize without equal, for it was the supreme object of their faith. To venerate it was their prescribed duty, for it was their God, before whom they would bow their foreheads to the ground, and to which their mouths sang hymns. They fainted at its appearance, they raised their eyes to contemplate it, they were consumed with passion when it was exhibited and boasted of nothing else when they had seen it. They went into ecstasies at its reappearance, they offered up their lives for it and sought comfort from it, so much so that they had copies made of it which they worshipped, before which they prostrated themselves in their houses and on which they called when they gave evidence. So when the Great Cross was taken great was the calamity that befell them, and the strength drained from their loins. Great was the number of the defeated, exalted the feelings of the victorious army. It seemed as if, once they knew of the capture of the Cross, none of them would survive that day of ill-omen. They perished in death or imprisonment, and were overcome by force and violence. The Sultan encamped on the plain of Tiberias like a lion in the desert or the moon in its full splendour.

THE CONQUEST OF THE CITADEL OF TIBERIAS

He sent men to the citadel to receive its surrender with a promise of safe-conduct, and established the Faith there in place of the falsehood that had dwelt there before. The Lady, the Countess of Tiberias, had defended it and carried there all her property and possessions. He granted her a safe-conduct for the journey for her companions and property, and she left with her women and men and luggage, taking everything to Tripoli, the city that belonged to the Count her husband. So once again Tiberias was inhabited in safety by the people of the Faith, and Sarim ad-Din Qaimāz an-Najmi, one of their greatest dignitaries, was appointed its governor. Meanwhile Saladin encamped outside Tiberias, after having cured all mankind of its ills, and his army covered the whole plain.

SALADIN'S TREATMENT OF THE TEMPLARS AND HOSPITALLERS, BEHEADING THEM AND CAUSING GENERAL REJOICING AT THEIR EXTERMINATION[1]

On the morning of Monday 17 rabīʿ II, two days after the victory, the Sultan sought out the Templars and Hospitallers who had been captured and said: 'I shall purify the land of these two impure races.' He assigned fifty *dinar* to every man who had taken one of them prisoner, and immediately the army brought forward at least a hundred of them. He ordered that they should be beheaded, choosing to have them dead rather than in prison. With him was a whole band of scholars and sufis and a certain number of devout men and ascetics; each begged to be allowed to kill one of them, and drew his sword and rolled back his sleeve. Saladin, his face joyful, was sitting on his dais; the unbelievers showed black despair, the troops were drawn up in their ranks, the amīrs stood in double file. There were some who slashed and cut cleanly, and were thanked for it; some who refused and failed to act, and were excused; some who made fools of themselves, and others took their places. I saw there the man who laughed scornfully and slaughtered, who spoke and acted; how many promises he fulfilled, how much praise

[1] This episode, described by our eye-witness with his usual stylistic embellishments, is a blot on Saladin's renowned magnanimity; the reason for the slaughter was the hatred aroused in the Muslim camp by the two warrior orders by conduct in war certainly no more humane and 'Christian' than that of their enemies.

he won, the eternal rewards he secured with the blood he had shed, the pious works added to his account with a neck severed by him! How many blades did he stain with blood for a victory he longed for, how many lances did he brandish against the lion he captured, how many ills did he cure by the ills he brought upon a Templar, how much strength did he give to the leaders whom he supported, how many banners did he unfurl against disasters that retreated! I saw how he killed unbelief to give life to Islām, and destroyed polytheism to build monotheism, and drove decisions through to their conclusion to satisfy the community of the faithful, and cut down enemies in the defence of friends!

The Sultan sent the Frankish King to Damascus with his brother, and Humphrey, and the ruler of Jubáil, and the Grand Master of the Temple and all the great barons who had been captured, to be imprisoned there and immobilized after all their activity; the army dispersed with its prisoners, and the embers of the assembled unbelievers faded and were extinguished.

Jerusalem Reconquered

(IBN AL-ATHĪR, XI, 361–6)

When Saladin had completed his conquest of Ascalon and the surrounding regions he sent for the Egyptian fleet and a large detachment of troops under Husām ad-Din Lu'lu' al-Hajib, a man well known for his courage, energy and initiative. This force set out by sea, intercepting Frankish communications; every Frankish vessel they sighted they attacked, and captured every galley. When they arrived and Saladin could rely on their support, he marched from Ascalon to Jerusalem. The venerable Patriarch,[1] who carried greater authority than the King himself, was there and so was Baliān ibn Barzān, ruler of ar-Ramla,[2] who was almost equal in rank to the King. The knights who had

[1] Heraclius. [2] Baliān of Ibelin.

survived Hittīn had also concentrated there. The inhabitants of that region, Ascalon and elsewhere had also gathered in Jerusalem, so there was a great concourse of people there, each one of whom would choose death rather than see the Muslims in power in their city; the sacrifice of life, possessions and sons was for them a part of their duty to defend the city. During that interval they fortified it by every means to hand, and then all mounted the walls, resolved to defend them with all their might, and showed determination to fight to the limit of their ability in the defence of Jerusalem. They mounted catapults to ward off attempts to approach the city and besiege it.

During Saladin's advance one of the amīrs went ahead with his band of men without taking any precautions to defend himself; a troop of Franks who had left Jerusalem on reconnaissance came face to face with him and in a battle killed him and some of his men, which caused great grief and sorrow to the Muslims. Half-way through rajab/September 1187 they besieged Jerusalem. As they approached they saw on the walls a terrifying crowd of men and heard an uproar of voices coming from the inhabitants behind the walls that led them to infer the number of people who must be assembled there. For five days the Sultan rode round the city to decide on the best point for the attack, for the city was more strongly defended than ever before. The only point at which to attack was on the north side, near the Bab 'Amuda and the Church of Zion. So on 20 rajab Saladin moved his army to the north side, and on the same evening began to mount his siege-engines. Next morning they were all ready and began their battery of the walls, from which the Franks replied with other machines that they had constructed there. Then began the fiercest struggle imaginable; each side looked on the fight as an absolute religious obligation. There was no need for a superior authority to drive them on: they restrained the enemy without restraint, and drove them off without being driven back. Every morning the Frankish cavalry made sorties to fight and provoke the enemy to battle; several of both sides fell in these encounters. Among the Muslim martyrs was the amīr 'Izz ad-Din Isa ibn Malik, one of the leading amīrs and the son of the ruler of Ja'bar. Every day he had led the attack himself, and at his death passed to God's great mercy; a man dear to Muslims both great and small, whose death brought grief and sorrow to many. They charged like one man, dislodged the Franks from their positions and drove them back into the city. When the Muslims reached the moat they crossed it, came up under the walls and began to breach them, protected by their archers and by continuous artillery fire which kept the walls clear of Franks and enabled the Muslims to make a breach and fill it with the usual materials.[1]

When the Franks saw how violently the Muslims were attacking, how continuous and effective was the fire from the ballistas and how busily the sappers were breaching the walls, meeting no resistance, they grew desperate, and their leaders assembled to take counsel. They decided to ask for safe-conduct out of the city and to hand Jerusalem over to Saladin. They sent a deputation of their lords and nobles to ask for terms, but when they spoke of it to Saladin he refused to grant their request. 'We shall deal with you,' he said, 'just as you dealt with the population of Jerusalem when you took it in 492/1099, with murder and enslavement and other such savageries!' The messengers returned empty-handed. Then Baliān ibn Barzān asked for safe-conduct for himself so that he might appear before Saladin to discuss developments. Consent was given, and he presented himself and once again began asking for a general amnesty in return for surrender. The Sultan still refused his requests and entreaties to show mercy. Finally, despairing of this approach, Baliān said: 'Know, O Sultan, that there are very many of us in this city, God alone knows how many. At

[1] Once they had cleared a tunnel they would fill it with combustible materials and set fire to it to bring down the wall above.

the moment we are fighting half-heartedly in the hope of saving our lives, hoping to be spared by you as you have spared others; this is because of our horror of death and our love of life. But if we see that death is inevitable, then by God we shall kill our children and our wives, burn our possessions, so as not to leave you with a *dinar* or a *drachma* or a single man or woman to enslave. When this is done, we shall pull down the Sanctuary of the Rock and the Masjid al-Aqsa and the other sacred places, slaughtering the Muslim prisoners we hold—5,000 of them—and killing every horse and animal we possess. Then we shall come out to fight you like men fighting for their lives, when each man, before he falls dead, kills his equals; we shall die with honour, or win a noble victory!' Then Saladin took counsel with his advisers, all of whom were in favour of his granting the assurances requested by the Franks, without forcing them to take extreme measures whose outcome could not be foreseen. 'Let us consider them as being already our prisoners,' they said, 'and allow them to ransom themselves on terms agreed between us.' The Sultan agreed to give the Franks assurances of safety on the understanding that each man, rich and poor alike, should pay ten *dinar*, children of both sexes two *dinar* and women five *dinar*. All who paid this sum within forty days should go free, and those who had not paid at the end of the time should be enslaved. Baliān ibn Barzān offered 30,000 *dinar* as ransom for the poor, which was accepted, and the city surrendered on Friday 27 rajab/2 October 1187, a memorable day on which the Muslim flags were hoisted over the walls of Jerusalem. At every gate Saladin set amīrs in charge of taxation to claim the appropriate ransom from the inhabitants. But they cheated in carrying out their duties, and divided among themselves money that would otherwise have filled the State treasury to the benefit of all. There were in fact exactly 70,000 cavalry and infantry in Jerusalem, not counting the women and children with them; not a surprising number when you consider that there were people there from Darūm, Ramla, Gaza and elsewhere, so many of them that they filled the streets and churches and walking was impossible. An indication of the numbers is the fact that most of them paid the ransom, and Baliān ibn Barzān freed 18,000, for whom he paid the 30,000, and yet apart from all these the number of those who could not pay and were taken prisoner came to exactly 16,000 persons, men, women and children.

A certain number of amīrs maintained that some subjects from their feudal estates were living in Jerusalem, and they freed them on payment of the tax to themselves. Others dressed Franks in the clothes of Muslim soldiers, got them out of the city, and ransomed them for a sum that they themselves decided. Others asked Saladin for the gift of a certain number of Franks, and when he granted them this made the men pay the tax to themselves. In fact only a small sum actually found its way into the treasury.

There was in Jerusalem a woman, married to a Byzantine king, who became a nun[1] and settled there with a great train of domestics, slaves and handmaids and a quantity of gold and precious stones. She asked for safe-conduct for herself and her dependants, and the Sultan granted it and let her go. In the same way he set at liberty the Queen of Jerusalem,[2] whose husband, imprisoned by Saladin, became King of the Franks through her agency and ruled the kingdom as her viceroy. He also let her take her possessions and dependants, and she asked permission to join her husband, who was then held prisoner in the fortress of Nablus. This was granted and she went and stayed with him. The wife of the Prince Arnat of al-Karak whom Saladin had killed with his own hand on the day of Hittīn also came before him to intercede for her son[3] who was a prisoner.

[1] This detail makes it difficult to identify her as Maria Comnena, widow of Amalric I and later wife of Baliān of Ibelin.

[2] Sibylla, wife of Guy of Lusignan.

[3] Stephanie, mother of Humphrey of Toron.

Saladin said: 'If you will give me al-Karak, I will let him go.' She went to al-Karak, but the Franks there would not let her yield the fortress, so Saladin refused to give up her son, but only her possessions and followers.

The Grand Patriarch of the Franks left the city with the treasures from the Dome of the Rock, the Masjid al-Aqsa, the Church of the Resurrection and others, God alone knows the amount of the treasure; he also took an equal quantity of money. Saladin made no difficulties, and when he was advised to sequestrate the whole lot for Islām, replied that he would not go back on his word. He took only the ten *dinar* from him, and let him go, heavily escorted, to Tyre.

At the top of the cupola of the Dome of the Rock there was a great gilded cross. When the Muslims entered the city on the Friday, some of them climbed to the top of the cupola to take down the cross. When they reached the top a great cry went up from the city and from outside the walls, the Muslims crying the *Allāh akbar* in their joy, the Franks groaning in consternation and grief. So loud and piercing was the cry that the earth shook.

Once the city was taken and the infidels had left, Saladin ordered that the shrines should be restored to their original state. The Templars had built their living-quarters against al-Aqsa, with storerooms and latrines and other necessary offices, taking up part of the area of al-Aqsa. This was all restored to its former state. The Sultan ordered that the Dome of the Rock should be cleansed of all pollution, and this was done. On the following Friday, 4 sha'bān/9 October, the Muslims celebrated the communal Friday prayers there. Among them was the Sultan, who also prayed at the Mosque of the Rock,[1] with Muhyi ad-Din ibn az-Zaki, qadi of Damascus,

[1] We have already noted that al-Aqsa and the Dome of the Rock, the so-called Mosque of 'Umar, were close together but separate. In this passage there is no doubt that the great ceremony was held in al-Aqsa and that Saladin *also* prayed in the Dome of the Rock, as is clear from 'Imād ad-Din's account.

as imām and preacher. Then Saladin appointed a qadi and an (ordinary) imām for the five canonic prayers, and ordered that a pulpit should be built for him. He was told that Nur ad-Din had once had one made in Aleppo, which he had commanded the workmen to embellish and construct to the best of their ability, saying: 'We have made this to set up in Jerusalem.' The carpenters had taken so many years to make it that it had no rival in the whole of Islām. Saladin had it brought from Aleppo and set up in Jerusalem, more than twenty years after it was made. This was one of the noble deeds of Nur ad-Din and one of his good works, God have mercy on him![1]

After the Friday prayer Saladin gave orders for the restoration of al-Aqsa, giving every encouragement to its embellishment and having it faced with stone and fine mosaics. Marble of an unrivalled quality was brought, and golden tesserae from Constantinople and other necessary materials that had been kept in store for years, and the work of restoration was begun. To hide the pictures that covered the walls, the Franks had set slabs of marble over the Rock, concealing it from sight, and Saladin had them removed. It had been covered with the marble because the priests had sold a good part of it to the Franks who came from abroad on pilgrimages and bought pieces for their weight in gold in the hope of benefiting by its health-giving influences. Each of them, on his return home with a piece of this stone, would build a church for it and enclose it in the altar. One of the Frankish Kings of Jerusalem, afraid that it would all disappear, had it covered with a slab of marble to preserve it. When it was uncovered Saladin had some beautiful Qur'āns brought to the mosque, and magnificent copies of the sections of the Holy Book for use in worship. He established reciters of the Qur'ān there, heaping them with bountiful endowments. So Islām was restored there in full freshness

[1] As we have seen before, Ibn al-Athīr let slip no opportunity of expressing his attachment to the Zangid dynasty supplanted by Saladin.

and beauty. This noble act of conquest was achieved, after 'Umar ibn al-Khattāb[1]—God have mercy on him!—by no one but Saladin, and that is a sufficient title to glory and honour.

The Frankish population of Jerusalem who had not departed began to sell at very low prices all their possessions, treasures and whatever they could not carry with them. The merchants from the army and the non-Frankish Christians in Jerusalem bought their goods from them. The latter had asked Saladin's permission to remain in their homes if they paid the tax, and he had granted them this, so they stayed and bought up Frankish property. What they could not sell, beds and boxes and casks, the Franks left behind; even superb columns of marble and slabs of marble and mosaics in large quantities. Thus they departed.

('IMĀD AD-DIN, 47–69)

Saladin marched from Ascalon to Jerusalem, victorious in his decision, accompanied by victory, escorted by glory. He had tamed the indomitable colt of his desires, and made fertile the meadow of his wealth. His hope had an easy passage, his paths were fragrant, his gifts poured out, his sweetness perfumed the air, his power was manifest, his authority supreme. The glory of his army flooded like an ocean over the plain and filled the desert, pouring out thanks and gratitude. The dust raised by his hosts had spread its cloak over the dawn; the cloud of it seemed to have replaced the clear morning hour with the shadows of evening. At times the earth groaned under the squadrons, the heavens received with joy the particles of dust. He marched on, rejoicing by his presence the surrounding regions, and the points of his lances related stories of his conquests from the

[1] The second Caliph (634–44), under whom the Muslims took Jerusalem for the first time, in 637.

mountain tops; to the scenes his hopes described he could add those that his success had made reality. Sweet and lofty fruits and flashes of light appeared from the roots of victory and from his success. Islām wooed Jerusalem, ready to lay down lives for her as a bride-price, bringing her a blessing that would remove the tragedy of her state, giving her a joyful face to replace an expression of torment, making heard, above the cry of grief from the Rock, calling for help against its enemies, the reply to this appeal, the prompt echo of the summons, an echo that would make the gleaming lamps rise in her sky, bring the exiled Faith back to her own country and dwelling-place and drive away from al-Aqsa those whom God drove away with his curse. Saladin marched forward to take up the reins of Jerusalem that now hung loose, to silence the Christian clappers and allow the muezzin to be heard again, to remove the heavy hand of unbelief with the right hands of the Faith, to purify Jerusalem of the pollution of those races, of the filth of the dregs of humanity, to reduce the minds to silence by silencing the bells. The news flew to Jerusalem, and the hearts of its inhabitants beat with terror and their chests palpitated and throbbed with fear of the army of Islām. The Franks, as the news spread, wished that they had never been born. Thus it was with the Frankish leaders Baliān ibn Barzān and the Grand Patriarch and the heads of the Orders of the Temple and the Hospital. Baliān was troubled, and fires of anguish consumed him; the glow of Patriarchal pride was extinguished, and all felt uneasy in their houses, as if every one of them had become a trap set for the unbelievers. They wanted to take action in their calamitous situation, but the minds of the unbelievers could not agree. The Franks despaired of finding any relief from their situation and decided all to give their lives (in defence of Jerusalem).

THE CHURCH OF THE RESURRECTION[1]

The Franks said: 'Here our heads will fall, we will pour forth our souls, spill our blood, give up our lives; we shall endure blows and wounds, we shall be prodigal of our spirits in defence of the place where the Spirit dwells. This is our Church of the Resurrection, here we shall take up our position and from here make our sorties, here our cry goes up, here our penitence is performed, our banners float, our cloud spreads. We love this place, we are bound to it, our honour lies in honouring it, its salvation is ours, its safety is ours, its survival is ours. If we go far from it we shall surely be branded with shame and just censure, for here is the place of the crucifixion and our goal, the altar and the place of sacrifice, the place of assembly and the sanctuary, the place of descent and of ascent, the flight of steps and the observation-post, the symposium and the theatre, the place for ornament and decoration, the prologue and epilogue, the food and the nourishment, the works of marble and intaglio, the permitted and the forbidden places, the pictures and the sculptures, the views and configurations, the lions and the lion-cubs, the portraits and likenesses, the columns and slabs of marble, the bodies and souls. Here are pictures of the Apostles conversing, Popes with their histories, monks in their cells, priests in their councils, the Magi with their ropes,[2] priests and their imaginings; here the effigies of the Madonna and the Lord, of the Temple and the Birthplace, of the Table and the fishes, and what is described and sculpted of the Disciples and the Master, of the cradle and the Infant speaking.[3] Here are the

[1] In Arabic *al-Qiyama*, but the Muslim writers of the time felt obliged to turn it derisively into *al-Qumama*, the dung-heap, and it appears in this form in 'Imād ad-Din; it is the Holy Sepulchre.

[2] A reference to Qur'ān XX, 69, where the Egyptian Magi, casting their ropes down before Moses, make them appear to be serpents.

[3] There are two Qur'ānic references here: the table is that of the Eucharist, which according to Muhammad descends miraculously from heaven (Q.V), and the Christ child speaking is influenced in its turn by the *Evangelium infantiæ* (Q. XIX, 31).

effigies of the ox and the ass, of Paradise and Hell, the clappers and the divine laws. Here, they say, the Messiah was crucified, the sacrificial victim slain, divinity made incarnate, humanity deified. Here the dual nature was united, the cross was raised, light was extinguished and darkness covered the land. Here the nature was united with the person, the existent mingled with the non-existent, the adored Being was baptized and the Virgin gave birth to her Son.[1]

They continued to attach errors like this to the object of their cult, wandering with false beliefs far from the true forms of faith, and said: 'We shall die in defence of our Lord's sepulchre, and we shall die in fear of its slipping from our hands; we shall fight and struggle for it: how could we not fight, not contend and join battle, how could we leave this for them to take, and permit them to take from us what we took from them?' They made far-reaching and elaborate preparations, stretching out endlessly to infinity. They mounted deadly weapons on the walls, and veiled the face of light with the sombre curtain of walls. They sent out their demons, their wolves ran hither and thither, their impetuous tyrants raged; their swords were unsheathed, the fabric of their downfall displayed, their blazing firebrands lit. They burned with enthusiasm and surged like a wave, they launched appeals and their hostile bands rode out, their loathesome vipers glided about, their priests aroused their passions, their leaders cheered them on, their hearts were stirred. Their spies brought them messages of disaster, telling them of the advance of al-Malik an-Nasir[2] and his victorious troops, with banners displayed, swords in hand, plucked from the sheaths, bloodstained lances, troops in serried ranks, chargers

[1] This curious jumble of Christian dogmas and rites betrays the Muslim author's lack of real information and his preconceived hostility. But apart from the stylistic frills this description, to us almost a caricature, is the usual picture of Christianity painted by mediaeval Muslims. Nor can we say that the Christian view of Islām was any more accurate.

[2] 'The King who brings victory to the Faith' was, as has been mentioned before, Saladin's official name.

trained to wreak vengeance on enemies, souls inflamed with the fire of the True Faith, with burning resolution, their odd-toed horses on leading-reins, their swords stained with blood. The hills were dewy, the scabbard-bearers raged, lance-points were sharpened, the chargers' reins slackened, their burden now secure. The valleys flowed down from their hills, the champions curvetted amid their standards; their squadrons blocked the mountain passes like waves scattering the dust, like eagles overshadowing the sun; the blades of their javelins could have ignited wicks. They were like winds blowing about the mountains, they carried their lances as if they had been cords. They were the lion's claws lurking in the thicket; their ranks advanced in the strength of their uncrushable resolution. Each believer made a covenant with his Lord, and was ready to ward off his approaching doom, prompt to soothe the troubles in his heart and to pour out generously its irrigating flood; rebutting all evil from behind the shelter of his breastplate, full of gallantry and valour, drawing the daughter of the sheath from her scabbard, washing the thirsty blade with enemy blood, grasping in his hands the white blades of India, bringing talk of disaster to an end with his lights and his thunder, his destiny as piercing as the sword with which he laboured. Each young man longed for the fire of battle, each man of the Faith was jealous for the Lord's religion, each army was like a tempestuous sea, everyone who stained a sharp sword with blood was defending the True Faith, everyone who believed in the other life hated this lower one and asked God for martyrdom, drawn away from desire for earthly survival and ready to pour out his wealth in the holy cause. The Sultan advanced in the authority he had won, with his valiant knights, with the lesser kings his sons and brothers, with the lion-cubs his mamlūks and pages, with his noble amīrs, his great friends, in squadrons ranked according to their merit, in platoons drawn up in solemn cavalcades, with lances whose metal points gleamed like stars, with serried ranks bearing their sharp swords, with yellow standards that would bring disaster to the Banu l-Asfar,[1] with white swords and brown lances, ready to bring crimson death to the blue-eyed enemy, with pavilions and tribes, with lances and darts, with neighing chargers pawing the earth, with pliant spear-points and knights on horseback, and people all ready, for jealous love of their Faith, to give their souls and their precious possessions. (When Saladin reached Jerusalem) he at once asked to see the Masjid al-Aqsa and wanted to know the nearest road leading to it, and who were its most distinguished devotees, expressing the noble sentiments with which God nobly inspired him.

DESCRIPTION OF JERUSALEM

The Sultan said: 'If God gives us the grace to drive His enemies from Jerusalem what happiness will be ours! What blessings shall we owe to Him if He chooses to assist us! For Jerusalem has been in enemy hands for ninety-one years,[2] during which time God has received nothing from us here in the way of adoration, while the zeal of (Muslim) sovereigns to ransom her languished and the generations followed one another and the Franks were settled here in power. And God has reserved the merit of conquest for a single house—the Ayyubid—to unite all hearts in appreciation of its members. He has chosen in particular the age of the Imām an-Nasir li Din Allāh to be given an advantage over other ages, and has chosen to give Egypt and its army an advantage in this over every other country. And how could He not assist in the conquest of the mighty Jerusalem and of the Masjid al-Aqsa, founded in piety, since she is the seat

[1] The *Banu l-Asfar* (the Arabic could mean 'sons of the yellow', hence the pun about 'yellow standards', although the real derivation is from the Biblical Sofer, Esau's nephew), is the Arabs' name for the ancient Romans, and by extension the Latins, the man of the West. In the next line they are called 'blue eyed', referring either to an ethnic characteristic or to its traditionally evil significance.

[2] The lunar years of the *hijra*, from 492/1099 to 583/1187.

of the prophets, the home of the saints, the place where the pious adore their God, the place that the great saints of the earth and angels of heaven visit. From there the great assembly and diaspora take place and crowd upon crowd of ambassadors of the pious friends of God go there. There is the Rock, whose eternal splendour has been preserved from any deterioration, from which the Road of the Ascension (of the Prophet to Heaven) leaves the earth; above it the proud Dome rises like a crown, there the lamp has shone and from there Burāq[1] departed, there the night of the heavenly journey, with the descent of the light-giving torch, illumined the whole world. Within its gates is the Gate of Mercy;[2] he who enters by it gains the right to dwell eternally in Paradise. Within it are the Seat of Solomon and the Oratory of David, and the Fountain of Aloes, which represents for those who go down to drink it the (heavenly) river Kauthar. Jerusalem is the first of the two *qibla*, the second of the two Houses of God, the third of the Sacred Zones.[3] It is one of the three places of prayer of which the Prophet says in his sayings that horsemen face in their direction to mount, and ally their hopes to them. And who knows that God will not, by means of us, restore her to her former beauty, as He honours her by mentioning her among His most noble creations at the beginning of the sura[4] in which He says: 'Praise Him who took His servant on a journey by night from the Sacred Mosque (at Mecca) to the Remote Mosque (in Jerusalem).' She has prayers and virtues innumerable; the

[1] The heavenly charger on whose back Muhammad left the Rock on his ascent (mi'rāj) and his miraculous voyage beyond the tomb. In this panegyric of Jerusalem eloquent hints come through even 'Imād ad-Din's rhetoric of the reasons why the place was, and is, so sacred to the pious and warlike zeal of Islām. See also the letter from Saladin to Richard for a more sober development of the same theme.

[2] Bab ar-Rahma, now the Golden Gate, one of the gates of the temple precinct.

[3] The *qibla* is the direction of prayer, originally ordained by Muhammad to be the direction of Jerusalem before he changed it definitely to Mecca. Jerusalem is God's second house after the *Ka'ba* at Mecca, and the third sacred precinct after Mecca and Medina.

[4] Qur'ān XVII, 1, the verse referring to the Prophet's nocturnal journey from Mecca to Jerusalem and from there to heaven.

holy journey by night took place to and from her, over her heaven was opened wide, she is referred to in the accounts of the prophets, the thanksgiving of the saints, the tombs of the martyrs, the miracles of the bountiful, the symbols of the scholars. Here is the home of pious acts and the theatre of joys. Her lofty Rock is the first *qibla*, from which the Prophet's foot ascended, bringing eternal benediction. Beside it our Prophet prayed with the prophets, accompanied by the faithful Spirit, and from it he ascended. Here is the oratory of Mary, of whom God says: 'Each time that Zacharias entered the room to her....'[1] Jerusalem is the city that David founded and advised Solomon to build, and in her honour God revealed the verse: 'Praise be....' She it was that al-Farūq[2] conquered and with which a sura of the Revelation begins. How illustrious and great is she, how noble and proud, high and gleaming, lofty and glorious! O blessed are her benedictions and blessed her auspices, noble her states and sweet her beauties! God has made manifest her nobility and position in the words of the Qur'ān: 'Whose precinct we have blessed.'[3] O how many miracles God has shown to the Prophet here, and now He has set before our eyes her virtues that formerly we had only heard of!'

Thus the Sultan described her distinctions and beauty, which, as he undertook and swore, he would bring back to the brilliance they used to have, and he took an oath not to depart until he had honoured his word and raised his standard on her highest point, and had visited with his own feet the place where the Prophet had set foot, and heard the call from the Rock, for he longed to light up the faces of his family[4] with the joyful news. So he advanced, certain of absolute victory and of the end of all difficulties, while the anguish of the Franks was clear to see. He reached the western side of Jerusalem on Sunday 15 rajab/

[1] Qur'ān III, 32.

[2] Honorific surname of 'Umar, see p. 146 n.

[3] Qur'ān XVII, 1.

[4] I.e. the Ayyubid house.

20 September. The hearts of the unbelievers thudded, the faction of polytheists was in a confusion of breathless anguish, destiny performed the miracle. There were in Jerusalem at the time 70,000 Frankish troops, both swordsmen and archers, and champions of error armed with lances, their pliant points quivering, ready to defend the city. They challenged (us) to combat and barred the pass, they came down into the lists like enemies, they slaughtered and drew blood, they blazed with fury and defended the city, they fumed and burned with wrath, they drove us back and defended themselves, they became inflamed and caused us harm, groaned and incited, called for help in a foreign tongue, entrenched themselves and acted like men enraged with thirst, whirled about and crossed, advanced and retreated, rolled about and grieved, cried out and yelled in the conflict, immolated themselves in their tragedy and flung themselves on death. They fought grimly and struggled with all their energy, descending to the fray with absolute resolution, they wielded the sockets of their spears to give their thirsty points the water of the spirit to drink; they dealt with those that had lost their nerve, and passed round the goblets of death; they hurled themselves into battle to cut off limbs, they blazed and set fire to things, they clustered together and obstinately stood their ground, they made themselves a target for arrows and called on death to stand by them. They said: 'Each of us is worth twenty, and every ten is worth a hundred! We shall bring about the end of the world in defence of the Church of the Resurrection, we shall despise our own safety in desire for her survival.' So the battle continued and the slaughter with spear and sword went on.

On Friday 20 rajab/25 September the Sultan moved to the northern side and pitched his tent there, cutting the Frankish lines and opening up the way to death. He mounted catapults, and by this means milked the udders of slaughter, making the Rock groan under the impact of missiles; his reward was the hosts of evil behind the wall. They could no longer put a head outside the gates without meeting death and the day of disaster, and casting their souls into perdition. The Templars clamoured, the barons leapt to their destruction in Hell, the Hospitallers went to damnation, the 'Brethren' found no escape from death. No band of soldiers cast itself between the stones from the catapults and their objective; in every heart on either side burned the fire of longing, faces were exposed to the blade's kiss, hearts were tormented with longing for combat, hands cleaved to the hilts of their bloody swords, minds were intent upon finding those whose spirit was slow to devote itself fully to the cause. The bases of the walls and the teeth of their battlements were battered and broken down by stones from the catapults' slings; they seemed like madmen throwing stones at random, impregnable gallant knights, mountains crossed with ropes, living beings aided by others, mothers of disaster and death, pregnant with calamity. Their missiles were invincible, all precautions against them were useless. Their darts vibrated with menace, their flight nourished on the bile of perceptive men.[1] How many boulders came down out of heaven upon them, how many blocks of sandstone plunged into the earth, how many blazing firebrands bespattered them! The damage caused by the catapults, the extraordinary extent of their devastation, the effects of their concentration, the whistling wind of their flight, the extent of their range were beyond compare. The attack from their catapults never ceased, the battery of their mangonels, the drawing of water with their ropes, the parading in their halters, the attacking and defending, prostrating and slashing open, shaking their buckets, becoming downcast at their misfortunes, dissolving the composure of strong men with the boulders that they shot one after another, smashing the

[1] This seems to mean: they induced terror, devouring bile ducts, in those who understood their lethal power. But as in all these metaphors meaning is subservient to the puns and plays on the sound that are almost all lost in translation.

huddles of buildings, breaking them down into ruins, demolishing their foundations, breaking up their joints by hauling them within their ropes, exhausting the wells by drinking from them with their own cups, until they reduced the walls to a single line of bricks and drove their defenders away. The enemy's ordnance was smashed and broken, the moat crossed and the attack sustained. The victory of Islām was clear, and so was the death of Unbelief. The breach was taken, the problem resolved. Every onslaught was energetic and achieved its object, the goal was reached, the enemy wounded, hindrances blown away, the work completed, the target set up for them achieved and surpassed, the task accomplished. The enemy feared that it would be crushed, and its strong morale gave way to distress. The city became Muslim and the infidel belt around it was cut. Ibn Barzān came out to secure a treaty with the Sultan, and asked for an amnesty for his people. But the Sultan refused and upheld his claims, saying: 'Neither amnesty nor mercy for you! Our only desire is to inflict perpetual subjection upon you; tomorrow will make us your masters by main force. We shall kill and capture you wholesale, spill men's blood and reduce the poor and the women to slavery.' He absolutely refused to grant them an amnesty, and their response was without bravura; they feared the consequences of a sudden decision, and communicated their fear. They said: 'If we must despair of your mercy and fear your power and lose all hope of your magnanimity, and if we are sure that there is no escape or way out, no peace or safety, no grace or generosity, then we shall seek death, and shall fight like men who sell their lives dearly. We shall face life with death, and advance like men going with bowed heads to perdition; we shall hurl ourselves like men who rush into the attack expecting instant death, we shall cast ourselves into the fire, but we shall not bring about our ruin and dishonour at our own hand. No one will be wounded before he has first wounded ten men himself, no one will shake hands with death before he has been seen to stave off destruction with open hands. We shall burn the houses and pull down the Dome, and leave to you the shame of reducing us to slavery. We shall tear up the Rock and leave you to enjoy the grief of losing it; we shall kill every Muslim prisoner in our hands, and we have thousands, since it is well known that each one of us spurns dishonour and honours his reputation. As for our possessions, we shall destroy them rather than hand them over, and as for our sons, we shall be quick to slay them; you shall not find us slow to do it. What advantage do you gain from this ungenerous spirit of negation, you who would only lose everything by such a gain? What delusions are born of the hope of success, when only peace will repair the evil! How many men, forced to make a journey in the dark, have wandered from the path in the gloom of night before the dawn appeared!'

Then the Sultan called a council meeting and sent for the leaders of his victorious hosts, consulting with them on the question, discussing with them in secret and in the open. He begged them to reveal to him their innermost thoughts and to display their hidden opinions; he wanted to light the spark in them, he asked to know their minds, he beguiled them into pronouncing the best solution and conferred with them on the most profitable peace treaty. 'We have been offered a chance,' he said, 'of which we should take the best advantage. The result that we begged God to secure for us is ours. If we let it go it will not return; if it slips away we shall never be able to seize it again.' And they said: 'God has reserved good fortune for you, and has elected you to this (His) worship. Your counsel is just, your judgment pursues the victory we have been looking for. Your commanding power brings together the scattered advantages and the means by which we might achieve success. The advice of every one of us to you in this situation is to pluck the fruits of victory.' So after repeated requests and consultations and messages and importunings and intercessions an amount was fixed that satisfied us and would act as a weighty caution, for which they were to ransom themselves and their possessions and save their men, women and children. Under the treaty, at the end of forty days whoever was unable to pay what he owed or refused to pay it was to become our slave by right and come into our possession. The tax was ten *dinar* for each man, five for a woman and two for a boy or girl. Ibn Barzān and the Patriarch and the Grand Masters of the Temple and the Hospital stood guarantee, and Ibn Barzān gave 30,000 *dinar* for the poor, fulfilling his word faithfully and without default. Every man who paid left his house in safety, never to return to live there again.

Once the tax had been fixed they surrendered the city on Friday 27 rajab/2 October, surrendering it under duress like ill-gotten gains rather than a legitimate deposit. There were more than 100,000 persons in the city, men, women and children. The gates were closed upon them all, and representatives appointed to make a census and demand the sum due. An amīr or representative was appointed to each gate, to keep count of those coming and going; those who paid, went out, while those who did not settle their debt remained prisoners within. If this money had been kept in the proper way the public treasury would have received a large share of it, but there was great negligence and widespread peculation, and anyone who paid a bribe was allowed to get out, for the officials strayed from the path of honesty to accept bribes. Some people were let down from the walls on ropes, some carried out hidden in luggage, some changed their clothes and went out dressed as (Muslim) soldiers, and some had the benefit of exemption, from an authority whom no one could disobey.

There was in Jerusalem a Greek princess who became a nun and sought the consolations of Christian worship. Her ardour therein comforted her in her misfortunes and she clung tenaciously to her faith. Her tearful sighs rose up on high and her tears fell like rain from a cloud. She held an exalted position and had wealth, possessions, servants, furnishings and a train of followers. The Sultan allowed her and hers to go free and to carry off all her wealth in bags and boxes. She went cheerfully, even though her heart wept for sadness.

Again, the wife of an imprisoned King, the daughter of King Amalric[1] lived near Jerusalem with all her serving women, domestics and handmaidens. She too left unhindered, with all her band of followers and all she needed to support the whole company. Also the Princess, daughter of Philip and mother of Humphrey,[2] was exempted from payment, and her wealth and treasure left untouched. The ruler of al-Bira begged to be allowed to free about 500 Armenians who, he said, came from his country and had come to Jerusalem for religious reasons. Muzaffar ad-Din ibn 'Ali Kuchūk claimed about 1,000 on the ground that they came from Edessa, and the Sultan granted their release as he desired.

The Sultan had set up a certain number of offices, each manned by a certain number of Egyptian and Syrian officials. Anyone who received a receipt for a completed payment from one of these officials could go free with those who were ransomed on exhibition of his receipt to the officials and employees at the gate. A person whose word I do not doubt said that he was in one of those offices and saw how things were done; often they would write a receipt for someone whose money went into their own pockets, and their deceit went undiscovered. They were conspirators, not real employees of the public treasury, which they defrauded of the wealth and profits that should have come to it; ill-gotten gains! In spite of all this the State treasury gained 100,000 *dinar*, and the rest of the population remained as prisoners in servitude, awaiting the time when the prescribed

[1] Queen Sibylla.

[2] Stephanie, daughter of Philip of Milly, widow of Reynald of Châtillon and mother of Humphrey of Toron.

period expired and they would still be unable to pay the required sum.

THE DAY OF CONQUEST, 17 RAJAB

By a striking coincidence the date of the conquest of Jerusalem was the anniversary of the Prophet's ascension to heaven. Great joy reigned for the brilliant victory won, and words of prayer and invocation to God were on every tongue. The Sultan gave an audience to receive congratulations, and received the great amīrs and dignitaries, sufis and scholars. His manner was at once humble and majestic as he sat among the lawyers and scholars, his pious courtiers. His face shone with joy, his door was wide open, his benevolence spread far and wide. There was free access to him, his words were heard, his actions prospered, his carpet was kissed, his face glowed, his perfume was sweet, his affection all-embracing, his authority intimidating. His city radiated light, his person emanated sweetness, his hand was employed in pouring out the waters of liberality and opening the lips of gifts; the back of his hand was the *qibla* of kisses[1] and the palm of his hand the *Ka'ba* of hope.

Sweet was it for him to be victorious; his throne seemed as if surrounded by a lunar halo. Qur'anic reciters sat there reciting and admonishing in the orthodox tradition. Poets stood up to declaim and to demand, banners advanced to be displayed, pens scribbled to spread the joyful news, eyes wept with great joy, hearts felt too small to contain their joy at the victory, tongues humbled themselves in invocations to God. The secretaries prepared long and ornate dispatches; eloquent stylists, both prolix and concise, tightened up or opened out their style. I could not compare my pen to anything but the collector of the honey of good news,[2] nor liken my words to anything other than the

[1] The direction of worship, see p. 152, n. 3.

[2] Here begins an auto-panegyric of the pen-virtuoso, the secretary who faithfully transmits his sovereign's will.

messengers of the divine graces, nor make my pen run except to apply itself to letters, to accompany virtue, divulge benefits, give widespread accounts and lengthy divulgence of superiority; for its arguments are long, even if its length is short, its words make it powerful although in itself its power to alarm is small, it reveals its master as well-fed although it itself is thin, it makes the army's weight felt, although it is light itself, by making clear the brilliance of the white star in the darkness of inky night, by revealing the splendour of light from the path of the shadow, by sending out decrees of death or reward, commands to bind or loose, by opposing or yielding, enslaving or freeing, promising and holding to it, enriching and impoverishing, breaking and mending, wounding and healing. It is indeed the pen that brings armies together, elevates thrones, alarms the confident and gives confidence to the discouraged, raises up the stumbler and causes the upright to stumble, sets the army against the enemy for the benefit of friends. Thus with my quills I gave good news to the four quarters of the earth, and with the prodigies of my pen I expressed the marvels of memorable events; I filled the towers with stars[1] and the caskets with pearls. This joyful news spread far and wide, bringing perfume to Rayy and to the evening conversation at Samarkand;[2] it was welcomed with enthusiasm and its sweetness surpassed candied fruits and sugar. The world of Islām was ready and adorned for a festival to celebrate the fall of Jerusalem. Her merits were illustrated and described and the duty to visit her explained and specified to everyone.

THE CONDITION OF THE FRANKS ON THEIR DEPARTURE FROM JERUSALEM

The Franks began selling their possessions and taking their

[1] A pun on the meanings of *burj:* 'tower, fortress' and 'sign of the Zodiac'.

[2] Here too there is an untranslatable play on the sound and meaning of the words: the sense is that the news cheered even the Persian and Central Asian Muslims.

precious things out of safe-keeping to sell them for nothing in the market of abjection. People made bargains with them and bought the goods at very low prices. They sold things worth more than ten *dinar* for less than one and were forced to put together all that they could find of their scattered possessions. So they scavenged in their own churches, stripped them of their ornaments and carried off candelabra and vases of gold and silver, gold and silken curtains and draperies. They broke open and emptied the boxes in the churches[1] and took from the storage chests the treasures they contained. The Grand Patriarch gathered up all that stood above the Sepulchre, the gold plating and gold and silver artifacts, and collected together the contents of the Church of the Resurrection, precious things of both metals and of the two sorts of fabric. Then I said to the Sultan: 'These are great riches, their value is quite clearly 200,000 *dinar*; free exit is permitted to personal property but not to that of churches and convents; do not allow these rascals to keep this in their grasp.' But he replied: 'If we interpret the treaty to their disadvantage they will accuse us of breaking faith and of being ignorant of the true essence of the thing. I prefer to make them obey the letter of the treaty, so that they are then unable to accuse the Believers of breaking their word, but will tell others of the benefits we have bestowed upon them.' So they left the heavy objects and carried away the most precious and the lightest, and shook from their hands the dust of their heritage and the sweepings of their 'dung-heap'.[2]

Most of them went to Tyre, to swell shadow with shadow. About 15,000 were unable to pay the tax, and slavery was their lot; there were about 7,000 men who had to accustom themselves to an unaccustomed humiliation, and whom slavery split up and dispersed as their buyers scattered through the hills

[1] The 'boxes' appear in the Arabic only for the sake of alliteration; the author is not referring explicitly to poor-boxes and the like.

[2] The Holy Sepulchre, see p. 148, n. 1.

and valleys. Women and children together came to 8,000 and were quickly divided up among us, bringing a smile to Muslim faces at their lamentations. How many well-guarded women were profaned, how many queens were ruled, and nubile girls married, and noble women given away, and miserly women forced to yield themselves, and women who had been kept hidden stripped of their modesty, and serious women made ridiculous, and women kept in private now set in public, and free women occupied, and precious ones used for hard work, and pretty things put to the test, and virgins dishonoured and proud women deflowered, and lovely women's red lips kissed, and dark women prostrated, and untamed ones tamed, and happy ones made to weep! How many noblemen took them as concubines, how many ardent men blazed for one of them, and celibates were satisfied by them, and thirsty men sated by them, and turbulent men able to give vent to their passion. How many lovely women were the exclusive property of one man, how many great ladies were sold at low prices, and close ones set at a distance, and lofty ones abased, and savage ones captured, and those accustomed to thrones dragged down!

When Jerusalem was purified of the filth of the hellish Franks and had stripped off her vile garments to put on the robe of honour, the Christians, after paying their tax, refused to leave, and asked to be allowed to stay on in safety, and gave prodigious service and worked for us with all their might, carrying out every task with discipline and cheerfulness. They paid 'the tax for protection permitted to them, humbly'.[1] They stood ready to accept whatever might be inflicted on them, and their affliction grew as they stood waiting for it. Thus they became in effect tribute-payers, reliant upon (Muslim) protection; they were used and employed in menial tasks and in their position they accepted these tasks as if they were gifts.

[1] Qur'ān IX, 29, according to F. Rosenthal's interpretation.

SALADIN'S GOOD WORKS IN JERUSALEM, AND THE EVIL WORKS THAT HE EFFACED

When Saladin accepted the surrender of Jerusalem he ordered the *mihrāb*[1] to be uncovered, and issued a decisive command to that effect. The Templars had built a wall before it, reducing it to a granary and, it was said, a latrine, in their evil-minded hostility. East of the *qibla* they had built a big house and another church. Saladin had the two structures removed and unveiled the bridal face of the *mihrāb*. Then he had the wall in front of it taken down and the courtyards around it cleared so that the people coming on Friday should have plenty of room. The pulpit was erected, the cleaned *mihrāb* exposed to the light of day again and the structures between the columns demolished. The spaces created were carpeted with deep carpets instead of matting, candelabra were hung, readings of the revealed text given, and thus truth triumphed and error was cancelled out. The Qur'ān was raised to the throne and the Testaments cast down. Prayer-mats were laid out and the religious ceremonies performed in their purity; the canonic prayers were heard and pious orations given continually; benedictions were scattered and sorrow was dispersed. The mists dissolved, the true directions came into view, the sacred verses were read, the standards raised, the *adhān* spoken and the clappers silenced,[2] the muezzins were there and not the priests, corruption and shame ceased, and men's minds and breaths became calm again. The propitious stars rose and the unpropitious set, faith made a stranger's return to her natural home, virtue was to be found once more at its natural centre. The Qur'anic readers arrived, the official prayers were read, the ascetics and pious men congregated,

[1] The *mihrāb* (niche marking the direction of prayer) of the Masjid al-Aqsa, to which the whole of this description applies. Compare Ibn al-Athīr.

[2] The *adhān* is the Muslim call to prayer, and the wooden clapper was the eastern Christians' equivalent of a bell.

with the great saints and the 'pillars'.[1] The Unique One was adored and the adorers proclaimed his unity. They joined in groups to pray and prostrate themselves, humbling themselves and beating their breasts, dignitaries and ascetics, judges and witnesses, zealots and combatants in the Holy War, standing and sitting, keeping vigil and committed to prayer by night, visitors and ambassadors. The pulpit raised its voice, the preacher expounded his truths; the crowd met and surged in, the resurrection and the supreme unity was celebrated. The traditionists recited, the holy orators comforted men's souls, the scholars disputed, the lawyers discussed, the narrators narrated, the traditionists transmitted canonic traditions. The spiritual guides performed pious exercises, the pious ascetics acted as guides, the worshippers adored God with devotion, the sincere devotees lifted their prayers to heaven. The dispensers of indulgences(?) were zealously prodigal, the commentators epitomized, the epitomizers commented, the virtuous assembled, the preachers stood before the throng. There were many candidates to lead the ritual prayer, successful men, famous for eloquence, distinguished for their seriousness; all were men who aspired to this grade and had given courses in preaching; authors of amazing perception and stylists of splendid eloquence, well-suited to the tasks of producing well-shaped discourses, reciters of original and superior flights of eloquence. There were some among them who offered me their sermons[2] and asked me to nominate them, each desiring his worth to be the most valued and to succeed in his undertaking, so that his desire might be fulfilled before he died. Each one stretched out his neck to get what he wanted and sweated with ardour to achieve it; they

[1] Strictly 'tent-pegs' or 'tent-poles': a title of one of the grades in the hierarchy of Muslim mystics and saints. In the same way we have translated *al-Abdāl*, literally 'the substitutes', as 'the great saints'.

[2] I.e. 'they offered themselves to me as preacher', asking the Sultan's secretary for his influential support and intercession. This whole episode of anxious rivalry and competition for the post is full of lively wit in spite of the literary affectations with which the author has clothed it.

were all prepared and on the alert, they solicited supporters and recommendations, sought audience and begged, searched out intercessions and put them into motion. Each had put on his dignity and made his clothing worthy of the occasion; each tried to play the game astutely and raised his eyes to that supreme position. But the Sultan still made neither appointments nor explanations, neither nominated nor promulgated. Some said: 'If I could preach the sermon on the first Friday, I should obtain the greatest favour! If I had the luck to achieve that, I should not care who came after me. . . .' When Friday 4 sha'bān arrived, people began to ask the Sultan to appoint a preacher; the Great Mosque filled with people, the meeting-places were crowded, eyes and ears were alerted, men wept with the strength of their emotions, stupendous marvels appeared to adorn this ceremony and the splendour of its beauty, voices were raised in deepest joy, as men clothed themselves in the mantle of delight. The courts were packed with the people gathered there, eyes fixed, thoughts ranging. People said: 'This is a noble day, a universal blessing, a high solemnity, a day in which prayers are heard, benedictions are profuse, tears are poured out and failings are pardoned, the negligent rouse themselves and the diligent permit themselves to give advice. Blessed is the man who has lived long enough to see this day on which Islām has arisen and taken wing! Beautiful is this crowd here present, this pure company, this victorious community, noble this victory of an-Nasir, this stock of Islām, this profession of Abbasid loyalty,[1] this Ayyubid kingdom, Saladin's dynasty! Is there anywhere in Islām an assembly more noble than this that God, by His help, has done the honour of allowing to obey Him in this way?' They discussed who would preach the sermon and who would be appointed to the office and to whom it should be entrusted, and discussed it openly and

[1] Saladin, strictly orthodox, maintained his theoretical subjection to the Abbasid Caliphate, and destroyed the heretical Fatimid Caliphate in Egypt.

by allusion. Standards were raised high, the pulpit was draped with gorgeous cloths, voices were lifted, groups assembled, throngs crowded together, waves beat upon one another, the devotees made the uproar that 'pilgrims at 'Árafa' make,[1] until the hour arrived at which the sun began to set, the midday equilibrium failed and the call to prayer rang out, and the people thronged together. Then the Sultan with his rescript named the preacher, making his choice known after mature consideration. He ordered the Qadi Muhyi ad-Din Abu l-Ma'ali Muhammad ibn Zaki ad-Din Ali al-Qúrashi to ascend the pulpit steps, causing by his choice the foreheads of the other candidates to break out into sweat. I myself presented him with a black robe of honour, the Caliph's honorific gift, so that he had, in perfection, the honour of the grace bestowed on him and gained by him. He mounted the staircase as he was told, and was well received. The sides of the pulpit shook, and the assembly rose from height to height of enthusiasm. He addressed them and they listened, he spoke and they were silent, he was eloquent and expressive, fluent and ornate, unsurpassed and marvellous, concise and diffuse; he exhorted in his double sermon and preached in his double address. He explained the significance of Jerusalem and its holiness, of the Masjid al-Aqsa from its foundation, of its purification after profanation, of having reduced their clappers to silence and expelled their priests. He prayed for the Caliph and the Sultan and concluded with the words of God: 'God commands good and the doing of good.' Then he came down and prayed at the *mihrāb*, and began the 'In the name of God' that begins the first sura of the Qur'ān,[2] leading the whole community in prayer. Thus perfect mercy fell from heaven and absolute grace was given. When prayers were over the people dispersed in conspicuous cor-

[1] 'Arafa, near Mecca, is a stopping place for the Pilgrimage where the pilgrims camp and stand in worship from noon to sunset.

[2] The 'Mother of the Qu'rān', called the first sura or *fātiha* (opening), which begins with the eulogy 'In the name of God, the merciful, the forgiving'.

diality; the general consensus was established and the analogical reasoning began.[1] A seat for homilies was set before the *qibla* in order that some distinguished person could inaugurate it. There sat Zain ad-Din Abu l-Hasan 'Ali ibn Naja and advised those who feared and those who hoped, the fortunate and the distressed, those destined for damnation and those on the way to salvation. He intimidated those endowed with reason with apt arguments and dispatched the doubters' gloom with the light of his pious exhortation, brought every pious warning to bear on the sleepers to waken them, to incite wrath for the wicked, tenderness for friends and harshness for the enemies of God. The cries of men weeping, the babble of lamentation, rose up far and near; hearts melted and cares were lightened, cries rose up and tears fell down. Sinners repented, the wicked were converted, penitents groaned, those who had turned to God lamented for themselves. Brilliant mystic ecstasies and sweet revelations occurred, prayers rose on high, supplications were heard, examples of divine love were collated and many blessings of divine providence were confirmed. The Sultan prayed in the Dome of the Rock amid throngs of believers who occupied the whole extent of the atrium, the whole community supplicating God to continue their victories. To him were turned the faces raised to the *qibla*; hands were raised to God and prayers went up to heaven for him. Saladin also appointed a preacher to a permanent post in the Masjid al-Aqsa.

A DESCRIPTION OF THE SACRED ROCK —GOD PRESERVE IT!

As for the Rock, the Franks built over it a church and an altar, so that there was no longer any room for the hands that wished to seize the *báraka*[2] from it or for the eyes that longed to see it.

[1] The 'consensus' of scholars and 'analogical reasoning' in establishing a judicial ruling are two of the basic principles of Muslim law.

[2] The healthful influence flowing from a sacred person or object.

They had adorned it with images and statues, set up dwellings there for monks and made it the place for the Gospel, which they venerated and exalted to the heights. Over the place of the (Prophet's holy) foot they set an ornamented tabernacle with columns of marble, marking it as the place where the Messiah had set his foot; a holy and exalted place, where flocks of animals, among which I saw species of pig,[1] were carved in marble. But the Rock, the object of pilgrimage, was hidden under constructions and submerged in all this sumptuous building. So the Sultan ordered that the veil should be removed, the curtain raised, the concealments taken away, the marble carried off, the stones broken, the structures demolished, the covers broken into. The Rock was to be brought to light again for visitors and revealed to observers, stripped of its covering and brought forward like a young bride. He wanted the pearl extracted from its shell, the full moon brought from behind the clouds, the prison torn down, the condemned ransomed, its beauty revealed, its blessed aspect allowed to shine, its true face made clear, its genuine honour brought to light, its fine state restored, its high honour and standing brought back. Surely it is something whose beauty consists in being unadorned, whose nakedness is clothing and whose clothing is nakedness. It was restored to its former state and the outstanding splendour of its beauty was brought into the open. Before the conquest only a small part of the back of it was exposed, and the Unbelievers had cut it about shamefully; now it appeared in all its beauty, revealed in the loveliest of revelations. Candelabra gleamed upon it, light on light, and over it was placed an iron grille.

Even up to this day concern for its adornment has not come to an end, but still grows. The Sultan appointed an imām for the Dome of the Rock; one of the finest readers of the Qur'ān, a man of the highest eloquence, clarity of voice, reputation for

[1] Romanesque animal carvings (on capitals, bas-reliefs?); the pigs may really have been there, or the author may be referring to the Christians.

religious piety and knowledge of the seven—no, of the ten Qur'anic readings,[1] and one who breathed the sweetest odour of sanctity. He gave him money and satisfaction and the benefit of his favour in the office assigned to him. He gave him a house and a garden as a pious endowment to his office, and conferred copious benefits upon him. He had brought to the Dome of the Rock and the *mihrāb* of al-Aqsa complete copies, portions and venerated sections of the Qur'ān, now raised up on their lecterns and placed on their shelves in view of the visitors. What is more he set up for the Rock in particular and Jerusalem in general custodians to keep it all in good condition. He nominated only men of piety and devotion, dedicated to the worship of God. O the glorious nights there, the crowds assembled, the great candles blooming, conspicuous humility, devoted contrition, the tears of the pious falling fast, the hearts of the devotees glowing in their breasts. Here was every friend of God who venerated his Lord and hoped for blessing and bounty from him, and every poor, ill-clad, obscure wretch who, if he swore an oath in God's name, carried it out, everyone who passed the night in prayer and exalted the divine truth and exposed it to view, everyone who held regular, intoned recitals of the Qur'ān, who drove out the devil and convicted him of falsity, who was well known in the mornings for his religious exercises and familiar by night for his recital of the offices and his prayers. O happy day for this sanctuary, when the angels moved against its invaders and the sun reached it again with its light and its blooms, and hearts brought their secrets to it, and sinners cast down their burden of sin there, and the dawn of every day begged it as a gift to reveal itself! O victorious one who undertook to purify it, O pure one who sought to bring it back into the light!

The Franks had cut pieces from the Rock, some of which

[1] Readings of the Sacred Book, handed down in seven or more slightly differing versions.

they had carried to Constantinople and Sicily and sold, they said, for their weight in gold, making it a source of income. When the Rock reappeared to sight the marks of these cuts were seen and men were incensed to see how it had been mutilated. Now it is on view with the wounds it suffered, preserving its honour for ever, safe for Islām, within its protection and its fence. This was all done after the Sultan left and after an ordered pattern of life had been established. Saladin also had the *mihrāb* of al-Aqsa lined with marble in a magnificent and splendid manner,[1] and the Ayyubid sovereigns vied with each other in the liberality of the good works they performed here, assuring themselves of the love of men's hearts and the gratitude of their tongues. Not one of them but has showered largesse and benefits upon it to the heights of his powers, illuminating and glorifying it, ornamenting and beautifying it, tending and adorning it, enriching and providing for it, perfecting and completing it, preferring and patronizing it. Thus al-Malik al-'Adil Saif ad-Din Abu Bakr[2] had works of art executed for it worthy of the deepest gratitude, and increased its resources with copious benefits, gracious and conspicuous concessions and praiseworthy generosity, with the virtuous acts he was well known for and the meritorious service that ensured its success. Al-Malik al-Muzaffar Taqi ad-Din 'Umar[3] performed there every deed of universal and widespread munificence, with prohibitions and commands, constructions and restorations. Among his laudable acts and famous deeds of generosity was his appearance one day at the Dome of the Rock with a band of noble princes of his house carrying rose-water and money for charity and public donation. He seized the opportunity to perform this original act of virtue, taking water and sprinkling the courts and colonnades with his own hand,

[1] The commemorative inscription, still in position, records for posterity the great Sultan's names.

[2] Saladin's brother (Saphadin), Sultan of Egypt and Syria until 1218.

[3] Saladin's nephew, ruler of Hamāt (1178–91).

washing them several times with water until they were clean. After the water he sprinkled the place with rose-water, so that the courts were impregnated with the fragrance; thus he washed the walls and cleaned the pavements. Then he called for censers of perfume and perfumed the mosque, and the believers breathed in all this sweetness, entirely against the will of the enemy. Nor did he and his followers cease for the whole of that day purifying that blessed precinct until they were sure that it was purified, that its sweetness was clear and its cleanness pleasing, and that no one could contemplate it without admiring it. Then he distributed the money to the deserving and was proud to surpass even generous men in his expenditure. And al-Malik al-Afdal Nur ad-Din 'Ali[1] was the cause of all shining light, pious generosity, glowing liberality, prosperous grace, pure munificence and sweet heady perfume, extraordinary gifts and unimaginable generosity, unusual largesse and conspicuous support. Thus he performed deeds that have immortalized his fine face and caused tongues to speak his praise, he poured blessings on this sanctuary and spread deep carpets, guided and gave, gave again, illumined and endowed, poured out generosity and broke the seal of liberality, and emptied his purse to the bottom so that we believed that his money was exhausted and had failed completely.

More will be said later about the wall of Jerusalem built by him and of the moats he dug, but he was already unsurpassable for his amazing acts of generosity and bounty, in which no one could possibly equal him, and in which no one could dominate the lists but he. Finally, al-Malik al-'Azīz 'Uthmān;[2] his beneficence was a source of strength to the Faith; when he returned to Egypt after having been present at the conquest and the victory he left his whole arsenal of arms to Jerusalem, not thinking to order me to take it away after he returned to Egypt. There

[1] Saladin's son and his successor in Syria (1186–96).

[2] Another of Saladin's sons and his successor in Egypt (1193–98).

were mounds of money, mountains of baggage, ample provisions, defensive weapons, great coats of mail, sharp swords, helmets and casques, lances and javelins, spears and missiles,[1] chargers and lances, ballistas and bows, Yemenite, Indian and Yazanite lances, lances from Rudaina and Mashrafite swords,[2] stockades and palisades, shields and lances, iron spears and Macedonian sarrisas, ordnance, multiple and flame-throwing ballistas, tubes of naphtha and stonebreakers, equipment for breaching walls and every other form of military gear. The city was reinforced with this arsenal and its defences made secure. In addition, one of the conditions of the surrender was that the Franks should leave us their horses and harnesses, and should leave the city without waiting for the rest to exhaust the time limit for paying the ransom. In this way Jerusalem acquired ample munitions and had no need of help (from outside).

CONCERNING THE ORATORY OF DAVID AND OTHER NOBLE SANCTUARIES. THE CHURCHES ARE SUPPRESSED AND 'MADRASAS' INSTITUTED

The Oratory of David outside the Masjid al-Aqsa was in a fortified stronghold near the city gate. It was set up on high in a commanding position, and was used by the governor. The Sultan took charge of its restoration and established there an imām, muezzins and guards. It is a centre for the pious, the goal of visitors morning and evening. It was Saladin who gave it new life and beauty and enabled visitors to enjoy it. As well as this, he gave orders for all the mosques to be renovated and all the sanctuaries to be guarded, and for the goals aimed at to be achieved under happy auspices, and for the water to be purified

[1] *Qanabil* now means 'bombs', but must then have referred to some other sort of arms or projectiles that we cannot identify more closely.

[2] Yazanite lances and those from Rudaina were highly prized by the ancient Arabs, as were Mashrafite swords from the Syrian hinterland.

for the benefit of travellers and pilgrims. The place where this fortress was built had been the house of David and Solomon (God's blessing on both of them), where people went to find them. Al-Malik al-'Adil had encamped in the Church of Zion and his troops were at its gates. The Sultan's household, pious scholars and men of virtue, spoke to him about establishing a *madrasa* for Shafi'ite lawyers[1] and a convent for sufis; he set aside for the use of the *madrasa* the church dedicated to Saint John near the Gate of the Tribes, and for the convent the Patriarch's house near the Church of the Resurrection. He endowed both liberally, thus benefiting both these communities. He also set aside sites for *madrasas* for the various (other) communities, to add to the benefits they had already received. He had the Church of the Resurrection closed to Christian visitors even as a refuge. Many discussions were held with him about its fate; some advised him to demolish it and abolish all trace of it, making it impossible to visit, removing its statutes, driving away its errors, extinguishing its lights, destroying its Testaments, eliminating its false allurements, declaring its affirmations to be lies. 'When its buildings are destroyed,' they said, 'and it is razed to the ground, and its sepulchre opened and destroyed, and its fires spent and extinguished, and its traces rubbed out and removed, and its soil ploughed up, and the Church scattered far and wide, then the people will cease to visit it, and the longings of those destined to damnation will no longer turn to seeing it, whereas if it is left standing the pilgrimage will go on without end.' But the majority said: 'Demolishing and destroying it would serve no purpose, nor would it prevent the infidels from visiting it or prevent their having access to it. For it is not the building as it appears to the eyes but the home of the Cross and the Sepulchre that is the object of

[1] The *madrasa* is an advanced school of theology and Islamic law. The first to be established in Jerusalem was the Shafi'ite because this was the chief school of law in Egypt and Syria, but the Sultan also made provision for the others (Malikite, Hanafite and Hanbalite), if this is what is meant by the 'communities' referred to a few lines on.

worship. The various Christian races would still be making pilgrimages here even if the earth had been dug up and thrown into the sky. And when 'Umar, prince of the believers, conquered Jerusalem in the early days of Islām, he confirmed to the Christians the possession of the place, and did not order them to demolish the building on it.'

CHAPTER THREE

The character of Conrad of Montferrat, saviour of Tyre and moving spirit of the Third Crusade, impressed itself upon the minds of contemporary Muslim historians more deeply than any apart from that of Richard of England. Here Ibn al-Athīr describes his adventurous arrival at Tyre and reproaches Saladin, perhaps justifiably, for not attacking the city with sufficient determination; the survival of Tyre made the Christian military resurgence and the siege of Acre possible.

CONRAD OF MONTFERRAT AT TYRE; SALADIN'S FRUITLESS SIEGE

(IBN AL-ATHĪR, XI, 358–9, 366–8)

When Count Raymond, Prince of Tripoli, fled from Hittīn, he stopped at Tyre, one of the strongest and best defended cities in Syria. When he saw that the Sultan had taken Tibnīn, Sidon and Beirūt he was afraid that he would decide to march on Tyre, stripped as it was at that moment of troops to defend it, while he was without the means of resisting him, so he left and went to Tripoli. Thus Tyre lay open and undefended from the Muslims, and if Saladin had attacked it first, before Tibnīn and elsewhere, he would have taken it easily. But he thought that its natural defences would make it difficult to capture and wanted first to secure its surrounding territories in order to take it more easily, and this was why it survived unconquered, this being God's will. It happened that a Frank from Outremer called 'the Marquis'—God damn him!—set out by sea with great wealth on a pilgrimage and trading mission, unaware of the disaster that had befallen the Franks. When he entered the harbour at Acre his suspicions were aroused by the absence of the manifestations of joy, ringing of bells and so on, that usually met the arrival in port of a Frankish vessel, and also by the style of dress of the people there. He dropped anchor, uncertain what might have happened. The wind had fallen. Al-Malik al-Afdal for his part sent his men out in a small boat to see who it was and what he wanted. When the boat came alongside the Marquis, not recognizing it as one of their own, asked what had been happening, and the men on board told him of the Frankish defeat, the fall of Acre and other cities, and informed him at the same time that Tyre and Ascalon and certain other towns were still in Frankish hands, giving him the full details. Since the lack of wind prevented his moving the Marquis sent the messenger back with a request for permission to enter the city in safety with his merchandise and money. This was granted, but he sent the messenger back again and again, each time with new requests, to gain time until the wind should rise and he could use it to escape. In the course of these comings and goings the wind began to blow again and he at once set sail for Tyre. Al-Malik al-Afdal sent a galley after him in pursuit but it failed to catch him and he reached Tyre, where a great number of Franks was gathered. For when Saladin took each town, Acre, Beirūt and the others mentioned above, he had allowed the populations to leave freely, and they had all come to Tyre. So the place was thronged, but it lacked a leader to unite it and a commander to lead it in battle. The people were not warriors, and were talking of making a treaty with Saladin and offering to surrender the town to him when the Marquis arrived and dissuaded them from such an act and gave them new hope by promising to defend the city himself. He distributed the money he had with him on condition that the city and its territory belonged to him and no one else. When they agreed he made them swear to it, and after that took up residence there and governed the city. He was a devil incarnate in his ability to govern and defend a town, and a man of extraordinary courage.

His first act was to strengthen the city's defences: he renewed the entrenchments, set the walls in order, and increased the armaments. The citizens agreed to defend the city and to fight for it.

When Saladin had taken Jerusalem he remained outside the city until 25 sha'bān, dealing with its re-organization, establishing convents and *madrasas*. He set up the Shafi'ite madrasa in the house of the Hospitallers; a beautiful building. When he had finished his work in Jerusalem he moved on to Tyre, where many Franks had gathered and of which the Marquis had become lord and governor, ruling it very well and reinforcing its defences out of all recognition. Saladin got as far as Acre and stayed there for a few days, and when the Marquis heard of his arrival there he immediately set about repairing the walls of Tyre and deepening the moats, and established a link between the sea on one side of the city and on the other, so that the city was like an island in the midst of the water, inaccessible and impregnable.

Leaving Acre, Saladin reached Tyre on 9 ramadān/13 November 1187 and stopped beside a stream within sight of the city, waiting for the rest of his army to catch up with him. On 22 ramadān he marched on and encamped on a hill close to the walls of Tyre so that he could follow the fighting. He ordered that battalion whose turn it was for action to make ready and arranged that each detachment should be on duty in turn so that the defenders would be under continuous attack. But the area from which they fought was small and only a small band of those within the walls was necessary to defend it, the more so because of the trenches running from sea to sea so that not even a bird, so to speak, could fly over the city. Tyre was like a hand stretched out into the sea, with an arm joining it to the mainland but with sea all around it. The attackers could only advance along that arm of land. The Muslims mounted an attack with catapults, ballistas and siege-engines. Saladin's own family took their turn in the battle: his son al-Afdal, his other son az-Zāhir Ghazi, his brother al-'Adil ibn Ayyūb, his nephew Taqi ad-Din; and so did the rest of the amīrs. The Franks had galleys and fire-ships with which they held the sea on either side of the isthmus along which the Muslims were attacking the city. They attacked the Muslim flanks with ballistas, which was a grave disadvantage to our armies, who were being attacked in front by the citizens and on either side by the soldiers posted on the galleys. The isthmus was so narrow that their arrows crossed from one side to the other. Many Muslims were wounded and killed, but they failed to gain the fort.

Saladin ordered the ten Egyptian galleys lying at Acre to sail to Tyre with their crews and soldiers and all their equipment. These prevented the Tyrian ships from coming out to attack the Muslims, who were then able to come up under the fort and attack it by land and sea. Victory was within their grasp. But destiny decreed that an accident should befall them. Five Muslim galleys were guarding the port one night, to cut off the enemy's lines of communication; they were commanded by 'Abd as-Salām al-Mághribi, a brave and experienced man. After spending the night on the watch they felt that the dawn brought safety, and slept. Suddenly Frankish galleys bore down on them, attacked them and killed as many as they wanted, taking the rest prisoner in their ships and towing them into the port of Tyre under the eyes of the Muslims watching from the land. Some Muslims cast themselves into the sea from the captured galleys, some surviving and some drowning. Saladin ordered the rest of the galleys to Beirūt, for so small a number was not safe. The eager Franks pursued them. When the Muslims saw the entire Frankish fleet behind them they drove their ships on to the shore and escaped, leaving them there. Saladin had the ships seized and destroyed, and returned to attacking Tyre by land only, which was almost useless because of the lack of space to manœuvre. One day the Franks made a sortie and attacked the Muslims from behind their trenches. The battle raged until sunset from the early afternoon. A great and famous knight of theirs was captured after a frenzied and murderous attack on him when he fell from his horse. He was taken and killed. The situation continued for several days. Finally Saladin realized that it was going to take a long time to conquer Tyre, and withdrew. It was a habit of his to tire of a siege when a town put up a firm resistance, and to move on. Throughout the whole of this year he had never stopped for long to attack a city, but had taken them all, as we have remarked, within a few days without any trouble or difficulty. Thus when he and his advisers saw that Tyre was a problem of a different order they grew bored and decided to leave. The sole responsibility for Tyre's resistance lies with Saladin, who had sent all the Frankish forces rushing off there and reinforced them with men and money from Acre, Ascalon, Jerusalem and elsewhere, as has been described above, for he allowed them all to depart freely and sent them to Tyre, where as a result there was a concentration of Frankish knights from Palestine with their money as well as the wealth of the merchants and the others. All these defended the city and wrote to the Franks abroad asking their help. This they were promised, and were ordered to hold on to Tyre as a focus of foreign aid and a place of rescue and protection. This impressed on them all the more the need to hold firm and defend the fort. Later, God willing, we shall tell the end of the story, to show that a king should not abandon forceful action even when fate seems to be on his side. Failure accompanied by firm conduct is preferable to success acquired with feebleness and lassitude, and makes the King less to blame in men's judgment.[1]

[1] This is only one of the passages in which an ill-disguised hostility to Saladin can be seen in the Mesopotamian historian's writings, caused by his preference for the Zangid dynasty supplanted by Saladin. We shall never know what basis there was for his criticisms of Saladin's conduct of the war; Ibn al-Athīr reveals himself as a very subtle man, and one who is capable of recognizing, even perhaps in spite of himself, the greatness of Islām's champion.

When Saladin was deciding to leave he called a council of his amīrs, whose advice was confused. Some said that departure was advisable, given their heavy losses, dead and wounded, and that the troops were tired and the provisions exhausted: 'Winter is coming,' they said, 'and the goal is far from being within our reach. Let us go away and rest throughout the cold weather, and in spring let us take up the fight again against this and the enemy's other strongholds.' This was the advice given by the amīrs, as if they were afraid that Saladin would extort the taxes they owed him to finance the army if they stayed there, for the exchequer and treasury were empty, because Saladin spent everything that came into it. The other faction wanted to stay and take the city by storm. This fort was vital to the Franks, and once it had gone the Franks abroad would no longer lust after this our land, and would surrender the other territories they held without bloodshed. Saladin wavered between staying and going, and when the retreating faction saw his uncertainty they sabotaged the jobs assigned to them, in battle or with the artillery, and excused themselves by saying that their troops were discontented, that some had been sent to find provisions, forage for the animals and food for themselves, and other similar excuses, until in the end they were sitting idle and doing no fighting. So Saladin was forced to go, and left at the end of shawwāl/end of December. By the beginning of January he was at Acre, where he gave the whole army permission to return home and rest for the winter and told them to meet him there in the spring. The contingents from the East, Mosul, Syria and Egypt went home, while Saladin's bodyguard stayed in Acre. He lived in the citadel and entrusted the command of the city to 'Izz ad-Din Jurdīk, one of Nur ad-Din's great mamlūks, an honourable man whose piety was as great as his courage.

CHAPTER FOUR

The loss of Jerusalem, and the Marquis of Montferrat's courageous defence of Tyre, set in motion the Third Crusade. But the most important event of the Crusade, the long siege of Acre, began long before the arrival of Philip II Augustus and Richard of England, who simply provided the final impetus that reaped the harvest of three hard years' blockade of this Palestinian port, taken by Saladin in 1187. Note the double siege of the city, first by the Franks, and then by Saladin, from outside, of the besieging Franks. Logistic difficulties prevented Saladin from maintaining the contact he had established with the beleaguered Muslims and forced him to stand by, almost impotently, throughout the city's long agony. The accounts of the siege and the attempts to break it are full of unusual and graphic incidents, examples of which have been taken from Bahā' ad-Din, 'Imād ad-Din and Ibn al-Athīr.

THE FRANKS MARCH ON ACRE AND BESIEGE IT

(IBN AL-ATHĪR, XII, 20–6)

We have already spoken of the great concentration of Frankish troops at Tyre. The cause of this was that Saladin allowed them to depart freely from every city and fort that he took and sent them to Tyre with their possessions, women and children. This created an enormous concourse of Franks and an inexhaustable supply of money, in spite of the very heavy expenses of the siege. Here monks and priests and a crowd of Frankish knights and nobles dressed themselves in black and expressed great grief at the loss of Jerusalem. The Patriarch of Jerusalem took them with him on a journey through the Frankish domains calling on the people to help, invoking their aid and inciting them to avenge the loss of Jerusalem. Among other things, they made a picture showing the Messiah, and an Arab striking Him, showing blood on the face of Christ—blessings on Him!—and they said to the crowds: 'This is the Messiah, struck by Mahomet the prophet of the Muslims, who has wounded and killed Him.' This made a deep impression on the Franks and they flocked to the Patriarch, even the women. There were in fact in the army at Acre a certain number of women, who challenged their enemy's warriors to single combat, as we shall describe later; a man who could not himself fight put a substitute into the field or gave money to the limit of his capacity. In this way they collected immense quantities of troops and money.

A Muslim living at Hisn al-Akrād told me the following story—he was one of the garrison that had handed the fort over to the Franks a long time ago, and who then repented of having given the Franks help in attacking Muslim territory and having fought and battled at their side—this man told me that he had gone with a group of Franks from Hisn al-Akrād in four galleys to the Frankish and Greek lands beyond the sea to seek help (for the Crusade). 'Our trip', he said, 'took us at length to Rome, that great city, which we left with our galleys full of silver.' And a Frankish prisoner told me that he was his mother's only son, and their house was their sole possession, but she had sold it and used the money obtained from it to equip him to go and free Jerusalem. There he had been taken prisoner. Such were the religious and personal motives that drove the Franks on. They flocked to battle by any means they could, by land and sea, from all directions. If God had not shown his grace to Islām in the death of the German King on his way to attack Syria, as will appear later, it would have been said one day that Syria and Egypt *had once been* Muslim lands.

So their troops mustered at Tyre, which was flooded with the multitudes and their great wealth, and received constant naval reinforcements of food, arms and men from the Frankish lands, so that Tyre, within and without the walls, could no longer hold them all. At first they wanted to attack Sidon, but we have already described what happened,[1] and so they returned and agreed to move on Acre and besiege it tenaciously. They marched all their troops there, clinging as far as possible to the coast, through easy and impassable terrain, broad or narrow, while their ships, loaded with arms and ammunition, moved parallel to them by sea to support them. If they had met an insuperable obstacle they could have embarked and returned home. They left on 8 rajab (585/22 August 1189) and reached Acre at the end of the month, harassed on the way by Muslim bands attacking them and capturing stragglers.

News of their departure was brought to Saladin, who marched off to meet them. As the two armies approached one another, he consulted with his amīrs about whether they should take them by the heel and attack them on the march, or meet them face to face by taking a different route from theirs. The amīrs said: 'There is no need for us to take the trouble to follow them by their route, for the road is difficult and narrow and we could not easily take them as we want. It is better to proceed by the broader road and attack them from the rear as they approach Acre, where we will disperse them and cut their army to pieces.' Saladin realized that they preferred the easy way, and he finally acquiesced, although he was himself in favour of accompanying the Franks on their march and attacking them on route: 'If the Franks reach their destination,' he said, 'and get a firm hold of the territory, it will not be easy for us to dislodge and overcome them. It is better to attack before they reach Acre.' But they opposed him and in the end he followed their advice and took the road by Kafar Kannā, and the Franks arrived (at Acre) before them. Now Saladin had detailed a group of amīrs to contact the Franks, with instructions to accompany them on their march and harass them. The Franks dared not turn upon them, however few they were, and thus if the army had followed Saladin's advice to follow the enemy

[1] They had been driven back by Saladin in an earlier encounter.

and attack before they reached and invested Acre his aim would have been achieved and the Franks prevented from reaching the city. But when God wills something He disposes its determinant causes in conformity (with his will).

When Saladin arrived at Acre he saw that the Franks were deployed from sea to sea before the city, leaving the Muslims no way of access to it. So they took up their position facing the Franks and pitched Saladin's tent on the Tall Kaisān. His left wing extended as far as the Tall al-'Ayadiyya, his right wing to the river. The baggage was at Saffuriyya. The Sultan sent messengers to the various provinces asking for troops, which arrived from Mosul, Diyār Bakr, Sinjār and other regions of Mesopotamia. His nephew Taqi ad-Din arrived, and so did Muzaffar ad-Din ibn Zain ad-Din, Prince of Harrān and Edessa. Reinforcements reached the Muslims by land and the Franks by sea. During the time of the siege a number of encounters, great and small, took place between the two sides; pitched battles and lesser affrays occurred, apart from small skirmishes of which no record is necessary. When Saladin arrived he could not make contact with Acre until the end of rajab. He fought there until the beginning of sha'bān/half-way through September without achieving his object. The troops passed the night drawn up for battle and on the next day Saladin attacked with all his forces, completely encircling the Franks on all sides, from dawn to midday. Both sides showed an amazing obduracy. At midday Taqi ad-Din led a terrible charge against the enemy facing him on the right wing and dislodged them from their position. They fell over one another in their retreat, not pausing even to help a brother in their flight to safety with near-by companies. They joined their ranks and left half the field empty. Immediately Taqi ad-Din occupied the area they had abandoned and made contact with the city. The Muslims were able to go in and out, communications were established and the blockade of the inhabitants was broken. Saladin was able to send in all the men, munitions, money and arms he wanted, and if the Muslims had kept up the attack until nightfall they would have gained their objective, for it is the first attack that is the most terrifying. But having gained this success they wanted to rest and stop fighting. They said: 'We will attack them tomorrow morning and exterminate them.' Among the amīrs whom Saladin sent into Acre was Husām ad-Din Abu l-Haijā the Fat, one of the army's greatest generals, a Kurd from Arbela. A great many Franks were killed on this day.

ANOTHER BATTLE, AND AN ATTACK BY THE ARABS

The following day (6 sha'bān/19 September) the Muslims attacked the Franks, determined to use every effort to exterminate them. Advancing toward the Frankish lines they saw the enemy on guard and on the defensive, and repented of the slackness of their watch last night. All the Frankish positions were heavily defended, and they had begun to dig a ditch that prevented the Muslims from closing with them. The Muslims persistently offered battle, but the Franks refused either to fight or to abandon their position. So the Muslims turned back.

A band of Arabs had news that the Franks were getting through at a point on the other side to cut wood and perform other tasks; they laid an ambush at the point where the river curves, and when the Franks came out as usual they attacked and killed them all, seized their possessions and took their heads to Saladin, who gave them rewards and robes of honour.

THE PITCHED BATTLE BEFORE ACRE

After this encounter the Muslims spent the days until 20 sha'bān/3 October going down every morning and evening to offer battle to the Franks, who however refused even to leave their camp. The Franks called a council and said: 'The Egyptian army has not yet arrived and we are already menaced by Saladin; what will happen when the Egyptians come? Our best course is to confront the Muslims tomorrow in the hope of defeating them before fresh troops and reinforcements reach them.' At that time a good part of Saladin's army was elsewhere: some before Antioch, some preventing Prince Bohemond's marauding bands from raiding the province of Aleppo and some in the district of Hims, before Tripoli, also on patrol. Another party was at Tyre; a part of the Egyptian army was defending the Damietta region, Alexandria and so on, and the rest had not yet arrived, for they had taken the longer route and were delayed. All this persuaded the Franks to come out and fight the Muslims.

The following morning the Muslims were employed as usual, some in coming down to offer battle, others in their tents, others about their various activities such as visiting a friend or procuring provisions for their companions or their horses when suddenly the Franks were seen leaving their tents like a great swarm of locusts skimming over the surface of the land that they filled far and wide. They attacked the Muslim right wing, which was under the command of Saladin's nephew Taqi ad-Din. When he saw that they were heading in his direction he put himself on the defensive, advanced a little toward them and then stopped quite still. When Saladin saw this he sent a reinforcement from his own troops, for the men from Diyār Bakr and other eastern contingents were drawn up to one side of the central block of troops. When the Franks saw that the centre was only weakly guarded and that many of its men had gone to reinforce the right wing they turned toward the centre, galloping as one man. The Muslim army fled before them. Only a few stood firm, of whom many were killed for the Faith, like the amīr Mujalli ibn Marwān, and Zahīr ad-Din brother of the *faqīh* Isa, governor of Jerusalem, who combined military virtues with religious learning, and the chamberlain Khalīl al-Hakkari and other brave men, who stood firm in the fight. So there was no one left in the centre to confront the Franks, who made for the hill where Saladin's tent was, killing and plundering as they went. They killed several men close to the tent itself, among them our Shaikh Abu 'Ali ibn Rawaha al-Hámawi, a learned man and a good poet; he was the heir to martyrdom, for his ancestor 'Abdallah ibn Rawaha, a Companion of the Prophet, was killed by the Greeks at the battle of Mu'ta,[1] and this (his grandson) was slain by the Franks at the battle of Acre. So the Franks killed him and others and came down the opposite slope of the hill, slaughtering whomever they encountered. It was only by God's grace that they did not cut down Saladin's tent, for if they had the whole Muslim army would have realized how far they had got and that the centre of their own army had fled before the enemy, and this would have led to a general flight.

At this point the Franks looked behind them and saw that their reinforcements were unable to follow them, so they turned back for fear of being cut off from their companions. What held the reinforcements up was the fact that our right wing was still resisting, thus obliging a detachment of Franks to confront them, while the Muslim left wing had charged the Franks. The reinforcements, occupied with their own battle, had been unable to join the main body of troops and so had retreated to their trenches. Then our left wing charged the Franks who had reached the Sultan's tent as they were retreating, and pages from the camp attacked them impetuously. Saladin had gone back to his men when the centre had collapsed, persuading and commanding them to reorganize themselves and launch a counter-attack. When he had collected a good number of them

[1] In Transjordan in 629, when an expedition sent by Muhammad to the boundaries of his territory was surprised by the Byzantines.

around him he attacked the Franks from behind while they were engaged with our left wing. The swords of the faithful faced them on every side, and none of them escaped. Most were killed, the rest taken prisoner, among them the Grand Master of the Temple,[1] who had been captured and released once already by Saladin. Captured a second time, he was put to death. The number of dead, not counting those at sea, was 10,000, and these at Saladin's command were thrown into the river from which the Franks drew their water. Most of the dead were Frankish knights, for the infantry had not caught up with them. Among the prisoners were three Frankish women who had fought from horseback and were recognized as women only when captured and stripped of their armour. Of the Muslims who fled some returned by way of Tiberias, others crossed the Jordan and returned to their homes, others reached Damascus. If these troops had not dispersed after their flight they could have exterminated the Franks at their leisure. The rest, for their part, performed prodigies in their attack on the Franks, and all tried to reach the Franks in their camp, hoping that they would have lost heart. Suddenly they heard a cry that their goods had been pillaged. This is how it happened: at the sight of the rout our army had loaded its baggage on to pack-horses, but the rabble and the pages fell on them and looted the contents. Saladin would have liked to pursue and engage the enemy, but he saw that his men were concentrating on running here and there to collect up and reassemble their lost possessions. He issued a proclamation saying that everything that had been taken was to be brought to him, and the amount brought covered the earth: carpets and loaded bags, clothes, arms and the rest, all of which was returned to its real owners. So Saladin failed to achieve his aim on this occasion and the Franks, recovered from their fear, succeeded in re-forming battle lines from their survivors.

[1] Gerard of Ridfort, captured at Hittīn and ransomed.

SALADIN WITHDRAWS FROM THE FRANKS, WHO ARE ABLE TO RENEW THE SIEGE OF ACRE

After all those Franks had been killed the air was heavy with the smell of them and they caused infections that began to affect the health of the army. Saladin himself was ill, tormented by the colic from which he suffered from time to time. The amīrs had an audience of him and advised him to leave the area and lift his pressure on the Franks. They presented their advice in the best possible light: 'We have surrounded the Franks so closely that even if they wanted to retreat they could not. Now it would be advisable to retire and give them a chance of withdrawing and going away. If they go, we shall be rid of each other, and if they stay we can return and fight them from our old position. You are not well and are in great pain; if word got about (that you are ill) it would be the end of all of us. So our best course is to move off.' As the doctors too gave the same advice Saladin finally yielded, divining, that is, what God had decided should happen: '. . . and when God wishes evil for a people no power can avert it and no one else can protect them.'[1] So they left for Kharruba on 4 ramaḍān/16 October. The Sultan ordered the Muslims in Acre to defend themselves, with the gates shut and a guard posted, and he explained the reason for his departure.

Once he and his troops had gone the Franks felt safe and at ease there and continued to blockade Acre. They surrounded it by land from coast to coast, and used their ships to blockade it by sea as well. They began to build a trench and a revetment with earth from the trench, and took other unexpected measures. Every day Muslim outposts came up to their lines, but they neither gave battle nor moved their position, intent only on

[1] Qur'ān III, 12; another of Ibn al-Athīr's criticisms of Saladin's conduct of the war.

digging the trench and building the wall to protect themselves from Saladin when he came back to attack them. Now it was clear how well-advised Saladin had been to retire. . . . Every day the spies informed Saladin of what the Franks were doing, and revealed to him the full gravity of the situation, while he, sunk in his illness, was in no state to move in to attack. Someone advised him to send his whole army to Acre to prevent the Franks from digging the trench and building the wall and to attack them, while he stayed behind, but he said: 'If I am not there with them they will achieve absolutely nothing, and it might cause much more harm than good.' So things dragged on until he was better, and the Franks were able to take their time and do what they wanted. They consolidated and reinforced their position by all available means, while the citizens of Acre made daily sorties, attacking them and killing them outside the city walls.

THE ARRIVAL OF THE EGYPTIAN ARMY AND OF THE FLEET BY SEA

Half-way through shawwāl/at the end of November the Egyptian army arrived under the command of al-Malik al-'Adil Saif ad-Din Abu Bakr ibn Ayyūb. Hearts lifted at his arrival with his companions, bringing quantities of siege weapons, shields and wooden spears and arrows and bows, and a large body of infantry. Saladin too mustered infantry in great numbers from the Syrian provinces and decided to march them all against the enemy. After al-'Adil the Egyptian fleet arrived, commanded by the amīr Lu'lu', a brave and energetic man, a naval and military expert full of useful initiative. He appeared unexpectedly, seized a Frankish ship and plundered it, capturing a lot of goods and provisions, and sent it to Acre, whose inhabitants felt reassured and heartened by the fleet's arrival.

(BAHĀ' AD-DIN, 140–7)

On Wednesday 24 sha'bān/4 October 1189 the Frankish forces began an unexpected manœuvre, using cavalry and infantry, great and small. They were drawn up outside their tents in a central block with left and right wings. In the centre was the King, before whom the Testament was carried under a baldacchino of satin borne by four men, who advanced with it. The Frankish right wing appeared all of a sudden in front of the Muslim left wing and all of the enemy's left wing in front of our right. They occupied the tops of the hills, their furthest right at the river, their extreme left at the sea. In the Muslim army the Sultan commanded the heralds to cry out amid the troops: 'For Islām, forward the monotheist army!' They all mounted, having sold their lives in exchange for Paradise, and posted themselves before their tents. Like theirs, our army extended from the river to the sea. The Sultan had previously had the tents pitched in the order of the battle line, so that there would be no need to take up new positions when the alarm was given. Saladin was in the centre; to the right of him was his son al-Malik al-Afdal, his other son, al-Afdal's brother al-Malik az-Zahir, the Mosul regiments under Zahīr ad-Din ibn al-Bulunkari, the Diyār Bakr regiments under Qutb ad-Din ibn Nur ad-Din of Hisn Kaifā, then Husām ad-Din ibn Lajīn of Nablus, then the eunuch Qaimāz an-Najmi with his close-packed ranks linking the centre with the extreme right wing. Here, with the sea on his right, was al-Malik al-Muzaffar Taqi ad-Din with his troops. Immediately to the left of centre was Saif ad-Din 'Ali al-Mashtūb, the great Kurdish prince and general, the amīr Mujalli with his Mihranite and Hakkarite troops,[1] Mujahid ad-Din Baranqash commanding the Sinjār regiments and a band of mamlūks, then Muzaffar ad-Din ibn

[1] Kurdish tribes.

Zain ad-Din and his men, and on the extreme left wing the great Asadite mamlūks[1] like Saif ad-Din Yazkug and Arslān Bughā and the other Asadites whose valour is legendary. The centre was commanded by the *faqīh* Isa. The Sultan himself moved about among the battalions inciting them to battle and strengthening their faith in God and victory.

The Muslims and the enemy advanced when the sun was high, at about the fourth hour. This was when the enemy attacked the Muslim right, and al-Malik al-Muzaffar sent out the archers of the advance guard, who met with varied fortunes. As the enemy was pressing al-Malik al-Muzaffar fiercely in his position on the extreme right by the sea he retreated a little before them to inveigle them away from their companions and then to fall on them. When Saladin saw this he attributed it to weakness and sent a large number of battalions from the centre to his aid. So the enemy left wing retreated, and reassembled on a hill overlooking the sea, while those facing the centre saw it weakened by the loss of the troops sent to the right wing, took heart and attacked at that point, infantry and cavalry charging like one man. I myself saw the infantry advancing at the same pace as the cavalry, who did not move ahead of them —indeed, at times the infantry was in front. The brunt of the attack fell on the Diyār Bakr contingents, who being inexperienced fighters yielded before it and fled headlong in a state of panic that communicated itself to most of our right wing. The enemy pursued them as far as al-'Ayadiyya and encircled the hill; some of the enemy got up as far as Saladin's tent and killed one of his cup-bearers whom they found there. On that day Isma'il al-Mukabbis and Ibn Rawaha fell as martyrs for the Faith, God have mercy on them. Meanwhile our left wing stood firm and unshaken by the enemy charge. The Sultan moved among the battalions exhorting them with fine promises, urging them to fight for the Faith and raising the cry:

[1] I.e. bearing the name of Saladin's uncle, the general Asad ad-Din Skirkūh.

'For Islām!' With only five men beside him he moved among the battalions and through the lines. From there he returned to the bottom of the hill on which his tent was pitched. The rout of the Muslims had reached Uqhuwana on the far side of the bridge of Tiberias, and some of the men even got as far as well-guarded Damascus. The enemy cavalry followed them as far as al-'Ayadiyya, but when they saw that they had gained the hill they turned back toward their own lines. They fell upon a band of servants, mule-tenders and palfreymen who were fleeing on some of the pack-mules, and killed many of them. When they reached the top of the market-place they killed others, and some of their own men were killed in their turn, for there was a crowd of armed men there. As for those who reached Saladin's tent, they found absolutely nothing there except for the men they murdered, as we mentioned, three in all. When they saw that the Muslim left wing was standing firm they realized that it was not a total rout, and so descended the hill in the hope of regaining their own battalions.

The Sultan with a small band of men was at the bottom of the hill, rallying his men for a counter-offensive. They saw the Franks riding down the hill and wanted to attack them, but he ordered them to wait until the Franks had ridden past them on their way to find their regiments. Then the Sultan gave the signal at the top of his voice, and they rode after them and sent several of them flying. As the idea of pursuing them spread, the crowd grew until the Franks reached their regiments with a rabble snapping at their heels. When the others saw their side in flight and hordes of Muslims at their backs they assumed that all the commanders had been killed and that only this few had survived to flee. So they all took to their heels, and our left wing moved in against them. Al-Malik al-Muzaffar in his turn led his right wing to victory, and our side stood firm and cried out in its turn, flowing back to the fight from all sides. God put the devil to flight and gave victory to the Faith. Our army stayed to slaughter and kill, to strike and wound, until the escaping fugitives reached their army. Here the Muslims fell upon them even in the midst of their own tents, but some battalions, kept in reserve for fear of such a development, emerged and drove the Muslims off. Our army was now tired and sweating, so after the afternoon prayer they turned back through a sea of blood and corpses, happy and contented to their own tents. The Sultan too went back to his tent where he took counsel with his amīrs, adding up the number of losses. The number of unknown mamlūks dead was a hundred and fifty; among the famous who fell was Zahīr ad-Din, brother of the *faqīh* Isa; I saw the latter sitting and smiling while people offered their condolences and turning them aside with the words: 'This is a day of rejoicing, not of condolence!' he himself had fallen from his horse and been set back in the saddle by those near him, and several of his close friends had been killed defending him. On the same day the amīr Mujalli was killed. These were the Muslim losses. The enemy, God damn them! lost 7,000 men. I saw them being carried to the river to be thrown in, and the estimate was 7,000.

When the Muslims suffered that initial defeat and their servants saw their tents standing empty of anyone to resist them—the army was either in flight or fighting, and there was no one left behind in the tents—they believed that it was a general rout and that the enemy would loot the tents, so they began the job themselves and stripped the tents of their contents. They seized quantities of Muslim money, goods and arms, more than even defeat would have cost. When Saladin returned to his tent and saw the double damage, the looting and the flight of part of the army, he hurriedly sent written messages and messengers to bring back the fugitives and round up the disbanded soldiers. The messengers took their messages as far as the hill of Fiq, where they caught up with the fugitives and cried: 'To the counter-attack! To the Muslim recovery!' They turned back, and the Sultan gave orders that everything should be taken from the servants and assembled before his tent, even to the horses' saddle-cloths and nose-bags. There he sat, with his men about him, and commanded that if a man recognized something as his, and gave his word on it, he was to have it. He faced all these events with steadfastness and serenity, with open eyes and wisdom that did not wander blindly; he was intent on gaining merit before God and determined to bring victory to the Faith. The enemy, for their part, retired to their tents, having seen their valiant men lost and their champions destroyed.

The Sultan sent for wagons from Acre to carry the enemy dead to the river and tip them in. One of the men working on the wagons told me that there were about 4,100 Franks dead on the left wing, but he had not been able to count those from the centre and the right wing as someone else was dealing with them. After this encounter those of the enemy who were left to defend themselves shut themselves into their camp, unaffected by Muslim attacks. Of the Muslim forces, many disappeared in the flight: the only ones to return were well-known men who had much to fear (from the consequences of desertion); all the rest escaped to wherever the road led.

The Sultan collected the stolen property and restored it to its rightful owners. I happened to be there on the day when the objects were distributed to their owners, and I saw the best court of law the world has ever seen. It was Friday 23 sha'bān/6 October. After this episode, when everything was calm again, the Sultan ordered the baggage to be taken to a place called Kharruba, for fear that the stench of the corpses would make his soldiers ill. This was a place near the battlefield but further off than where they had been encamped so far. A tent was pitched for him by the baggage, and he told the outposts to stay at the site of the earlier camp. This happened on the 29th of the month. He called together the amīrs and counsellors at the end of the month, (I was among them,) and invited them to hear what he was about to say.

'In God's name,' he said, 'Praise to God and blessing to the Prophet; know that this enemy of God and of ourselves has invaded our country and seized the territory of Islām. Signs are already appearing of the victory that we shall win over them, God willing. Now they are left with very small forces, and it is our task to try at any cost to exterminate them, as a duty imposed upon us by God. You know that these are our entire forces, and that we shall have no reinforcements except for al-Malik al-'Adil who is on his way. If the enemy stay where they are and hold on until communications by sea can be reopened, they will get large reinforcements. My feeling, therefore, is that we should not hesitate to attack them. Each of you will now give his opinion about this.'

The date was 13 tishrīn according to the solar calendar (13 October). Various opinions were voiced and discussed, and they reached the conclusion that the best plan would be to withdraw with the army to Kharruba and allow the men to rest for a few days from carrying arms and the fatigue that it entailed, to gain strength and graze their horses. The men had been in the front line for fifty days, and the horses were exhausted with the fighting and the strain imposed on them. After a short rest they would recover their breath. 'Al-Malik al-'Adil will arrive and give us his advice as well as his support. We shall round up the deserters and muster the infantry so that they will be ready to face the enemy.'

The Sultan was very ill with various troubles exacerbated by the weight of the arms he bore and the constant wearing of a helmet, so he decided to follow their advice. The army was moved up to join the baggage on 3 ramadān. The Sultan moved on the same night, and his health began to improve. The troops were mustered, and waited for his brother al-Malik al-'Adil, who arrived on 10 ramadān/22 October.[1]

THE SIEGE-TOWERS ARE BURNT DOWN

(IBN AL-ATHĪR, XII, 28–30)

During the siege of Acre the Franks built three lofty wooden towers, each one sixty cubits tall. They had five floors, each crowded with soldiers. The wood for them had been brought from abroad, as a very special kind was needed for these towers. They were covered with skins, vinegar, mud and fire-resisting substances. The Franks cleared a path for their advance and brought all three up under the walls of Acre. The assault began on 20 rabī' I (587/27 April 1190). They towered over the walls, and the men inside them fought the defenders on the walls, and pushed them back, while the Franks began to fill up the moat. Thus the city was on the point of being taken by assault. The people of Acre sent a man to escape by swimming and tell Saladin what was happening, and that capture seemed imminent. The Sultan ordered his army to mount and advanced on the enemy, engaging them on all sides in fierce and unceasing combat, and endeavoured by this means to distract them from their attack on the city. The Franks divided their forces, one part to attack Saladin and the other the city, and so the pressure on Acre was relieved.

The fighting lasted for eight days on end, until the 28th of the month/5th May, when the exhaustion of both sides after eight days of continuous day and night fighting brought it to an end. The Muslims were now convinced that the Franks would take the city, seeing that the defenders could not fend off attacks from their siege-towers. They had exhausted every stratagem to no avail, and followed this by showering the towers

[1] The date is more than a month earlier than that given by Ibn al-Athīr and his source 'Imād ad-Din (half-way through shawwāl).

with Greek fire, but made no impression on them. They were convinced therefore that they were doomed, when God aided them and enabled the towers to be burnt.

It happened like this: there was a man from Damascus who was a passionate collector of pyrotechnic devices and ingredients for reinforcing the effect of fire. His friends reproached and rebuked him for his passion, but he replied that it was an occupation that did no harm to anyone and which interested him as a hobby. By a strange coincidence this man was in Acre, and when he saw the towers being built for use against the city he began to collect together the ingredients that he knew would increase the effectiveness of fire and make it inextinguishable by earth, vinegar or any other substance. When he had everything ready he presented it to the amīr Qaraqūsh, commander and governor of Acre, and told him to order the artillery to aim one of their catapults at a tower and fire off what he had given him, and it would set the tower alight. Qaraqūsh was out of his mind with fear that the city would fall, with a frenzy that almost killed him. The man's words drove him to even greater fury and he raged at him: 'These men have used all their skill to hit the towers with Greek fire and everything else, without success!' But some of those present said: 'Who knows that God has not put our salvation in this man's hands? There is no harm in doing what he proposes.' So Qaraqūsh consented and told the artillery to obey the man's orders. They shot a certain number of containers full of naphtha and other things without starting a fire, and the Franks, seeing that when the containers fell they did not burn anything, called out and danced about and made jokes from the top of the tower. When the inventor saw that the containers shot from the catapult really hit the tower he sent over one that was filled with his invention, and at once the tower went up in flames. He shot a second and a third time; the fire spread through the tower, preventing the men on the five platforms from escaping to safety. Thus it was burnt with everyone in it, as well as a store of cuirasses and arms. The Franks, seeing that the first containers were ineffective, had been inclined to stay calm and make no effort to save themselves, until God gave them a foretaste of Hell-fire. When the first tower was burnt the Muslims turned to the second, whose soldiers fled in fear, and the third, and burnt them both, making this a day to stand out in the memory. The Muslims looked on and rejoiced, their faces lit up with joy again after sorrow, for the victory and preservation from death of their co-religionists, for every one of them had a friend or relation in the city. The inventor was brought before Saladin who offered him great wealth and honour, but he refused to take anything. 'I did it for love of God,' he said, 'and I want no other reward than Him.' The joyful news travelled through the provinces, and the Sultan sent for reinforcements from the East. First to arrive was 'Imād ad-Din Zangi ibn Maudūd ibn Zangi, ruler of Sinjār and the Jazira, then 'Alā' ad-Din son of 'Izz ad-Din ibn Maudūd ibn Zangi, ruler of Mosul, sent by his father to command the Mosul army, then Zain ad-Din Yusuf of Arbela. As soon as each arrived he attacked the Franks with his troops and fought with the rest of the army, and after that pitched his tents.

Various Incidents during the Siege

(BAHĀ' AD-DIN, 178–9, 201–3, 211)

A SHIP FROM BEIRŪT REACHES ACRE BY MEANS OF A RUSE

The Franks, God damn them! had posted their ships all round Acre to blockade the harbour against Muslim shipping. The besieged were in dire need of food and provisions. A group of Muslims embarked at Beirūt with a cargo of four hundred sacks of grain, cheese, onions, mutton and other provisions.

They dressed in Frankish clothes, shaved their beards, put some pigs on the upper deck where they could be seen from a distance,[1] set up crosses, weighed anchor and made for the city from the open sea. When they came into contact with enemy ships the Franks accosted them in small boats and galleys saying: 'We see that you are making for the city,' thinking that they too were Franks. The Muslims replied: 'But haven't you taken it yet?' 'Not yet.' 'Then we will make for the Frankish army. But there was another ship travelling with us on the same wind; warn it not to enter the city.' There was in fact a Frankish ship behind them on the same route, making for the army. The patrol-boat saw it and made off to warn it. Thus the Muslim ship was free to follow its own course, and entered port on a favourable wind, safe and sound by God's grace. They brought great joy, for the inhabitants were now suffering severe hardships. This happened in the last ten days of rajab (586/August–September 1190).

THE STORY OF THE SWIMMER ISA

One of the most strange and amazing incidents of the siege was this: a Muslim swimmer called Isa used to come into the city by night with messages and money carried in his belt, eluding enemy surveillance. He would dive down, and come up on the other side of the boom. One night, carrying three purses containing a thousand *dinar* and messages for the army in his belt he set out on his swim, but met with an accident from which he died. It was some time before we learnt of his death. It was his custom, on entering the city, to send up a messenger-pigeon to tell of his arrival. When the bird did not appear we realized that he must be dead. One day some time later a group of people was on the beach by the city when the sea cast up a body on the shore. Examination revealed that it

[1] Unclean animals that a Muslim would never eat.

was Isa the swimmer. In his belt they found the gold and the wax-paper containing the letters; the gold was used as payment for the troops. This is the only man who has faithfully carried out his duties even after death. This too happened in the last ten days of rajab.

AN AMBUSH

On 22 shawwāl (586/22 November 1190) the Sultan decided to stage an ambush for the enemy. He selected a group of warriors and gallant knights chosen from a great number, and told them to leave camp by night and wait at the foot of a hill to the north of Acre, not far from the enemy camp, where al-Malik al-'Adil had been stationed in the battle that was called after him. A few of them were to allow the enemy to see them, and by going up to the tents to provoke them, and then, when the Franks came out to get them, to escape in the direction of the Muslims. The detachment obeyed and marched off to arrive at the hill by night and take up their positions. Saturday 23rd dawned and a small band, mounted on swift horses, emerged and made for the enemy tents, firing arrows at them. Provoked by this persistent attack about two hundred Frankish knights in full armour, with fine horses and weapons, appeared and attacked without infantry. The smallness of the Muslim band had beguiled them into giving battle. The Muslims fled before them, fighting and retreating at the same time, until they reached the ambush. At their arrival the hidden warriors burst out and with one shout fell on the Franks like lions on their prey. The Franks resisted and fought nobly, but they were put to flight. The Muslims overcame them, killed many and unseated and captured a good number and took their horses and arms.

The good news reached the Muslim camp, and voices were raised in praise and jubilation to God. The Sultan rode out to meet the heroes (I was on duty at his side) as far as Tall Kaisān, where he met the leaders of the band. There he stopped to inspect the prisoners, while the people praised and thanked him for his gesture. The Sultan examined the prisoners and ascertained who they were. Among them was the commander of the King of France's army, whom the latter had sent to help before his own arrival. In the same way the King's treasurer was taken prisoner. The Sultan returned to his tent happy and contented, sent for the prisoners, and had the herald summon all who had captured one to bring him into his presence. They all appeared with their prisoners; I was present on the occasion. Saladin treated the most important and distinguished prisoners with respect and gave them robes of honour. He gave the captain of the King's guard a special fur robe, and to each of the others one from Jarkh, for it was very cold and they were suffering from it. He sent for food for them, which they ate, and had a tent pitched for them near his own. He continued to show honour to them and sometimes invited the commander to his table. Then he had them sent to Damascus, whither they were conducted with honour. He gave them permission to write to their companions and send for clothes and other necessities from the camp. This they did, and then left for Damascus.

SALADIN'S HUMANITY

Forty-five Franks taken at Beirūt were brought before Saladin on their arrival there that day.[1] On this occasion I was able to observe his unparalleled generosity with my own eyes. Among the prisoners was a very old man, without a tooth in his head or the strength to do more than get himself about. The Sultan told the interpreter to ask him: 'What brought you here at such an advanced age, and how far is this place from your own land?' He replied: 'My own land is many months' voyage away from

[1] At Tall al-'Ayadiyya, near Acre, on 9 rabi' I 587/6 April 1191.

here, and my journey here was a pilgrimage to the Holy Sepulchre.' The Sultan was moved by this to thank him and do him the honour of giving him his liberty and sending him back to the enemy camp on horseback. His small sons asked his permission to kill one of the prisoners, but he refused. They asked me to ask him why, and he said: 'One does not accustom children to shedding blood thus lightly, when they are still incapable of distinguishing a Muslim from an infidel.' Observe the clemency, conscientiousness and scrupulousness of this King![1]

FRANKISH WOMEN OF PEACE AND WAR[2]

('IMĀD AD-DIN, 228–30)

There arrived by ship three hundred lovely Frankish women, full of youth and beauty, assembled from beyond the sea and offering themselves for sin. They were expatriates come to help expatriates, ready to cheer the fallen and sustained in turn to give support and assistance, and they glowed with ardour for carnal intercourse. They were all licentious harlots, proud and scornful, who took and gave, foul-fleshed and sinful, singers and coquettes, appearing proudly in public, ardent and inflamed, tinted and painted, desirable and appetizing, exquisite and graceful, who ripped open and patched up, lacerated and mended, erred and ogled, urged and seduced, consoled and solicited, seductive and languid, desired and desiring, amused and amusing, versatile and cunning, like tipsy adolescents, making love and selling themselves for gold, bold and ardent, loving and passionate, pink-faced and unblushing, black-eyed and bullying, callipygian and graceful, with nasal voices and fleshy thighs, blue-eyed and grey-eyed, broken-down little fools. Each one trailed the train of her robe behind her and bewitched

[1] This is one anecdote in which the Saladin of history and of legend meet.

[2] There follows a page of baroque pornography that may be of interest to connoisseurs of literary teratology.

the beholder with her effulgence. She swayed like a sapling, revealed herself like a strong castle, quivered like a small branch, walked proudly with a cross on her breast, sold her graces for gratitude, and longed to lose her robe and her honour. They arrived after consecrating their persons as if to works of piety, and offered and prostituted the most chaste and precious among them. They said that they set out with the intention of consecrating their charms, that they did not intend to refuse themselves to bachelors, and they maintained that they could make themselves acceptable to God by no better sacrifice than this. So they set themselves up each in a pavilion or tent erected for her use, together with other lovely young girls of their age, and opened the gates of pleasure. They dedicated as a holy offering what they kept between their thighs; they were openly licentious and devoted themselves to relaxation; they removed every obstacle to making of themselves free offerings. They plied a brisk trade in dissoluteness, adorned the patched-up fissures, poured themselves into the springs of libertinage, shut themselves up in private under the amorous transports of men, offered their wares for enjoyment, invited the shameless into their embrace, mounted breasts on backs, bestowed their wares on the poor, brought their silver anklets up to touch their golden ear-rings, and were willingly spread out on the carpet of amorous sport. They made themselves targets for men's darts, they were permitted territory for forbidden acts, they offered themselves to the lances' blows and humiliated themselves to their lovers. They put up the tent and loosed the girdle after agreement had been reached. They were the places where tent-pegs are driven in, they invited swords to enter their sheaths, they razed their terrain for planting, they made javelins rise toward shields, excited the plough to plough, gave the birds a place to peck with their beaks, allowed heads to enter their ante-chambers and raced under whoever bestrode them at the spur's blow. They took the parched man's sinews to the well, fitted arrows to the bow's handle, cut off sword-belts, engraved coins, welcomed birds into the nest of their thighs, caught in their nets the horns of butting rams, removed the interdict from what is protected, withdrew the veil from what is hidden. They interwove leg with leg, slaked their lovers' thirsts, caught lizard after lizard in their holes, disregarded the wickedness of their intimacies, guided pens to inkwells, torrents to the valley bottom, streams to pools, swords to scabbards, gold ingots to crucibles, infidel girdles to women's zones, firewood to the stove, guilty men to low dungeons, money-changers to *dinar*, necks to bellies, motes to eyes. They contested for tree-trunks, wandered far and wide to collect fruit, and maintained that this was an act of piety without equal, especially to those who were far from home and wives. They mixed wine, and with the eye of sin they begged for its hire.[1] The men of our army heard tell of them, and were at a loss to know how such women could perform acts of piety by abandoning all decency and shame. However, a few foolish mamlūks and ignorant wretches slipped away, under the fierce goad of lust, and followed the people of error. And there were those who allowed themselves to buy pleasure with degradation, and those who repented of their sin and found devious ways of retracing their steps, for the hand of any man who shrinks from (absolute) apostasy dares not stretch out, and it is the nature of him who arrives there to steal away from them, suspecting that what is serious, is serious, and the door of pleasure closes in his face. Now among the Franks a woman who gives herself to a celibate man commits no sin, and her justification is even greater in the case of a priest, if chaste men in dire need find relief in enjoying her.

Another person to arrive by sea was a noblewoman who was

[1] This is a hint of the true nature of these camp-followers, represented in the rest of the passage as fanatical hierodules of the Christian faith; but even this metaphor from the market, the request with the eye (or the coin) of sin, could be understood in other than a literally venial sense.

very wealthy. She was a queen in her own land, and arrived accompanied by five hundred knights with their horses and money, pages and valets, she paying all their expenses and treating them generously out of her wealth. They rode out when she rode out, charged when she charged, flung themselves into the fray at her side, their ranks unwavering as long as she stood firm.

Among the Franks there were indeed women who rode into battle with cuirasses and helmets, dressed in men's clothes; who rode out into the thick of the fray and acted like brave men although they were but tender women, maintaining that all this was an act of piety, thinking to gain heavenly rewards by it, and making it their way of life. Praise be to him who led them into such error and out of the paths of wisdom! On the day of battle more than one woman rode out with them like a knight and showed (masculine) endurance in spite of the weakness (of her sex); clothed only in a coat of mail they were not recognized as women until they had been stripped of their arms.[1] Some of them were discovered and sold as slaves; and everywhere was full of old women. These were sometimes a support and sometimes a source of weakness. They exhorted and incited men to summon their pride, saying that the Cross imposed on them the obligation to resist to the bitter end, and that the combatants would win eternal life only by sacrificing their lives, and that their God's sepulchre was in enemy hands. Observe how men and women led them into error; the latter in their religious zeal tired of feminine delicacy, and to save themselves from the terror of dismay (on the day of Judgment) became the close companions of perplexity, and having succumbed to the lust for vengeance, became hardened, and stupid and foolish because of the harm they had suffered.

[1] Ibn al-Athīr has the same story. Clearly there was more than one Clorinda in the Christian camp; but from a passage in Usama we learn that Muslim women too were capable of taking up arms if necessary.

CHAPTER FIVE

The expedition of Frederick Barbarossa, which ended in the waters of the Calycadnus and the epidemics of northern Syria, was followed with greater success by those of the kings of France and England. Despite all Saladin's efforts to mobilize all the forces of Islām in a counter-crusade (we owe to Abu Shama the text of one of his impassioned appeals on the subject), in 1191, her food and her army gone, Acre submitted. Bahā' ad-Din paints for us a vivid picture of the last hours and the tragedy of the surrender with its bloody epilogue, a disgrace to the name of Cœur de Lion, when the Muslim prisoners were massacred in cold blood.

CONRAD OF MONTFERRAT AND THE THIRD CRUSADE

(BAHĀ' AD-DĪN, 181)

. . . the Marquis, the ruler of Tyre, was one of the most cunning and experienced of the Franks, and his was the chief responsibility for luring the crowds of Crusaders from overseas. He had a picture of Jerusalem painted showing the Church of the Resurrection, the object of pilgrimage and deepest veneration to them; according to them the Messiah's tomb is there, in which he was buried after his crucifixion.[1] This sepulchre was the object of their pilgrimage, and they believed that every year fire came down upon it from heaven at one of their feasts.[2] Above the tomb the Marquis had a horse painted, and mounted on it a Muslim knight who was trampling the tomb, over which his horse was urinating. This picture was sent abroad to the markets and meeting-places; priests carried it about, clothed

[1] We have already remarked on the Docetist theories of Muslim Christology.

[2] The fire ceremony on Holy Saturday, celebrated at the Holy Sepulchre until the last century.

in their habits, their heads covered, groaning: 'O the shame!' In this way they raised a huge army, God alone knows how many, among them the King of Germany with his troops.

FREDERICK BARBAROSSA'S CRUSADE AND HIS DEATH

(IBN AL-ATHĪR, XII, 30–2)

In 586/1190 the King of Germany left his country, which was inhabited by one of the most numerous and vigorous of the Frankish tribes. Troubled by the fall of Jerusalem to the Muslims, he marshalled his army, equipped them fully and left his land for Constantinople. The Byzantine emperor sent word of his coming to Saladin and promised that he would not let him pass through his lands. When the King of Germany reached Constantinople the Emperor was in no position to prevent his passage because of the size of his army, but he denied him any provisions and forbade his subjects to supply the army with what it needed, so that they found themselves short of food and provisions. They crossed the Bosporus and landed on Muslim soil, in the kingdom of Qilij Arslān ibn Qutlumīsh ibn Seljūq.[1] They had barely set foot there before the Turcomans attacked them, and they continued to keep up with them on their march, killing stragglers and plundering where they could. It was winter and the cold in those parts is intense. The snow settled, and cold, hunger and the Turcomans took their toll of the army and reduced its numbers. When they approached Konya, King Qutb ad-Din Malikshāh ibn Qilij Arslān came out to bar their way, but he could do nothing against them and so returned to Konya and his father. This son had stripped his father of his power, and the other sons had dispersed through his lands, each seizing a part of the kingdom. As Qutb ad-Din retreated before them the German army moved quickly in his wake and set up

[1] The Seljuqid Sultan of Iconium.

camp outside Konya. Then they sent a gift to Qilij Arslān with the message: 'Your country is not our objective, but Jerusalem,' and asking him at the same time to allow his subjects to provide them with food and other necessities. He gave his permission and they got whatever they needed, satisfied themselves, gathered together provisions for the journey and set off. Then they asked Qutb ad-Din to order his subjects not to molest them, and to consign to them as hostages a certain number of his amīrs. He was sufficiently afraid of them to hand over about twenty amīrs whom he disliked, and they took them off. Since the brigands and others were not in fact restrained from attacking and harassing the expedition, the King of Germany had the hostages seized and put in chains, and some of them died in prison, while others succeeded in ransoming themselves. The King of Germany reached Lesser Armenia, whose King was called Leo, son of Stephen son of Leo, and he supplied them with food and provisions, welcomed them as lords in his country and showed them obedience. From here they advanced toward Antioch, but found a river in their path, beside which they camped. The King went down to the river to wash himself, and was drowned at a place where the water was not even up to his waist. Thus God liberated us from the evil of such a man.

He had with him a young son,[1] who became King in his place and continued the march to Antioch. But his companions had lost their undivided loyalty to him; some wanted to turn back and go home, others wanted his brother as King, and they too split away from the main party. He went on with the remainder of his army that was faithful to him. They numbered 40,000 when he reviewed them, for death and epidemics had decimated them. They reached Antioch looking like disinterred corpses, and the ruler of the city, who was not pleased to see them, sent them off to join the Franks besieging Acre. On their

[1] Frederick, soon to die before Acre.

journey through Jabala, Laodicea and other regions in Muslim hands they were attacked by troops from Aleppo and elsewhere; many were taken prisoner and even more died. They reached Tripoli and stayed there for several days, but the pestilence fell upon them and left not more than a thousand. These made their way to the Franks at Acre. When they got there and realized the losses they had suffered and the discord there was among them they decided to return home, but their ships were wrecked and not one escaped.

King Qilij Arslān had written to Saladin advising him of their arrival and promising to prevent their passage through his lands, so when they had got through and left him behind them he sent his excuses for having failed to prevent them—his sons had seized control, stripped him of his power and dispersed, evading their obligation to him. As for Saladin, when he heard of the arrival of the King of Germany he took counsel with his companions. Many of them advised him to march against them and confront them before they reached Acre, but he said that it was better to wait until they came nearer to the Muslim armies before attacking them, in case the Muslim troops at Acre should think of surrendering. He sent contingents from Aleppo, Jabala, Laodicea, Shaizar and elsewhere into the region of Aleppo to protect it from enemy attacks. The Muslims found themselves in the state of which God says: 'When they attacked you from above and below, and your eyes were distracted and your hearts came up into your throats, and you thought on God in all sorts of ways. Then the Believers were put to the test and seriously shaken.'[1] But God freed us of their evil and turned their plotting upon themselves.

So great was the fear they aroused that this story was told: one of Saladin's amīrs had a village in the Mosul area, administered by my brother. When the harvest was reaped, barley and

[1] Qur'ān XXXIII, 10–11, referring to the siege of Medina by the pagan confederacy in the fifth year of the hijra/627.

straw, he sent to his lord to discuss the sale of the crop, but got in reply a letter saying; 'Do not sell a single grain, and make sure to reap the largest possible amount of straw.' This was followed by a letter from the amīr telling him to go ahead and sell the crop, as they had no further need of it. When the amīr came to Mosul we asked him why he had forbidden the sale and then soon afterward authorized it. He replied: 'When we had news that the King of Germany had come we were convinced that we should no longer be able to hold Syria, and so I wrote to prevent the sale of the harvest so that there would be food in reserve when we came to you. But when God destroyed them and there was no longer any need for reserves of food I wrote to you to sell it and invest the money.'

THE ARRIVAL OF THE KINGS OF FRANCE AND ENGLAND

(BAHĀ' AD-DIN 212–14, 220)

(In the spring of 1190) when the sea became navigable again and the weather was fine, the time came for both sides to return to the fray. The first of the Muslims to arrive was 'Alam ad-Din Sulaimān ibn Jandar, one of al-Malik az-Zahir's amīrs, an old and distinguished man, the veteran of many battles, a wise counsellor, esteemed and honoured by the Sultan, of whom he had for years been a companion at arms. After him came Majd ad-Din ibn 'Izz ad-Din Farrukhshāh, ruler of Baalbek, and then other Muslim contingents arrived from all directions. As for the enemy army, they warned our spies and outposts of the imminent arrival of the French King,[1] a great and honoured ruler, one of their mightiest princes, whom all the armies obeyed. He was to assume supreme command of them on his arrival. He arrived as they promised he would, six ships carrying him and his supplies, the horses they would need and his

[1] Philip II Augustus.

closest companions. This was on Saturday 23 rabī' I/20 April 1191.

He brought with him from his homeland an enormous white falcon of a rare species; I never saw a finer specimen. The King held it dear and showed it great affection. One day it escaped from his hand and flew away. He called it back but it did not respond, and instead flew over the wall of Acre, whose inhabitants seized it and sent it to the Sultan. Its arrival brought great joy, and its capture was seen as a good omen of victory for the Muslims. The Franks offered a ransom of a thousand *dinar* for it, but the offer was refused. After the King came the Count of Flanders,[1] a famous military leader, of whom it was said that he had laid siege to Hamāt and Harīm in the year of the fall of ar-Ramla. . . .

The King of England[2] was a very powerful man among the Franks, a man of great courage and spirit. He had fought great battles, and showed a burning passion for war. His kingdom and standing were inferior to those of the French King, but his wealth, reputation and valour were greater. For example, when he reached Cyprus, he refused to proceed any further until the island was his. So he laid siege to it and gave battle, while its ruler, with a great host of warriors, moved out against him and offered strenuous resistance. The King of England sent to Acre to ask for help in taking the island, and King Guy[3] sent his brother and a hundred and seventy knights, while the Franks at Acre waited to see the outcome of the conflict. . . .

On Saturday 13 jumada I/8 June 1191 the King of England arrived, after coming to terms with the King of Cyprus and taking possession of the island. His arrival made an enormous impression: he appeared with twenty-five ships full of men, arms and equipment, and the Franks made a great display of joy and lit fires that night among their tents. The fires were im-

[1] Philip of Alsace. [2] Richard Cœur de Lion.
[3] The text has 'Godfrey' for Guy.

pressive, and big enough to show what a vast amount of equipment he had brought with him.[1] The Frankish rulers had for a long time been telling us that he was coming, and those of them who had safe-conducts and could contact our side said that they had been waiting for his arrival to put into effect their plan to besiege the city with new vigour. The King was indeed a man of wisdom, experience, courage and energy. His arrival put fear into the hearts of the Muslims, but the Sultan met the panic with firmness and faith in God, consecrating all his actions to Him and dedicating to Him his sincere intention of fighting in the Holy War.

SALADIN'S SUMMONS TO THE HOLY WAR

(ABU SHAMA, II, 148)

'We hope in God most high, to whom be praise, who leads the hearts of Muslims to calm what torments them and ruins their prosperity. As long as the seas bring reinforcements to the enemy and the land does not drive them off, our country will continue to suffer at their hands, and our hearts to be troubled by the sickness caused by the harm they do us. Where is the sense of honour of the Muslims, the pride of the believers, the zeal of the faithful? We shall never cease to be amazed at how the Unbelievers, for their part, have shown trust, and it is the Muslims who have been lacking in zeal. Not one of them has responded to the call, not one intervenes to straighten what is distorted; but observe how far the Franks have gone; what unity they have achieved, what aims they pursue, what help they have given, what sums of money they have borrowed and spent, what wealth they have collected and distributed and divided among them! There is not a king left in their lands or islands, not a lord or a rich man who has not competed with his neighbours to produce more support, and rivalled his peers in

[1] Western sources too speak of these great bonfires of jubilation.

strenuous military effort. In defence of their religion they consider it a small thing to spend life and soul, and they have kept their infidel brothers supplied with arms and champions for the war. And all they have done, and all their generosity, has been done purely out of zeal for Him they worship, in jealous defence of their Faith. Every Frank feels that once we have reconquered the (Syrian) coast, and the veil of their honour is torn off and destroyed, this country will slip from their grasp, and our hand will reach out toward their own countries. The Muslims, on the other hand, are weakened and demoralized. They have become negligent and lazy, the victims of unproductive stupefaction and completely lacking in enthusiasm. If, God forbid, Islām should draw rein, obscure her splendour, blunt her sword, there would be no one, East or West, far or near, who would blaze with zeal for God's religion or choose to come to the aid of truth against error. This is the moment to cast off lethargy, to summon from far and near all those men who have blood in their veins. But we are confident, thanks be to God, in the help that will come from Him, and entrust ourselves to Him in sincerity of purpose and deepest devotion. God willing, the Unbelievers shall perish and the faithful have a sure deliverance.'

THE LAST ATTACK ON ACRE AND THE SURRENDER OF THE CITY

(BAHĀ' AD-DIN, 229–39)

The besiegers battered the walls ceaselessly with catapults, which was the only method of attack they used, and eventually the walls began to crumble, their structure collapsed, and exhaustion and vigilance wore the defenders out. There were few of them against a great number of enemy soldiers, and they underwent the most severe trial of endurance; in fact some of them went for several nights on end without closing their eyes, night or day, whereas the circle hemming them in consisted of a great number of men who took it in turns to fight. The defenders however were but few, and had had to share the duties of the wall, the trenches, the catapults and the galleys.

When the enemy realized this, and when the walls seemed to be tottering, their structure undermined, they began to attack on all sides, divided into groups and detachments that took it in turn to fight. Each time that a detachment exhausted itself it retired to rest and another took its place. On the seventh of the month (jumada II 586/12 July 1191) they began a great offensive, manning night and day all the mounds surrounding their trenches with infantry and combatants. The Sultan, who learnt of the assault from eye-witnesses and by an agreed signal from the garrison—a roll of drums—mounted his horse and ordered the army to mount and attack the enemy. A great battle was fought that day. As deeply concerned as a mother bereft of her child, Saladin galloped from battalion to battalion inciting his men to fight for the Faith. Al-Malik al-'Adil, they say, himself led two charges that day. The Sultan moved through the ranks crying: 'For Islām!' his eyes swimming with tears. Every time he looked toward Acre and saw the agony she was in and the disaster looming for her inhabitants, he launched himself once more into the attack and goaded his men on to fight. That day he touched no food and drank only a cup or two of the potion prescribed for him by his doctor. I was left behind and could not take part in the attack because of an illness that afflicted me. I was in my tent at Tall al-'Ayadiyya, and all the battle was spread out before my eyes. Night fell, the Sultan returned to his tent after the final evening prayer, exhausted and in anguish, and slept fitfully. The next morning he had the drums beaten, marshalled his army and returned to the battle he had left the night before.

On that day a letter arrived from the beleaguered men in which they said: 'We have reached such a pitch of exhaustion that we can do nothing but surrender. Tomorrow, the eighth of the month, if you can do nothing for us, we shall beg for our lives and hand over the city, securing only our personal safety.' This was one of the saddest messages ever received by the Muslims, and it stabbed them to the heart; the more so since Acre contained all the military equipment from Palestine, Jerusalem, Damascus, Aleppo, Egypt and all the Muslim lands, as well as the army's greatest amīrs, and such gallant champions of Islām as Saif ad-Din 'Ali al-Mashtūb, Saif ad-Din Qaraqūsh, and others. Qaraqūsh in particular had directed the defence of the town since the enemy first besieged it. The Sultan was smitten by the news as by no other blow that had ever struck him, to such an extent that his life was feared for. But he continued his unceasing prayers to God and turned to Him throughout the crisis, with patience and pious abnegation and tenacious energy: 'And God does not waste the hire of the doer of good.'[1] He wanted to try by assault to re-establish contact with the besieged men. The alarm sounded among the troops, the champions mounted their horses, cavalry and infantry assembled. But on that day the army did not support him in the attack on the enemy, for the enemy infantry stood like an unbreakable wall with weapons, ballistas and arrows, behind their bastions. Attacked on every side by the Muslims, they held firm and defended themselves most vigorously. A man who penetrated as far as their trenches told how there was a huge Frank there who leapt on to the parapet of the trench and chased back the Muslims; some men standing close to him handed him stones which he threw down on to the Muslims sheltering behind the parapet. More than fifty stones and arrows struck him without dislodging him from the defensive battle he had undertaken, until a Muslim pyrotechnician threw an incendiary bottle at

[1] Qur'ān III, 165.

him and burnt him alive. Another observant old soldier who penetrated the trenches that day told me that on the other side of the parapet was a woman dressed in a green mantle, who shot at us with a wooden bow and wounded many Muslims before she was overcome and killed. Her bow was taken and carried to the Sultan, who was clearly deeply impressed by the story. Thus the fighting continued until nightfall.

ACRE, INCAPABLE OF FURTHER RESISTANCE, NEGOTIATES WITH THE FRANKS

The attack on the city from all sides was intensified, with troops taking turns to fight, and the defenders were reduced to a handful of infantry and cavalry as a result of the great losses they had suffered. The survivors lost heart at the thought of the imminence of death, and felt incapable of any further defiance. Meanwhile the enemy captured their trenches and the wall of the first bastion. The Franks had tunnelled under it, filled the mines with combustible material and set fire to it. Part of the bastion crumbled and the Franks got in. But they lost more than a hundred and fifty men there, dead or captured, including six of their leaders. One of these cried: 'Do not kill me, and I will make the Franks retreat!' but a Kurd fell on him and killed him, and the other five were killed in the same way. The next day the Franks issued a proclamation: 'Return those six men, and we will grant freedom to all the city!' But the Muslims replied that they were already dead, which caused great grief to the Franks, who suspended the offensive for three days after this.

It was said that Saif ad-Din al-Mashtūb himself went out under safe-conduct to talk to the French King, and said to him: 'In the past we have taken many of your cities by storm. In every case, when the inhabitants asked for an amnesty it has been granted, and we have allowed them honourably to go into safety. Now we would surrender this city, and we hope that you will guarantee our lives.' The King replied: 'Those whom you captured in the past were our subjects, and in the same way you are our mamlūks and slaves. We shall see what is to be done with you.' To which al-Mashtūb, they say, replied harshly and at length, saying among other things: 'We shall not hand over the city until we are all dead, and not one of us will die before he has killed fifty of your leaders,' and he went away. When al-Mashtūb brought the news to the city some of the garrison were afraid, and climbing an embankment escaped to the Muslim camp by night. This was on 9 jumada II, and among the distinguished men in the party were 'Izz ad-Din Arsil, Ibn al-Jawali and Sunqūr al-Ushaqi. When Arsil and Sunqūr reached the camp they vanished without leaving the faintest trace, for fear of Saladin's wrath. Ibn al-Jawali was taken and thrown into prison.

On the following morning the Sultan mounted, intending to take the enemy by surprise, and took with him spades and other equipment for bridging the trenches. But the troops refused to support him in carrying out his plan, and said rebelliously: 'You want to place all Islām in jeopardy, but such a plan could not have a successful outcome.' That day three messengers came from the English King asking Saladin for fruit and snow, and saying that the Grand Master of the Hospital would come out the next day to discuss peace. The Sultan treated the messengers with honour, and they went to the market and walked about there, and returned to their own camp at nightfall. That day the Sultan told Sarim ad-Din Qaimāz an-Najmi to take his men and penetrate the enemy lines. He took a group of Kurdish amīrs such as al-Janāh, (al-Mashtūb's brother), and his friends, as far as the Frankish lines. Qaimāz himself raised the standard over the enemy trenches and fought a part of the day in defence of the oriflam. At the height of the battle that day 'Izz ad-Din Jurdīk an-Nuri arrived, dismounted and fought vigorously alongside his men. On Friday 10 jumada II/5 July the Frankish army took the initiative. They were completely surrounded by Muslims, who passed the night fully armed and in the saddle, looking for a chance to help their brothers in Acre who, they hoped, would be able to attack some point of the enemy lines, break through and get out; the army outside helping them to hold their position, so that some would escape and some be taken, according to their fate. But the besieged men who had agreed to the plan, could not get out that night because an escaped slave had informed the enemy and precautions were taken and strict watch kept. On Friday 10th three enemy messengers spent an hour with al-Malik al-'Adil and returned without reaching any agreement. The day ended with the Muslim army holding the plain facing the enemy, and thus the night passed.

On Saturday the 11th the Franks, in full panoply, moved forward and it appeared that they wanted a pitched battle with the Muslims. When they were drawn up about forty men came out of the gate below the pavilion and invited certain mamlūks, among them al-'Adl az-Zabdani of Sidon one of the Sultan's freedmen, to present themselves. Al-'Adl came up to them and began to negotiate for the garrison in Acre to be allowed to go free, but the terms were too stiff and the Saturday came to an end without any conclusion being reached.

LETTERS ARRIVE FROM THE CITY

On Sunday the 12th letters reached us (from Acre) saying: 'We have sworn an oath to one another to die. We shall fight until death. We shall not yield the city as long as we have a breath of life in us. See what you can do to distract the enemy from us and draw his fire. These are our decisions. Take care that you do not yield to the enemy. Our part is now over.' The messenger who swam out with this letter said that from the great noise heard in the city during the night the Franks thought that a great army had entered Acre. 'A Frank,' he said, 'came up to the wall and cried out to one of the guards: "In the name of your Faith, tell me how many soldiers came into your city last night." This was the night before the Saturday, during which a great uproar was heard that alarmed both sides, but its cause was not discovered.[1] "A thousand cavalry," replied the other. "No," he returned, "fewer than that; I saw them myself, and they were dressed in green robes"!'[2]

Repeated attacks by Muslim contingents were still able at this stage to turn the enemy attack away from the siege, even after the city was wide open to be taken. But the defenders grew weaker, the number of breaches in the walls increased although the defenders built up in place of the broken wall another internal wall from which they fought when the vulnerable section finally collapsed. On Tuesday 14th of the month there arrived Sabīq ad-Din of Shaizar, on Wednesday Badr ad-Din Yildirīm with a large band of Turcomans to whom the Sultan had sent a large sum of money to be distributed among them as pay, and on Thursday Asad ad-Din Shirkūh the younger. Through all this the Franks held firm, refusing to grant the besieged men their lives until every Frankish prisoner in Muslim hands had been returned, and all the cities of Palestine submitted to the Franks. They were offered the surrender of the town with everything in it except the defenders, and they refused it. They were offered the return of the True Cross, and still they refused, becoming increasingly greedy and more obstinate. No one knew any longer what expedient to use with them: 'They play at being cunning, and God too plays at being cunning, and He is the better player.'[3]

[1] There appears to have been a small earthquake.

[2] The usual heavenly warriors who according to Muslim piety so often intervene in battle.

[3] Qur'ān III, 47.

THE GARRISON AGREE TO SURRENDER IN RETURN FOR THEIR LIVES

On Friday 17 jumada II a swimmer got out of the city with letters saying that the defenders were at their last gasp. The breaches had grown and the people, unable to resist any longer, saw that death was certain and were sure that when the city was taken by storm they would all be put to the sword. They had therefore made an agreement handing over the city with all its equipment, munitions, and ships, in addition to 200,000 *dinar*, 500 ordinary prisoners and 100 important ones nominated by the Franks themselves, and also the True Cross. In return they were to be allowed to leave the city freely with their personal possessions, women and children. They also guaranteed 400 *dinar* to the Marquis (of Montferrat) who had acted as intermediary in the negotiations. On this basis agreement was reached.

THE ENEMY TAKES POSSESSION OF ACRE

When the Sultan learnt the contents of their letters he was extremely upset and disapproved strongly. He called his counsellors, informed them of the developments, and asked their advice on what should be done. He was given conflicting advice and remained uncertain and troubled. He decided to write that night and to send a message by the swimmer disapproving of the terms of the treaty, and was still in this state of mind when suddenly the Muslims saw standards and crosses and signs and beacons raised by the enemy on the city walls. It was midday on Friday 17 Jumada II/12 July 1191.

The Franks all together gave a mighty shout, and struck a heavy blow into Muslim hearts. Great was our affliction; our whole camp resounded with cries and lamentations, sighs and sobs. The Marquis took the King's standards into the city and planted one on the citadel, one on the minaret of the Great Mosque—on a Friday!—one on the Templars' tower and one on the Battle Tower, each one in place of a Muslim standard. The Muslims were all confined to one quarter of the city.

I was on duty, and came into the Sultan's presence, and he was like a parent bereft of a child. I offered him what comfort I could, and exhorted him to think of his duty to Palestine and Jerusalem, and to save the Muslims left as prisoners in the city. This was the night of Saturday the 18th. He finally decided to withdraw slightly from his present position, since the moment had passed for attacking the enemy at close quarters. He had the baggage removed to its first position at Shafar'am, remaining at his post with a small body of troops to observe the enemy and the defenders. The army carried out the move during the night, but Saladin stayed where he was in the hope that by God's will the Franks in their blindness would be inspired to attack him, so that by falling on them from behind he could inflict a blow on them; let God give the victory to whom He would. But the enemy did nothing of the sort, confining themselves to taking over the city. The Sultan stayed there until the morning of the 19th and then moved to the Tall.

MASSACRE OF THE MUSLIM PRISONERS

When the English King saw that Saladin delayed in carrying out the terms of the treaty he broke his word to the Muslim prisoners with whom he had made an agreement and from whom he had received the city's surrender in exchange for their lives. If the Sultan handed over the agreed sum, he was to allow them to go free with their possessions, wives and children, but if the money was refused him he was to take them into slavery as his prisoners. Now, however, he broke his word and revealed the secret thought that he was nurturing, and put it into effect even after he had received the money and the (Frankish) prisoners: it was indeed in these terms that his co-religionists spoke of him later on. On the afternoon of 27 rajab/ 20 August he and all the Frankish army, infantry, cavalry and turcopules, rode to the wells below Tall al-'Ayadiyya, (they had sent their tents ahead of them), and marched off to occupy the centre of the plain between Tall Kaisān and Tall al-'Ayadiyya, while the Sultan's outposts retired to Tall Kaisān. Then they brought up the Muslim prisoners whose martyrdom God had ordained, more than three thousand men in chains. They fell on them as one man and slaughtered them in cold blood, with sword and lance. Our spies had informed Saladin of the enemy's manœuvres and he sent some reinforcements, but by then the slaughter had already occurred. As soon as the Muslims realized what had happened they attacked the enemy and battle raged, with dead and wounded on both sides, continuing with increasing vigour until night fell and separated them. The next morning the Muslims wanted to see who had fallen, and found their martyred companions lying where they fell, and some they recognized. Great grief seized them, and from then on they did not spare (enemy prisoners), except for well-known persons and strong men who could be put to work.

Many reasons were given to explain the slaughter. One was that they had killed them as a reprisal for their own prisoners killed before then by the Muslims. Another was that the King of England had decided to march on Ascalon and take it, and he did not want to leave behind him in the city a large number (of enemy soldiers). God knows best.

CHAPTER SIX

Negotiations for peace, or the truce, according to the Muslim concept of the Holy War, took a whole year. Involved in the long, tortuous diplomatic game were Richard of England's matrimonial plans, his exchange of gentlemanly courtesies with Saladin (and even more with his brother al-'Adil), and the ceaseless military operations (Ascalon, Jaffa, Arsūf), in which the Frankish cruelty to the prisoners taken at Acre led to equally cruel reprisals by Saladin. Finally, *de guerre lasse*, came the agreement of September 1192 which in effect sanctioned the *status quo*. There was little in the agreement to remind the Muslims of the first great victories of 1187, and Saladin accepted it with reluctance and under pressure from a tired and undisciplined army. The plan to drive the Franks back to the sea, which had at one moment seemed a possibility, had to wait another century for its realization.

The chief sources for the treaty are Bahā' ad-Din and 'Imād ad-Din.

PEACE NEGOTIATIONS AND THE TREATY

(BAHĀ' AD-DIN, 274–5, 277–8, 283–4, 287–91, 294–5, 346–8)

On 26 ramadān (587/17 October 1191) al-Malik al-'Adil was on duty with the outposts when the King of England asked him to send over a messenger. He sent his secretary and favourite Ibn an-Nahhāl, a fine young man. He met Richard at Yazūr, whither the King had gone with a large detachment of infantry, which was now scattered over the plain. Richard had long private talks with him to discuss the peace, and Richard said: 'I shall not break my word to my brother and my friend', meaning al-'Adil, and the secretary reported his words to al-Malik al-'Adil. He also sent a letter to the Sultan, through an-Nahhāl, which said in effect: 'I am to salute you, and tell you that the Muslims and Franks are bleeding to death, the country is utterly ruined and goods and lives have been sacrificed on both sides. The time has come to stop this. The points at issue are Jerusalem, the Cross, and the land. Jerusalem is for us an object of worship that we could not give up even if there were only one of us left. The land from here to beyond the Jordan must be consigned to us. The Cross, which is for you simply a piece of wood with no value, is for us of enormous importance. If the Sultan will deign to return it to us, we shall be able to make peace and to rest from this endless labour.'

When the Sultan read this message he called his councillors of state and consulted them about his reply. Then he wrote: 'Jerusalem is ours as much as yours; indeed it is even more sacred to us than it is to you, for it is the place from which our Prophet accomplished his nocturnal journey and the place where our community will gather (on the day of Judgment). Do not imagine that we can renounce it or vacillate on this point. The land was also originally ours, whereas you have only just arrived and have taken it over only because of the weakness of the Muslims living there at the time. God will not allow you to rebuild a single stone as long as the war lasts. As for the Cross, its possession is a good card in our hand[1] and it cannot be surrendered except in exchange for something of outstanding benefit to all Islām.' This reply was sent to Richard by the hand of his own messenger.

* * *

On 22 ramadān/20 October al-Malik al-'Adil sent for me, together with 'Alām ad-Din Sulaimān ibn Jandar, Sabiq ad-Din of Shaizar, 'Izz ad-Din ibn al-Muqaddam and Husām ad-Din Bishara, and showed us the proposals that had been sent

[1] Text and meaning uncertain; another reading could mean 'that Jesus is dead is a falsehood for us', or else 'that it were destroyed would be an act of great merit for us'.

to the King of England by his messenger. He said that his plan was that he himself should marry the King's sister,[1] whom Richard had brought with him from Sicily where she had been the wife of the late King. Her brother had taken her along with him when he had left Sicily. She would live in Jerusalem, and her brother was to give her the whole of Palestine that was in his hands: Acre, Jaffa, Ascalon and the rest, while the Sultan was to give al-'Adil all the parts of Palestine belonging to him and make him their King, in addition to the lands and fees he already held. Saladin was also to hand over the True Cross to the Franks. Villages and forts belonging to the Templars were to remain in their hands, Muslim and Frankish prisoners were to be freed and the King of England was to return home by sea. In this way the problem was to be resolved.

Such were the proposals brought by al-'Adil's messenger to the King of England. Al-'Adil thought them feasible, and so he sent for us, and sent us with a message to that effect to the Sultan, charging me to speak and the others to listen. We were to present the project to the Sultan, and if he approved and thought it to the advantage of Islām we were to bear witness that he had authorized and approved the treaty, and if he disapproved we were to bear witness that negotiations had reached this point, and that the Sultan had decided not to confirm them. When we came before the Sultan I expounded the matter to him and read him the message, in the presence of the men I have already named. Saladin immediately approved the terms, knowing quite well that the King of England would never agree to them and they were only a trick and a practical joke on his part. Three times I repeated to him the formula of consent and Saladin replied 'Yes', calling on those present to bear witness. Now that we were sure of his views we returned to al-'Adil and told him what had happened, and the others told him that I had repeated to Saladin the declaration that took effect from the

[1] Joanna of Sicily, widow of William II.

oath taken by him, and that Saladin had insisted on authorizing it. In this way he firmly accepted the proposed terms.

* * *

On 13 shawwāl/3 November, the arrival was announced of the Prince of Sidon as ambassador from the Marquis of Tyre. Conversations had already been held between us on several occasions, the essence of which was that the Marquis and his men were tired of the Franks and of supporting them, and wanted to make common cause with us against them. This arose from a quarrel that had been blowing up between the Marquis and the Frankish Kings as a result of his marriage to the wife of King Guy's brother,[1] a scandalous affair according to certain tenets of their Faith. This led to a division of opinions, and the Marquis, fearing for his life, took his wife and fled by night to Tyre. There he had begun to incline to the Sultan, and made certain gestures of reconciliation toward him. The split between the Marquis and the Franks was of advantage to the Muslims, for he was the strongest and most experienced of their generals, as well as a good governor. When the news of their ambassador's arrival reached the Sultan he gave orders that he was to be treated with honour and respect. He had a tent erected for him, surrounded with an enclosure of cloth and containing as many cushions and carpets as are suitable when princes and kings meet. Saladin ordered that he should be shown to his quarters near the stores to rest, and then held a secret conference with him.

* * *

On 19 shawwāl/9 November the Sultan gave an audience and summoned the Prince of Sidon to hear his message and statement. He appeared with a whole group of companions—I

[1] Actually the sister of Guy's wife (Guy, not Godfrey, as Bahā' ad-Din always calls him). Isabella of Anjou was Queen Sibyllas' sister. She married first Humphrey of Toron, and was later taken from him and married to Conrad of Montferrat.

was present at the audience—and Saladin treated him with great honour. He entered into conversation with him and had a sumptuous banquet served for them. After the meal he led them aside; their proposal was for the Sultan to make peace with the Marquis with whom various great Frankish lords had made common cause, among them the Prince of Sidon himself and other distinguished persons. We have already stated his position. A condition of accepting his offer was that he should break openly with the Franks of Outremer, because of his great fear of them and because of the matter of his wife. The Sultan appeared to be disposed to accept his proposal on certain conditions, by which he hoped to create discord among the Franks and to set them at loggerheads. Now, after listening to him, the Sultan promised to give him a reply later, and the ambassador retired for the day to the tent erected for him.

That night an ambassador came from the King of England: the son of Humphrey, one of the great Frankish leaders and kings (in his train was an old man who was said to be a hundred years old). The Sultan sent for him and listened to what he had to say. His message was: 'The King says: your friendship and affection are dear to me. I told you that I would give these regions of Palestine to your brother, and I want you to be the judge between us in the division of the land. But we absolutely must have a foothold in Jerusalem. I want you to make a division that will not bring down on you the wrath of the Muslims, or on me the wrath of the Franks.'

The Sultan replied immediately with fine promises and allowed the messenger to return at once. He was impressed by the message. He sent someone after the ambassador to check on the matter of prisoners, which was treated separately from the terms of the peace. 'If there is peace,' he said,[1] 'it will be a general peace, and if there is no peace the matter of prisoners will be of no account.' The Sultan's real object was to under-

[1] Presumably the king of England's ambassador, but could possibly refer to Saladin

mine the foundations of peace on those terms. When the audience was at an end and the Franks had gone, he turned to me and said: 'When we have made peace with them, there will be nothing to prevent their attacking us treacherously. If I should die the Muslims would no longer be able to muster an army like this and the Franks would have the upper hand. It is better to carry on the Holy War until we have expelled them from Palestine, or death overtakes us.' This was his opinion, and he only moved toward peace in response to external pressures.

On 21 shawwāl[1] (11 November) the Sultan summoned his amīrs and counsellors and explained to them the terms of the agreement sought by the Marquis, which for his part he was inclined to accept. The terms were that they should hand Sidon over to him in return for his military support against the Franks in open warfare. On the other hand, he was impressed by the terms proposed by King (Richard)—that either he should have certain points on the coast and we the mountain region, or we should divide the total number of settlements in half. In both cases the Franks stipulated that their priests should have the churches and oratories of Jerusalem, and the King of England left us to decide between the alternatives. Saladin explained the situation to the amīrs and asked them to reveal their hearts to him and tell him which plan, the King's or the Marquis', seemed preferable to them, and if the former, which of the two divisions mentioned above, proposed by the King of England. The counsellors held that peace must be made with the King, since it was improbable that Franks and Muslims would live amiably side by side, and they had no security against treacherous attacks.

So the treaty (with the Marquis) came to nothing and the peace negotiations continued, ambassadors coming and going to settle the terms. A basic condition was that the King should give his sister in marriage to al-'Adil who would, as her hus-

[1] The text has 11th, which does not fit in with the preceding chronology.

band, acquire the whole of Palestine, Muslim and Frankish, the Frankish regions from the Princess' brother and the Muslim from al-'Adil's brother, the Sultan. But the King's final message on this matter said: 'The Christian people disapprove of my giving my sister in marriage without consulting the Pope, the head and leader of Christianity. I have therefore sent a messenger who will be back in three months. If he authorizes this wedding, so much the better. If not, I will give you the hand of one of my nieces, for whom I shall not need Papal consent.'[1] While all this was going on the hostilities continued and took their inevitable course.

The Prince of Sidon sometimes went riding with al-'Adil, and they would go and inspect the Frankish positions. Every time the Franks saw him they would reiterate their offers of peace, for fear of an alliance between the Muslims and the Marquis, and their strength of mind weakened. This continued until 25 shawwāl.

* * *

Yusuf, one of the Prince of Sidon's pages, came from the Marquis to seek peace from the Muslims. One of the conditions imposed by the Sultan was that the Marquis should undertake to fight his compatriots and to detach himself from them. The Frankish territories that he himself took after the peace were to be his, those taken by us alone were to be ours, and of those taken by both together, he should have the city and we the Muslim prisoners and whatever else the place contained. He was to release all the Muslim prisoners in his domains, and if the King of England should make him governor of the city by some agreement between them, peace between him and us should be based on the conditions laid down between us and the

[1] Because, as Bahā' ad-Din states elsewhere, whereas Richard's sister was a widow, Papal authorization was not necessary in the case of a virgin. In fact all these marriage projects were shipwrecked on Christian objections to marriage with a Muslim.

King of England, except for Ascalon and the region beyond, which should not be subject to the treaty. The coastal region was to be his and the region held by us, ours, and the area between was to be divided between us. The messenger left to carry these terms to the Marquis.[1]

★ ★ ★

(In sha'bān 588/late August 1192) al-'Adl[2] came to Jaffa and was lodged in a tent outside the city while the King was informed of his arrival. He was then sent for with the rest of the delegation, and presented the text of the treaty. The King, who was ill, said: 'I have not the strength to read it now. But I agree to the peace, and here is my hand on it.' The Muslim delegates conferred with Count Henry and Ibn Barzān[3] and submitted the document to them. They accepted the division of Lydda and Ramla, and everything else in the text. They agreed to take the oath on Wednesday morning, as they had already eaten that day and it is not their custom to take an oath after they have broken their fast. Al-'Adl sent the news to the Sultan.

On Wednesday 22 sha'bān/2 September the whole Muslim delegation was conducted into the King's presence. They took his hand and meant to take the oath with him, but he excused himself, saying that kings do not take oaths, and the Sultan was content with this declaration. So they took the oath at the hands of Count Henry and his nephew, whom he had made ruler of Palestine, and of Baliān ibn Barzān, Lord of Tiberias, with the agreement of the Templars, the Hospitallers and other Frankish leaders. In the course of that day they returned to the Sultan's tent and joined him for the evening prayer, accompanied from

[1] The assassin's dagger soon put an end to these intrigues with Conrad, who did not see the conclusion of the truce; see below.

[2] The Muslim plenipotentiary.

[3] Henry of Champagne, later King, and Baliān II of Ibelin.

the Frankish side by Humphrey's son, Ibn Barzān and a group of their generals. They were received with great honour and a tent worthy of them was erected. Al-'Adil presented his report to the Sultan. Next day, 23 sha'bān, the King's ambassador presented himself to the Sultan, took his noble hand and undertook to keep the peace on the terms laid down. They proposed that oaths to this effect should be sworn by al-Malik al-'Adil, al-Malik al-Afdal, al-Malik az-Zahir, 'Ali ibn Ahmad al-Mashtūb, Badr ad-Din Yildirīm, al-Malik al-Mansūr, and all the rulers whose territories bordered on those of the Franks, such as Ibn al-Muqaddam of Shaizar. The Sultan for his part promised that he would send a messenger with them to all their neighbours to extract the oath from them. The King's ambassador also took the oath on behalf of the Prince of Antioch and Tripoli, on condition that the Muslims did the same on behalf of the other Muslims. If not, the treaty was annulled. Then the Sultan ordered a proclamation to be issued to all military camps and markets stating that a general peace extended over the whole territory and that unrestricted coming and going was permitted between their land and ours. He also proclaimed that the route of the Pilgrimage through Syria was open and expressed his intention of going on the Pilgrimage himself, an idea that occurred to him when I was with him. He also sent a hundred sappers under the command of a great amīr to break down the walls of Ascalon[1] and to enable the Franks to evacuate it. A Frankish delegation was to accompany them until the walls were down, for fear that we should leave them standing.

It was a memorable day, one on which the two sides expressed unimaginable joy and happiness. But it is well known that the peace did not entirely please the Sultan. In conversation with me he said: 'I am afraid of making peace. I do not know what might happen to me,[2] and the enemy would gain strength

[1] One of the clauses of the treaty.
[2] This fear of death appears often in Saladin's speeches; see the next passage.

from my death because these lands are still in their hands: they would take the opportunity of attacking us and recovering the rest. You see how each of them is perched on his own hilltop', meaning their forts; and he concluded. 'As soon as I am gone, the Muslims will be destroyed.'

These were his words, and it happened just as he said. Yet he felt that the peace was a good thing in that the army was tired and openly hostile (to a continuation of the war). It was indeed a good thing, as God in his prescience knew, for Saladin died soon afterward, and if he had died during a campaign Islām would have been in danger. Peace was therefore an act of divine providence and a fortunate occurrence for Islām.

('IMĀD AD-DIN 434–6)

When the King of England perceived that the (Muslim) army was united, his own problems more serious, Jerusalem irrecoverable and (divine) punishment hanging over him, he submitted and humbled himself, his boasts became less outrageous and he realized that he could not overcome one who was aided by fortune nor stand up against the hosts drawn up against him. He therefore declared that if he did not obtain a truce he would stay there and seek death, going to meet the worst; whereas he had decided to return to his own country to settle some matters there. 'Now,' he said, 'the time is close when the sea becomes unnavigable and the crests of the waves swell up on high. If you agree to a truce and enable me to, I shall fulfil my desire (to go); but if you fight and oppose me I shall pitch my tents and fix my dwelling here. Both sides are tired, both companies[1] are exhausted. I have renounced Jerusalem and will now renounce Ascalon. But do not be misled by this mass of troops assembled from everywhere, for it is destined to disperse when winter comes. If we persist in our miserable conflict we

[1] I.e. the two antagonists.

shall destroy ourselves. So fulfil my desire and win my friendship; make a pact with me and let me go; agree with me and accept my respect.'

The Sultan called his amīrs and counsellors and consulted them on this development, explained the approach that had been made to him and asked their advice, expounding the situation fully to them. 'We,' he said, 'thanks be to God, are in a strong position and within sight of the victory we have longed for. Our auxiliaries who have migrated to our side[1] are men of faith, nobility and valour. We have become accustomed to fighting the Holy War and in it we have achieved our aim. Now it is difficult to break off what has become customary, and with God's help so far not one has broken with us. We have no other occupation and aim than that of making war, for we are not among those who are beguiled by games and led astray by dissipation. If we give up this work, what shall we do? If we destroy our hope of defeating them, what shall we hope for? I am afraid that with nothing to do death will overcome me; and how will he who is accustomed to being adorned become used to being unadorned? My feeling is to reject the idea of a truce, and in preferring war, to prefer my honour and make it my leader. I do not seek to stand idle if it means wanting my present state to change. This duty has been placed upon me; it is my job, and with God's help I shall take the most determined and resolute course.' To this the amīrs replied: 'It is as you say; you must act as you think, and the right decision is the one that you make.[2] Only what you settle stays firm, and what you establish remains stable. Divine grace assist you in all you bind and loose, all that you give and take away. But you (alone) have looked to yourself, as one accustomed to happiness, to the desire to serve God, to the acquisition of eternal virtue, to the

[1] A play on words alluding to the two categories of Companions of the Prophet: the Auxiliaries of Medina and the Emigrants of Mecca.

[2] Observe the Oriental method of beginning with an apparent agreement when about to express an opposing view.

taking of measures necessary to success, to disdain for idleness and dislike of keeping oneself aloof. In yourself you find force and tenacity, and your indestructible faith marks you out as the one to achieve the aims we strive for. But look too at the state of the country, ruined and trampled underfoot, at your subjects, beaten down and confused, at your armies, exhausted and sick, at your horses, neglected and ruined. There is little forage, food is short, supply bases are far away, the necessities of life are dear. All supplies have to come from Egypt, confronting the murderous perils of the desert. Again, this concentration of troops may well decide to disperse, and your lengthy explanation of the situation will in that case have little effect, with provisions cut off, roads blocked, the rich reduced to hunger, the poor to destitution, straw more precious than gold, barley unobtainable at any price. And if they fail to get their truce they will devote all their energies to strengthening and consolidating their position; they will face death with high courage in the course of achieving their aims, and for love of their Faith will refuse to submit to humiliation. The best thing is for you to remember the verse revealed by God: "and if they incline to peace, you too should incline to it".[1] Then the farmers and inhabitants will return to their lands, and harvests and fruits will abound during the time of the truce. The armies can renew their equipment and rest throughout the time of peace. When war returns again we too shall return, reinforced and augmented, with supplies of food and forage, untroubled by exhaustion and strife. During peacetime we shall prepare for war, and shall renew the means of striking a blow with point and blade. This does not mean abandoning the service of God, but is simply a means of increasing our usefulness and our strength and success. The Franks will not keep faith long, or abide by sworn treaties; therefore make a truce with them all, which will enable them to break up and disperse, enduring the blows they have suffered and

[1] Qur'ān VIII, 63.

leaving no one in Palestine capable of resisting and standing up to us.'

The assembly continued to impress this view on the Sultan until he gave way and consented to their demands. The distance between the two armies was not more than a day's march, and the clouds of dust were already gathering over the outposts; if we had moved we should have dislodged them and thrown them into complete confusion. But God's will prevailed, and the King of England's request for peace was granted. I helped to draw up the treaty and wrote the text, fixing the boundaries and specifying the terms, and this was Tuesday 21 sha'bān 588, which corresponds to 1 September (1192). The truce lasted three years and eight months. They believed that the breathing-space coincided with their arrival by sea and the possibility of continuous reinforcements of men arriving and settling there. So they stipulated a general truce by land and sea, plains and mountains, desert and cities. The Franks were assigned the land from Jaffa to Caesarea and from Acre to Tyre. The Franks, even when abandoning land formerly held by them, appeared happy and content, and included Tripoli and Antioch in the terms, and the near and distant provinces.

CHAPTER SEVEN

The gallant Marquis of Montferrat did not see this peace, nor did he grasp the royal crown that he had coveted. There is a certain disagreement in the Muslim texts about who armed the assassins who killed him at Tyre in April 1192: Bahā' ad-Din and 'Imād ad-Din expressly name Richard of England (into whose negotiations Conrad, as we have seen, insinuated himself with his own scheme, repeating the personal approach made to Saladin by the Count of Tripoli before Hittīn), whereas Ibn al-Athīr suggests Saladin himself, attempting to kill Conrad and Richard at the same time. This seems very unlikely (consider on this point 'Imād ad-Din's persuasive suggestion that Conrad died at an inopportune moment for the Muslims), but the episode is strangely reflected, in a manner that reinforces suspicion of Saladin, in a later account, corrupted by legend, of the murder of a Frankish King at Acre enjoined upon the faithful by the Watcher of the Mountain to please his friend the Sultan. This strange text, which here follows accounts by 'Imād ad-Din and Ibn al-Athīr, is from an Isma'ilite source: an anecdotal and edifying biography of the contemporary Grand Master of the Assassins, Rashid ad-Din Sinān. In fact the assassins tried more than once to kill Saladin, whose rigid orthodoxy was irreconcilable with their heterodox beliefs.

THE ASSASSINATION OF CONRAD OF MONTFERRAT

('IMĀD AD-DIN, 420–2)

On Tuesday 13 rabī' II (588/28 April 1192) he was entertained by the Bishop of Tyre and ate his last meal, for his last day was come. He who would cut off all his hope was even now at the door. He was condemned to Hell, where (the angel) Malik was awaiting his arrival, and Tartarus was on the watch for his coming; the deepest circle of Hell-fire was burning, the blaze blazed and the flame flamed as it waited for him. The moment was at hand when the abyss would receive him and the fires of Hell would burn for him, and the Angels of Justice were even now building the foul place where they would torment him. Hell had already opened its seven gates, gaping to engorge him. Meanwhile he lounged carelessly on his couch eating his food. He ate and made his collation, unaware of the precipice ahead of him; he ate and drank, sated and solaced himself, and went out and rode his horse. Suddenly two men fell upon him like two mangy wolves and with their daggers stopped his movement and struck him down near those shops. Then one of them fled and entered a church, having put out that vile soul. The Marquis, at death's door, but still with a flicker of life in him, said 'Take me into the church', and they took him in thinking that he was safe there. But when that one of the two murderers saw him, he fell on him to finish him off and struck him again, blow on blow. The Franks seized the two companions, and found that they were two apostates of the Brotherhood of Isma'ilites.[1] They asked them who had commanded them to commit this murder, and the assassins said it was the king of England. They also said that they had been Christians for six months and had begun a life of asceticism and purification, frequenting churches and living lives of rigorous piety. One was in service with Ibn Barzān and one with the Prince of Sidon so that they could both be close to the Marquis, ensuring his confidence in them by their constant presence. Then they seized hold of his saddle-bow and slaughtered him. They were both subjected to cruel punishments and were reduced to the depths of degradation. An extraordinary case of two Unbelievers shedding an Unbeliever's blood, two criminals killing a criminal!

When the Marquis was dead and hung head downward in Hell, the King of England assumed control of Tyre and conferred it upon Count Henry,[2] arranging it all with him. Henry

[1] I.e. the Assassins, considered to be outside the Faith by orthodox Muslims.

[2] Henry of Champagne.

married the Marquis' wife on the same night,[1] maintaining that he had first right to the dead man's wife. She was pregnant, but this did not prevent his uniting himself with her, something even more disgusting than the coupling of the flesh. I asked one of their courtiers to whom paternity would be awarded and he said: 'It will be the Queen's child.' You see the licentiousness of these foul Unbelievers!

The death of the Marquis in such circumstances was of little benefit to us, although he was one of the ringleaders of error, because he was one of the King of England's enemies, his rival for the kingdom and the throne and his competitor in all and for all. He was in contact with us in the hope of our help to get back what the King had taken from him. Whenever the King of England heard that the Marquis' ambassador was at the Sultan's court he at once sent messages full of humility and docility, and resumed negotiations for peace, and it was possible to hope that light would dawn on his night of error. When the Marquis was killed the fear in his heart was calmed, his troubled disquiet vanished, he became serene again, his affairs returned to normal and the evil he represented for Islām increased. In his opposition to the Marquis he had taken the part of the old King (Guy), showing him the affection of a loving relative and investing him with the island of Cyprus and all its territory, attempting by his appointment to cure all its ills. Once the Marquis was dead he realized that he had been wrong to support Guy, and was afraid that he would have to fly from his hostility and that he was not secure from attack by him. When his enemy vanished he found his calm again, tranquillity returned, his madness ebbed, his wrath dispersed, his good fortune excited him and he poured out all the brutality of the fountain of unbelief. In spite of all this he did not break off relations with Guy or discard him, but continued to send him pleasing messages and to try to charm and beguile him.

[1] He became governor of Tyre and married Isabella on the same night.

(IBN AL-ATHĪR, XII, 51)

In this year, on 13 rabī' II, the Frankish Marquis, the ruler of Tyre—God damn him!—was killed. He was the greatest devil of all the Franks. The cause of his death was Saladin's negotiation with Sinān,[1] leader of the Isma'ilites, to send a man to kill the King of England; if he then killed the Marquis he would get 2,000 *dinar*. It was not possible to kill the King of England, and it did not seem to Sinān to be in their interests, in that it would free Saladin of all worry about the Franks and he would then turn on the Isma'ilites themselves. On the other hand, he was anxious to have the money, and so he resolved to organize the death of the Marquis. He sent two men in monk's robes, who entered the service of Ibn Barzān of ar-Ramla and the Prince of Sidon. They stayed with them for six months, showing great devotion, and the Marquis felt secure and confident with them. After this time the Bishop of Tyre held a banquet for the Marquis. He went, ate at his table, drank his wine, and then left. The two Batinites[2] fell on him and inflicted mortal wounds upon him, then one of them fled and went into a church to hide. When he realized that the Marquis had been brought into the same church to have his wounds bandaged he fell on him and killed him. After his death the two assassins were also killed. The Franks attributed the murder to a command from the King of England, so that he could be sole ruler of Palestine. When he was dead Count Henry, a Frankish Count from abroad, became governor of Tyre and married the Queen (Conrad's widow) the same night, and consummated the marriage with her although she was pregnant, this being no impediment to marriage among them.

[1] The Old Man of the Mountain, or Grand Master of the Assassins; see the next section.

[2] Another name for the Isma'ilites, or Self-Sacrificers, or Assassins. Literally 'followers of esoteric doctrines'.

This Count Henry was a nephew of the King of France on his father's side and of the King of England on his mother's. He was to rule the Frankish parts of Palestine after the English King's return home, and he lived until 594 (1197), when he fell from a balcony and died. He was a capable man, pleasant and tolerant. When the King of England left for home, Henry sent a messenger to Saladin to conciliate him and win his good-will. He asked him for the gift of a robe of honour, and said: 'You know that to put on the *qabā* and the *sharbūsh*[1] is not approved of among us, but I would put them on if they came from you, because of the regard I have for you.' Saladin sent him sumptuous robes of honour, among them a *qabā* and a *sharbūsh*, and he wore them in Acre.

(MANAQIB RASHID AD-DIN, 463–6)

A trusted and virtuous Companion told us that when Saladin took Acre a Frankish King came against him from overseas with an army that attacked Acre and took it, killing all the Muslims there. Then a tent was put up for him opposite Saladin's and his army took up its position facing Saladin's army, so that war between them was imminent. Saladin no longer knew how to get rid of him. Then our Lord, who at that time was at the Fortress of Kahf[2] said—peace be to us from him!—[3] 'Our friend Saladin is now in a difficulty.' So he called two of his assassins whom he had taught to speak the Frankish language, and when they came he had them given two Frankish costumes and two Frankish swords. Then he said: 'Go to King Saladin with my letter. Go by night to such and such a place'—and he told them where to spend each night—'You will arrive at Acre

[1] The *qabā* is a sort of cassock, open at the front. The *sharbūsh* is a tall triangular biretta. Both were part of Oriental costume of the period.

[2] One of the Isma'ilite forts near Baniyās in northern Syria. 'Our Lord' is the Old Man of the Mountain, Rashid ad-Din Sinān, whose deeds are celebrated in this text.

[3] Note the heterodox formula used in place of the orthodox 'peace be upon him'.

on such and such a day at the hour of noon. If you do not arrive on the appointed day and hour you will not achieve your aim. When the time comes, God willing, and you are presented to Saladin, salute him from me, assure him of my regard, and hand over my letter. When he has read it and absorbed it and understood its meaning, tell him that I have sent you to his enemy the King of the Franks, to kill him that night. Leave Saladin at sunset, leave the (Muslim) army and approach the Frankish army along the seashore, mingling with them in the darkness of night. Find your way by night to the King's pavilion, and when you have found him, drunk and sleepy, with head drooping and no one at his side, cut off his head and take his sword-belt and sword. If anyone addresses you reply in Frankish, and no one will notice what you are doing. When you get back to Saladin, set the head before him with the sword-belt and sword. He will immediately attack the Frankish army, drive them off, cut them to pieces, please God, and kill many of them, and he will be victorious and happy. Then he will want to recompense you, and will ask you to express whatever desires you may have. You will not ask for gold, silver or any such thing, but will say simply: 'We are men who have thrown away our lives to obey God and have left behind the world and all its possessions and renounced them. We therefore desire none of them, but for one thing: when we left our families, our children had no flour. Would the King make a gift of some flour to each of us, that is all.' 'We obey,' answered the two assassins, and left our Lord Rashid ad-Din Sinān—peace be to us from him!—and went to Acre, obeying all the instructions given to them and acting according to all his precepts. They reached Acre precisely at the moment, and presented themselves to Saladin, handed over the letter, saluted him from their Lord, and said: 'Our Lord has commanded us to kill the Frankish King today, and has told us the precise moment, saying that we shall find him at that moment with his face on the ground, drunk, with no one at his side. He also said that if we do not find him precisely at the appointed moment we shall be unable to do anything, and shall not even reach him.'

When Saladin heard the speech they made he was very much cheered by it, and treated them with great honour. They stayed with him until the sun began to set, and then put their Frankish costumes on again and spoke to one another in the Frankish language. Saladin was amazed by the clothing and the language they used. He smiled, amused by the plan. The two set out and moved away from the two armies, then they turned toward the seashore and the Frankish army, and mixed with the soldiers in the darkness of night. They drew close to the (enemy) King, and at the time and moment appointed went in to Richard and found him dead asleep with his head on the ground, as the Lord had said, drunk, and without a living soul near him. They cut off his head, put it in a sack, took his sword and sword-belt, left the Frankish camp quickly and soon reached Saladin again. They put the head down before him with the sword and belt. He kissed both their foreheads and ordered the army to saddle up at once. He himself leapt into the saddle and attacked the Frankish army, putting it to flight, cutting it to pieces and almost exterminating it. Happy and content, the victorious conqueror, he asked for the two Faithful, and when they appeared he rose in their honour, showed them every courtesy, and his viziers and courtiers likewise rose to their feet. Then he gave them robes of honour, made them sit beside him, and said: 'Tell me whatever you desire, ask me for whatever you want. My duty is to content you.' They replied: 'God with His angels assist Your Majesty and cast your enemies into Hell! This world is nothing, and whoever deludes himself will repent when penitence is of no avail. We are of those who have turned away from worldly goods and renounced them. In truth, we ask nothing but two portions of flour, one for each of us, for our families.'

Then the Sultan Saladin ordained that in each province near the forts of the Company[1] of right guidance ten villages should be inscribed (as tributaries), and that in every city a 'House of the Company' should be built as a centre for the Company of right guidance. So in Cairo, Damascus, Hims, Hamāt, Aleppo and other centres this was done, and all the houses are known by the name of 'the Company'. As well as this he loaded the two Brethren with gifts and sent a splendid gift to our Lord Rashid ad-Din.

[1] Literally, mission, propaganda (*da'wa*), meaning here the Isma'ilite sect. 'Propaganda' would serve very well also a little further on, where the author speaks of the sect's centres in various cities.

CHAPTER EIGHT

Saladin's illness and death, shortly after the truce with the Franks, are described in the most minute detail by the faithful Bahā' ad-Din. Disregarding a certain pettiness and pedantry common to nearly all these Muslim sources, his account reveals a sincere devotion to its hero, and recognition that he was an exceptional person who won the regard of both East and West. His pious end, and the complete attachment to the spirit and letter of his Faith that marked Saladin's real life, banish Lessing's fantasies of the liberal and enlightened ruler.

SALADIN'S ILLNESS AND DEATH

(BAHĀ' AD-DIN, 361–9)

On the Friday evening he felt a great weariness, and even before midnight had an attack of bilious fever, more evident internally than externally. On the morning of Saturday 16 safar 589/21 February 1193 he woke up feeling weak and with traces of fever, but this was not apparent to the ordinary observer. The qadi al-Fadil and I presented ourselves, together with his son al-Malik al-Afdal, and we spent a long time with him. He complained of a disturbed night, and spoke cheerfully with us until almost midday. Then we left him, but we left our hearts with him. He invited us to a luncheon presided over by al-Malik al-Afdal; al-Fadil never attended luncheons, so he retired, and I went to the southern chamber where the meal was served. Al-Malik al-Afdal sat in his father's place. Then I too retired, unable to remain because of the turmoil in my soul; and indeed several people wept, taking as a sinister omen the sight of the son in the Sultan's place.

From that time the illness grew more serious. We continued

to present ourselves regularly morning and evening, and the qadi al-Fadil and I were admitted at various times during the day when the sickness abated somewhat. His illness was in the head; one of the signs that his life was now at an end was the absence of his personal doctor, who knew his constitution and looked after him at home and when he was travelling. The doctors decided to bleed him and did so on the fourth day, but the illness grew worse and the humours of his body, of which the dry predominated, began to fail. The progress of the illness eventually produced an extreme weakness.

On the sixth day we sat him up, supporting his back on a cushion, and sent for warm water for him to drink, shortly after he had drunk an emollient medicine. He found the water too hot and complained of it, so a second cup was brought, which he found too cold, but without becoming enraged or crying out. He simply said: 'Dear God, can no one produce water of the right temperature?' At this the qadi and I left the room, weeping hot tears, and the qadi said to me: 'What a spirit Islām is about to lose! By Allah, any other man would have thrown the cup at the head of whoever brought it. . . .'

On the sixth, seventh and eighth days the illness grew steadily worse, obscuring the lucidity of his mind. On the ninth day he lost consciousness and could not take his potion. Great fear spread through the city: the merchants, terrified, began to remove their wares from the markets,[1] and everyone was overcome by sadness and grief beyond words.

The qadi al-Fadil and I sat together every night until almost a third of the night had passed, and we would then present ourselves at the Palace gates and if the way were clear would go in to him to see how he was before retiring, or else we would get news of his condition and then retire. We would find people standing and waiting for us to come out, to judge his condition from our faces as we passed. On the tenth day he was twice

[1] The ruler's death was often the occasion of riots and looting.

given an enema, which gave him some relief, and he was able to take a little barley water. This news caused great public rejoicing. As usual, we waited until a part of the night had gone by and then went to the Palace gate, where we met Jamāl ad-Daula Iqbāl. We asked him to tell us what was happening, and he went in and sent al-Malik al-Mu'azzam Turanshāh to tell us that Saladin had begun to sweat at the legs. We gave thanks to God, and begged al-Malik al-Mu'azzam to feel the rest of his body and let us know how the sweating went. He examined him and came out to tell us that Saladin was sweating freely, so we went away very much relieved. But on the morning of the eleventh day of his illness, Tuesday 26 safar, when we came to the gate to ask for news we were told that he was sweating so copiously that it soaked the mattress and the matting and even the ground, and that the violence of his thirst was beyond belief, and caused the doctors to abandon hope.

When al-Malik al-Afdal saw his father's condition and was convinced that there was no hope he hurriedly arranged for the oaths of loyalty to be taken.[1] He held audience for the purpose in the Palace of Ridwān, so called because he[2] had lived there. He sent for the qadis and had ready a brief formula comprising an oath of loyalty to the Sultan as long as he lived and to al-Afdal after his father's death. He apologized for this in public, saying that the Sultan was worse and that he did not know what would happen but this was simply a precautionary measure following normal procedure among rulers. The first to be called on to take the oath was Sa'd ad-Din Mas'ūd,

[1] The details that follow show clearly the fragility of these empires based on an archaic military feudalism, when they found themselves without an energetic character like Saladin, or later al-'Adil and al-Kamil, as ruler. All the precautions taken here by the first-born, al-Afdal, to secure the succession in Syria and the dominant position throughout the Ayyubid empire fell to the ground chiefly because of the independence of the amīrs, whose only aim was personal advantage and privilege. The future betrayed the hopes of this and all Saladin's sons, and the primacy passed to his brother al-Malik al-'Adil.

[2] Amīr of Aleppo during the First Crusade.

brother of Badr ad-Din Maudūd and governor of the city. He took the oath immediately, without making any conditions. Then it was the turn of Nasir ad-Din of Sahyūn, who took the oath on condition that the fortress he held should continue in his hands. Next came Sabiq ad-Din of Shaizar, who omitted the divorce clause,[1] with the excuse that he never used that formula in an oath. Then came Khushtarīn Husáin al-Hakkari, then Nushirwān az-Zarzari, who made it a condition that he should receive a satisfactory fief, then 'Alkān and Mankalān. At this point luncheon was served and everyone ate. Proceedings were resumed in the afternoon. Maimūn al-Qasri and the old man Shams ad-Din Sunqur presented themselves, and said: 'We swear on condition that we are never asked to draw sword against any of your brothers', undertaking instead to defend their states. Maimūn al-Qasri said the same. Sunqur refused for a while to take the oath, then he said: 'You will receive my word as governor of Natrūn, on condition that I keep the city.' Then it was Sa'ama's turn, and he said: 'I have no fief: tell me what I have to swear by', and after some argument finally took the oath on condition that a satisfactory fief were given him. Sunqur the Disfigured took the oath on condition that he received satisfaction, and so did Aibek the Snub-nosed, who omitted the divorce clause. Finally came Husām ad-Din Bishara, leader of them all. Al-Afdal had not summoned any of the Egyptian amīrs or asked anything of them,[2] but only made those mentioned take the oath so as to have things in order. I may have omitted the names of one or two more obscure amīrs. The formula of the oath was; 'First, from this moment I dedicate and consecrate all my deepest feeling to al-Malik an-Nasir for as long as he lives, binding myself to sacrifice in the defence of his state myself, my possessions, my sword and my

[1] A common feature of Muslim oaths was for the taker to declare that if he broke his word his wives would be repudiated by him.

[2] In fact al-Afdal's direct sovereignty, as Saladin's heir, was valid only in Syria, the heir to Egypt being Saladin's brother al-'Adil.

men, in obedience to his orders and awaiting his pleasure; and after him to his son al-Afdal ʿAli and his heirs. In God's name I shall be loyal to him, defend his state and territory with my person, my wealth, my sword and my men, and obey his command and prohibition. This I both profess openly and inwardly adhere to. God is the guarantee of what I say.'

The night before Wednesday 27 safar 589, which was the twelfth of his illness, the Sultan's condition deteriorated, his strength diminished and the women who tended him would not allow us to visit him. That night the qadi al-Fadil, Ibn az-Zaki (qadi of Damascus) and I met together. Ibn az-Zaki did not usually come at this hour, and al-Malik al-Afdal invited us to spend the night with him. This did not seem a good idea to al-Fadil, as people were waiting for us to leave the citadel, and he was afraid that if we did not emerge alarmist rumours would run through the city and looting would follow. He advised us therefore to go down, and suggested that Shaikh Abu Jaʿfar, imām of al-Kallasa,[1] should be sent for. He was a good man, and could spend the night in the citadel in order to be at hand if God called Saladin to him that night. He would be able to keep the women away from Saladin, and to recall to him the formulas of the Muslim faith and the name of God. This was done, and we went away, each ready to offer his life for Saladin's. He passed the night, being now near his end, with Shaikh Abu Jaʿfar, who recited the Qur'ān at his bed-head and recalled Almighty God's name to his mind. On the night of the ninth day he had lost consciousness, recovering it only for brief intervals, and Shaikh Abu Jaʿfar told us that when he reached the passage: 'He is God, than whom there is no god, knower of the unseen and of the seen'[2] he heard the Sultan reply 'True'. It was an extraordinarily opportune recovery of consciousness and an act of divine providence toward him, God be praised for it!

[1] A small sanctuary near the Great Mosque of Damascus.

[2] Qur'ān LIX, 22.

He breathed his last after the hour of the morning prayer on Wednesday 27 safar 589/4 March 1193. The qadi al-Fadil came into his room just after dawn at the precise moment of his death, and when I arrived he had already passed into the bosom of divine grace. I was told that when Shaikh Abu Ja'far reached the words of the Qur'ān; 'There is no other God but He, and in Him is my trust,[1] the Sultan smiled, his face illumined, and he gave up his spirit to his Lord.

The day of his death was a day of grief for Islām and the Muslims, the equal of which they had not known since the days of the right-guided Caliphs. The citadel, the city and the entire world were overcome with a grief beyond words, and, by God, I had heard before of people who have desired to ransom those dear to them with their own lives, and had thought it just a figure of speech, not to be taken literally, but on that day I knew that if it had been possible to ransom him with our lives I and several others would have been ready. His son al-Malik al-Afdal held audience in the north chamber to receive condolences, and the gate of the city was shut to all but the amīrs closest to the family, and to the scholars and divines. It was a weary day; everyone was so deep in his own grief and sorrow and misery that he could pay attention to no one else. No poet's recital or preacher's discourse was of any use. His sons went out among the people crying out for pity; the sight of them was enough to make one's heart die of pain, and so it went on until after the midday prayer. Then we occupied ourselves with washing his body and clothing it in the funeral shroud, but we could use only equipment worth almost nothing for the purpose, unless we resorted to borrowing— even to the straw with which the clay is washed.[2] The lawyer ad-Dáula'i washed his body; I was invited to be present, but had not the strength of

[1] Qur'an IX, 130.

[2] Another example of Saladin's extreme austerity and probity. The function of straw and clay in the funeral ritual I do not know.

heart to witness such a scene. After the midday prayer he was carried out in a coffin draped simply with a length of material procured, like the other materials needed to shroud him, by the qadi al-Fadil from permitted sources known to him.[1] When men saw the dead Sultan being borne away, voices and lamentations rose on high. Men's grief was so great that it overcame them, and distracted them even from the prayer recited over him by men clothed in sackcloth. The first to act as imām was the qadi Muhyi ad-Din ibn az-Zaki. Then the body was carried back to the palace in the garden where he had lain during his illness and was buried in the west pavilion. He was laid in his tomb at about the hour of the evening prayer; God sanctify his spirit and illumine his sepulchre!

[1] The 'permitted', i.e. judicially impeccable, origin of the sources of food and of all the objects used by the faithful in life and death is a constant preoccupation of Muslim piety and casuistry.

Part Three

THE AYYUBIDS AND THE INVASION OF EGYPT

CHAPTER ONE

While the Fourth Crusade turned its attention to Constantinople (1203), Islām had another fifteen years of truce, which enabled al-Malik al-'Adil to unite his brother Saladin's kingdom firmly under his own control and to organize as one empire the Ayyubid domains from Egypt to Mesopotamia. The new Crusade had its eyes on Egypt itself, as the heart of Muslim resistance at a time when the Mongol threat loomed in the East, soon to grow to its full, terrible stature. Ibn al-Athīr, with his usual breadth of vision, rises above the level of a local chronicler to consider the fate of Islām as a whole, and perceives the gravity of the double threat. He expresses it both in his dramatic description of the Mongol invasion and in this history of the Fifth Crusade, uniting in one cogent account the four years of the Egyptian campaign (1217–21). As a complement to Ibn al-Athīr's account we include that of Ibn Wasil, an Ayyubid historian until recently almost inaccessible in his original form and therefore little studied.

The Fifth Crusade

THE FRANKS GATHER IN SYRIA, MARCH ON EGYPT AND TAKE DAMIETTA, WHICH IS RECOVERED BY THE MUSLIMS

(IBN AL-ATHĪR, XII, 208–9)

From beginning to end this episode lasted for four years less one month. We shall speak of it at this point (614/1217) because it was in this year that the Franks appeared, and we shall give the whole account as a continuous narrative because its various phases followed one another without intervals. In this year, then, the Frankish reinforcements arrived from overseas, from Rome and the other countries west and north of us, all under the control of the Lord of Rome (the Pope), who held a very high place in their society, so that they dared not disobey him or stray from the path ordained by him for good or ill. He sent the armies from his own states under a group of commanders, and ordered the other Frankish Kings either to go in person or to send an army. They obeyed his command and assembled in Acre, on the coast of Syria.[1]

THE FRANKS BESIEGE AND TAKE DAMIETTA

(IBN AL-ATHĪR, XII, 210–3)

When the Franks returned from the siege of at-Tur[2] they camped at Acre until the beginning of 615, and then set out for Damietta by sea, reaching it in safar/May 1218, and anchored at al-Jiza. The Nile was between them and Damietta, and one of its branches flowed into the sea near the city. At this point a tall and well-fortified tower had been built by the Egyptians, with massive iron chains slung across the river to the walls of Damietta to prevent ships arriving from the sea from travelling up the Nile into Egypt. The Franks disembarked at al-Jiza, with the Nile between them and Damietta, and built a wall on their side and dug out a trench to defend themselves from attack. Then they began to assault Damietta. They built siege-engines and mobile towers that they moved on ships to attack and seize the tower, which was full of defenders. Al-Malik al-Kamil, the son of al-Malik al-'Adil and ruler of Damietta and all Egypt, had camped in a place called 'Adiliyya, near Damietta, and sent continuous supplies of troops to Damietta to prevent the enemy from landing on his territory. The Franks, despite the unremitting attack on the tower, had no success and suffered the destruction of their own engines and machines of war. In spite of this they persevered in their attack, but spent fourteen months in unsuccessful attempts before they finally suc-

[1] With King John of Brienne, Andrew of Hungary, Hugh of Cyprus, etc.
[2] A Muslim fort near Acre.

ceeded and cut the chains so that their ships could enter the Nile and they could step safely ashore on to Egyptian soil. Al-Malik al-Kamil then had a great bridge built to prevent their getting any further up the Nile, and it cost them a fierce battle to break through it. Then he took a large number of cargo vessels and sank them in the Nile to impede the Franks' passage upstream. The Franks fell back on a canal called al-Azraq, through which the Nile used to flow in earlier times; they dredged it and deepened it upstream of the sunken ships, diverted the river into this channel to the sea, and sent their ships up that way as far as a place called Bura, also in the area of al-Jiza, facing the place where al-Malik al-Kamil was encamped, to attack him from there, for they had no other way of reaching him to attack him, as Damietta was situated between them and him. When they reached Bura they found themselves face to face with him and began to attack him across the river. Their repeated assaults had, however, no success, and made no impression on the situation at Damietta, which was being reinforced and supplied uninterruptedly, and had the Nile between itself and the Franks. The city stood safe and unharmed, its gates open, and suffered no hardship or damage from the siege.

Then in jumada II 615/August 1218, by God's decree, al-Malik al-'Adil died, as we shall describe, God willing. His death lowered public morale for he was the real Sultan and although his sons bore kingly titles they were subordinate to his command, by grace of which they governed the various provinces.[1] In this situation, under enemy attack, he died. One of the amīrs of Egypt was a man called 'Imād ad-Din Ahmad ibn 'Ali, known as Ibn al-Mashtūb, a Hakkarite Kurd. He was the leader of the Egyptian amīrs and had a great following among them, especially among the other Kurds, who all

[1] Al-'Adil had succeeded in uniting under his supreme command the various domains of his brother Saladin.

obeyed him docilely. Ibn al-Mashtūb hatched a plot with the other amīrs to depose al-Malik al-Kamil in favour of his brother al-Malik al-Fa'iz ibn al-'Adil, and through him to control the whole country. When al-Kamil heard the news he abandoned his position and went by night with a small detachment to a village called Ashmūn Tannāh, near which he made his camp. The army, its Sultan gone, was left to look after itself. No one gave a moment's thought to his nearest neighbour. They could only carry a little of the lightest gear in the way of tents, provisions, arms and equipment, so they left the rest where it was: stores, arms, horses and tents, and made their way toward al-Kamil.

The following morning the Franks could not see a single Muslim on the river-bank where they were used to seeing them. At first they were unsure what had happened, but when information reached them later on they crossed the Nile unopposed, without any incidents or any need to defend themselves, and set foot on the soil of Damietta. This was on 20 dhu l-qa'da 615/ 8 February 1219. They collected enormous, incalculable quantities of booty from the Muslim camp. Al-Malik al-Kamil was inclined to leave Egypt, for he did not trust a single member of his army and the Franks had seized everything without any effort or work on their part. But God was gracious to the Muslims, and al-Malik al-Mu'azzam Isa, the son of al-'Adil,[1] arrived two days after this, while everything was in turmoil. His arrival cheered and strengthened his brother, who held his position with renewed courage. Ibn al-Mashtūb, driven out into Syria, came to an understanding with al-Malik al-Ashraf and went to join his army.

When the Franks crossed to Damietta all the Arab nomads of the various tribes united to pillage the area around the city. They cut the roads and indulged in the most ruinous sort of brigandage, which caused the Muslims more damage than it

[1] Sultan of Damascus.

did the Franks themselves. The gravest disadvantage that the people of Damietta suffered was their lack of any local militia, for until then the Sultan and his troops had been within reach of the city to defend it from an enemy, but when this catastrophe occurred no soldiers were sent in to garrison the city. This was the fault of Ibn al-Mashtūb, whose just punishment was not long delayed, for he met a violent end, as we shall describe later, God willing. So the Franks laid siege to Damietta and attacked it by land and sea. They dug a trench in their usual way to defend themselves from Muslim attacks. After a prolonged struggle the defenders reached the end of their resources. They were almost without food, and exhausted by unending battle. The Franks were sufficiently numerous to take turns at the fighting, but Damietta lacked the soldiers to make this possible. In spite of this they held out amazingly and suffered great losses from death in battle, wounds and sickness. The siege lasted until 27 sha'bān 616/8 November 1219, when the survivors, few in number and without provisions, were unable any longer to defend their city. So they surrendered the city to the Franks in exchange for their lives. Some left, some stayed, unable to move; the city's inhabitants were scattered.

THE MUSLIMS RECONQUER DAMIETTA FROM THE FRANKS

(IBN AL-ATHĪR, XII, 213–6)

The Franks settled in Damietta after the conquest and sent out raiding parties into all the surrounding territories to pillage and slaughter. The population evacuated the region, and the Franks began to set things in order and to fortify the citadel most carefully in an effort to make it impregnable. Al-Malik al-Kamil for his part was stationed close to the enemy, on the borders of his own territory, ready to defend it. When the Franks at home learnt that the Franks had seized Damietta they hurried there from all directions, so that it became a centre for them when they emigrated. Al-Malik al-Mu'azzam returned to Syria and destroyed (the walls of) Jerusalem in dhu l-qa'da of that year, because of the general fear of the Franks.[1] The entire Muslim world, men and territories, seemed likely at this moment to be lost to the East on the one hand and the West on the other: from the East came the Tartars, who reached Irāq, Azarbaijān, Arrān and other provinces, as we shall narrate, God willing; while from the West came the Franks, who took a city like Damietta in Egypt because of its lack of fortifications to protect it from an enemy. All the rest of Egypt and Syria was on the point of collapse and everyone was terrified of the invaders and went in anticipation of disaster night and day. The population of Egypt was even ready to evacuate the country for fear of the enemy, but 'It was no time to escape',[2] surrounded as they were on all sides by the enemy. If al-Kamil had allowed them, they would have abandoned the country altogether, but impeded as they were they stood firm. Al-Malik al-Kamil sent a stream of letters to his two brothers al-Malik al-Mu'azzam of Damascus and al-Malik al-Ashraf who ruled the Jazira, Armenia and the rest, imploring their help and begging them to come in person, or at least to send him their troops. The Lord of Damascus went himself to al-Ashraf, but found him unable to send help to their brother because many of his vassals were in a state of rebellion, as will be explained under the year 615, following the death of al-Malik al-Qahir, ruler of Mosul. He therefore excused him and returned home, and the situation facing al-Malik al-Kamil remained unchanged.

Then the rebellions in al-Malik al-Ashraf's kingdom were put down and the rebellious Princes restored to obedience. This

1 Because he was afraid that he might have to hand the Holy City back to them (it was in fact offered to them at one point), and wanted at least to destroy its military significance.

2 Qur'ān XXXVIII, 2.

was accomplished by 618, at which time al-Malik al-Kamil was still confronting the Franks. At the beginning of 618 al-Kamil learnt that al-Ashraf's troubles had subsided and so he sent to his brothers to ask their help. The ruler of Damascus once again begged his brother to set out, and he did in fact start for Damascus with the troops at his disposal, commanding the rest to join him there, where he would halt and wait for them. Some of his amīrs and courtiers advised him to send the troops on and return home himself, for fear of an uprising there, but he rejected their advice: 'I have set out on a Holy War,' he said, 'and must carry it through to the end.' So he set off for Egypt.

The Franks with all their forces came out of Damietta to confront al-Malik al-Kamil. The two armies encamped facing one another but separated by a tributary of the Nile known as Bahr Ashmūn. The Franks attacked the Muslims with catapults and ballistas, and were, like everyone else, sure that they would gain control of the whole of Egypt. When al-Ashraf reached Egypt his brother al-Kamil learnt of his arrival and set out to meet him, delighting both himself and the other Muslims by this meeting, which all hoped would lead to success and (final) victory. (Even) al-Mu'azzam of Damascus came to Egypt and made for Damietta, thinking that his two brothers and their armies would already have laid siege to it. Others say that he heard that the Franks were making for Damietta[1] and went in that direction to confront them while the two brothers fell on them from behind; but God knows best. When al-Ashraf and al-Kamil met they decided to make for a branch of the Nile known as Bahr al-Mahalla, which they did, and pressed the Franks more and more closely. The Muslim galleys came down the Nile, attacked the Frankish fleet and took three ships with all their crew, cargo and arms. This delighted and encouraged the Muslims, who saw it as a good omen and drew from it the strength they needed to overcome the enemy.

[1] In an attempt to withdraw from the flooded Delta: see below, p. 262.

Meanwhile ambassadors passed between the two sides to discuss the terms of the peace. The Muslims offered the Franks Ascalon, Tiberias, Sidon, Jábala, Laodicea and all Saladin's conquests except al-Karak, in return for Damietta,[1] but the Franks refused and asked for 300,000 *dinar* as indemnity for the destruction of the walls of Jerusalem, to be used to rebuild them, and made no further moves, except to say that they could not give up their claim to al-Karak. In such a situation, being on the losing side, the Muslims could do nothing but continue the fight.

The Franks were confident of their own strength and had brought with them provisions for only a few days, thinking that the Muslim army would offer no resistance and that the whole of the cultivated area of Egypt would fall into their hands, so that they would be able to obtain whatever provisions they wanted; this was because of the divinely predestined intention (to destroy them). A detachment of Muslims crossed the river to the Frankish side and opened the flood-gates. The river flooded most of the area and left the Franks with only one way out, along a narrow causeway. Al-Kamil threw a bridge over the Nile at Ashmūn, and his troops crossed it and held the road along which the Franks would have to pass to reach Damietta. There was no escape. In this crisis a big cargo vessel called a *maramma* reached the Franks. It was defended by a convoy of fire-ships, all loaded with food, arms and reinforcements. The Muslim galleys attacked and fought them, and overcame and seized the *maramma* and all its fire-ships. When the Franks saw this they lost heart and realized that they had made a serious error in leaving Damietta to venture into unknown terrain, surrounded, harassed by arrows and attacked by Muslim forces on all sides. The situation became so serious for the Franks that

[1] This gives some idea of the relative importance of Damietta, and the wisdom of the Franks in attacking it. The al-Karak excepted from the towns offered (almost all the towns that Saladin conquered!) is al-Karak in Moab, a vital point on the line of communication between Syria and Egypt.

they burnt their tents, ballistas and luggage and decided to attack the Muslims in the hope of breaking through and getting back to Damietta. But the object of their longings was far off and their way to it restricted, by the mud and water surrounding them, to a single path, along which they would have to fight their way through the Muslims who held it.

When they realized that they were completely surrounded, that communications were very difficult and destruction imminent,[1] they lost heart, broke their crosses, and their devil abandoned them. They sent messages to al-Malik al-Kamil and al-Ashraf asking for their lives in exchange for Damietta with no indemnity. While negotiations were in progress they saw a great cloud of dust in the sky and heard a great noise from Damietta. The Muslims thought that it must be help coming for the Franks and were alarmed, but in fact it was al-Malik al-Mu'azzam from Damascus, who had taken the route to Damietta, as we mentioned. He reinforced the Muslims and caused the Franks still greater dread and despondency. They agreed to make peace in return for Damietta, and the agreement was reached and the oaths taken on 7 rajab 618/27 August 1221. The Frankish kings, counts and barons came from Damietta as hostages in the hands of al-Malik al-Kamil and al-Ashraf. There was the King of Acre, the Papal Legate, Louis[2] and others; twenty in all. They sent their priests and monks to Damietta to negotiate the surrender. The inhabitants yielded and handed the city over on the ninth, a memorable day for Islām. It is said that just when the Muslims received the city from the Franks help arrived for them by sea. If it had reached the city before the Muslims they would have refused to hand it over, but the Muslims arrived first because it was decreed thus by God. Of the population of Damietta only a few isolated individuals were left; they had all dispersed, some leaving the

[1] Literally: 'death was gnashing its teeth at them'.

[2] Duke of Bavaria (reading *Ludwīsh* for the *Kundrīsh* of the text).

city of their own free will, some dead, some prisoners of the Franks. When the Muslims entered they found it effectively fortified by the Franks in a way that made it impregnable. But Almighty God restored justice to him who waited and right to the righteous, giving the Muslims victory beyond their expectations. For their highest hope was to get Damietta in exchange for all their conquests in Syria, but God gave them Damietta while preserving Syria for them. Praise and thanks to God for His grace to Islām and the Muslims, for turning the enemy's attack aside and liberating them at the same time from the Tartar threat, as we shall narrate, God willing.

OTHER DETAILS OF THE FRANKISH SURRENDER

(IBN WASIL, FO. 209r–210r)

. . . The Franks sent ambassadors to al-Malik al-Kamil and his two brothers al-Malik al-Mu'azzam and al-Malik al-Ashraf asking for their lives to be spared in exchange for Damietta with no indemnity. Al-Malik al-Kamil consulted the princes of his House about this. Some advised him not to grant them an amnesty but to seize them at once, while they were in his control and made up the majority of the Unbelievers (on Muslim soil). When he had done this he could take Damietta and the parts of Palestine that they held. But the Sultan al-Malik al-Kamil disagreed, and said: 'There are other Franks; even if we destroy[1] them too it will take us a long time and a hard fight to win Damietta. The Franks beyond the sea will hear what has befallen them and will arrive in more than double the numbers of these here, and we shall have to face a siege.' At the time the troops were exhausted and tired of fighting,[2] for the Frankish

[1] Could also be read as 'capture'.

[2] These words could also be taken as a part of the preceding speech, in which case, for 'were' read 'care'.

occupation of Egypt had lasted for three years and three months. So they all accepted his decision to grant the Franks their lives in exchange for Damietta. He accepted the Frankish petition on condition that al-Malik al-Kamil held hostages from them until Damietta was handed over. They in their turn asked for one of al-Kamil's sons and a group of his nobles as hostages for the return of their King. So an understanding was reached and oaths were taken on 7 rajab 618. The Frankish hostages were the King of Acre, the Papal Legate who was the representative of the Pope in Rome the Great, King Louis and other lords, numbering twenty altogether. Al-Kamil's hostages were his son al-Malik as-Salih Najm ad-Din Ayyūb[1] and a group of his nobles. Al-Malik as-Salih was then fifteen, for he was born in 603. When the nobles presented themselves before al-Malik al-Kamil he held audience in great pomp, in the presence of all the kings and princes of his House. The Franks received a vivid impression of his royal power and majesty. . . .[2]

. . . (When Damietta surrendered) the Frankish and Muslim hostages were returned to their respective sides, and the Sultan entrusted the government of the city to the amir Shujā' ad-Din Jurdik al-Muzaffari an-Nuri, an experienced and worthy man. At the time of the peace the Franks found that they had at Damietta some enormous masts for their ships, and they wanted to take these away with them to their own land. Shujā' ad-Din refused permission for this, so they sent messages to al-Malik al-Kamil complaining about it and saying that these masts were their own property, and that according to the terms of the treaty they should be free to take them. Al-Malik al-Kamil wrote to Shujā' ad-Din commanding him to hand over the masts, but he persisted in his refusal: 'The Franks took the

[1] Later to rule Egypt 1240–49.

[2] A little earlier in this same campaign, 'in the presence of the mighty Sultan', St. Francis came forward and preached. A faint trace of this same episode is believed to have been discovered recently in an eastern source which speaks of a Muslim advising al-Kamil 'on the matter of the monk'.

pulpit from the Great Mosque of Damietta,' he said, 'and cut it up and sent a piece to each of their kings: let the Sultan command them to return the pulpit, and the masts will be theirs.' The Sultan did write to the Franks about this, referring them to what Shujā' ad-Din said, and the Franks, unable to return the pulpit, gave up their claim to the masts.

CHAPTER TWO

The bloodless Crusade of Frederick II, a diplomatic skirmish that was one episode in the rivalry of the Ayyubid princes who were al-'Adil's heirs, has left interesting traces in the Muslim histories of the epoch. Here the main sources are Sibt ibn al-Jauzi, himself a witness of and participant in the Muslim reaction to the surrendering of Jerusalem to the Hohenstaufen, and Ibn Wasil, who did not know Frederick personally, but was later ambassador to Manfred in southern Italy and has left personal and lively, if not always accurate, details of the Hohenstaufen's phil-Islāmic tendencies. The impressions of those who were close to the Emperor during his visit to Jerusalem and saw his pro-Islāmic bias in political matters and his religious scepticism and scorn would, if they had been known in Europe, have received a warm welcome as support for the Vatican-inspired anti-Frederick polemic then current. A comprehensive example of this is to be found among Frederick's diplomatic correspondence, in two letters in Arabic sent by him, shortly after his return to Italy, to a friend of his, an amir at the Ayyubid court. These have been preserved for us by an unknown eastern chronicler. Beneath the Arabic rhetoric, certainly the work of an Arab secretary, concrete historical references reveal the awareness of his imperial dignity and the fierce animosity to the Pope that are so clearly to be seen in the rest of his public utterances.

THE ARRIVAL AT ACRE OF THE EMPEROR FREDERICK, KING OF THE FRANKS

(IBN WASIL, FO. 119V–252R)[1]

In 625/1228 the Emperor Frederick arrived in Acre with a great company of Germans and other Franks. We have already described how the amīr Fakhr ad-Din, the son of the Shaikh ash-Shuyūkh, was sent to the King-Emperor from the Sultan

[1] The pages of the Paris MS. are in the wrong order here and elsewhere.

al-Malik al-Kamil. This was in the time of al-Malik al-Mu'azzam.[1] The idea of the approaches made to the Emperor, the King of the Franks, and of his invitation, was to create difficulties for al-Malik al-Mu'azzam and prevent his availing himself of the help offered to him by the Sultan Jalāl ad-Din ibn 'Alā' ad-Din Khwarizmshāh and Muzaffar ad-Din of Arbela, in his quarrel with al-Kamil and al-Malik al-Ashraf.

The Emperor made his preparations, and arrived with his army on the coast of Syria in the same year and disembarked at Acre. A great number of Franks had preceded him there but they could not move off for fear of al-Malik al-Mu'azzam and so they were waiting for their leader the Emperor. This word means in the Frankish language 'the King of the Princes'. His kingdom consisted of the island of Sicily, and Apulia and Lombardy in the Long Country (Italy).[2] It is the author, Jamāl ad-Din ibn Wasil, who speaks: I saw these parts when I was sent as ambassador of the Sultan al-Malik az-Zahir Rukn ad-Din Baibars, of blessed memory, to the Emperor's son, Manfred by name. The Emperor was a Frankish King, distinguished and gifted, a student of philosophy, logic and medicine and a friend to Muslims, for his original home was Sicily, where he was educated. He, his father and his grandfather were Kings of the island, but its inhabitants were mostly Muslims.

When the Emperor reached Acre, al-Malik al-Kamil found him an embarrassment, for his brother al-Malik al-Mu'azzam, who was the reason why he had asked Frederick for help, had died, and al-Kamil had no further need of the Emperor. Nor

[1] The ruler of Damascus and al-Kamil's brother, whom we have already met flying to his brother's aid against the Franks at Damietta. After this relations between them deteriorated, and it was the tension between them, caused by Jalāl ad-Din the Sultan of Khwarizm, and the amīr of Arbela, that had led al-Kamil to approach Frederick.

[2] The author was perhaps confusing 'Lombardy' and 'Longobardy', which according to the Arabic system of place-names in use at the time refer respectively to the region lying N.W. of the Capitanata (now Lucania) and the Murge (N.W. of the present Foggia), and the coastal region of 'Apulia'. In Frederick's Arabic titles both names appear, as will be seen in a letter translated below.

was it possible to turn him away and attack him because of the terms of the earlier agreement, and because this would have led him to lose the goals on which his heart was set at the time. He therefore made a treaty with Frederick and treated him with great friendship. What followed will be told later, God willing. . . . The Emperor settled at Acre and messengers came and went between him and al-Malik al-Kamil until the end of the year.

JERUSALEM IS HANDED OVER TO THE FRANKS

(IBN WASIL, FO. 253 r–v, 120r–121r)

Then followed the negotiations between al-Malik al-Kamil and the Emperor of which the object had been fixed earlier when al-Kamil and the Emperor first met, before the death of al-Malik al-Mu'azzam. The Frankish King refused to return home except on the conditions laid down, which included the surrender of Jerusalem and of part of the area conquered by Saladin,[1] whereas al-Malik al-Kamil was by no means prepared to yield him these territories. It was finally agreed that he should have Jerusalem on condition that he did not attempt to rebuild the walls, that nothing outside it should be held by the Franks, and that all the other villages within its province should be Muslim, with a Muslim governor resident at al-Bira, actually in the province of Jerusalem. The sacred precincts of the city, with the Dome of the Rock and the Masjid al-Aqsa were to remain in Muslim hands, and the Franks were simply to have the right to visit them, while their administration remained in the hands of those already employed in it, and Muslim worship

[1] Frederick was recalling the offer made by al-Kamil in 1220 to the Crusaders at Damietta (see above) to surrender Palestine. To the Emperor the Papal Legate Pelagius becomes, by a natural process, 'my representative, the chief of my servants. And you owe me now no less than you were prepared to offer him' (*Ta'rikh Mansuri*, 32, Maqrizi, 228-29).

was to continue there. The Franks excepted from the agreement certain small villages on the road from Acre to Jerusalem, which were to remain in their control unlike the rest of the province of Jerusalem.

The Sultan al-Malik al-Kamil maintained that if he broke with the Emperor and failed to give him full satisfaction the result would be a war with the Franks in which the Muslims would suffer irreparably, and everything for which they were working would slip from their grasp. So he was in favour of satisfying the Franks with a disarmed Jerusalem and making a temporary truce with them. He could seize the concessions back from them later, when he chose to. The amīr Fakhr ad-Din ibn ash-Shaikh conducted the negotiations for him, and many conversations and discussions took place between them, during which the Emperor sent to al-Malik al-Kamil queries on difficult philosophic, geometric and mathematical points, to test the men of learning at his court. The Sultan passed the mathematical questions on to Shaikh 'Alam ad-Din Qaisar, a master of that art, and the rest to a group of scholars, who answered them all. Then al-Malik al-Kamil and the Emperor swore to observe the terms of the agreement and made a truce for a fixed term.[1] In this way they arranged matters between themselves, and each side felt secure in its relations with the other. I was told that the Emperor said to the amīr Fakhr ad-Din: 'If I were not afraid that my prestige among the Franks would be destroyed I should not have imposed these conditions on the Sultan. I have no real ambition to hold Jerusalem, nor anything else; I simply want to safeguard my reputation with the Christians.'

After the truce the Sultan sent out a proclamation that the Muslims were to leave Jerusalem and hand it over to the Franks. The Muslims left amid cries and groans and lamentations. The

[1] Ten years, five months and forty days from 28 rabī' I 626/24 February 1229 (Maqrizi 230).

news spread swiftly throughout the Muslim world, which lamented the loss of Jerusalem and disapproved strongly of al-Malik al-Kamil's action as a most dishonourable deed, for the reconquest of that noble city and its recovery from the hand of the infidel had been one of al-Malik an-Nasir Saladin's most notable achievements—God sanctify his spirit!—But al-Malik al-Kamil of noble memory knew that the Muslims could not defend themselves in an unprotected Jerusalem, and that when he had achieved his aim and had the situation well in hand he could purify Jerusalem of the Franks and chase them out. 'We have only,' he said, 'conceded to them some churches and some ruined houses. The sacred precincts, the venerated Rock and all the other sanctuaries to which we make our pilgrimages remain ours as they were; Muslim rites continue to flourish as they did before, and the Muslims have their own governor of the rural provinces and districts.'

After the agreement the Emperor asked the Sultan for permission to visit Jerusalem. This the Sultan granted, and ordered the qadi of Nablus Shams ad-Din of blessed memory, who enjoyed great prestige and favour with the Ayyubid house, to be at the Emperor's service during the time of his visit to Jerusalem and his return to Acre. The author Jamāl ad-Din ibn Wasil says: 'The Qadi of Nablus Shams ad-Din of blessed memory told me: "I took my place beside him as the Sultan al-Malik al-Kamil had ordered me to and entered the Sacred Precinct with him, where he inspected the lesser sanctuaries. Then I went with him into al-Aqsa, whose construction he admired, as he did that of the Dome of the Rock. When we came to the *mihrāb* he admired its beauty, and commended the pulpit, which he climbed to the top. When he descended he took my hand and we went out in the direction of al-Aqsa. There he found a priest with the Testament in his hand about to enter al-Aqsa. The Emperor called out to him: 'What has brought you here? By God, if one of you comes here again without permission I shall have his eyes put out! We are the slaves and servants of al-Malik al-Kamil. He has handed over this church to me and you as a gracious gift. I do not want any of you exceeding your duties.' The priest made off, quaking with fear. Then the King went to the house that had been prepared for him and took up residence there." The Qadi Shams ad-Din said: "I recommended the muezzins not to give the call to prayer that night, out of respect for the King. In the morning I went to him, and he said: 'O qadi, why did the muezzins not give the call to prayer last night in the usual way?' 'This humble slave,' I replied, 'prevented them, out of regard and respect for Your Majesty.' 'You did wrong to do that,' he said: 'My chief aim in passing the night in Jerusalem was to hear the call to prayer given by the muezzins, and their cries of praise to God during the night.' Then he left and returned to Acre." '

When news of the loss of Jerusalem reached Damascus al-Malik an-Nasir began to abuse his uncle al-Malik al-Kamil for alienating the people's sympathies, and ordered the preacher, shaikh Shams ad-Din Yusuf, the nephew (*sibt*) of shaikh Jamāl ad-Din ibn al-Jauzi, who was in great public favour as a preacher, to preach a sermon in the Great Mosque in Damascus. He was to recall the history of Jerusalem, the holy traditions and legends associated with it, to make the people grieve for the loss of it, and to speak of the humiliation and disgrace that its loss brought upon the Muslims. By this means al-Malik an-Nasir Dawūd proposed to alienate the people from al-Malik al-Kamil and to ensure their loyalty to himself in his contest with his uncle.[1] So Shams ad-Din preached as he was told to, and the people came to hear him.[2] It was a memorable day, one on which there rose up to heaven the cries, sobs and groans of the crowd.

[1] We have already had an account of the clash between al-Malik al-Kamil and al-Malik al-Mu'azzam of Damascus that had led to Frederick's being summoned. An-Nasir, who succeeded his father in Damascus, was now seeking to use the emotions aroused by the loss of Jerusalem to bolster his declining power.

[2] Sibt ibn al-Jauzi himself refers to the episode in the next passage.

I myself was one of the crowd there, and among the matters to which I heard him refer was a *qasida* composed by him, rhyming in 't', into which he had inserted a few lines by the poet Di'bil al-Khuza'i,[1] of which I recall the following:

In the Sanctuary of the Ascent and of the Rock, which surpasses in glory
every other rock in the world.
There are Qur'anic schools now deprived of recitations of the sacred verses,
and a seat of revelation in the now deserted courtyards.

On that day one saw nothing but weeping men and women. Now that the truce between al-Malik al-Kamil and the Emperor had been ratified the latter weighed anchor and returned home.[2]

MUSLIM GRIEF IN DAMASCUS. FREDERICK IN JERUSALEM

(SIBT IBN AL-JAUZI, 432–4)

News of the loss of Jerusalem spread to Damascus, and disaster struck all the lands of Islām. It was so great a tragedy that public ceremonies of mourning were instituted: al-Malik an-Nasir Dawūd invited me to preside over a meeting in the Great Mosque of Damascus and to speak of what had occurred in Jerusalem. I could not refuse him, considering obedience to his desire as one of my religious duties and part of my zeal for the cause of Islām. So I ascended (the pulpit) of the Great Mosque of Damascus, in the presence of al-Malik an-Nasir Dawūd, at the gate of Mashhad 'Ali. It was a memorable day, for not one of the people of Damascus remained outside. In the course of my oration I said: 'The road to Jerusalem is closed to the companies of pious visitors! O desolation for those pious men who live there; how many times have they prostrated themselves

[1] A poet at the time of Harun ar-Rashīd (eighth–ninth centuries). The preacher has taken a line from one of his laments for the 'Alids and adapted it to the loss of Jerusalem (the second of the two quoted here.)

[2] At the end of jumada II/May 1229, according to Maqrizi.

there in prayer, how many tears have they shed there! By Allāh, if their eyes were living springs they could not pay the whole of their debt of grief; if their hearts burst with grief they could not diminish their anguish! May God burnish the honour of the believers! O shame upon the Muslim rulers! At such an event tears fall, hearts break with sighs, grief rises up on high . . .' and so on throughout a long discourse. The poets too composed many works on the same subject.

The Emperor entered Jerusalem while Damascus was under siege.[1] During his visit various curious incidents occurred: one was that when he went into the Dome of the Rock he saw a priest sitting near the imprint of the Holy Foot, and taking some pieces of paper from the Franks.[2] The Emperor went up to him as if he wanted to ask a benediction of him, and struck him a blow that knocked him to the ground. 'Swine!' he cried. 'The Sultan has done us the honour of allowing us to visit this place, and you sit here behaving like this! If any of you comes in here again in this way I shall kill him!' The scene was described by one of the custodians of the Dome of the Rock. They said too that the Emperor looked at the inscription that runs round the inside of the sanctuary, saying: 'Saladin purified this city of Jerusalem of the polytheists. . . .' and asked: 'Who would these polytheists be?' 'He also asked the custodians: "What are these nets at the doors of the sanctuary for?" ' They replied: 'So that the little sparrows should not come in.' He said: 'God has brought the giants here instead!'[3] When the time came for the

[1] By al-Kamil and al-Ashraf, united against their nephew an-Nasir.

[2] It is not clear what the pieces of paper were that the priest was taking from the Franks in this version (certainly not paper money as alms). Ibn Wasil's version says that he held a copy of the New Testament; Amari thinks that there is a lacuna here.

[3] The Arabic word *jabbarīn* means 'giants' and also 'potentates, tyrants'. Amari here reads, with an easy textual emendation, *khanazīr*, 'pigs'. Both words are jibes at the Crusaders by the materialist Emperor. The reading *khanazīr*, with its aural similarity to the preceding *asafīr*, ('sparrows'), makes one think not of a translation but of a pun *in Arabic* made by Frederick, whose knowledge of the language is borne out by both eastern sources.

midday prayer and the muezzins' cry rang out, all his pages and valets rose, as well as his tutor, a Sicilian with whom he was reading (Aristotle's) Logic in all its chapters, and offered the canonic prayer, for they were all Muslims. The Emperor, as these same custodians recall, had a red skin, and was bald and short-sighted. Had he been a slave he would not have been worth two hundred *dirham*. It was clear from what he said that he was a materialist and that his Christianity was simply a game to him. Al-Kamil had ordered the Qadi of Nablus, Shams ad-Din, to tell the muezzins that during the Emperor's stay in Jerusalem they were not to go up into their minarets and give the call to prayer in the sacred precinct. The qadi forgot to tell the muezzins, and so the muezzin 'Abd al-Karīm mounted his minaret at dawn and began to recite the Qur'anic verses about the Christians, such as 'God has no son',[1] referring to Jesus son of Mary, and other such texts. In the morning the qadi called 'Abd al-Karīm to him and said: 'What have you done? The Sultan's command was thus and thus.' He replied: 'You did not tell me; I am sorry.' The second night he did not give the call. The next morning the Emperor summoned the qadi, who had come to Jerusalem as his personal adviser and had been responsible for handing the city over to him, and said: 'O qadi, where is the man who yesterday climbed the minaret and spoke these words?' The qadi told him of the Sultan's orders. 'You did wrong, qadi; would you alter your rites and law and faith for my sake? If you were staying in my country, would I order the bells to be silenced for your sake? By God, do not do this; this is the first time that we have found fault in you!' Then he distributed a sum of money among the custodians and muezzins and pious men in the sanctuary; ten *dinar* to each. He spent only two nights in Jerusalem and then returned to Jaffa, for fear of the Templars, who wanted to kill him.[2]

[1] Qur'ān XXIII, 93.

[2] Reading *ad-Dawiyya* for *ad-duna* (for these Christian intrigues against Frederick see Amari, *Storia dei Musulmani di Sicilia*, 2nd ed., III, p. 660 and n. 3.

LATER RELATIONS BETWEEN THE HOHENSTAUFEN AND THE AYYUBIDS. THE LATERHOHENSTAUFEN

(IBN WASIL, 1211–1231)

The Emperor was a sincere and affectionate friend of al-Malik al-Kamil, and they kept up a correspondence until al-Kamil died—God have mercy on him!—and his son al-Malik al-'Adil Saif ad-Din Abu Bakr succeeded him.[1] With him too the Emperor was on sincerely affectionate terms and maintained a correspondence. When al-'Adil died in his turn and his brother al-Malik as-Salih Najm ad-Din Ayyūb[2] succeeded him, relations were unchanged: al-Malik as-Salih sent to the Emperor the learned shaikh Sirāj ad-Din Urmawi, now qadi of Asia Minor, and he spent some time as the Emperor's honoured guest and wrote a book on Logic for him. The Emperor loaded him with honours. After this, still in high favour, he returned to al-Malik as-Salih. In 647/1249, when the King of France, one of the great Frankish kings, attacked Egypt, the Emperor sent him a message in which he tried to dissuade him from the expedition and warned him of the consequences of his action, but the French king did not take his advice. Sir Berto[3] (he was master of ceremonies to the Emperor's son Manfred) told me that Frederick had sent him on a secret embassy to al-Malik as-Salih Najm ad-Din Ayyūb to tell him that the King of France had decided to attack Egypt and to put him on his guard and advise him to prepare to resist the attack, which al-Malik as-Salih did. Sir Berto said that his journey to Egypt had been made in the guise of a merchant, and that no one heard a whisper of his visit to the Sultan and the Franks never realized that the Emperor was intriguing with the Muslims against them. When al-Malik

[1] 1238–40.

[2] 1240–49.

[3] On the name of this master of ceremonies (*mihmandār*, actually the man responsible for entertaining ambassadors and other important guests) the Arabic text is clear only about the final letters; 'Sir Berto' is just a guess based on the group of symbols s.r. ?r.d.

as-Salih died and the King of France met the fate he deserved—the defeat and destruction of his army by death and capture, his own capture by al-Malik al-Mu'azzam Turanshāh, his release after al-Malik al-Mu'azzam was murdered and his return home—[1] the Emperor sent to remind him of the advice he had given him and of the sorrow he had brought upon himself by his obstinacy and disobedience, and reproached him harshly for it.

The Emperor died in 648/1250, a year after al-Malik as-Salih Najm ad-Din Ayyūb, and was succeeded by his son Conrad. When he too died his brother Manfred came to the throne. All three were hated by the Pope—the Frankish Caliph—because of their sympathy with the Muslims; the Pope, the Caliph of the Franks, and Manfred went to war, and Manfred the son of the Emperor was victorious.

The qadi Jamāl ad-Din, chief qadi of Hamāt, says in his history: I went as ambassador to Manfred from the Sultan al-Malik az-Zahir Rukn ad-Din Baibars of blessed memory, in ramadān 659/August 1261, and was entertained by him in the highest honour in a city called Barletta in Apulia, which is in the Long Country, next to Spain.[2] I had dealings with him on several occasions, and found him a remarkable man, who loved the dialectical sciences and knew the ten books of Euclid off by heart. Near the town where he lived was a city called Lucera, whose inhabitants were all Muslims from the island of Sicily; they hold public prayer there on a Friday and make open profession of the Muslim Faith. This has been so since the time of the Emperor Manfred's father Frederick. He had undertaken the building of a scientific institute there[3] for the study of all the branches of speculative science; most of his officials and

[1] See below for St. Louis' Crusade in Egypt.

[2] No one looking at one of Idrisi's maps would be surprised at this Muslim notion that Italy and Spain are contiguous.

[3] Valuable information, not known before, about the cultural life of the Muslim community in Lucera. The founder of this *dar al-'ilm* was apparently Manfred, but the sentence could, strictly, apply to either father or son.

courtiers were Muslims, and in his camp the call to prayer, and even the canonic prayers themselves, were openly heard.

When I returned home, news came that the Pope—the Prince of Rome the Great—together with the brother of the King of France mentioned earlier,[1] was gathering an army to attack him. Rome was five day's journey from the town where I had stayed. The Pope had already excommunicated Manfred for his Muslim leanings and for having dishonoured Christian religious law. His brother and his father the Emperor had also been excommunicated by the Pope of Rome for the same thing. They say that the Pope of Rome is for them the vicar of the Messiah, and his representative, with authority to decide what is permitted and what is forbidden, to cut off and to separate. It is he who crowns their Kings and sets them on the throne, and everything in their law needs his approval. He is a priest,[2] and when he dies he is succeeded by the man who is endowed as he was with this sacerdotal quality.

While I was in their land I was told a strange story according to which the title of Emperor, before the time of Frederick, was held by his father, who died when his son was a boy in early adolescence. Several of the Frankish kings aspired to be Emperor and each hoped that the Pope of Rome would bestow the title on him. Frederick, who was a German—the Germans are one of the Frankish nations—was a man of astute cunning. He met each of the aspirants privately and said to him: 'I do not want this title; I am not worthy of it. When we see the Pope, tell him that you leave the choice to Frederick and that you will stand by his decision, he being the son of the dead Emperor. I will choose you alone of them all, and my intention is to support you and be your ally.' Frederick confided this to each of them, and each one believed him and trusted his sincerity. They all met in the city of Rome the Great, Frederick among

[1] Charles of Anjou, brother of King Louis IX.

[2] The Arabic has 'monk, friar'.

them. Frederick had ordered a large band of his German nobles to mount their horses and wait near to the great church in Rome where the council was meeting. When the kings assembled the Pope said: 'What do you think about this office; which of you is the most worthy of it?' and he placed the royal crown in front of them. Each replied: 'I leave the decision to Frederick. What he decides I will accept and recommend in my turn, since he is the Emperor's son and the most appropriate person to give the council advice on the matter.' Then Frederick stood up and said: 'I am the Emperor's son and the most worthy of his title and his throne, and all have chosen and accepted me.' Then the Pope, who chose only according to the will of the assembly, put the crown on his head. They all stood bemused while Frederick, the crown on his head, left hurriedly and mounted his horse with the whole company of Germans whom he had ordered to be near the church door. With them he galloped as fast as they could go back to his own land. Later he committed acts that incur excommunication among them, and was excommunicated.

I was told that at Acre the Emperor said to the amīr Fakhr ad-Din ibn ash-Shaikh of blessed memory: 'Explain to me what your Caliph is.' Fakhr ad-Din said: 'He is the descendant of our Prophet, whom God bless and save,[1] who has received the title of Caliph from his father, and his father from his father, so that the Caliphate has remained in the Prophet's house and has not moved outside its members.' 'How fine that is!' he said. 'But these stupid men'—meaning the Franks—'take a man from the sewer,[2] without any bond of blood or relationship with the Messiah, ignorant and incapable of making himself understood, and they make him their Caliph, the representative of the Messiah among them, a man who could not possibly

[1] The definition applies to the members of the dynasty of the 'Abbasids, who were descended from Muhammad's uncle, 'Abbās.

[2] Literally: 'dung-heap'.

be worthy of such an office. Whereas your Caliph, a descendant of the Prophet, is clearly more worthy than any other man of the dignity invested in him!'[1]

The Pope and the King of France's brother attacked Manfred, the Emperor's son, and in a pitched battle destroyed his army and took him captive. The Pope ordered that he should be killed, and it was done. The King of France's brother[2] reigned over the lands that had belonged to the Emperor's son and held possession of them. This occurred, I think, in 663/1265.

TWO ARABIC LETTERS WRITTEN BY FREDERICK

(TA'RĪKH MANSURI, 34–7)

In the year 627/1229 an ambassador to al-Kamil came to Harrān[3] from the Emperor with a letter to Fakhr ad-Din, the son of the Shaikh ash-Shuyūkh,[4] which ran as follows:
Heading and dedication:

The august Caesar, the Roman Emperor Frederick, son of the Emperor Henry, son of the Emperor Frederick, by God's grace victorious, powerful in His might, exalted in His glory, King of Germany and Lombardy, Tuscany and Italy, Longobardy and Calabria and Sicily, and of the Syrian Kingdom of Jerusalem, support of the Roman Pontifex,[5] champion of the Christian faith.

In the name of God, the merciful, the forgiving

We departed, and left behind us our heart, which stayed (with you) detached
from our body, our race and our tribe.

[1] It is clear from this and other passages that an awareness of certain parallels between the Caliphate and the Papacy was widespread at the time in spite of the profound religious and constitutional differences between the two institutions.

[2] Text had 'his brother', obviously a *lapsus* for 'brother of the King of France': Charles of Anjou, as stated elsewhere by Abu l-Fidā' after Ibn Wasil.

[3] Harrān, in Mesopotamia, was also a part of the Ayyubid domains.

[4] Al-Kamil's plenipotentiary and the Emperor's guide in the Holy Land (see above).

[5] One of the ironies of protocol.

And it swore that its love for you would never change, eternally, and escaped,
fleeing from its obedience to me.[1]

If we set ourselves to describe the great desire we feel and the sorrowful sensations of solitude and nostalgia we endure for the high excellency of Fakhr ad-Din—may God lengthen his days and extend his years, and make his feet firm in power, and keep the affection He has for him and do him honour, and give his desires fulfilment, and direct his actions and his words and heap him with abundant graces, and renew his safety night and morning—we should exceed by far the limit of an exordium and err from the path of reason. For we have been smitten, after a time of tranquility and ease, with a bitter anguish, and after pleasure and peace with the torment of separation; all comfort seems to have fled, the cord of strong-mindedness is cut, the hope of meeting again turned to despair, the fabric of patience slashed. At our parting[2]

If I had been given the choice between life and death I should have said:
'It is death that calls me.'
Death is tired of us, he has taken others in our place; he has chosen to leave
us and seems to have forgotten our love.

We are consoled by the words of Abu t-Tayyib:[3]

When you part from those who could have prevented that parting, it is they
who are really going away.

Now, to talk about ourselves, and in the knowledge that Your Highness likes to hear good news of us and our affairs and to learn of our noble deeds, we inform you: that as we explained (to you) in Sidon, the Pope has treacherously and deceitfully taken one of our fortresses, called Montecassino, handed over to him by its accursed Abbot. He had promised to do even more harm(?), but could not, for our faithful subjects expected our return. He was forced therefore to spread false news of our death, and made the Cardinals swear to it and to say that our return was impossible. They sought to deceive the populace by these tricks and by saying that after us no-one could administer our estates and look after them for our son so well as the Pope. So, on these men's oaths who should be High Priests of the Faith and successors of the Apostles, a rabble of louts and criminals was led

[1] For the whole of this first section of the letter verse and rhymed prose alternate, expressing in the far-fetched images that characterize Arabic rhetoric grief at the departure and absence of a friend. The text is often far from clear.

[2] Amari makes the following lines prose, but the mutilated text seems to reveal glimpses of poetry, particularly in the first line.

[3] Al-Mutanabbi, the great romantic poet of the tenth century.

by the nose. When we arrived at the gates of well-defended Brindisi we found that King John and the Lombards had made hostile raids into our domains,[1] and doubted even the news of our arrival because of what the Cardinals had sworn to them. We sent letters and messengers announcing our safe return, and our enemies now began to feel perturbed, troubled and alarmed, and turned tail in disorder and retreated for a distance of two days' march, while our subjects became submissive again. Then the Lombards, who made up the greater part of their army, could not endure to be found rebellious and breaking faith with their Lord, and all turned back. As for King John and his companions, shame and fear seized them and they crowded together in a narrow pass from which they feared to move or come out, for the new loyalty of the whole countryside towards us made it impossible for them. Meanwhile we had collected a large army of Germans who were with us in Syria and of those who left the Holy Land before us but whom the wind had cast upon our shores, and of other loyal men and officials of our state; with these we have marched off by long stages towards our enemy's territories.

Finally we inform Your Highness of our desire for frequent letters from you revealing your happy state, your interests and your needs, and of the salutations that we would have transmitted to the commanders of (your army) and to all your pages, mamlūks and courtiers. On your health be God's blessing and mercy. Written at Barletta 23 August of the second indiction[2] (1229).

This is the text of the second letter, which is headed in the same way as the first, and contains the following news:

We have assembled a great army and are in haste to fight those who await us and have not fled (like the others) before us. Now what we anticipated has come about: they had besieged one of our forts[3] using catapults, mobile siege-engines and instruments of war, but when they heard of our advance, in spite of the great distance separating us they immediately burnt all their weapons and fled before us, while we advanced rapidly to catch up with them and to disperse and destroy them. The Pope chose to claim those whom we found there, and has sent them back, afraid for their lives(?) and

[1] The 'Clavisignati' (Schlüsselsoldaten), the Papal army under the command of ex-King John of Brienne, who in Frederick's absence had invaded and devastated his kingdom.

[2] A fiscal period of fifteen years.

[3] Probably Caiazzo, besieged in September 1229.

repenting of their plot. What other news we have we shall write to Your Highness, God willing.

We have copied these letters here to show clearly the nature of the Kings who surrounded the King-Emperor, and the extent of his power. In fact no one in Christendom from the time of Alexander until today has ruled a kingdom the equal of his, particularly when one considers his power, his behaviour to their Caliph, the Pope, and his audacity in attacking him and driving him out.

CHAPTER THREE

The final offensive of the Crusades was Louis IX's Egyptian expedition, which came back to make another attempt to take the places vainly besieged thirty years before by Pelagius and John of Brienne. The most important Arabic historians for this period are Ibn Wasil and Maqrizi: the first a contemporary and sometimes an eye-witness of the events he records, the second rather later, but here as elsewhere the compiler of earlier material. He follows Ibn Wasil's account quite closely but enriches it with various details taken from different sources, or from a common, unknown source. We rely here on Ibn Wasil's version for the dramatic events of the Crusade, and take from Maqrizi only certain documents and Muslim comments on the arrival of the French King, and as a final word, an outline of the Tunisian expedition of twenty years later, on which Louis lost his life.

Saint Louis' Crusade

THE FRANKS ARRIVE IN EGYPT AND OCCUPY DAMIETTA

(IBN WASIL, FO. 356r–357r)

At the second hour of Thursday 20 safar 647/5 June 1249 the great Frankish fleet, including all the ships from the Syrian coast, arrived and dropped anchor at the mouth of the Nile, facing the Muslims. The King of France's tent was pitched (it was red in colour). The enemy was attacked by some detachments of Muslim troops, and among them was a man who fell a martyr for the Faith that day, the amīr Najm ad-Din ibn Shaikh al-Islām. We have already mentioned the fact that he and his brother Shihāb ad-Din accompanied al-Malik as-Salih to al-Karak on the orders of al-Malik an-Nasir Dawūd. Another Egyptian amīr to fall among the brave was a certain al-Waziri. In the evening the amīr Fakhr ad-Din Yusuf ibn Shaikh ash-Shuyūkh[1] marched out at the head of the Egyptian troops and cut the bridge crossing to the eastern shore where Damietta stood so that the western shore was now entirely in Frankish hands. Then the next morning the army, led (to defy discipline) by al-Malik as-Salih's serious illness, and with no encouragement or incitement, marched out toward Ashmūn Tannāh. Even Fakhr ad-Din made off in that direction, and so the eastern shore too was without Muslim troops to defend it.

The people of Damietta feared for their own lives if they were besieged. There was of course a garrison of brave Kinanites in the city, but God struck terror into their hearts and they left Damietta, together with the population, and marched all night. They abandoned the city without a living soul in it, man, woman or child. They all left under cover of night, accompanied by the troops, and fled toward Ashmūn Tannāh. The behaviour of the people, of Fakhr ad-Din and of the troops was shameful: if Fakhr ad-Din Yusuf had prevented their flight and stood firm Damietta would have been able to defend itself, for when the Franks attacked it the first time, in the reign of al-Malik al-Kamil, it was even worse provisioned and armed, yet the enemy failed to take it for a whole year. It was in fact besieged in 615/1218 and taken in 616/1219, and the enemy had no success until the population was decimated by plague and famine. If the Kinanites and the people of Damietta had shut the gate and entrenched themselves within them, after the army had gone to Ashmūn Tannāh, the Franks could not have overcome them. The army would have been behind them and could have defended them. They had provisions, munitions and arms in great quantity, and could have defended the city for at least

[1] He who twenty years earlier had conducted the negotiations with Frederick, and had now been put in charge of Egyptian defence by the sick Ayyubid Sultan al-Malik as-Salih.

two years. But when God ordains something there is no way of avoiding it. The people of Damietta however are not to blame if when they saw the troops in flight and heard of the Sultan's illness they were afraid to face a long siege and to die of hunger, as happened the last time.

On the morning of Sunday 23 safar the Franks appeared before Damietta and found it deserted, with the gates wide open. They occupied it without striking a blow and seized all the munitions, arms, provisions, food and equipment that they found there. It was a disaster without precedent. The author of this history says: on the Sunday morning a messenger brought the news to the amīr Husām ad-Din Muhammad ibn Abi 'Ali al-Hadhbani, with whom I was staying. There was great grief and amazement, and despair fell upon the whole of Egypt, the more so because the Sultan was ill, too weak to move, and without the strength to control his army, which was trying to impose its will on him instead. As well as all this, when the people of Damietta and the Kinanites reached the Sultan he was extremely angry with the Kinanites and ordered that they should all be hanged, which was done. He was also distressed by the behaviour of Fakhr ad-Din and his troops, but circumstances compelled him to muster them again and pass over what they had done.

AL-MALIK AS-SALIH WITHDRAWS AND ENCAMPS AT MANSURA

(IBN WASIL, FO. 357r–v)

After these events the Sultan al-Malik as-Salih Najm ad-Din Ayyūb set out with his army on the direct route for Mansura, where he encamped. It was here that his father al-Malik al-Kamil had encamped during the first attack on Damietta. The town stood on the eastern bank of the Nile, facing Jarjīr, with the canal of Ashmūn Tannāh dividing it from the peninsula on which Damietta is situated.[1] We have already stated that al-Malik as-Salih had the camp set up here and a wall built between it and the Nile. His father al-Malik al-Kamil had a great palace here on the Nile, and al-Malik as-Salih halted there and had his tent pitched beside it. The Sultan took up position at Mansura on Tuesday 25 safar; the army began to make such buildings as still stood inhabitable and set up markets. The wall facing the Nile was rebuilt and faced with a curtain wall, galleys and fire-ships brought up, loaded with ammunition and troops and anchored under the wall, and uncountable numbers of irregular infantry and volunteers for the Faith flocked to Mansura. A number of Bedouin Arabs also came and began to make raids and attacks on the Franks. They, for their part, fortified the walls of Damietta and filled the city with soldiers.

On Monday 28 rabī' I/13 July forty-six Frankish prisoners, among them two knights, came to Cairo, captured by the Bedouin and their followers. On Saturday 5 rabī' II thirty-nine others, taken by the Arabs and the men from Khwarizm, arrived and then twenty-two others, taken unexpectedly, entered the city on 7 rabī' II. Finally, on Wednesday 15 rabī' II, thirty-five more arrived, among them three knights. On Friday 24 rabi' II news came that al-Malik as-Salih's troops in Damascus had attacked Sidon and accepted the Frankish surrender. After this fresh groups of Frankish prisoners arrived every moment; for instance, fifty came in on Friday 18 jumada I/30 August. Meanwhile al-Malik as-Salih was weakening, his strength wasting away. The doctors, who were at his pillow day and night, now despaired of his life. His strength of mind and will remained as powerful as ever, but two grave diseases combined to overcome him: an ulcer in the groin and phthisis.

[1] 'Peninsula' refers to the long strip of land between the Nile and Lake Manzala at the end of which stands Damietta.

THE FRANKS ADVANCE AND TAKE UP POSITION FACING THE MUSLIMS

(IBN WASIL, FO. 364r–365r)

When the Franks heard of al-Malik as-Salih's death (15 sha'bān 647/24 November 1249) they left Damietta in full force, while their fleet moved upstream parallel with them and anchored at Fariskūr before proceeding another stage up the river. This was Thursday 24 sha'bān 647. On Friday a letter reached Cairo from the amīr Fakhr ad-Din warning the people and urging them to join the Holy War. It was signed with a stamp (*sijíll*) similar to that of al-Malik as-Salih,[1] to persuade the people that the letter came from him. It began: 'Come out, heavily or lightly armed, and fight for God's cause with your money and your life. It will be better for you, if you could only understand this!'[2] It was an eloquent letter, composed I think by Bahā' ad-Din Zuháir,[3] full of fine exhortations to come and fight the infidel. It said that the Franks were moving in full force against Egypt and the Muslim territories, thirsting for conquest, and that it was the duty of all Muslims to rush to arms and drive them out. This letter was read out to the people from the pulpit of the Great Mosque in Cairo. The people wept bitterly and grew frenzied, and from Cairo and all Egypt a great crowd set out (for the Holy War). The death of al-Malik as-Salih caused great grief, and meanwhile the Franks holding Damietta realized that if the Muslim army encamped at Mansura could be induced to withdraw even a short distance, the whole of Egypt would be theirs at once.

On Tuesday 1 ramadān/8 December 1249 a fierce skirmish

[1] Whose death he was trying to conceal until his son al-Malik al-Mu'azzam arrived and was safely enthroned. The royal stamp (*'alama*) was the autograph signature of the sovereign on State documents.

[2] Qur'ān IX, 41

[3] Well-known poet, secretary to the Ayyubids.

took place between the Franks and the Muslims, in which we lost one of the court officials, the amīr al-'Ala'i, as well as other soldiers. The Franks made their camp at Sharimshāh. On Monday 7 ramadān they camped at Baramūn, and this caused great alarm (in the Muslim camp), for now the Frankish King was very close to the Muslim army. On Sunday 13 ramadān the enemy reached the end of the Damietta peninsula and so found itself face to face with the Muslim forces. The bulk of the army was in Mansura, on the eastern bank, but a part, with the sons of al-Malik an-Nasir Dawūd, al-Malik al-Mu'azzam's[1] son, that is al-Malik al-Amjad, al-Malik az-Zahir, al-Malik al-Mu'azzam and al-Malik al-Awhad with their elder brothers, occupied the western bank. There were twelve of al-Malik an-Nasir's sons, of varying ages, in Cairo for the occasion. Also on the same side of the river were al-Malik an-Nasir's brother al-Malik al-Qahir, and also al-Malik al-Mughīth. When they reached the end of the Damietta peninsula in full force and came face to face with the Muslims, the Franks began to dig themselves a wall protected by screens, and set up catapults to attack the Muslims, whose galleys were across the river from Mansura. This led to a battle for the control of the land and the sea.

A SURPRISE ATTACK ON THE MUSLIMS AT MANSURA. THE DEATH OF THE AMĪR FAKHR AD-DIN YUSUF. THE SUBSEQUENT MUSLIM VICTORY

(IBN WASIL, 365v–366v)

We have already described how the Franks came face to face with the Muslims and how fighting broke out between the two

[1] This al-Mu'azzam, whom we have already met as the brother of al-Kamil and the father of an-Nasir Dawūd of Damascus and later of al-Karak, should not be confused with al-Mu'azzam Turanshāh, son of as-Salih, who had now succeeded his father and was to be the last Ayyubid in Egypt. These Ayyubid names are often confusingly duplicated.

sides, separated by the Ashmūn, a branch of the Nile. The Ashmūn is a small canal with a few narrow fords. A Muslim showed the Franks where one of the fords could be safely crossed, and on the morning of Tuesday 5 dhu l-qa'da/10 February 1250 the Franks mounted their horses and moved down to the ford. The Muslims suddenly found that the Franks were in their camp. The amīr Fakhr ad-Din Yusuf ibn Shaikh ash-Shuyūkh was washing himself in his bath when he heard the cry go up that the Franks had taken the Muslims by surprise. Frenziedly he leapt into the saddle, without weapons or any means of defending himself, and a band of Franks[1] fell on him and killed him—God have mercy upon him! He was a worthy amīr, learned and cultivated, generous and wise, high-minded and magnanimous, without peer among his brothers or any other men. He had been very successful in his career and had risen to a high position, next in rank to al-Malik as-Salih Najm ad-Din Ayyūb. His ambition reached to the throne itself,[2] but God ended his life as a martyr for the Faith.

The Frankish King penetrated Mansura and reached the Sultan's palace. The Franks spread through the narrow streets of the town, while the civil and military population scattered in all directions. Islām was about to suffer a mortal blow, and the Franks were now sure of their victory. It was lucky for the Muslims that the Franks dispersed through the streets. At the moment of supreme danger, the Turkish battalion of the mamlūks of al-Malik as-Salih, Bahrites and Jamdarites,[3] lions in war and mighty in battle, rode like one man upon the enemy in a charge that broke them and drove them back. The Franks were massacred one and all with sword and club. The Bahrites

[1] A band of Templars, according to Maqrizi's more detailed account.

[2] He was in fact regent of Egypt between as-Salih's death and al-Mu'azzam's coronation, on his arrival from Mesopotamia.

[3] The Bahrites, from whom came the first Mamlūk dynasty, were so called because they were quartered at Cairo on the Nile (*bahr*). The Jamdarites ('gentlemen of the wardrobe') were another mamlūk regiment.

slaughtered them and drove them back through the streets of al-Mansura, and the Franks lost 1,500 of their finest cavalry there. Meanwhile their infantry had reached the bridge of al-Mansūr over the Ashmūn canal and were preparing to cross. If the defence there had been weak the Frankish infantry could have crossed in force to the Muslim side and terrible damage would have been caused, for in these numbers they could have defended their cavalry. (But it did not happen) and had it not been for the restricted field of battle, for we were fighting in alleys and narrow streets, the Muslims would have exterminated the Franks to a man. Instead of this some survivors succeeded in escaping and fled to Jadila, where they reassembled while the darkness of night separated the two sides.

The Franks built a wall at Jadila and dug a trench to defend themselves. Some stayed on the eastern side, and held the roads along the peninsula leading to Damietta, protected by trench and wall. This battle was the source of victory and the key to the final success. Messages announcing it reached Cairo and were brought to Husām ad-Din Muhammad ibn Abi 'Ali[1] on the afternoon of the day of battle. They said that while messenger-pigeons were being sent off the enemy had attacked Mansura and a violent battle had followed. That was all, and we and the Muslims were in complete confusion, everyone already imagining disaster for Islām. At sunset Muslim fugitives from the battle arrived, and the Bab an-Nasr[2] stayed open all night, the night of Tuesday to Wednesday. Military and civilians, secretaries and officials entered the city in flight from Mansura, knowing nothing of the situation after the Franks had entered the town. Among them was Taj ad-Din, known as Ibn bint al A'azz, director of the Diwān as-suhba, and he reported to Husām ad-Din. We remained in suspense until the sun rose on Wednesday and the joyful news of victory reached

[1] Governor and then vizier of Cairo and Ibn Wasil's employer.
[2] A gate into Cairo, still in existence.

us. The city prepared for a feast and the glad tidings were announced by a roll of drums. The victory over the Franks caused great joy and exultation. This was the first battle in which the Turkish lions defeated the infidel dogs. The good news reached al-Malik al-Mu'azzam while he was on his way, and made him march even faster toward Egypt.

THE MUSLIM FLEET ATTACKS AND CRIPPLES THE FRANKISH FLEET

(IBN WASIL, FO. 368r–v)

While the Franks stabilized their positions, reinforcements were reaching them from further up the Nile, from Damietta. The Muslims took some ships on camel-back up to the Bahr al-Mahalla,[1] and there launched them and embarked troops. There was water at that time from the flooding of the Nile, stagnant, but communicating with the Nile itself. When the Frankish vessels coming upstream from Damietta passed close to the Bahr al-Mahalla the Muslims, who were lying in wait, fell on them and gave battle. The Muslim squadron from al-Mansura came downstream to join the fight and they surrounded the Franks and captured them and their ships. Fifty-two Frankish men-of-war were taken, with about a thousand men on board and all the provisions they were carrying. The prisoners were taken on camels to the Muslim camp. For the Franks the defeat broke their supply-line and seriously weakened their position. They found themselves very short of provisions and blockaded without the means either of staying put or of leaving their position. The Muslims had the upper hand, and now nourished plans to attack.

On 1 dhu l-hijja/7 March 1250 the Franks took seven Muslim fire-ships on the Bahr al-Mahalla, but the Muslims escaped with their gear. On the second, al-Malik al-Mu'azzam

[1] A backwater of the Nile, mentioned in operations in the Fifth Crusade.

ordered the amīr Husām ad-Din to enter Cairo and take up residence in the vizier's palace and to perform all the usual functions of the Sultan's viceroy. The Qadi Jamāl ad-Din ibn Wasil, the author, says: The Sultan gave robes of honour to me and also to a group of lawyers who presented themselves to do him homage. Al-Malik al-Mu'azzam's liberality extended in this way to anyone who presented himself at his gate. So I entered Cairo with the amīr Husām ad-Din. On Monday 9 dhu l-hijja, the day of 'Arafa,[1] Muslim galleys attacked the Frankish supply-ships. The encounter took place near the Mosque of Victory and the Muslims took thirty-two vessels from the Franks, of which seven were galleys. This weakened the Franks even more, and supplies in the camp were even scarcer. Then the Franks opened negotiations for a truce with the Muslims. Their ambassadors arrived and went into consultation with the amīr Zain ad-Din, a *jamdār* amīr, and the Grand Qadi Badr ad-Din. The Franks wanted to exchange Damietta for Jerusalem and a part of the Syrian coast, but this was not acceptable. On Friday 26 dhu l-hijja the Franks burnt all their encampments, sparing only the ships, and decided to take refuge in Damietta. At the end of the year (647) they were still in the same position, facing the Muslims.

TOTAL ROUT OF THE FRANKS, AND THE CAPTURE OF THE KING OF FRANCE

(IBN WASIL, FO. 369r–370r)

On the night before Wednesday 3 muharram 648/7 April 1250, the resplendent night that disclosed a great victory and a stupendous triumph, the Franks marched out with all their forces towards Damietta, which they counted on to defend them, and their ships began to move downstream in convoy.

[1] A solemn festival during the Muslim Pilgrimage.

When the Muslims heard the news they set out after them, crossed to the Frankish bank of the river and were soon at their heels. As Wednesday dawned the Muslims had surrounded the Franks and were slaughtering them, dealing out death and captivity. Not one escaped. It is said that the dead numbered 30,000. In the battle the Bahrite mamlūks of al-Malik as-Salih distinguished themselves by their courage and audacity: they caused the Franks terrible losses and played the major part in the victory. They fought furiously: it was they who flung themselves into the pursuit of the enemy: they were Islām's Templars.[1] The accursed King of France and the great Frankish princes retreated to the hill of Munya, where they surrendered and begged for their lives. They were given assurances by the eunuch Jamāl ad-Din Muhsin as-Sālihi, on the strength of which they surrendered. They were all taken to Mansura, where chains were put on the feet of the King of France and his companions. They were imprisoned in the house where the secretary Fakhr ad-Din ibn Luqmān was living, and the eunuch Sabīh al-Mu'ázzami, a servant of al-Malik al-Mu-'azzam Turanshāh, son of al-Malik as-Salih Najm ad-Din Ayyūb, was set to guard them; he had come with his master from Hisn Kaifā and had been promoted and shown great honour.

Referring to this episode, the imprisonment of the King of France in Fakhr ad-Din ibn Luqmān's house, and the appointment of the eunuch Sabīh to look after him, Jamāl ad-Din ibn Yahya ibn Matrūh wrote:

Speak to the Frenchman, if you visit him, a true word from a good counsellor:
'God requite you for what has happened, the slaughter of the Messiah's adorers!
You came to the East boasting of conquest, believing our martial drum-roll to be a mere breath of wind.

[1] Their enemy's highest praise for the Order's military valour.

And your stupidity has brought you to a place where your eyes can no longer see in the broad plain any way of escape.
And of all your company, whom you commanded so well that you led them into the tomb's embrace,
Of fifty thousand not one can be seen that is not dead, or wounded and a prisoner.
God help you to other similar adventures: who knows that in the end Jesus will not breathe freely (of your impious worship[1])!
If your Pope is content with this, how often is a statesman guilty of deceit!'
And say to them, if they ever think of returning to take their revenge, or for any other reason:
'The house of Ibn Luqmān is always ready here, and the chain and the eunuch Sabīh are still here.'

After this al-Malik al-Mu'azzam and the victorious army advanced to Damietta and camped at Fariskūr in the province of Damietta. The Sultan's tent was erected, and beside it a wooden tower which from time to time al-Malik al-Mu'azzam would climb to while away the time, putting off the capture of Damietta. If he had surrounded and entered it quickly and forced the King of France to surrender all his possesions, he would have taken it very quickly. But the evil conduct to which he abandoned himself deterred him, and indeed his fate was already sealed.

THE ASSASSINATION OF AL-MALIK AL-MU'AZZAM TURANSHĀH

(IBN WASIL, FO. 371r–v)

When the soldiers, especially the Bahrite mamlūks belonging to his father, lost their loyalty to him,[2] as we have described, a

[1] For the Muslims Jesus Christ is a prophet, the miracle-working servant of God. The Christian cult must therefore appear sacrilegious to Christ himself, according to this view.

[2] In favour of other elements whom they had brought with them from Mesopotamia, for example the eunuch Sabīh mentioned above.

group of them decided to kill him. On the morning of Monday 30 muharram 648/2 May 1250 al-Malik al-Mu'azzam gave an audience in his tent. He sat on his couch while all the others ate, and he ate with them, as usual. After the meal the amīrs dispersed to their houses and he got up and went toward his little tent. Then Rukn ad-Din Baibars came forward. He was one of al-Malik as-Salih's *Jamdariyya*, known as al-Bunduqdari, and was later to become ruler of Egypt under the name al-Malik az-Zahir and to defeat the Mongols at 'Ain Jalūt with the aid of al-Malik al-Muzaffar Qutūz; and once on the throne, to reconquer most of the Frankish domains, for example Safad, ash-Shaqīf, Antioch and the Isma'ilite territories, and to defeat the Mongols on several occasions.[1] This man struck al-Malik al-Mu'azzam with a sword and wounded him in the shoulder and threw the sword away. Al-Malik al-Mu'azzam turned around in his audience chamber, and his courtiers and servants flocked round him, as well as some of his father's mamlūks, asking what had happened. 'One of the Bahrites has wounded me.' Ruqn ad-Din Baibars al-Bunduqdari was there and said: 'It must have been an Isma'ilite,'[2] but the Sultan replied: 'No, it was a Bahrite alone who did this to me'. Then the Bahrites were afraid, and dreaded what he might do. The Sultan climbed into his tower and sent for a surgeon to attend his hand. Meanwhile his father's mamlūks assembled, stricken with horror to hear the attempt (on the Sultan's life) was blamed on them. To this was added their resentment that he had set them aside, so they surrounded the tower. The Sultan opened the windows and called to the people for help, but no one responded, and none of the Egyptian amīrs would come to his aid, for he had lost their loyalty completely. Fire

[1] So magniloquent an introduction to Baibars is understandable coming from someone like Ibn Wasil, who was dependent on him for his livelihood. What he says is plain historical fact, but it fails to lighten the impression created by the murky scene that follows (told with even more macabre detail in other sources), the beginning of the future Sultan of Egypt's career.

[2] A heretical sect specializing in political assassinations; see Part Two.

was brought to burn down the tower, so he came down (and left it). Al-Bunduqdari, who had already wounded him, fell upon him, and he fled to the river bank where some of his fire-ships were, hoping to reach them in time to get on board and defend himself. But Faris ad-Din Aqtay caught up with him and killed him with a blow from his sword—God have mercy on him! He was still young, not yet thirty, I think, but I have been unable to discover the date of his birth. He ruled over Egypt for two months.

THE DECISION TO PUT THE PRINCESS SHAJAR AD-DURR, THE MOTHER OF KHALĪL, ON THE THRONE, WITH ʻIZZ AD-DIN THE TURCOMAN AS MILITARY COMMANDER

(IBN WASIL, FO. 372r–v)

When al-Malik al-Muʻazzam was killed the amīrs and Bahrites assembled near the Sultan's palace and agreed that the functions of Sultan and ruler (of Egypt) should be assumed by Shajar ad-Durr, mother of Khalīl and wife of al-Malik as-Salih Najm ad-Din Ayyūb.[1] The Sultan's decrees were to be issued at her command and in her name, and marked with her royal stamp. They had already made this offer to Husām ad-Din Muhammad ibn Abi ʻAli,[2] saying: 'You were al-Malik as-Salih's most trusted statesman and so are the most worthy of this responsibility.' But he declined and suggested that the more suitable man was the eunuch Shihāb ad-Din Rashīd

[1] She was a Turkish slave who had borne al-Malik as-Salih a son, al-Khalīl, who died in childhood. The elevation of this lady to throne with the title of Sultan, an event without precedent in the history of Islām, as Ibn Wasil points out, was a brief transitional compromise between the last trace of Ayyubid legitimism and the military regime of the Mamlūks, who now installed themselves in Egypt in name as well as in fact. The commander Aibek soon married Shajar ad-Durr and founded the Mamlūk dynasty.

[2] From what immediately precedes this, one would expect it to apply to the power of the Sultan, but what follows suggests that it refers to the position of army commander. The two were in any case soon united.

al-Kabīr. It was offered to him, but he too refused. So they agreed on the name of 'Izz ad-Din Aibek at-Turkumani as-Sālihi, and all took the oath of loyalty to him. He came to Cairo, went up to the citadel and announced the news to al-Khalīl's mother, the wife of al-Malik as-Salih. From that time she became titular head of the whole state; a royal stamp was issued in her name with the formula 'mother of Khalīl', and the *khutba*[1] was pronounced in her name as Sultana of Cairo and all Egypt. This was an event without precedent throughout the Muslim world: that a woman should hold the effective power and govern a kingdom was indeed known; there was for example the case of Daifa Khatūn, daughter of the Sultan al-Malik al-'Adil,[2] who governed Aleppo and its province after the death of her son al-Malik al-'Azīz for as long as she lived, but in this case the *khutba* was pronounced in the name of her grandson al-Malik an-Nasir.

After his death al-Malik al-Mu'azzam's body lay abandoned on the river bank and no one dared to approach it until some boatmen passing by on the west bank gave him a burial there.

THE RECONQUEST OF DAMIETTA

(IBN WASIL, FO. 372V–373V)

When the amīrs and the army had taken oaths of loyalty and affairs were settled as we have described, the surrender of Damietta was discussed with the King of France. The man who conducted the negotiations was the amīr Husām ad-Din ibn Abi 'Ali, for everyone agreed to rely on his advice and opinion because of his reputation for wisdom and experience, and because of the trust that al-Malik as-Salih had in him. So he and the King of France held a series of conversations and

[1] The Friday address from the pulpit in the Mosque, in which the name of the ruling sovereign is mentioned.

[2] Wife of az-Zahir, Sultan of Aleppo. He died in 1216 and his son al-'Azīz in 1236, and from that date the grandmother ruled as Regent for her grandson.

finally agreed that Damietta should surrender and that the King should go free. The Qadi Jamāl ad-Din ibn Wasil, the author of this history, says:

> The amīr Husām ad-Din told me: 'The King of France was an extremely wise and intelligent man. In one of our conversations I said to him: "How did Your Majesty ever conceive the idea, a man of your character and wisdom and good sense, of going on board ship and riding the back of this sea and coming to a land so full of Muslims and soldiers, thinking that you could conquer it and become its ruler? This undertaking is the greatest risk to which you could possibly expose yourself and your subjects." The King laughed but did not reply. "In our land," I added, "when a man travels by sea on several occasions, exposing himself and his possessions to such a risk, his testimony is not accepted as evidence by a Court of Law." "Why not?" "Because such behaviour suggests to us that he lacks sense, and a man who lacks sense is not fit to give evidence."[1] The King laughed and said: "By God, whoever said that was right, and whoever made that ruling did not err." '

The author of this history says: What Husām ad-Din says here is indeed the opinion of several scholars, but in fact it is not valid, for in most cases men return from sea voyages quite unharmed. On this subject there are two replies possible to the question whether, when a man has no other route to Mecca than one involving a sea voyage, the Pilgrimage is obligatory for him. One reply is that it is not, as the danger and risk involved in a sea voyage are so great; the other is that it is, as in most cases the traveller returns unharmed.

When agreement was reached between the King of France and the Muslims on the surrender of Damietta, the King sent to order his henchmen in Damietta to hand the city over. They, after objections, and messengers coming and going between them and the King, finally obeyed, and handed the city over to the Muslims. The Sultan's standards entered the city on Friday 3 safar 648/May 1250, and were raised on the walls, proclaiming once again the rule of Islām. The King of France

[1] See above, in the section on Saladin's 'zeal in the Holy War'.

was set free and went, with the remains of his army, over to the western shore. The next day, Saturday, he went aboard and set sail for Acre. He stayed some time in Palestine and then returned home. So God purified Egypt of them, and this victory was many times greater than the first,[1] because of the large number of the enemy killed and captured; so many that the prisons of Cairo were full of Franks. The joyful news spread to all the other countries, and public manifestations of joy and happiness were seen.

After the King of France left, the army marched straight to Cairo and entered the city. There, for many days on end, rolls of drums announced the glad tidings of the Muslim victory over the Franks and the recovery of the province of Damietta, pearl of Islām and frontier of Egypt. This was the second time that the infidels had taken it and lost it again and had fled in defeat and disarray.

PROLOGUE AND EPILOGUE TO ST. LOUIS' CRUSADE

(MAQRIZI, 334–5, 356–8)

(Disembarking in Egypt) the King of France sent a letter to the Sultan (al-Malik as-Salih). After the (introductory) heretical phrases[2] he continued:

You will be aware that I am the head of the Christian community, as I acknowledge that you are the head of the Mohammedan community. You know also that the (Muslim) population of Andalusia pays tribute to us and gives us gifts, and we drive them before us like a herd of cattle, killing the men, widowing the women, capturing their daughters and infants, emptying their houses.[3] I have given you sufficient demonstration (of our strength),

[1] At the time of the Fifth Crusade.

[2] I.e. after the Christian eulogies.

[3] This reference to Andalusia seems to Reinaud irrelevant to the document. He thinks that Maqrizi must have inserted it, taking it out of some other context in the history of the reconquest. But one might also imagine that King Louis naturally recalled, to frighten his enemy, St. Fernando's recent triumphs against the Muslims in Spain; the fall of Seville (November 1248) occurred a few months before the Crusade landed.

and the best advice I can offer. Even if you were to promise me anything on oath and to appear before the priests and monks and carry a candle before me as an act of obedience to the Cross, it would not deter me from attacking you and fighting you on the land that is dearest to you. If this country falls into my hands, it will be mine as a gift. If you keep it by victory over me, you may do as you will with me. I have told you about the armies obedient to me, filling the mountains and the plains, numerous as the stones of the earth and poised against you like the sword of Destiny. I put you on your guard against them.

When this letter arrived and was read to the Sultan his eyes filled with tears and he exclaimed: 'We belong to God, and to Him we return!' Then he had a reply composed by the Qadi Bahā' ad-Din Zuháir, head of Chancellery. After an introductory formula with the name of God and benedictions on God's apostle Muhammad, his family and companions, the letter went on:

Your letter has reached us in which you threaten us with the size of your armies and the number of your warriors. Now we are a war-like race; never is one of our champions cut down without being replaced; never has an enemy attacked us without being destroyed. Fool! If your eyes had seen the points of our swords and the enormity of our devastations, the forts and shores that we have taken (from you) and the lands that we have sacked in the past and the present, you would gnaw your fingers in repentance! The outcome of the events you are precipitating is inevitable: the day will dawn to our advantage and end in your destruction. Then you will curse yourself: 'and the wicked shall know the fate that awaits them'.[1] When you read my letter, let your response comply with the Sura of the Bees: 'You shall see God's command brought about; do not hurry it."[2] (Remember) too the Sura of *Sad*: 'You shall know what this signifies after some time!'[3] We have recourse to God's word, for he declares most truthfully: 'How many times has a small band defeated a large army, with God's support! For God is with the patient,'[4] and to the words of the wise, according to whom: 'The man of might is brought down in the end'; so your might will finally be brought down, and will bring catastrophe upon you. Greetings.

[1] Qur'ān XXVI, 228.
[2] Qur'ān XVI, 1.
[3] Qur'ān XXXVIII, 88.
[4] Qur'ān II, 250.

(After the victory at al-Mansura the Sultan Turanshāh) wrote to the amīr Jamāl ad-Din ibn Yaghmūr, his commander in Damascus, a letter in his own hand which said:

Praise is due to God, who has lifted our sorrow from us! Victory comes from God alone. On that day the faithful will rejoice in the help of God. Speak of the grace received from your Lord! If you wish to count God's graces, you will not be able to number them.[1]

We inform His Excellency Jamāl ad-Din and all Islām of the victory bestowed by God over the enemies of the Faith. Their threat grew and grew, their evil was already established in the land, and the believers despaired of the fate of their country, their wives and their children. 'But do not despair of God's aid.'[2] On Monday, the first day of this blessed year, God poured out his blessing on Islām's behalf. We opened our treasures, scattered wealth, distributed arms and summoned the desert Arabs, the volunteers and a multitude whose number God alone knows, from every deep valley and distant place. On the Tuesday night the enemy abandoned their tents, their possessions and their baggage and fled to Damietta, pursued all night by our swords, beyond shame, crying out in anguish. When Wednesday morning dawned we had killed 30,000, apart from those who cast themselves into the waves. As for the prisoners, it is impossible to count them. The Franks took refuge in al-Munya and begged for their lives, and this was granted them. We made them our prisoners, treated them honourably, and recovered Damietta with God's help and assistance, His majesty and highness. . . .

and so on at length.

With the letter the Sultan sent the King of France's mantle, and the amīr Jamāl ad-Din ibn Yaghmūr put it on. It was of scarlet red, trimmed with ermine. Shaikh Najm ad-Din ibn Isra'īl said of it:

The mantle of the Frenchman, sent in homage to the Prince of Amīrs was white as paper, but our swords have stained it the colour of blood.

and also:

Lord of all the Kings of this time, You have seen fulfilled the divine promises of victory.

May our Lord always triumph over his enemies, and clothe his servants in a king's booty!

[1] All the foregoing are Qur'anic phrases: XXXV, 31; III, 121; XXX, 3; XC III, 11; VI, 18.

[2] Qur'ān XII, 87.

SAINT LOUIS IN TUNISIA

(MAQRIZI, 364–5)

It happened that this Frenchman, after escaping from the hands of the Muslims, decided to attack Tunisia in the land of Africa,[1] profiting by the plague and famine that were rife there, and he sent to summon the Christian kings to arms. He also sent to the Pope, the vicar of the Messiah according to them, who wrote calling on the Christian kings to join the campaign with King Louis, giving them a free hand with the Church's wealth of which they could take what they wanted. The kings who came were the Kings of England, Scotland, Toulouse, Barcelona (who was called 'King of Aragon') and a whole host of other Christian princes. The (Hafsid) Sultan Abu Abdullāh Muhammad al-Mustansir bi-llāh, son of the amīr Abu Zakariyya Yahya, son of Shaikh Abu Muhammad 'Abd al-Wahid, son of Shaikh Abu Hafs, King of Tunisia,[2] prepared to resist the attack and sent his ambassadors to sue for peace, offering 8,000 *dinar*. They took the money but did not make peace, and attacked Tunisia on 28 dhu l-qa'da 668/21 July 1270, disembarking at Carthage with 6,000 cavalry and 30,000 infantry. They remained there for six months.[3] The Muslims kept up the fight until mid-muharram 669/the end of August, with violent battles in which many of both sides died. The Muslims were almost defeated when God liberated them. One morning[4] the King of France was found dead. Succeeding events led to the signing of the peace treaty and the departure of the Christians. It is interesting to note that a Tunisian, one Ahmad ibn Isma'il az-Zayyan, composed the following lines:

O Frenchman, this land is Egypt's sister; prepare for your certain fate!

[1] Properly Ifrīqiya, the Roman province of Africa, i.e. Tunisia.
[2] King of Tunis 1249–77.
[3] Incomprehensible in view of the dates of this conflict.
[4] 25 August.

Here Ibn Luqmān's house will be a tomb, and the eunuchs (to guard you) will be Munkar and Nakīr.[1]

This seems like a prophecy for the French King, for he did die. This King of France was an intelligent man, cunning and deceitful.

[1] Alluding to Louis' prison and his guardian in Egypt. Munkar and Nakīr are the Muslim angels who interrogate the spirits of the newly dead.

Part Four

THE MAMLŪKS AND THE LIQUIDATION OF THE CRUSADERS

CHAPTER ONE

Between 1265 and 1291 three Mamlūk Sultans, Baibars (1260–77), Qalawūn (1279–90) and al-Ashraf (1290–93), destroyed what was left of the Crusaders' achievements. The main source for all three, although incomplete and for the most part still unedited, is the contemporary Ibn 'Abd az-Zahir. For the conquests of Baibars we have his biography written by Ibn 'Abd az-Zahir as well as the later chronicles of Ibn al-Furāt, al-Maqrizi and al-'Aini. The passages given here, among them the famous victory letter to Bohemond IV after the fall of Antioch, come from these sources.

BAIBARS AGAINST TRIPOLI AND ANTIOCH. HIS LETTER TO BOHEMOND VI

(IBN 'ABD AZ-ZAHIR, FO. 105V–111V)

This fortress (Syrian Tripoli) belonged to the Muslims in times past; the last of them to hold it were the Banu 'Ammār. One of the Frankish kings besieged it for many years and built a castle in front of it for as long as the siege lasted.[1] The Banu 'Ammār, reduced to dire straits, left one of their tribe in the city and went to find help and succour. But he was an apostate; he climbed the city wall and invited the Franks to enter and take possession of the city. In this way they conquered the fortress.[2] The last of the Franks to hold it was Prince Bohemond (VI), son of Bohemond. When al-Malik az-Zahir (Baibars), whose biography this is, came to the throne he began to hear rumours of acts of manifest tyranny committed by Bohemond, and of his frequent acts of hostility and aggression toward those who entered his domain; he even went so far as to lay hands on

[1] The Mount Pilgrim built by Raymond of Saint-Gilles in 1103.

[2] In fact taken by storm in 1109.

some ambassadors from Georgia whose ship had been wrecked, imprisoning them and seizing the letters to the Sultan that they carried. He sent both men and letters to Hulagu, King of the Mongols, bringing ruin upon them and those who sent them. He did the same to other princes. Zeal for Islām and religious fervour forced the Sultan to attack Tripoli. He ordered the preparations to be made in secret, and finally set off across mountains and valleys to launch the Muslim army against the enemy. The troops surrounded the enemy city with a circle of fire and iron, capturing, pillaging and storming. The Sultan seized most of the region and then, following the best counsel, retired.

Concerning his incursion into Tripoli we have described how the Sultan made a hard fight of it, and by his subterfuges left everyone uncertain of what his aims had been when he withdrew, for he had ordered a certain number of tents to be pitched so that their entrances faced in different directions, so as to confuse those who thought (to divine his plans). Next he attacked Antioch, which was part of the domains of the Prince of Tripoli. The Muslims advanced, killing and capturing and pillaging the land. The Sultan himself led the march on Antioch, and laid siege to it on 1 ramadān 666/12 May 1268. His major-domo (*ustadār*) the amīr Shams ad-Din Aqsunqur al-Farqani came to blows during the advance with a squadron of cavalry from Antioch. He exterminated them in battle and captured the Constable who commanded the city. Muslim troops swarmed toward Antioch from all directions; the word was given for the assault, the walls were broken down and the city was taken with much bloodshed. The Muslims then besieged the citadel and took it after guaranteeing the lives of the beleaguered men, and so it came safely into Muslim hands.

The Sultan ordered a letter to be written to the Prince announcing the fall on the city and the loss that he had suffered through its acquisition by the Sultan. The letter was composed by the author of this history[1]—God have mercy upon him!—as the greatest expert in the epistolary style who ever lived, the master of the most telling and felicitous expressions, experienced in the finesse demanded by chancellery affairs, with the subtlest power of divining his Sovereign's intentions and aims! The Franks give the title of Prince only to the ruler of Antioch, and so the author refers to Bohemond as a Count only, since Antioch was no longer his.[2] This is an opportunity to describe an episode passed on to me by the author himself: the Sultan, he said, sent me with the amīr Atā-beg Faris ad-Din as ambassador to Tripoli when the truce was under negotiation.[3] Now the Sultan al-Malik az-Zahir himself entered the city with his two ambassadors, disguised as an equerry (*silahdār*), to explore the town and find out the points at which it could be stormed. When we came into the Prince's presence to discuss the terms of the truce and reached an agreement the Sultan stood looking down at the Atā-beg and listening. He[4] began to write: 'Terms of the truce between our Lord the Sultan and the Count ...' without putting in 'Prince'. The Lord of Tripoli glanced at the writing, disapproved, and said: 'Who is this Count?' 'You,' I said. 'No,' he replied, 'I am the Prince!' 'The Prince is the Sultan al-Malik az-Zahir; the title of 'Prince' refers to the ruler of Jerusalem, Antioch and Alexandretta, all of which now belong to our Lord the Sultan.' He cast a glance at his warriors standing there, and the door of the chamber was barred. Then the Sultan kicked the Atā-beg, who said: 'O Muhyi ad-Din, you are right, but our Lord the Sultan has graciously conceded to this man the title of Prince, as he has allowed him to remain in his kingdom.' 'If that is so,' I said to the Atā-beg, 'then that is all right'; and I wrote 'Prince' in place of 'Count'. 'When we had

[1] The reference here is to Ibn 'Abd az-Zahir, whose nephew compiled his uncle's work.

[2] During the reign of Bohemond IV (1177–1233) the principate of Antioch and the county of Tripoli were united under the dynasty of Antioch.

[3] 1271, three years after the fall of Antioch.

[4] Muhyi ad-Din ibn 'Abd az-Zahir, author and narrator.

left,' continued the author, 'and our Lord the Sultan reached his own camp, His Majesty began to tell the story to the amīrs at court, laughing and saying as he turned to me; "He certainly chose a good moment! To the devil with the Prince *and* the Count!" ' This is the end of the story, so we will return to the text of the letter, which was as follows:

Count Such-and-Such,[1] head of the Christian community, reduced to the title of Count—God inspire him with wisdom and make good his aim and good counsel his treasure—knows already how we attacked Tripoli and devastated the very centre of his domains; he saw the ruins and the slaughter that we left behind at our departure; the churches themselves were razed from the face of the earth, every house met with disaster, the dead were piled up on the seashore like islands of corpses, the men were murdered, the children enslaved, the free women reduced to captivity, the trees cut down leaving only enough to be used, God willing, for catapults and walls,[2] goods pillaged, together with women, children and herds, so that the poor are enriched, the single man has gained a family, the servant has servants and the infantryman a horse.

All this happened before your eyes, while you stood like a man overcome by a mortal disaster, and when you regained your voice you cried in fear: 'This calamity is my fault!' You know too that we left you, but only to return, that we have deferred your total destruction, but only for a certain number of days; you are aware that we have left your country without an animal remaining in it, for we have driven them all before us, nor a girl, for all are in our power, nor a column, for our crowbars have tumbled them all, nor a field under cultivation, for we have reaped them all, nor a single possession, for we have taken them. The caves at the tops of these high mountains, these valleys cutting across frontiers and touching the imagination; these can give no defence. You know how we left you to appear unexpectedly before your city of Antioch while you were still hardly daring to believe that we had withdrawn: (this time) if we depart we shall surely return to where our feet rested before!

[1] So in Ibn 'Abd az-Zahir's compilation, but other sources give a more sonorous heading ('the noble and exalted Count, the valiant lion, pride of Christendom, leader of the Crusaders, whose title, with the fall of Antioch, has changed from "Prince" to "Count",' etc.). In spite of their pompous and polemical tone these epithets were apparently too much for the compiler, who allowed them to drop. In Professor Gabrieli's translation the often corrupt text of Ibn 'Abd az-Zahir is emended from that of an-Nuwairi (Quatremère: *Sultans Mamlouks*, I, II, pp. 190–91).

[2] Referring to the threatened return of the Muslim army to Tripoli.

Our purpose here is to give you news of what we have just done, to inform you of the utter catastrophe that has befallen you. On Wednesday, 24 sha'bān we left you at Tripoli and on the first of the holy month of ramadān we besieged Antioch. While we were taking up our position in front of the city your troops rode out to measure themselves against us in combat. They were defeated; they came to one another's aid but failed to win the day, and their Constable became our prisoner. He asked to be allowed to negotiate with your men and went to the city, to return with a band of your monks and principal satellites, who negotiated with us. But we saw that they were inspired with your own spirit, wickedly intent on murderous designs, at loggerheads in a good cause but united in a bad one. When we saw that their fate was irremediably sealed and that their destiny from God was death we dismissed them, saying; 'We shall lay siege to you at once, and this is the first and last warning that we shall give you.' Thus they returned, behaving like you, in the belief that you would be coming to their aid with your cavalry and infantry: but in time the Marshal was done away with,[1] fear seized the monks, the Castellan bowed his head to disaster and death overwhelmed them from every side. We took the city by storm in the fourth hour of Saturday, the fourth day of the holy month of ramadān (18 May), bringing despair to all those whom you had chosen to garrison and defend it. Not one of them but had certain wealth, and now there is not one of us but owns one of them *and* his money. You would have seen your knights prostrate beneath the horses' hooves, your houses stormed by pillagers and ransacked by looters, your wealth weighed by the quintal, your women sold four at a time and bought for a *dinar* of your own money! You would have seen the crosses in your churches smashed, the pages of the false Testaments scattered, the Patriarchs' tombs overturned. You would have seen your Muslim enemy trampling on the place where you celebrate the mass, cutting the throats of monks, priests and deacons upon the altars, bringing sudden death to the Patriarchs and slavery to the royal princes. You would have seen fire running through your palaces, your dead burned in this world before going down to the fires of the next, your palace lying unrecognizable, the Church of St. Paul and that of the Qusyān[2] pulled down and destroyed; then you would have said: 'Would that I were dust, and that no letter had ever brought me such tidings!' Your soul would have left your body for sadness; you would have quenched its fires with the water of your tears.

[1] The following passage contains many untranslatable puns of the type already noted in the passages from 'Imād ad-Dinal-Isfahani.

[2] The Cathedral of Saint Peter, centre of the religious and municipal life of Christian Antioch.

If you had seen your dwellings stripped of your wealth, your chariots seized at Suwaidiyya[1] with your ships, your galleys become (as your enemy's property) detesters of you, you would then be convinced that the God who gave you Antioch has taken it away again, the Lord who bestowed that fortress on you has snatched it away, uprooting it from the face of the earth. You know now that we, by God's grace, have taken back from you the fortresses of Islām that you seized, Derkūsh and Shaqīf Kafar Dubbīn, as well as all your possessions in the province of Antioch; that we have brought your troops down from the citadels and have seized them by the hair and scattered them far and wide; that there is no one who could be called a rebel this side of the river; that if it could it would not call itself by that name any longer[2] and weeps for penitence. Its tears at first ran clear, but now the blood spilt into it has dyed them red.

This letter we send brings you the good news that God granted you safety and long life by causing you not to live in Antioch at this time and allowing you to live elsewhere, for otherwise you would be dead, or a prisoner, or wounded, or knocked about. To be alive is something upon which all but the dead must congratulate themselves. Who knows if God saved your life so that you could make amends for your former disobedience and disrespect to Him! Since no survivor has come forward to tell you what happened, we have informed you of it, and since no one is in a position to give you the good news that you have saved your life at the loss of everything else, we bring you the tidings in a personal message to you, to give you accurate information about what really happened. After reading this letter you will have no reason to say that any of our news is false, just as after reading this dispatch you will need to ask no one to give you the details.

When this letter reached Bohemond he flew into a great rage. This was the only news he received of the fall of Antioch.

NEGOTIATIONS WITH HUGH III, KING OF CYPRUS AND JERUSALEM

(IBN AL-FURĀT, VI, 146r–147r)

After the fall of Shaqīf the Franks in Acre wanted a king capable of defending their interests. There was a child-king in Cyprus,[3]

[1] The port of Antioch, at the mouth of the Orontes.

[2] The Orontes is called by the Arabs *al-'Asi*, 'the rebel', because of its course from south to north.

[3] Hugh II, who died in 1267 at the age of 14.

with a regent who was commander of the army and whose name was Hugh, son of Henry. He was less than thirty years old, a cousin of the Prince of Tripoli and the son of the (former) King of Cyprus' sister,[1] the aunt of the boy-king. The child died, and the kingdom fell to the young man, who was related through his wife to the lords of Arsūf[2] and through his mother to his cousin.[3] The latter had a greater right to the throne because his mother was the elder sister and the Frankish custom is for the son of the elder sister to take precedence, but he was abroad, at Sis,[4] so the younger man seized Cyprus. The Franks then invited him to come to Acre, for the kingdom of Acre was linked to that of Cyprus. He came, and the people of Acre swore obedience to him. A letter arrived (at Baibars' court) from the Prince of Tyre announcing the King's arrival and saying that he was a man of discretion who, as soon as he arrived, had realized that Frankish opinion was in favour of doing everything possible to secure good relations with their neighbour the Sultan, and had said that he had no reason for hostility toward him. The Prince of Tyre concluded by asking the Sultan to make peace with him.

When the Sultan returned to Damascus from the Antioch campaign, as we have said, the King's ambassadors appeared, with a detachment of about one hundred Frankish cavalry, bringing gifts of goldsmiths' work, wild animals and other objects. A circumscribed agreement was reached between al-Malik az-Zahir (Baibars) and this King affecting the city and province of Acre, which comprises thirty-one villages. It was agreed that Kaifa and three villages should remain in Frankish hands and that the rest of its district should be divided in two; the province of Carmel was to be divided; 'Athlīth with three villages was to go (to the Franks?) and the rest was to be divided;

[1] Isabella, younger sister of Henry I.
[2] Hugh III married Isabella of Ibelin.
[3] Hugh of Brienne, son of Maria, the elder sister of Henry I.
[4] In Cilicia or Lesser Armenia.

al-Qurâin with ten villages was to go (to the Franks?) and the rest to the Sultan; of the province of Sidon the lowlands were to go to the Franks and the mountains to the Muslims, and there was to be peace in the kingdom of Cyprus. Such were the territorial provisions of the treaty, which was to last for ten years, unaffected by foreign invasion or the arrival of any king from overseas. Finally (the Sultan) persuaded him to release the hostages taken from various cities.

The Qadi Muhyi ad-Din ibn 'Abd az-Zahir, author of the *Life of Baibars*, recalls: 'I went as an ambassador with the amīr Kamāl ad-Din ibn Shith to get the King to sign the truce. The Sultan sent with us a gift of twenty prisoners from Antioch, priests and monks. We entered Acre on 24 shawwāl (666/7 July 1268) and were very well received. The Sultan had told us not to humiliate ourselves either in posture or in speech. When we entered we saw the King with his generals seated on a bench, and so we refused to sit down until a bench was set for us in front of him. His vizier put out his hand for the document but we would put it into the hand of no one but the King himself. He took it, and paused to make observations on certain points: one was that he wanted a separate treaty for Cyprus and that the peace should last as long as there was no foreign invasion and no king from abroad appeared, also that the Isma'ilites should not be included in the truce. He also asked for dispensations in the matter of hostages as well as other details. The Sultan's ambassadors returned without the King's signature to the treaty and the matter stood in abeyance. Every time that this King of Acre opened his mouth he said: "I am afraid of King Charles, the King of France's brother, and for fear of him I cannot conclude a peace treaty."[1] God knows best.'

[1] Charles of Anjou was already beginning to assert his rights to the nominal crown of Jerusalem (which meant, in effect, the Kingdom of Acre) acquired from Maria of Antioch and officially proclaimed in 1277.

(IBN 'ABD AZ-ZAHIR, FO. 117V–118V)

At the time of the truce, Acre had no king and was ruled from Cyprus by one of the Franks. When he assumed control of Acre he wrote in a tone of humble supplication to the Sultan asking for his friendship and inviting him to sign a truce on the terms already agreed. He also sent precious gifts of great value. The Sultan was not displeased by such an offering, and accepted his friendship and sent him gifts in exchange. The King asked that the truce should be in his name and expressed his obedience and submission to it. The Sultan acceded to his request, signed the truce and sent Muhyi ad-Din, author of the *Life*, and Kamāl ad-Din ibn Shith to the Frankish King with the truce to be signed. Muhyi ad-Din[1] told me: 'When this King granted us an audience we found him sitting on a lofty throne and he declared that he would sit up on high and we lower down. The honour of Islām did not permit us to accept this, so we were raised to his level, and began our discussions with him. He began to cavil and wander from the point, to which I objected. He looked angrily at me and said to the interpreter: "Tell him to observe whom we have standing behind him." I looked, and saw that he had his army drawn up in full battle array. "Say to him," said the King to the interpreter, "that he should look at this multitude." I looked, and bowed my head. He said again: "Say to him: What do you think of what you have seen?" "May I speak with impunity?" "Yes." "Then tell the King," I said, 'that in our Flag Store, which is a prison in the Sultan's realms, in Cairo, there are more Frankish prisoners than all these.' The King was furious and made the sign of the Cross as he said: "By God, I will not spend any longer today listening to an embassy from such a people!" So we went away. Later, however, he received us again and we got him to sign the truce,

[1] The compiler is speaking.

which lasted as long as the Sultan al-Malik al-Mansūr Qalawūn lived.'[1]

THE DESTRUCTION OF HISN AL-AKRĀD[2] (IBN AL-FURĀT, FO. 189r–190v)

In ancient times this fortress was called *Hisn as-Safh* (Fortress of the Mountainside). Concerning the name given to it later by the Kurds Mūntakhab ad-Din Yahya ibn Abi Tayy an-Najjār al-Hálabi[3] says in his history that the amīr Shibl ad-Daula Nasr ibn Mirdās, ruler of Hims, sent a Kurdish garrison force there in 422/1031, and that the fort took its name from them. In the time of the Ata-beg Tughtikīn of Damascus a truce was signed by him and the Franks, one of its conditions being that the forts of Masyaf and Hisn al-Akrād were included in it and that their inhabitants paid an annual tax to the Franks. This situation continued for some time. Then, says Ibn 'Asakir,[4] (Raymond of) Saint-Gilles—God curse him!—began to beleaguer Tripoli and at the same time subjected the fort and others in its neighbourhood to continual attacks. In 496/1103 he besieged and almost subdued it. He was on the point of taking it when Janāh ad-Daula the ruler of Hims was murdered. Raymond wanted Hims, so he abandoned Hisn al-Akrād. At his death his son Bertrand[5] continued his father's policy of harrying the fort and devastating its surrounding countryside, which kept its inhabitants in a state of terror. Then he went off to

[1] Thus a treaty was signed with Hugh III in 1268, contrary to what would appear from Ibn al-Furāt's account, quoted by Ibn 'Abd-az-Zahir himself. But the reference to the truce's lasting until the time of Qalawūn more probably refers to the truce of Caesarea (May 1279) between Baibars and Acre, later renewed by Qalawūn (see below).

[2] In Arabic 'fortress of the Kurds', in French 'Krak des Chevaliers', the great fortress of the Hospitallers north-east of Tripoli.

[3] Lost Shi'ite historian of the twelfth century, quoted on several occasions by Ibn al-Furāt.

[4] Twelfth-century historian of Damascus.

[5] See above.

besiege Beirūt and Tancred, Prince of Antioch, took over most of the region and was by some means kept at bay by the Syrians. He too besieged this fort, and reduced its inhabitants to such straits that the ruler surrendered it, hoping that Tancred would allow him to stay there as a reward for having given him a warmer welcome than he had to Saint-Gilles. Tancred, however, cleared the city of its inhabitants, whom he took away with him, and established there a garrison of Franks, or so Ibn 'Asakir says. According to another version Tancred, Prince of Antioch left that city, besieged Hisn al-Akrād and received the citizens' surrender at the end of 503/1110, and it remained in Frankish hands until the events that we are about to relate, God willing. Ibn Munqidh in his *Kitāb al-Buldān*[1] says that the champion of the Faith al-Malik al-'Adil Nur ad-Din Mahmud ruler of Damascus—God bless him!—had contacts with one of the Turcoman infantrymen in the service of the Franks who ruled Hisn al-Akrād, with whom he arranged that when Nur ad-Din attacked the fort the man and a group of his companions would support him, raise his banner on the walls and shout his name. This Turcoman had several sons and a brother, all of whom enjoyed the confidence of the Franks in the fort. The signal agreed between him and Nur ad-Din was that he should stand on top of one of the ramparts. But, it is said, Nur ad-Din informed no one of the plan, and so when the troops were advancing and saw the man standing there they shot at him and killed him; on his death his supporters were all taken and the plot came to nothing.

Hisn al-Akrād was not among the cities taken by Saladin but remained in Frankish hands until al-Malik az-Zahir Rukn ad-Din Baibars led the 669/1271 expedition against Tripoli of which we have already spoken. He besieged Hisn al-Akrād on 9 rajab/21 February: on 20 rajab/4 March the suburbs were

[1] Lost work by Usama ibn Munqidh, famous author of the *Autobiography*. All these references reveal Ibn al-Furāt as a habitual compiler.

taken and al-Malik al-Mansūr, ruler of Hamāt,[1] arrived with his army. The Sultan went to meet him, descended from his horse when al-Mansūr did and advanced beneath his banners without bodyguards or equerries as a gesture of courtesy to the Lord of Hamāt. At his command a tent was brought and pitched for him. The amīr of Sahyūn, Saif ad-Din, and Najm ad-Din the Grand Master of the Isma'ilites also arrived.

At the end of rajab work was completed on a large number of catapults. On 7 sha'bān/22 March the bastions were taken by storm and an emplacement was built from which the Sultan could draw a bow at the enemy. Then Baibars began to distribute gifts of money and robes of honour.

On 16 sha'bān/31 March a breach was made in one of the towers of the fortress, our soldiers went up to attack, got up into the fort and took possession of it, while the Franks withdrew to the keep. A whole group of Franks and Christians was then set free by the Sultan as a pious offering in the name of al-Malik as-Sa'īd.[2] The catapults were then moved into the fortress and directed on the keep. At this point the Sultan wrote certain letters as if they had been written by the Frankish general in Tripoli, ordering them to surrender. They begged that their lives should be spared, which was granted on condition that they returned to their homelands. On Tuesday 24 sha'bān/7 April the Franks left the fort and were sent home, and the Sultan took possession of it.

He wrote a letter to the Grand Master of the Hospital, the ruler of Hisn al-Akrād, to give him the news of the victory. These were his words: 'This letter is addressed to *frère* Hugues[3] —God make him one of those who do not oppose destiny or rebel against Him who has reserved victory and triumph for His army, and do not believe that any caution is sufficient to

[1] Uncle of the historian Abu l-Fidā'.

[2] Baibars' eldest son, a young man who later succeeded his father for two years (1277–79) on the throne of Egypt.

[3] Hugh of Revel.

save men from what God has decreed, or that they can protect themselves from it within the shelter of buildings or walls of stone—to inform him of the conquest, by God's grace, of Hisn al-Akrād, which you fortified and built out and furbished—you would have done better to destroy it—and whose defence you entrusted to your Brethren. They have failed you; by making them live there you destroyed them, for they have lost both the fort and you. These troops of mine are incapable of besieging any fort and leaving it able to resist them, or of serving an unfortunate Sa'īd' ('happy, *felix*')[1].

The Sultan named the amīr Sarim ad-Din al-Kāfiri as his commander in Hisn al-Akrād and entrusted the restoration work to 'Izz ad-Din al-Aqram and 'Izz ad-Din Aibek. During the siege he arrested two assassins who had been sent from al-'Ullaiqa to the ruler of Tripoli,[2] who had ordered them to make an attempt on Baibar's life. When the Grand Master Najm ad-Din arrived he reproved them for it, but then let them both go.

AN UNSUCCESSFUL ATTACK ON CYPRUS

(AL-'AINI, 239–42)

Ibn Kathīr[3] says that when al-Malik as-Sa'īd, az-Zahir's son, took Hisn al-Akrād he turned its church into a mosque and held divine worship there on Fridays, while the Sultan nominated a qadi and a governor for the fort and ordered that it should be restored to its former state. The Sultan was encamped there when he received the news that the ruler of the island of Cyprus

[1] A pun in Arabic, one of the many on the name of the hereditary prince.

[2] 'Ullaiqa was one of the Syrian forts belonging to the Isma'ilites. Their fearful power had diminished after the blows they had suffered from the Mongols and now they steered a course between the Crusaders and Baibars, sometimes paying tribute to both, but they had not yet lost the habit of assassination.

[3] Fourteenth-century chronicler. Al-'Aini too merely compiled passages from earlier sources.

had set out with an army for Acre, fearing that he would be attacked by al-Malik az-Zahir. The Sultan, keen to profit by this, sent a large expedition with sixteen galleys to take the island of Cyprus in its ruler's absence. The ships sailed away with all speed, but as they approached the island a treacherous wind seized them and sent them colliding into one another. Eleven were wrecked—by the decree of Almighty God!—many men were drowned and about 1,800 soldiers and sailors taken prisoner. To God we belong and to Him we return!

Baibars[1] says in his chronicle: The following disaster struck the Muslims after the conquest of al-Quráin. The Sultan left Damascus at the end of the manœuvres in that region, during the last ten days of shawwāl/first ten days of June 1271, and attacked and besieged al-Quráin[2] on 2 dhu l-qa'da/13 June. He stormed the ramparts, and the defenders begged him to spare their lives, which he did. It was agreed that they should leave and go wherever they wanted but should take neither possessions nor arms with them. The Sultan then took possession of the fortress and had it demolished before retiring to Lajūn. From there he sent orders to his commanders in Egypt to arm galleys and send them to Cyprus. They did so and sent them off under the command of an admiral, and a captain of each ship. When the fleet reached the port of Limassol on the southern coast of Cyprus, and night had fallen, the first ship went ahead to enter port but struck a shoal in the darkness and was wrecked. One after another the rest of the galleys followed, unaware of what had happened, and the darkness of night sent them all to their doom. The Cypriots seized their possessions. The admiral, Ibn Hassūn, had given them advice in which men saw a bad omen, for he told them to smear the ships with pitch and hoist crosses up on high, which would make them

[1] Mamluk amir not to be confused with the Sultan of whom he was a younger contemporary (died 1335) and author of an important chronicle of his own times.

[2] The Frankish 'Montfort', north-east of Acre, and another stronghold of the Hospitallers.

look like Frankish ships and save them from attack by the enemy, but this change of colours brought about the shipwreck that God had ordained. A letter from the King of Cyprus soon reached the Sultan informing him that the Egyptian galleys had reached Cyprus and eleven of them had been wrecked and seized by the King. The Sultan ordered a reply to be written, and so the following letter was sent:

To His Highness King Hugh, formerly Regent—whom God make to be one of those who give each man his due, not boasting of a victory unless it yields, then or later, some advantage or profit worth (the outlay)—we inform him that when God intends to make a man happy He relieves him of the burden of his destiny with some small misfortune[1] and makes him take appropriate measures to withstand the blows of fate. You have informed us that the wind has wrecked a certain number of our galleys; you call this a personal achievement and congratulate yourself on it. Now we in our turn send you the news of the fall of al-Quráin; quite a different matter from the incident by which God has chosen to deliver our kingdom from an evil fate. In your case, there is nothing remarkable for you to boast about in having taken possession of some iron and wood: to seize mighty castles is really remarkable! You have spoken, and so have we, and God knows that our words are true. You trusted (in your God) and we (in ours); he who trusts in God and his sword is different from him who trusts in the wind. Victory brought about by the action of the elements is less noble than victory by the sword! In a single day we could send out more galleys, whereas you could not rebuild a single bit of your castle. We can arm a hundred ships, but in a hundred years you could not arm a single fortress. Anyone who is given an oar can row but not everyone given a sword is capable of using it. If a few sailors are missing we have thousands more, but how can those who wield an oar in mid-ocean compare with those who wield a sword in the midst of the (enemy's battle-)lines? For you, horses are ships; for us, ships are horses: there is a great deal of difference between the man who rides chargers like the waves of the sea and the man who stands still aboard a ship even as it arrives in port: between the man who rides Arab steeds when he goes hunting with falcons and those who boast of having been hunting on a crow![2] If

[1] Variant and emendation of the old concept of divine envy.

[2] The 'crow' was a sort of light vessel; here and in the rest of the passage the usual puns and double meanings are to be found.

you have taken one of our broken ship's timbers (*qarya*) how many populous villages (*qarya*) have we taken from you! If you have captured a rudder (*sukkān*) how many of your lands have we emptied of inhabitants (*sukkān*)! How much have you gained, and how much have we? It is clear which of us has gained the most. If it were possible for kings to keep quiet, you should have kept silent and refrained from boasting.

CHAPTER TWO

Qalawūn's sultanate, no less humane and valiant than Baibars', is notable in its relations with the remaining Christian states in Syria for a series of treaties between the Sultan and the Templars, the people of Acre and Margaret of Tyre, of which Ibn 'Abd az-Zahir has preserved the text in his *Life of the Sultan* (*Tashrīf al-ayyām wa l-'usūr*).

But Qalawūn continued the erosion of the Latin domains in the Holy Land; his greatest triumph was the conquest of Tripoli in 1289, of which Abu l-Fidā' was an eye-witness. (There is another version in Maqrizi but clearly from an earlier source.) After the fall of Tripoli, the Franks retained only Acre and a few other coastal towns.

QALAWŪN'S TREATY WITH THE TEMPLARS AT TORTOSA

(IBN 'ABD AZ-ZAHIR, TASHRĪF, 38v–44r)

In 681/1282 a truce was signed between our Lord al-Malik al-Mansūr (Qalawūn) and his son al-Malik as-Salih 'Alā' ad-Dunya wa'd-Din 'Ali on the one hand and the Grand Master *frère* William of Beaujeu, Grand Master of the Order of the Temple in Acre and the Litoral, and all the Templars in Tortosa on the other.[1] Peace was to last for ten years, entire, continuous and consecutive, and ten months, beginning on Wednesday 5 muharram 681 from the Prophet Muhammad's *hijra*, corresponding to 15 nisān 1593 of the era of Alexander son of Philip the Greek[2]/15 April 1282. It applied to the territories of our Lord al-Malik al-Mansūr and of his son al-Malik as-Salih

[1] The text of the document is here clumsily welded to the preamble.

[2] The Seleucid era, beginning in 311 B.C.

'Alā' ad-Din 'Ali[1] and to everything that came under their authority: Egypt with its provinces, borders and ports; Syria with its districts, castles, fortresses, shores and ports; the province of Hims with its surrounding territory; the Isma'ilite forts and their surrounding territory; the province of Sahyūn and Balātunus; Jábala, Laodicea and the territories under their control; the province of Hamāt and its environs, the province of Aleppo and its environs, the Euphrates province and its territory; the (recent) conquests in Syria, the city of Hisn al-Akrād and its environs and everything therein or dependent on it or counted as part of it at the time of the signing of the present treaty in the way of cities, villages, arable fields, pastures, terrains, fortifications, mills, etc.; the province of Safithā and its surrounding regions, villages and walls, and all the other villages and cities in its possession or added to it in the future; Mai'ār and its territory, al-'Uraima and its territory, with everything that comes under its control; Halabā and its territory, 'Arqā and its territory, Tibū and its territory, the fort of Hisn al-Akrād and its territory, al-Qulai'āt (lit., the small fortresses) and their territory; Maraqiyya and the whole of its lands, the region of al-Marqab, of which both sides agree to hold half each, and everything included in the treaty made with the Christians by al-Malik al-Mansūr. The treaty embraces, in these regions far and near, neighbouring and bordering, every zone, cultivated or not, flat and hilly, land and sea, ports and shores, with their mills, towers, gardens, waters, trees and wells and all that God conquered by the hand of our Lord al-Malik al-Mansūr and his son the Sultan al-Malik as-Salih and the commanders of his armies, in the way of forts, cities, villages and every region in between, flat and mountainous, cultivated or not, waters and gardens, ports and shores and plains. On the other hand the truce applies to Tortosa, which is held by the

[1] Qalawūn's appointed heir who, however, died before him, in 1288, when the succession passed to his younger brother al-Ashraf.

Order of the Temple, and to their lands recognized in perpetuity in the act of signing this blessed truce; as well as the annexed territories of al-'Uraima and Mai'ār, according to a truce signed by al-Malik az-Zahir[1] whose terms are transferred to this treaty. The treaty applies then to all the territories of our Lord the Sultan (with security for them) on the part of the Grand Master *frère* William of Beaujeu, Grand Master of the Order of the Temple, and all the Brethren of Tortosa, knights and turcopoles and other categories of Franks.

No one from Tortosa and its port and coast shall invade the lands of our Lord al-Malik al-Mansūr and his son al-Malik as-Salih, or their forts and castles and cities, whether or not they have been mentioned in the treaty. In return Tortosa and the regions mentioned in the treaty, with the Brethren and knights and their subjects living there or visiting, shall enjoy security and tranquillity from our Lord the Sultan al-Malik al-Mansūr, his son, their armies and subjects. No one shall invade Tortosa or its territory, or cause harm to or attack any of its inhabitants for as long as the truce shall last. All matters coming under prohibition shall be subject to the same prohibition.

Whenever a ship from the lands of our Lord the Sultan or one going thither from any other land or nation is wrecked or suffers damage in the port of Tortosa or its coasts and lands included in this treaty, all those on board the ship shall be kept safe, and also their goods and merchandise. Where the owner of the damaged ship is available, his ship and his property shall be handed over to him; if death or drowning have made this impossible, his property shall be sent under guard to a representative of our Lord the Sultan. The same rule shall apply to ships from Tortosa wrecked in the realms of our Lord the Sultan.

In the territory of Tortosa mentioned in the treaty no fort or

[1] We do not possess a copy of the truce with Baibars referred to here.

fortification is to be repaired, nor any reinforcement, entrenchment or the like built.

THE TREATY WITH ACRE

(IBN ʿABD AZ-ZAHIR, TASHRĪF, 69r–85v)

In 682/1283 our Lord the Sultan agreed to grant a request from the people of Acre, after their ambassadors had appeared before him time after time, in Syria and Egypt, asking for peace. He forbade them to travel overland, inviting them to come by sea only, whenever they should desire an audience of him. This they did. The agreement reached was that they should submit themselves to the will of the Sultan, although before this, at the the expiration of the truce (of al-Malik az-Zahir[1]), they had put forward exorbitant claims. In safar of this year/May 1283 delegates and notabilities came from Acre and signed the truce. The Sultan took the oath in the presence of the Frankish ambassadors, who were: two Brethren of the Order of the Temple, two of the Order of the Hospital, two royal knights, the governor-general William and the vizier Fahd. The text was as follows:

A truce is declared between our Lord the Sultan al-Malik al-Mansūr (Qalawūn) and his son al-Malik as-Salih ʿAlā' ad-Dunya wa'd-Din ʿAli—God make their power eternal—and the authorities of the Commune of Acre, Sidon, ʿAthlīth and the dependent territories, over which the truce extends. These are: the Seneschal Odo, *bailli* of Acre,[2] the Grand Master *frère* William of Beaujeu, Grand Master of the Order of the Temple, the Grand Master *frère* Nicholas Lorgne, Grand Master of the Order of the Hospital, and the Marshal *frère* Conrad, representative of the Grand Master of the Teutonic Hospital. The truce is to last ten whole years, ten months, ten days and ten hours, beginning on Friday 5 rabīʿ I 682 of the *hijra* of the Prophet, which corresponds to 3 hazirān 1594 of the era of Alexander son of Philip the Greek/3 June 1283. The truce is to be effective throughout all

[1] The truce of 1272 with Baibars.

[2] Odo Poilechien, Charles of Anjou's representative.

the states of our Lord al-Malik al-Mansūr and of his son al-Malik as-Salih 'Alā' ad-Dunya wa'd-Din 'Ali: forts, castles, territories, provinces, cities, villages, farmed and unfarmed land. This includes:[1]

The kingdom of Egypt with all its regions and Muslim forts and castles, the district of Damietta, the district of Alexandria, Nastarawa, Santariyya and every port and coast and town connected with them; the district of Fuwwa and of Rosetta: the country of the Hijāz; the well-guarded district of Gaza with all its harbours and territories; the province of Karak, Shaubak and its territory, as-Salt and its territory, Bustra and its territory; the province of the Friend of God (Hebron)—on which be God's blessing!—the province of Jerusalem the noble and its territories, of the Jordan, of Bethlehem and its territory, with all the towns included in it and taken into account; Bait Gibrīl; the province of Nablus and its territory; the province of Alatrūn and its territory; Ascalon and its territory, harbours and coasts; the province of Jaffa and Ramla, its port and territory; Arsūf, its port and territory; Caesarea, its port and coastline and territory; the fort of Qaqūn and its territory; Lydda and its territory; the al-'Aujā zone and the salt works therein; the zone of the blessed conquest, with its territory and its farmland; Baisān and territory, at-Tur and territory, al-Lajūn and territory, Jubnīn and territory. 'Ain Jalūt and territory, al-Qaimūn and territory with all regions dependent on it; Tiberias with its lake and territory; the province of Safad and its dependencies; Tibnīn and Hunīn with all their towns and territories; ash-Shaqīf, known as Shaqīf Arnūn, with its territory and dependencies; the town of al-Qarn and its dependencies, apart from those specified in this treaty; half of the city of Alexandretta and of the suburb of Marūn with their villages and vineyards and gardens and fields—and the rest of the above-mentioned Alexandretta shall all, including all its confines and lands, be subject to our Lord the Sultan and to his son—while the other half shall go to the kingdom of Acre; al-Biqā' al-'Azizi[2] and its territory, Mashghar and

[1] The long, monotonous list that follows, enumerating the dominions of the Mamlūk Sultan of Egypt from south to north, has the eloquence of fact when one compares it with the brief description, a little further on, of the territories belonging to the other party to the treaty. The 'kingdom of Jerusalem' was in effect reduced to a narrow coastal strip extending from a short distance north of Acre as far as Carmel. Apart from this, Tyre and Sidon, Beirūt and Tripoli and a few forts in Syria still held by the Templars and Hospitallers were all that remained of the Crusaders' achievements. The list of Qalawūn's possessions, beginning with the Holy City, is in fact a list of all the territories that the Crusaders had lost during the last century, or had attacked in vain.

[2] Al-Biqā' is the region of Syria east of Mount Lebanon; the epithet *al-'Azizi* (singular because the originally plural meaning of the word—the districts—has been forgotten) refers to al-Malik al-'Aziz, Saladin's son.

territory, Shaqīf Tirūn and its territory; all the caves, Zalaya and the rest; Baniyās and its territory; the fort of as-Subaiba with its lakes and territory; Kaukab and its territory; the fort of 'Ajlūn and its territory; Damascus and its province with its forts and towns and districts and territories; the fortress of Baalbek and its territory; the province of Hims with its territory and confines; the province of Hamāt with its city and fort and lands and confines; Balātunus and its territory; Sahyūn and its territory; Barzayya and its territory; the conquests of Hisn al-Akrād and its territory; Safithā and its territory; Mai'ār and its territory; al-'Uraima and territory; Maraqiyya and its territory; Halabā and its territory; the fort of 'Akkār and its territory and lands; al-Qulai'a and its territory; the fort of Shaizar and its territory, Apamea and its territory; Jábala and its territory, Abu Qubais and its territory; the province of Aleppo, with all the forts, cities, towns and castles connected with it; Antioch and its territory, with everything that made up that blessed conquest;[1] Baghrās and its territory, Darbsāk and its territory, Rawandān and its territory, Harīm and its territory, 'Aintāb and its territory, Tizīn and its territory, Saih al-Hadīd and its territory; the fort of Najm and its territory, Shaqīf Dair Kush and its territory; ash-Shughr and its territory, Bakās and its territory, as-Suwaida and its territory; al-Bab and Buza'a and their territories; al-Bira and its territory, ar-Rahba and its territory, Salamiyya and its territory, Shumaimīs and its territory, Tadmur and its territory; and everything connected with these places, whether specified or not.

(The safety of all these places is guaranteed) by the authorities of the kingdom of Acre, i.e. the *bailli* of the Kingdom, the Grand Master of the Templars *frère* William of Beaujeu, the Grand Master of the Hospitallers, *frère* Nicholas Lorgne and the Marshal *frère* Conrad, representative of the Grand Master of the Teutonic Hospitallers; as well as all the Franks, Brethren and knights obedient to them and members of their State of Palestine; and by all the Franks without distinction who inhabit Acre and the coastal regions included in the treaty, and anyone of them to arrive there by land or sea, whatever his race or condition.

The territories of our Lord the Sultan al-Malik al-Mansūr and of his son the Sultan al-Malik as-Salih, their castles, forts, towns, villages and armies, Arab, Turcoman and Kurdish, and their subjects of every race, with all their possessions, flocks, goods, crops and everything else, shall have to fear no harm, injury or encroachment, attack or assault. This shall apply to all

[1] Baibars' fairly recent conquests. It is not clear what is meant by the 'zone of the blessed conquest' mentioned a few lines earlier.

conquests of our Lord the Sultan al-Malik al-Mansūr and of his son al-Malik as-Salih, by their own hand or by means of their armies and their commanders of castles and forts and provinces, by land and by sea, in the plains or in the mountains.

In the same way all the coastal lands of the Franks to which this treaty applies (shall be guaranteed their safety); to wit: the city of Acre, with the gardens, terrain, mills and vineyards dependent upon it, including the taxes received from its administrative area, and the regions agreed under this treaty, numbering seventy-three districts with their fields; all without dispute in possession of the Franks. In the same way Kaifa and its vineyards and gardens, with seven dependent districts. In the same way Marina and the region known by that name shall belong to the Franks. In the same way they shall hold the monastery of Sayāj(?) and that of Mar Elias. Of the area of Carmel our Lord the Sultan shall take for himself 'Afā and al-Mansura, while the rest, consisting of thirteen districts, shall belong to the Franks. Of 'Athlīth the fort and the city and the gardens that have been harvested, the vineyards and the cultivated land and terrains shall go to the Franks, with sixteen districts; our Lord the Sultan shall take the village of al-Haramis herein mentioned, with its taxes and farmlands; the rest of the territory of Athlīth shall be divided in half, apart from that which is in our Lord the Sultan's private possession: eight districts. The Hospitallers' estates in the province of Caesarea shall be Frankish property with everything that they contain. A half of the city of Alexandretta and the suburb of Marūn with all its contents shall belong to the Franks, and the rest to our Lord the Sultan; all the taxes and crops of Alexandretta and the suburb of Marūn shall be divided between them. In the case of Sidon, the fort and the city, the vineyards and the administrative area with all that it involves shall belong to the Franks; they shall take possession of fifteen districts with all their rivers, waters, springs, gardens, mills, canals flowing streams and dikes, by which the land is watered according to ancient usage; the rest of the entire mountain region shall be in the sole possession of our Lord the Sultan and his son. All these territories belonging to Acre, and those specified in the treaty, shall be given guarantees of safety by our Lord the Sultan and his son on behalf of their armies and troops, whether the region is partly or wholly in Frankish hands; the guarantee shall apply to property and inhabitants.

Outside Acre, 'Athlīth and Sidon and the walls of these three places the Franks may not rebuild walls, forts, fortifications or castles, whether old or new.

The galleys of our Lord the Sultan and his son that have been fitted out and sent to sea are forbidden to cause any harm to the coastal territories under treaty. When the above-mentioned galleys are bound for a country other than those whose ruler is linked by treaty with the authorities of the Commune of Acre the galleys may not drop anchor or take on provisions in countries affected by this treaty; if however the ruler of the country for which they are bound is not linked by treaty with the authorities of the Commune of Acre the galleys may drop anchor and take on provisions in the afore-mentioned countries. If ever, which God forbid, one of these galleys should be wrecked on a harbour or on a coast affected by the treaty, if making for an ally of the Commune of Acre and its ruler, the *bailli* of the kingdom of Acre and the Grand Masters of the Orders must take it into custody, enable the crew to take on provisions and to repair the damage to the ship, and send it back to Muslim territory. The original objective of the ship that has been wrecked and cast up on the shore shall be cancelled. If however the country for which the ship was bound is not linked by treaty with the Commune of Acre, the wrecked ship may take on provisions and crew in countries affected by the treaty and may proceed toward the original objective. This clause shall obtain equally in the case of Frankish ships cast up on Muslim territory.

Whenever one of the Kings of the Franks or of Outremer shall leave his land and invade the territory of our Lord the Sultan or of his son, where that territory is under treaty, the *bailli* of the Commune and the Grand Masters of Acre shall undertake to give notice of their movements to our Lord the Sultan two months before their arrival; in the event of their arrival after the two months have elapsed the *bailli* of the Commune of Acre and the Grand Master shall be exempt from any obligations in the matter.

In the case of attack by the Mongols or other enemies whichever of the two signatories is the first to receive news of it shall inform the other. If an enemy force, which God forbid, whether Mongol or from some other hostile power, should attack Syria by the overland route and drive the (Sultan's) armies before it as far as the coastal territories affected by this treaty and invade these lands, the *bailli* of the Commune of Acre and the Grand Masters shall have the right to make provision by means of treaties for the defence of their persons, their subjects and their territories, to the best of their ability.

If, God forbid, sudden panic should cause Muslims to flee from their own lands into the coastal territories affected by the treaty, the *bailli* of the Commune of Acre and the Grand Masters shall give protection and defence to these fugitives, and defend them from their pursuers, so that they and their possessions may be safe and secure. The *bailli* of the Commune of Acre and the Grand Masters shall instruct all the other coastal territories under treaty not to permit pirates to take on food or water in their ports, to hold them if they capture them, and in the case of a pirate ship coming to sell its booty they shall detain the brigands until the rightful owner shall come to take back his property. The same conditions shall apply to the Sultan.

The church at Nazareth and four houses close to it shall be reserved for the use of Christian pilgrims, great and small, of whatsoever race and station, coming from Acre and the coastal lands affected by the treaty. In the church priests and friars shall perform their offices, and the houses shall be reserved for the use of visitors to the church of Nazareth, who shall have complete freedom of movement within the area under treaty. Concerning the stones of the church, those that are picked up (having fallen from their place) shall be cast away, and stone shall not be set upon stone to rebuild the church; nor shall unlawful gifts be solicited by priests and friars for this purpose.[1]

The treaty contained the usual stipulations. When our Lord the Sultan had taken the oath on it the amīr Fakhr ad-Din Ayāz, *amīr hajib* 'lord chamberlain', and the Qadi Bahr ad-Din ibn Razīn took it to the Franks, who also swore to it, and so the truce was concluded.

FORMULA OF THE OATH TAKEN BY THE SULTAN, SWEARING TO KEEP THIS TRUCE

(IBN AL-FURĀT, VII, 181v–182r)

By Allāh by Allāh by Allāh, in the name of Allāh of Allāh of Allāh, the witness being Allāh Allāh Allāh, great and pursuing, inflicting and bestowing, constructive and destructive, aware of what is revealed and of what is concealed, of the secret and of the manifest, merciful, forgiving; by the Qur'ān and He who revealed it and him to whom it was revealed, Muhammad son of 'Abdallāh, God bless and save him, and by all that is stated therein, chapter by chapter, verse by verse; by the month of ramadān: I bind myself to uphold this blessed truce agreed between myself and the Commune of Acre and the Grand Masters who live there; a truce that is valid for Acre,

[1] Muslim law tolerated the existence of Christain churches on Islamic territory but did not permit them to be repaired or new ones to be built. Naturally, the local authorities wrung 'gifts' from the clergy in exchange for allowing such restorations.

'Athlīth and Sidon and the territories under their control. The duration of the truce shall be ten years, ten months, ten days and ten hours, beginning on Friday 5 rabī' I of the year of the *hijra* 682. I will observe the truce from first to last, I will keep it and abide by all the conditions laid out in it, basing my actions on its precepts for the duration of the time set out in it. I will not raise difficulties over it or any of the conditions it contains, nor will I seek legal advice in order to break it,[1] for as long as the authorities of Acre, Sidon and 'Athlīth, to wit the *bailli* of the Commune of Acre, the Grand Master of the Temple and he of the Hospital and the representative of the Grand Master of the Teutonic Hospital, in person or those who succeed them in the Regency of Acre or the Mastership of the Orders in the above-mentioned kingdom, shall keep their oath that they swore to me, to my son al-Malik as-Salih and to my other sons, to keep the truce here formulated, applying the conditions laid down in it for as long as it is valid and obeying its precepts. If I should break this oath, my penance shall be to make the Pilgrimage to the House of God at Mecca thirty times, barefoot and bareheaded, and to fast the whole time, apart from the days on which fasting is forbidden.

The other clauses of the oath having been recited, it concludes:

and Allāh is the guarantor of that which we are saying here.

FORMULA OF THE FRANKISH OATH

(IBN AL-FURĀT, VII, 182r–183r)

By God by God by God, in the name of God of God of God, the witness being God God God, by the Messiah the Messiah the Messiah, by the Cross the Cross the Cross, by the three persons of one substance, designated the Father and the Son and the Holy Spirit and forming a single God; by the blessed Divinity[2] dwelling in the august Humanity, by the pure Testament and all that it contains, by the four Gospels transmitted by Matthew, Mark, Luke and John, by their prayers and benedictions; by the twelve Apostles and the seventy-two Disciples and the three hundred and eighteen (Fathers of Niceae) gathered into the Church; by the voice that descended from Heaven over the river Jordan and which drove back its waves; by God who

[1] An old method, not only Muslim, of escaping from a sworn undertaking.

[2] Text has 'the Cross'; an obvious error; the emendation is Quatremère's.

revealed the Good Tidings to Jesus son of Mary, Spirit and Word of God; by the Madonna, Holy Mary mother of the Light; by John the Baptist; by Saint Martha and Saint Mary; by the Lenten fast; by my Faith and the God whom I adore; and by the Christian dogmas in which I believe, and which have been impressed upon me by the Father and Priest who baptized me. From this moment and this hour I consecrate my whole intention and my deepest resolve to upholding, with regard to the Sultan al-Mansūr, his son al-Malik as-Salih and their sons, all the articles of the blessed truce by which peace is concluded and reigns in the Kingdom of Acre, Sidon and 'Athlīth and their dependent territories as included in this truce and specified therein. The duration of the truce shall be ten years, ten months, ten days and ten hours, beginning on Friday 3 hazirān of the year 1594 of the era of Alexander son of Philip the Greek. I will observe all the stipulations set out in the treaty, one by one, and bind myself to keep faith in every clause included in the above-mentioned truce for as long as it applies. By God God God, by the Messiah and the Cross and my Faith, I will cause no harm or injury to any of the states belonging to the Sultan and his son, nor to any of the persons who live therein, nor to any of them who may visit any of the countries to which the truce applies, in respect of their persons or their possessions. By God, by my Faith, and by Him whom I adore, I will follow the path of the sincere confederate, committed to avoiding any act of violence or hostility toward persons or property, in loyally upholding the treaty and the truce, in sincere friendship, in defence of the Muslim people and of those who come and go from the Sultan's states. I bind myself to keep faith in all the stipulations of this truce for as long as it is valid, as long as al-Malik al-Mansūr keeps the oath that he swore to this same truce. I shall not break my oath or any part of it, nor shall I make any exceptions to it or to any part of it with the aim of violating it. If I should contravene or break it, I shall be an outcast from my religion and my Faith and the God whom I adore, and a rebel against the Church; my penance shall be to perform thirty pilgrimages to Jerusalem the noble, bareheaded and barefoot; I shall be obliged to release a thousand Muslim prisoners from the Frankish prisons and shall be cut off from the Divinity handed down in Humanity. This is my oath, sworn by me, So and So. My intention in all this is the same as that of the Sultan al-Malik al-Mansūr and of his son al-Malik as-Salih, and as his who takes the oath before them on my account, swearing on the noble Testament. This is my only intention. God and the Messiah are witnesses to our statement here.

THE FALL OF AL-MARQAB

(TASHRĪF, FO. 149r–160r)

This is a great and mighty castle, which had long been a challenge to our Lord the Sultan al-Malik al-Mansūr—God grant him victory. He studied every means of securing it for Islām and supported every plan or method for conquering it and overcoming it. Up to this time he had refused to authorize an attack by any of the (Muslim) rulers, none of whom was capable of getting anywhere near the place, much less besieging it. Al-Malik az-Zahir (Baibars) had led several offensives against it but God had not decreed or agreed to its conquest; He had not assigned it to him as his lot or hastened (its fall?): on one occasion he marched toward it from Hamāt, but snow and rain fell and combined with the difficult terrain to make it impossible to reach the objective. Another time he tried to attack it from a different base, but was unable to bring up enough artillery. In fact God had reserved it for our Lord the Sultan (Qalawūn), that it might be his glorious conquest and that he might crown his splendid life with it. The Hospitallers who held it were daily becoming more insolent, dangerous and murderous, to such a degree that the people of the neighbouring forts were confined to them as if imprisoned or even entombed. The Franks believed that it was unassailable by any combination of force and cunning, and that no one was clever enough to get the better of it. So they went on with their haughty ways, broke their oaths, and in the incident at al-Qulai'āt[1] committed every possible crime and perfidy, rapine and robbery. But our Lord the Sultan al-Mansūr lay in wait for them like a man-eating lion, and went about it without attracting the attention of the castle, illumined by the heavenly guide every time that they lit

[1] The latin *Coliat*, near 'Araq, the object of an attack by the Hospitallers just before the date of the treaty.

a fire of war. He brought siege-engines from Damascus without anyone knowing where they had been sent to or were destined for; armies were mobilized from the various countries in uncountable number, with their stores, equipment and commanders. Some said that the expedition was bound for Greeks' Fortress,[1] and others held other opinions. The Sultan had sent for a great arsenal from Egypt, with great bundles of arrows and other arms, and issues of arrows were made to the amīrs and troops to carry with them and use when given the word; iron implements and flame-throwing tubes were procured, such as exist only in the royal magazines and arsenals. All these were assembled before the army moved off on its march. A number of experts on the art of siege and the techniques of blockade were also enlisted. The catapults of the neighbouring forts were requisitioned and mobilized without any fuss that might attract the attention of the fort. Catapults and fighting gear were carried on men's shoulders. Eventually, our Lord the Sultan left his camp at 'Uyūn al-Qasab and by forced marches arrived to besiege al-Marqab on Wednesday 10 safar (684/17 April 1285).

Immediately the catapults were brought up, carried on men's shoulders, and the fort was surrounded by a murderous circle of weapons, which began their attack under the gaze of the greatest of Sultans. Catapults of the 'Frankish' and 'qarabugha' types were brought up; they had three of the great 'Frankish' type, three 'qarabughas' and four 'devils' surrounding the fort on all sides. These began a formidable, murderous assault with stones, while excavations were started on each side to undermine the walls. The 'Frankish' catapults broke up those of the enemy, and the Muslims were able to bring theirs up close under the walls. But the Franks repaired their catapults, aimed them at the Muslims and smashed some of theirs, killing some of the Muslims who operated them. It is incontestable that the

[1] Qal'at ar-Rum, on the upper Euphrates.

fortunes of war ebb and flow and that not everyone can save his skin. When the Sultan's tunnel under the wall was finished the wood was put into it and set on fire on Wednesday 17 rabīʿ I/25 May; the fire reached mid-tunnel under the tower at the angle of the bastion and the Muslims moved in to attack the walls themselves, but after violent fighting the attacking force proved insufficiently powerful to scale the wall. At sunset the tower fell, which in the opinion of our army increased the difficulty of gaining a foothold in the fortress. Thus the night passed in great confusion, for the use of catapults was made impossible by what had happened, and everything that could be done with mines had been done. Now God alone could exterminate the enemy. On the following Friday God did indeed send down His blessing and His grace and sent us the help of the angels closest to Him as well as all the hosts of heaven, who came down to bring victory to Islām. God made the Franks think that the tunnels under the entire wall were all equally far advanced, that they had reached the moats, then the towers, and from there were undermining the walls themselves. In fact the tunnels, travelling in conduits under the moats, had reached as far as the towers, but the Franks were unaware of this. When they did discover it they lost their courage and presence of mind and gave themselves up for lost. They thought that they were trapped, and asked that their lives should be spared in exchange for their surrender, and that they should be treated with generous indulgence. Having chosen death rather than life, they now preferred life to death and were convinced that if they did not now take thought for their lives they would certainly lose them.

They begged our Lord the Sultan to show mercy and pardon them. In the circumstances it was most important for the Sultan to be sure of taking this great castle without a prolonged siege, for he judged that if he delayed the best moment would pass, and that it was better to seize the immediate advantage. For even if the Franks in the fort were saved from the fire of death in battle they would not in the end escape death in some form. So he agreed to grant them pardon and amnesty, and they, in the faith that our Sultan's word was worth more than any oaths, sent their leaders to the tent of victory and asked only for their lives and nothing more. They agreed to take away with them no property or arms belonging to the fortress and only those who happened to have possessions of their own received permission to take them away with them. The amīrs interceded for them; they kissed the ground before our Lord the Sultan and begged that their request should be heard. The Sultan therefore made the following concessions: for their leaders' journey twenty-five horses and mules with the equipment necessary for them, and the sum estimated as the value of the owners' property, 2,000 Tyrian *dinar*. Safe-conducts were issued for them and they returned to the citadel accompanied by the amīr Fakhr ad-Din al-Muqri al-Hajib, who witnessed the oaths of the Castellan and all the knights. They surrendered the fort in its entirety at the eighth hour of Friday 18 rabī' I/25 May. The Sultan's victorious standard rose over the battlements and a universal chorus of blessing was raised to our Lord the Sultan al-Mansūr, in whose time it was granted to us to see this victory, for so long unattainable at no matter what cost, and for which the Muslims had for so long struggled in vain.

The Muslims went up (to take possession of the fort) and from the heights of the citadel the call to prayer resounded with praise and thanks to God for having cast down the adorers of the Messiah and freed our land of them. Messages announcing the good news were written to all the provinces and couriers were sent to bear them in all directions. Our Lord the Sultan (himself) went up to the castle on the Saturday. The chief amīrs met in his presence and a council was held under his presidency to decide whether or not to destroy the fort. Opinions differed, but the Sultan's inspired judgment was to preserve it for his own protection and safety, and to repair and restore it. He determined to keep it for the destruction of the infidels and the support of the neighbouring castles; he therefore stationed, 1,000 *aqjiyya*(?) infantry there, catapulters and fighting men, and 400 craftsmen, a group of amīrs 'with bands', and Bahrite, Salihite and Mansurite mamlūks;[1] 550 men in all. Then he had transferred to the castle the catapults that until now had been attacking it. Now their job was to attack the enemy from its ramparts. The same applied to the equipment, timbers, arrows, combustible materials, naphtha and all the other siege equipment belonging to His Highness. He made the command of the fort a feudal position giving the holder control of the Kafartáb area, the city of Antioch, Laodicaea and its port and the area already dependent on al-Marqab itself, as well as what had already been his fief before the conquest. The total income of this territory once it had been put in order was a million *dirham*. The cost of repairing it and paying the garrison's wages was spread out over the country[2] until the fort was back in working order and the local population returned. When he had seen to all this the Sultan—God grant him victory!—departed to the plains and the city of Bulunyās.

THE FALL OF MARAQIYYA

(TASHRĪF, FO. 172r–178v)

When our Lord the Sultan—God grant him victory!—had dealt with Marqab and gone down to the plains, as we have said, he turned his attention to the castle of Maraqiyya and studied ways of taking it. He perceived that it was like a wedge

[1] Amīrs 'with bands' were those with their own military orchestras (*tablkhane*) to perform in their honour. The Bahrite mamlūks were, as has been noted, those based on the Nile (*Bahr*), and the Salihites and Mansurites were those instituted in the names of al-Malik as-Salih and al-Malik al-Mansūr, i.e. Qalawūn.

[2] I think this means, over the whole vast economic and administrative unit so formed, as it seems unlikely that the cost of the repairs would be borne by the actual region in need of rehabilitation.

inserted between the other forts and that he could enjoy neither peace nor security while it flourished. Its ruler was called Bartholomew, and was one of the leading Franks. When Hisn al-Akrād was taken (by the Muslims) he could no longer make a living in that part of the world, so he went over to the Mongols for protection, support and assistance, and enjoyed their patronage for several years. When al-Malik az-Zahir died he profited by the occasion to return to his land and began to fortify Maraqiyya. His resources were not great enough however, and fearing that it would be taken from him he built and fortified a large castle in front of the city with the help of the ruler of Tripoli and other Franks, the Hospitallers of Marqab and others. This fort lay between Tortosa and Marqab and faced Maraqiyya from a position in the sea, two bow-shots or more from the shore. It was almost square in shape; each side was twenty-five and a half cubits long, with walls seven cubits thick. It had seven storeys and was built on ships loaded with stones and sunk in the sea. Under each corner were sunk nine-hundred(?) shiploads of stones; the blocks were held together by two continuous iron bands covered with an iron network. Within the citadel was a great cistern over which a vault was built, and above that some wooden beams supporting battering-rams and covered with fine gravel, a layer of sacking and hempen ropes fixed in such a way that if the fort were attacked by catapult from *terra firma* it would be able to smile at such a bombardment, for the stones would roll off the protective roof into the water. It had a garrison of a hundred. Behind it and attached to it was a small second fort defended by three mounted catapults. The place was in effect unassailable by siege or blockade. The (Muslim) commanders of Hisn al-Akrād, watching the fort being built and unable to prevent it, because the materials and tools came by sea, were forced to build another nearby in the village of Mai'ār, with a garrison of about fifty, but this had no effect whatsoever.

When our Lord the Sultan saw this fort, so strong and impregnable, when he realized that the castle built to oppose it had been more of a disadvantage than a benefit to its builders, that it was impossible to besiege a fort set in the midst of the sea, that the Muslims had no fleet strong enough to cut the supply-lines and prevent traffic reaching the fort, that it was likely to be a long fight but at the same time that it was urgent—of the most absolute and particular importance—and that wit and not force was the agent necessary to its conquest; when he had taken account of all this he sent the following message to the Prince of Tripoli: 'My troops are free (from any other commitment) and their sole objective is you. You are the real builder of the fort, for it would not have been constructed without your aid, so the responsibility for it falls upon you. Either you demolish it or we shall take so much of your territory in revenge that the Lord of Maraqiyya will be of no help to you. You will repent then, when repentance is no longer of any use; the cover will be lifted and the gift taken back.'

When the Prince[1] read this terrible judgment he was convinced that his lands, his castles and his whole state would be laid waste as the message promised, that the ruler of the land with his great armies was already at the gates of his city, encamped upon his land, and that the only alternatives were to lose his kingdom or to demolish the fort. He therefore took the course of surrendering the castle and demolishing it. He paid off its commander with all the money and land available, which was accepted after a certain amount of resistance. The commander's son was secretly smuggled into the Sultan's camp with a plan to hold the fort and hand it over to him. Still in secret he made for Acre by post-horse, but was arrested there by the officials. The news reached his father, who hurried from Tripoli to Acre, got hold of the boy and killed him with his own hand before the people of Acre; that was the end of the

[1] The contested title is here restored to him, as the former ruler of Antioch.

plot. In the end, however, when the Prince intervened as mediator, the commander agreed to bow his head and hand over the fort to the Muslims. The Prince sent a certain number of Franks to help with the demolition, by which means the word of God was fulfilled: 'They cast down their dwellings with their own hands, and with the hands of the believers.'[1] The ruler of Tripoli sent one of his high officials to supervise the demolition as the leader of a band of Franks sent for this purpose, and also to put an end to excuses about having to find demolition tools, chains and so on. The amīr Badr ad-Din Baktāsh an-Najmi, a *jamdār* amīr, was also sent with a hundred engineers[2] for the demolition. The *sipahsalār* amīr Rukn ad-Din Taqsū al-Mansuri was stationed before Jábala with a body of troops, and the Sultan ordered him to take his men to the top of the fort to assist with the demolition. Stone by stone it came down, so zealously demolished that no trace of it remained, but the labour needed for the task made the spades groan, hardened the stones and exhausted the men for as long as the work took. Thus God was pleased to remove the traces of the fortress and to destroy its foundations, freeing the faithful from the threat of it and dissipating its menace, while in its place, in the hearts of Unbelievers, was only grief.

THE FALL OF TRIPOLI

(ABU L-FIDĀ', 162)

The Sultan al-Malik al-Mansūr Qalawūn's campaign began in muharram of this year (688/February 1289) when he led his Egyptian troops into Syria. With his combined Egyptian and Syrian armies he besieged the Syrian city of Tripoli on the first Friday of the month of rabī' I/25 March. Most of the city is

[1] Qur'ān LIX, 2.

[2] In Arabic *hajjarīn*, 'stonecutters' and also 'stone throwers', those who look after the ballistas, and so half-way between artillery and engineers.

surrounded by sea; the only approach by land is from the west along a narrow bridge of land. The Sultan beleaguered the city with a large number of catapults, big and small. He enforced a stringent blockade and after a violent struggle took the city by storm on Tuesday 4 rabī' II 688/27 April. The Muslim troops forced their way in and the citizens fled to the harbour. A few got to safety on ships, but most of the men were killed and the children taken captive. The Muslims took quantities of booty from the place. When the killing and looting were over, the city, on the Sultan's orders, was demolished and razed to the ground.

In the sea, a short distance from Tripoli, is a small island with a church on it called the Church of Saint Thomas. It is separated from the city by the harbour. When Tripoli was taken a great many Franks fled with their women to the island and the church. The Muslim troops flung themselves into the sea and swam with their horses to the island, where they killed all the men and took the women, children and possessions. After the looting I went by boat to this island, and found it heaped with putrefying corpses; it was impossible to land there because of the stench.

When the Sultan finished taking and demolishing Tripoli he returned to Egypt. Tripoli had been in Frankish hands for 185 years and some months.[1]

(MAQRIZI, 746–8)

On Thursday 10 muharram/4 February 1289 the Sultan camped outside Cairo, and on the 15th he departed, leaving his son al-Malik al-Ashraf Khalīl as commander in the Citadel,[2] and the amīr Baidar as his son's general and vizier. On his departure he wrote to the provinces of Syria to muster troops for the attack on Tripoli. He made for Damascus, entered it on 13 safar/

[1] According to the Muslim lunar calendar (502–688), or 180 solar years (1109–1289).
[2] The Citadel on the hill of al-Muqattam, the Sultan's home in Cairo.

7 March and on the 20th set out for Tripoli and laid siege to it. Four galleys came from the King of Cyprus to assist the town. The Sultan kept up continuous fire from his siege-engines and pressed his attack on the walls until at the seventh hour of Tuesday 4 rabīʿ II,[1] after a siege of thirty-four days, he took the city by storm. He had used nineteen catapults and employed 1,500 artillerymen and bombardiers. The citizens tried to escape to an island that faced the city but the Muslims, cavalry and infantry together, threw themselves into the sea, captured and killed the fugitives and seized their goods. The swordsmen and palfreymen took many who had got on to boats but whom the waves[2] had cast on to the beach. There were many prisoners; so many of them that 1,200 of them had to be kept in the Sultan's arsenal. Among the Muslims who fell were the amīr ʿIzz ad-Din Maʿn and the amīr Rukn ad-Din Mankuras al-Farqani, with fifty-five of the Sultan's guard. On the Sultan's orders Tripoli was demolished. The thickness of the walls was such that three horsemen could ride their horses side by side along it. The population was extremely wealthy, and 4,000 weaver's looms were found.

The Sultan confirmed the ruler of Jubáil (Byblos) in his position, in return for the tribute paid by him; he took Beirūt[3] and Jábala and the surrounding forts and returned to Damascus half-way through jumada I/June 1289. The army camped as usual at Hisn al-Akrād, under the command of its general the amīr Saif ad-Din Balbān at-Tabakhi, and the vanguard went down from Hisn al-Akrād to Tripoli, which now came under at-Tabakhi's control. With him were 150 soldiers, ten amīrs 'with bands' and fifteen amīrs 'of ten', who received fiefs. The Sultan later built a new city near the river; a great and beautiful city which now bears the name of Tripoli.

[1] The MS. has 'first', which can be emended from the context and from Abu l-Fidā'.
[2] The MS. has 'the Franks', correctly emended by Quatremère.
[3] Beirūt really fell two years later, after Acre (see below).

CHAPTER THREE

In 1291 al-Ashraf, Qalawūn's son, completed his father's work (Qalawūn died while preparations for the campaign against Acre were in progress) and the work of all his predecessors in the struggle against the Christian invader. The bloody conquest of Acre after a strenuous resistance is described here by Abu l-Fidā', who took part in it as one of the Sultan's vassals. His account is consistent with that of the 'Templar of Tyre', the best known Western source for the episode that marked the end of Christian rule in the Holy Land. The treacherous slaughter of the heroic defenders after the surrender is shown by a later Egyptian chronicler, Abu l-Mahasin, to reflect a similar massacre of Muslim prisoners under treaty committed a hundred years before by Richard Coeur de Lion, also at Acre. This harsh application of the old law closes the last act of the drama of the Crusaders.

THE FALL OF ACRE

(ABU L-FIDĀ', 163–5)

In 690/1291 the Sultan al-Malik al-Ashraf marched on Acre with his Egyptian troops and sent word to the Syrian army to join up with him and to bring the siege-engines. The ruler of Hamāt, al-Malik al-Muzaffar, set out with his uncle al-Malik al-Afdal[1] and the whole of Hamāt's army for Hisn al-Akrād, where we collected a huge catapult called 'the Victorious'; a hundred wagons were needed to transport it. (It was dismantled and the pieces) distributed through the army. The part consigned to me was only one wagon-load, since at the time I was an 'amīr of ten'.[2] It was the end of the winter when we

[1] The author's cousin and father respectively. Abu l-Fidā' was to become in his turn ruler of Hamāt.

[2] One of the lowest ranks in the feudal hierarchy.

marched off with the wagons; rain and snowstorms struck us between Hisn al-Akrād and Damascus, causing great hardship, for the wagons were heavy and the oxen weak and dying of cold. Because of the wagons it took us a month to march from Hisn al-Akrād to Acre, usually an eight-day ride. The Sultan ordered all the other fortresses to send catapults and siege-engines to Acre, and in this way a great number of large and small artillery concentrated under its walls, more than had ever before been assembled in one place.

The Muslim troops mustered at Acre in the first days of jumada I 690/beginning of May 1291, and the battle raged furiously. The Franks did not close most of the gates; in fact they left them wide open and fought in front of them in their defence. The Hamāt army was in its usual position on the extreme right wing. This meant that we were on the seashore, with the sea on our right when we faced Acre. We were attacked by troops landing from boats protected by wood-faced frames covered with buffalo-hides, from which they shot at us with bows and ballistas. Thus we found ourselves fighting on two fronts, the city and the sea. A ship came up with a catapult mounted on it that battered us and our tents from the sea. We were severely hindered by it, but one night when a fierce wind blew up the ship was buffeted on the waves and the catapult broke up and was not rebuilt.

One night during the siege the Franks made a sortie, put the outposts to flight and reached the tents, where they became tangled up in the guy-ropes. One knight fell into the latrine-trench of one of the amīr's detachments and was killed. Our troops turned out in overwhelming numbers and the Franks turned tail and fled back to the city, leaving a number of dead accounted for by the Hamāt army. The next morning al-Malik al-Muzaffar, Lord of Hamāt, had a number of Frankish heads attached to the necks of horses we had captured and presented them to the Sultan al-Malik al-Ashraf.

The blockade was continually reinforced, until God granted to the attackers victory over the city on Friday 10 jumada II/17 June 1291. As the Muslims stormed the city some of the citizens took to the sea in boats. Within the city was a number of well-fortified towers, and some Franks shut themselves inside them and defended them. The Muslims killed vast numbers of people and gathered immense booty. The Sultan forced all those in the towers to surrender, and they submitted to the last man, and to the last man were decapitated outside the city walls.[1] At the Sultan's command the city was razed to the ground.

An amazing coincidence occurred; the Franks seized Acre from Saladin at midday on 17 jumada II 587, and captured and then killed all the Muslims therein; and God in His prescience destined that this year it should be reconquered at the hand of another Saladin, the Sultan al-Malik al-Ashraf.[2]

After the conquest of Acre God put despair into the hearts of the other Franks left in Palestine; they abandoned Sidon and Beirūt, which (the amīr) ash-Shuja'i took over at the end of rajab/end of July. The population of Tyre also abandoned the city and the Sultan sent troops to occupy it. He received the surrender of 'Athlīth on the first of sha'bān/30 July, and that of Tortosa on 5 sha'bān of the same year. So this Sultan had the good fortune, granted to none other, to conquer without effort and without striking a blow these great, well-fortified cities, all of which were at his command demolished.

With these conquests the whole of Palestine was now in Muslim hands, a result that no one would have dared to hope for or to desire. Thus the whole of Syria and the coastal zones were purified of the Franks, who had once been on the point of conquering Egypt and subduing Damascus and other cities. Praise be to God!

[1] Abu l-Fidā' says nothing about the guarantee of safety given by the Sultan and later violated by this massacre. But see below for Abu l-Mahasin's account.

[2] He also bore, like his illustrious predecessor, the title Salah ad-Din.

(ABU L-MAHASIN, FO. 24V–25r)

At the beginning of 690 al-Malik al-Ashraf began preparations for his departure for Syria. He called up his troops, assembled siege-engines and employed craftsmen to put them all in order. Then on 3 rabīʿ I/6 March 1291 he left Egypt, and began his siege of Acre, on 4 rabīʿ II, which corresponds to 5 April. A vast army concentrated at Acre, of which more soldiers were volunteers than were regular troops or members of the Sultan's private army. There were also fifteen great 'Frankish' catapults, capable of throwing a load weighing a Damascene quintal or more, and other, lighter machines as well as a good number of 'devils' and the like. Some tunnels were dug for mines. The King of Cyprus himself came to help the people of Acre, who on the night of his arrival lit great fires, greater than were ever seen before, as a sign of their joy. But he stayed only three days before returning home, for he realized their desperate position and the disaster looming over them.

The city was besieged and vigorously attacked until the defenders' morale began to crumble and weakness destroyed their unity. There was fighting every day and a certain number of Muslims fell as martyrs for the Faith. At dawn on Friday 17 jumada II[1] the Sultan and his troops, mounted on their horses, moved in to attack before sunrise. They beat their drums, creating a terrible, terrifying noise, and the army massed under the walls. The Franks fled and the city was taken by storm. Not three hours of the day had passed before the Muslims entered Acre and made themselves masters of it, while the Franks cast themselves into the sea, trampled on by the Muslim troops who killed and captured them. Only a few escaped. The

[1] The dates given in the text in the following pages are Professor Gabrieli's emendation of the text from which he was obliged to work (see his note on Abu l-Mahasin in the section on the authors). The Cairo edition offers the emendations given in the notes.

Muslims took all the booty they could find, goods, treasure and arms, and the population was killed or taken prisoner. Templars, Hospitallers and Teutonic Hospitallers made a last stand in four lofty towers in the middle of the city, where they were besieged. On Saturday 19th of the month,[1] two days after the fall of the city, regular troops and others attacked the house and tower where the Templars were. The Templars begged for their lives, which the Sultan granted them. He sent them a standard which they accepted and raised over the tower. The door was opened and a horde of regulars and others swarmed in. When they came face to face with the defenders some of the soldiers began to pillage and to lay hands on the women and children who were with them, whereupon the Franks shut the door and attacked them, killing a number of Muslims. They hauled down the standard and stiffened their resistance. The siege continued. On the same day the Teutonic Hospitallers asked for an amnesty and this was granted to them and their women by the Sultan, by the hand of the amīr Zain ad-Din Kitbughā al-Mansuri. The battle against the Templars' tower continued until Sunday 20 jumada II[2] when they and the defenders of the other two towers sued for their lives. The Sultan granted them permission to go where they liked, but when they came out he killed more than 2,000 of them, took an equal number prisoners and sent the women and children as slaves to the gate of the Sultan's pavilion. One reason for the Sultan's wrath against them, apart from their other crimes, was that when the amīr Kitbughā al-Mansuri had gone up (to receive their surrender) they had seized and killed him. They had also hamstrung their horses and destroyed everything they could, which increased the Sultan's wrath against them. The army and volunteers made a vast haul of prisoners and booty.

1 Actually the 18th.

2 Sunday 19th (preserving the Jumada I of the MS. and noting that the two MSS. have 29th).

When the remaining Franks realized what had happened to their companions they decided to keep up their resistance to the end. They rejected the assurances offered them and fought desperately, and when they captured five Muslims threw them down from the top of the tower. One alone escaped; the other four died. On Tuesday 18th of the same month of jumada[1] the last of the towers to keep up a resistance was taken. The defenders abandoned it in return for their lives, for the tower had been mined from all sides. When the Franks had come out and most of the contents had been removed the tower collapsed on a group of sightseers and on the looters within, killing them all. After that the Sultan set the women and children apart and decapitated all the men, of whom there was a great number.

It is marvellous to observe that Almighty God permitted the Muslims to conquer Acre on the same day and at the same hour as that on which the Franks had taken it: they gained control of Acre in 587/1191 after the famous siege on Friday 17 Jumada II[2] at the third hour of the day, promised to spare the lives of the Muslims and then treacherously killed them. God permitted the Muslims to reconquer them this time at the third hour of 17 jumada II,[3] the Sultan gave his word to the Franks and then had them slaughtered as the Franks had done to the Muslims. Thus Almighty God was revenged on their descendants.

When the Sultan had taken Acre he sent a body of troops under the amīr 'Alam ad-Din Sanjar as-Sawabi al-Jashnighīr[4] in the direction of Tyre to patrol the roads, collect information and blockade the city. While they were doing this the ships fleeing from Acre arrived and tried to enter the harbour at Tyre. The amīr prevented them, and the people of Tyre asked for an amnesty and were granted security for themselves and

[1] Actually, Tuesday 28.

[2] Text has 17 Jumada I, which destroys the coincidence in day and hour of the Frankish and Muslim conquests of Acre.

[3] According to whether Jumada I or II is right, Acre fell in May or June 1291.

[4] 'Taster' or 'steward'; a title in the court hierarchy.

their possessions. So they surrendered the city, which is among the best situated and fortified. It was not taken by the Sultan Saladin as one of his conquests in Palestine; when he took a town and granted the inhabitants their lives he sent them to Tyre, because of the strength of its fortifications. But now God filled the hearts of its inhabitants with despair and they surrendered it without a battle or siege of any sort, whereas al-Malik al-Ashraf had in fact had no intention of attacking it. When he received the surrender he sent men to organize its demolition, to pull down the walls and buildings, and he gained from this a good quantity of marble and salvage. With Tyre so easily taken al-Malik al-Ashraf confirmed his intention to proceed with the conquest of all the remaining (Frankish territories).[1]

[1] I.e. Beirūt, Sidon, 'Athlīth and Tortosa, all of which surrendered or were abandoned without a fight in the summer of the same year (see Abu l-Fidā'). The small island of Ruwād facing Tortosa remained in the Templars' hands until 1303.

INDEX